ENCOUNTERS IN HISTORY

ENCOUNTERS IN HISTORY

PIETER GEYL

Meridian Books
THE WORLD PUBLISHING COMPANY
Cleveland and New York

PIETER GEYL

Pieter Geyl, who was born on December 15, 1887, at Dort, in the Netherlands, is one of the world's most distinguished living historians. For a long period his work dealt mostly with Dutch subjects, but since the war he has given much attention to the problems of European and even of American history as well as to the theory of history. Dutch is naturally the language in which he generally expresses himself, but he has achieved an enviable mastery of English idiom and style. This is not unaccountable, given the fact that Professor Geyl was London correspondent for a leading Dutch newspaper from 1914 to 1919, and then Professor of Dutch History at University College, London, from 1919 to 1935. His works include, besides *Encounters in History*, *The Revolt of the Netherlands* (1932; third impression, 1953), *The Netherlands Divided* (1936; second impression, 1961), *Napoleon For and Against* (1949; paperback edition to be published in 1962), *Use and Abuse of History* (1955), and *Debates with Historians* (1958, Meridian Books, M57). In 1958 Professor Geyl retired as Professor of Modern History at the University of Utrecht.

AN ORIGINAL MERIDIAN BOOK

Published by The World Publishing Company
2231 West 110 Street, Cleveland 2, Ohio

First printing August 1961
Library of Congress Catalog Card Number: 6 -11475
Manufactured in the United States of America
Typography and design by Elaine Lustig

CONTENTS

I

SHAKESPEARE AS A HISTORIAN: A FRAGMENT

PREFACE

I feel that an apology, or at least an explanation, is due for the inclusion in this volume of the following essay on Shakespeare.

First, because it is a fragment that will never be completed. Second, because for a discussion of Shakespeare more expert knowledge might be desired than that which I have at my command.

The essay is the result of a number of months of intensive reading—rereading of the plays and reading of such literature on Shakespeare as I could lay my hands on.

It was in the winter of 1944-45, that is to say, during the worst period of the German occupation, that I indulged in this fascinating occupation. I had been released from internment in February 1944 and had spent the spring and summer of that year writing *Napoleon For and Against*. In one respect circumstances were ideal.

I had been dismissed from my professorial post. No classes, no examinations, no reading and discussing of essays. No telephone. Apart from occasional trips to Amsterdam or The Hague and animated discussions with like-minded friends on what might be made of the future, there was nothing but work to while away the months of weary waiting and sometimes excruciating suspense. So in that last winter, while famine was laying a heavy hand on us all, sitting by the one old-fashioned stove to which the dearth of fuel was compelling us to resort, the same stove on which my wife cooked our scanty meals, I read Shakespeare and about Shakespeare; I read the French and Dutch dramatists of the seventeenth century and about *them*; and I made extensive notes, which very soon kindled in my mind the idea of a book.

The liberation came while I was in the middle of these activities. In fact I had had to interrupt them some two weeks earlier and go into hiding with my wife—just before the German military police descended on my house. On returning I recovered the Shakespeare notes from the awful mess to which what was left of my belongings had been reduced, but life had suddenly become too crowded and active again to give them much attention.

It was not until a year or more afterward that I looked at them more closely and felt so gripped again by the promise of the subject that I sat down to work them out. But when I had written the fragment I published in the *Nieuw Vlaams Tijdschrift* in 1947, and some years later included in my volume of essays *Tochten en Toernooien*, the notes gave out, and my attention, or at least my creative powers, engaged by many more actual and pressing matters, did not allow me to resume the work where I had left off in the spring of 1945.

The fragment, then, will remain a fragment. Reviewers of the Dutch original have been kind to it; American readers of the translation have encouraged me. If I cannot compete with the experts, perhaps the spontaneous (or must I say, naive?) reactions of a historian to the inexhaustible manifestations of Shakespeare's genius may still be of some interest.

(Utrecht, 1960)

A
Shakespeare's Attitude toward State and Society

AN INTRODUCTORY NOTE ON THE HISTORY PLAYS

Although I shall not, in trying to delineate Shakespeare's attitude toward history and his powers as a historian, confine myself to the evidence provided by the history plays proper, a note giving some details about these plays may be useful. Of the thirty-five or thirty-six plays that may be regarded as actually written by Shakespeare, a full dozen can be so described. (As drawn up by E. K. Chambers, *William Shakespeare: A Study of Facts and Problems* [1930], the list of Shakespeare's plays contains thirty-eight titles. Of these, *Pericles, Prince of Tyre* and *The Two Noble Kinsmen* seem to me doubtful, while to *Henry VIII*, which otherwise would increase the number of history plays to thirteen, Shakespeare certainly contributed no more than a few scenes. *Henry VI*, *First Part*, was also at one time considered to contain no more than a few scenes by Shakespeare, while the *Second Part* and the *Third Part* were regarded as no more than recastings; I shall refer to this farther on in the text.) Apart from the twelve, history has served Shakespeare in a good many of his other plays, comedies and tragedies alike, if only to provide a background and a setting for their plots. Among these I count the Greek plays *Troilus and Cressida* and *Timon of Athens*, and even *Titus Andronicus*, a melodrama (belonging to the poet's early period) that, though it deals with a Roman theme, cannot well be described as a history play.

The twelve history plays proper fall into two groups. There are nine dealing with English subjects and three inspired by Roman history. Among the nine named after English kings are some of the earliest plays known to have been composed by Shakespeare; all nine belong to the first ten years of his career as a dramatist, the whole of which covered not much more than twenty years (1590 to 1612 or 1613). Of the Roman plays, one followed immediately after the English series, but the two others belong to a later period, coming even after the great tragedies.

Here is the entire list, with, for the reader's convenience, the years of the reigns of the kings after whom the English plays are named. The *New Cambridge Shakespeare*, edited by J. Dover Wilson, and the *New Arden Shakespeare*, edited by Una Ellis-Fermor, editions that appeared since Chambers wrote, have been consulted for the dates of the plays, some of them presumptive.

King John	(1199-1216)	1591 (?)
Henry VI, First Part / *Henry VI, Second Part* / *Henry VI, Third Part*	(1422-1461)	before the summer of 1592
Richard III	(1483-1485)	1593 (?)
Richard II	(1377-1399)	1595
Henry IV, First Part / *Henry IV, Second Part*	(1399-1413)	1597 / 1598
Henry V	(1413-1422)	1599
Julius Caesar		1599 (?)
Antony and Cleopatra		1607-1608
Coriolanus		1607-1608

Leaving *King John* to one side, eight English plays cover a century of history (1377-1485) which as seen by the author forms a coherent episode, significant to him and to his contemporaries. Actually, these plays fall into two groups of four, that covering 1377 to 1422 written after that covering 1422 to 1485, the reverse of historical chronology.

The downfall of Richard II, with which the poet ushered in the events preliminary to the period already treated in his first four plays, did indeed mean the end, for a number of generations, of the old legitimate royalty, which had just attained to glory under Richard's grandfather Edward III, the conqueror of France. Richard's deposition by Bolingbroke, Duke of Hereford, son of the fourth of Edward's sons, John of Gaunt, may have been explicable by Richard's incapacity and by that dreamer's self-glorification; Bolingbroke's assuming the royal dignity was nonetheless a violation of the legitimate order of succession. This tampering with the sacred order made itself felt the more painfully because, although Richard himself (who was soon murdered) left no children, there were descendants, in the female line it is true, of Edward's third son. However forceful a ruler Bolingbroke-Lancaster, Henry IV, may have been, he was severely troubled by revolts, which shook his usurped throne. His son Henry V, who won the glorious victory over the French at Agincourt, and who seemed to be reviving the great days of Edward III, was ever conscious of the wrong done to Richard II. Shakespeare reveled in the glory of that celebrated warrior, nor did he belittle the piety and virtuousness that, after his wild youth, Henry displayed when he was King.

But for all that, Shakespeare never forgot that Henry V's greatness was to be followed by the disastrous reign of Henry VI: in the epilogue to *Henry V* he recalls having already (some seven years earlier) put this on the stage. The infraction of the order must be avenged. This young and feeble king, a pious bookworm rather than a king, completely lacking his father's sanguine courage and energy, was unable to restrain the quarrels of the high nobles, his relatives mostly, until finally a party was formed under the Duke of York, grandson of Edward III's fifth son (and through his mother the great-great-grandson of the third), a party that disputed Henry's right to the crown. So it came to what is known as the feud between Lancaster and York—for the King, the descendant of Bolingbroke-Lancaster and of Gaunt-Lancaster, now was made to appear a pretender, on an equal footing with his rival, at the head of a connection of high nobles. The so-called Wars of the Roses, between the Red Rose (Lancaster) and the White Rose (York), were characterized by pitiless executions and inhuman horrors, resulting in the extermination of a large part of the highest English nobility.

In the end Henry VI became the captive of York's sons—York himself having been killed—and had to give up the crown to the elder, who thus became Edward IV. The deposed king, like Richard II sixty years earlier, was soon murdered, as was his young son. More than Edward IV his younger brother Richard, the hunchback, was the perpetrator of these crimes. Edward IV died a natural death, still in middle age, after a relatively quiet reign of twenty years' duration. But now Richard, robbing Edward's young sons of their rights, made himself master of the kingdom and (according, at least, to the reading of history universally accepted in Shakespeare's time) had the two princes, his nephews, murdered in the Tower. After these events the conjurations and the revolts began afresh, against Richard this time, until he was defeated by Henry Tudor, Earl of Richmond, and got killed during his flight.

Richmond's mother was a direct descendant of John of Gaunt, and consequently, Richmond was a Lancaster, but he married the daughter of Edward IV, the York king, sister of the little princes murdered by Richard. Lancaster and York could thus be regarded as united under Richmond, Henry VII; at any rate, with him there came an end to the protracted and murderous civil war. With him, and under the Tudor dynasty, a new period of strong and undisputed royal power opened for England, which in Shakespeare's own lifetime seemed to be culminating in the brilliant reign of Elizabeth, daughter of Henry VII's son Henry VIII.

SHAKESPEARE'S BELIEF IN A MORAL COSMIC ORDER

Shakespeare awoke to literary consciousness at a time when the stage was much used in order to bring before the public the great events of English history. It was done in a spirit of lively national pride. As against the Continent, torn by war and civil war, England was aware of its unity and prosperity and enthusiastically accepted the Tudor kingship, both as representing and as safeguarding those boons. The writers of chronicle plays did not look for much more in history than the colorful or the shocking event, that which could be staged for the amusement of the spectators and to the glory of England. From the preceding survey of Shakespeare's eight plays, it must have become clear that he intended to do more. He subordinated incident to a conception. All the crowded variety of a century of English history he attempted to view as a unity.

This, then, is the first feature to be noted in Shakespeare's treatment of historical subject matter, distinguishing it at once from the more primitive chronicle fashion employed by most writers. Not that this approach of his was entirely original. England possessed a rich historiography, and on more than one side a reflective interpretation of events, a tracing of their connections with an all-embracing cosmic order, was being attempted. It has been customary to stress above all Shakespeare's debt to Holinshed, whose large chronicle went into a second edition in 1587. No doubt the chronicle play in general owed much to that work, and Shakespeare as well as other dramatists made use of it. But besides, he must have found mental nourishment in the ideas of more philosophically inclined and moralizing writers, like Hall and the authors of the *Mirror for Magistrates*, who addressed themselves to the intellectual elite of the day.[1]

The old classicist picture of Shakespeare as the barbarian of genius—inevitable in an age that identified all civilization with conformity to its own rules, transitory as they were—has long been assailed and sapped of its authority.[2] The critics are, however, still engaged in uncovering the cultural wealth of that amazing *oeuvre*. Of late years they have been assisted by a reaction—and a similar one is evident in Homeric criticism—against the "disintegrators," as they have been somewhat acidly described—the eighteenth- and nineteenth-century critics who splintered the unity of the Shakespeare canon as it has been handed down to us, ascribing to other writers, wholly or in part, a number of plays, especially among the earlier ones, or degrading these plays to mere imitations of lost works. It is only since, in particular, the *Henry VI* trilogy has been boldly restored to his hand, that justice can be done to the intellectual formation of the youthful Shakespeare.[3] New studies continue to bring important contributions, helping us realize that from his youth on, Shakespeare, far from being a child of nature, or a mummer who had learned to decorate his fabrications for the stage with the fine-sounding phrases of the intellectual movement of his period, took his full share in that movement and integrated it into his plays. And in truth integrated it. Ideas were so taken up in the full tide of his dramatic imaginings that only with the help of a profound familiarity with late-sixteenth-century philosophy and theology and politics and historiography—a familiarity in which earlier generations of readers and critics were deficient—can they be isolated and valued.

The belief in a moral cosmic order permeates the whole of Shakespeare's work.[4] This is the life breath of the tragedies as well as of the history plays, and when years came in which the poet seemed above all conscious of the contrast presented by harsh reality, this is reflected in an almost despairing gloom.

> As flies to wanton boys, are we to the gods;
> They kill us for their sport.

But these words of Gloucester's, by which doubt seems to be thrown on everything, are not the last spoken in *King Lear*. After the death of the unhappy old king, who was himself unable to find sense in the end to which his innocent daughters came, Kent and Edgar are still called upon to sustain "the gor'd state."

In the English history plays, at any rate, even doubt is not yet voiced, and the order reflects itself for all to see, not only in the moral world, but in the forms of earthly society. Connected with the entire ordinance of things, and supplying to it indispensable support, there is in the community of man a fixed hierarchy of superior and inferior. Nowhere do we find this conception indicated more emphatically than in that well-known parallel of the solar system with which Ulysses in *Troilus and Cressida* tries to demonstrate the necessity of "degree"—*Troilus and Cressida*, which nevertheless was written in those gloomy years and gives of the Greek world an almost grotesque and certainly unattractive picture (not, in fact, taken direct from Homer, but derived from medieval adaptations).

The parallel of the solar system, however, is not meant for more than a parallel. In Shakespeare's mind, especially as it realized itself through the imagination in his dramas, the social order is neither rigid nor mechanical: it depends on moral, on human, factors, which may fail. It cannot help, therefore, but be frequently disarranged, but forever undismayed there springs from the human mind an urge to overcome these confusions. That is the drama.

SHAKESPEARE AND KINGSHIP

Shakespeare's treatment of kingship—of authority—reflects a dynamic conception, a sense for the human problematics of social relationships. Kingship has a claim to recognition. In itself the claim is absolute: rebellion is a wholly unjustifiable sin. This was the general attitude of the age; the detestation of rebellion was deeply felt. In England, a sermon "Against Disobedience and Willful Rebellion" had been included in 1574 in the official *Book of Homilies*. But not in England alone; throughout the whole of Europe the intellectuals, even without the exhortations of religion, were keenly aware of the dangers that state and society might incur from rebellion, whether coming from the mob, from religious fanatics, or from turbulent noblemen. It is important to note—for without it Shakespeare's dramatic powers could not have attained their depth—that in Shakespeare's view the holder of regal authority was himself subject to the moral order. With all due reverence for the office, Shakespeare was nevertheless able to retain freedom of judgment with regard to the king's person and the king's actions: the law is valid for the king, too; he, too, is accountable for his misdeeds.

To realize the significance of this attitude and the wealth of dramatic tensions it released, contrast the doctrine proclaimed by Corneille—a doctrine that must have strait-jacketed his freedom of judgment. (It is Caesar speaking, but Corneille sides with him unhesitatingly.)

Of all these crimes of State committed to obtain the crown,
We are absolved by Heaven when it gives it to us,
And in the sacred rank where Heaven's favor has placed us
The past becomes guiltless and the future lawful.
He who can attain that rank cannot be guilty;
Whatever he may have done or does, he is inviolable.[5]

A doctrine suited to tyrants; small wonder that Napoleon (as Talleyrand assures us in his memoirs) knew these lines from *Cinna* by heart and liked to quote them.

In the absolute rejection of rebellion Shakespeare was typical of the European civilization of his age—insofar as the theory of Machiavelli did not embolden people to eliminate all moral restraints from politics, which became thereby a mere game of power—but in his freedom of judgment, which in the final reckoning discerned the human being in king and rebel alike and assigned to both their places in the same order, he was a child of his own country. In England the universal triumph of state absolutism was still accompanied by a recognition of the sovereignty of law.

In Shakespeare's own world, as he fashioned it in the untrammeled liberty of his imagination—in a play like *Measure for Measure*, for instance, where he could let his mind play with the problem of authority in a purely fanciful environment—this law assumes a broadly moral and human sense and is tempered by mercy and love. There, when the Duke of Vienna is concerned, or rather, a sanctimonious nobleman who, placed in the Duke's position, extends the privileges of authority to the breaking point and soon misuses them for his lust, the poet can afford to mock the entire spectacle of earthly power.

> . . . man, proud man,
> Drest in a little brief authority,
> Most ignorant of what he's most assur'd,
> His glassy essence, like an angry ape,
> Plays such fantastic tricks before high heaven
> As make the angels weep; who, with our spleens,
> Would all themselves laugh mortal.

But the historic kings of England, too, are far from being to Shakespeare the mere symbolic bearers of an inviolable right. They are men, subject not only to the moral obligations, but to the weaknesses, of men, and their being men helps us to understand their vicissitudes, even to understand the rebellions that—however unjustifiable—are sometimes directed against them. It is true that in nearly the whole of the period Shakespeare chose for his series of eight plays, the kings are themselves sired by rebellion, their titles are often doubtful, and their misfortunes can be regarded as retribution for old misdeeds, misdeeds perhaps committed by a preceding generation. In connection with my present argument, therefore, no play (with perhaps the exception of *King John*, which, however, on account of the period to which it transfers the reader, falls outside the continuity of the series) is as important as *Richard II*, the tragedy of the last indisputably legitimate Plantagenet.

King John

The two plays just mentioned, *Richard II* and *King John*, differ not a little. In *King John* the King behaves like a villain when he orders his little nephew to be killed and like a coward when he tries to throw the guilt on his henchman. His selling England to the Pope is no more surprising than that his nobles rise against him and plot with France. But although the King's person is not spared, the office of king is left uncompromised. England's humiliation and peril constitute the play's proper theme, and the character who rises above all national calamity is he who at the play's end, expressing national self-confidence no less than aversion to rebellion, utters the famous words:

> This England never did, nor never shall,
> Lie at the proud foot a conqueror,
> But when it first did help to wound itself.
> Now these her princes are come home again,
> [The King has by then died repentant; the rebellious
> nobles have mended their ways.]
> Come the three corners of the world in arms,
> And we shall shock them. Nought shall make us rue,
> If England to itself do rest but true.

A most remarkable character this Bastard! Even though the picture lacks finish, he has, from his first entrance, when, with easy-tempered mockery, he glories in his illegitimate birth and the paternity of Richard the Lion-Hearted, the marks of Shakespeare's great creative powers upon him. Not the King, but *he* is the impersonation of the England Shakespeare wanted to hold up for the public's love and veneration, the merry, vital England longing for deeds, the England of his own day. It is as if, by placing that man as the true hero over and against the wearer of the crown, he gave rein to his feeling of the relative importance of "degree," in the cult of which at the same time he participated. At all events, when the Bastard finally becomes the mouthpiece of an emphatic loyalism, it is rather the English nation symbolized by the kingship than the kingship itself that supplies the animating force. With what a striking absence of respect, at once daring and simple-minded, had the Bastard given his impression of the great ones of the earth whom it had been his lot to meet: "Mad world! mad kings! . . . he that wins of [i.e., governs] all . . . kings . . . beggars, old men, young men, maids [is] That smooth-fac'd gentleman . . . Commodity"—that is to say, interest.

King Richard II

King Richard II is constructed upon the same antithesis as *King John:* kingship as a divine institution and the king as a human being. If the play nevertheless shows sharp contrast with *King John,* which was written some years earlier, it is but a sign of the incomparable width of Shakespeare's artistic power. It is the character of the King that occupies, from the third act on, at least, the central position.

At first, in a play whose outlines, forceful and vivid, impress by strength rather than subtlety, the verse heavily rhetorical, a good measure of somewhat forced metaphors and verbal ingenuity, the lines stepping purposefully, without any enjambments, the whole built up by lines, frequently rhymed—at first, Richard, too, has nothing that surpasses the ordinary. He is a tyrant, given to abuse of his power, unfair, arbitrary, thinking only of his own convenience, rude to his uncles. But when, later, he is shown in his distress, soon in his humiliation, a personality entirely his own, a personality such as only a great poet can create, breaks through that regularity, that humdrum quality, finding a voice fitted to the most unusual conception. The unbalanced weakling turns out to be possessed of the finest sensibility and imaginative power. His change from exalted belief in the saving quality of his royalty to abject prostration, from a sort of unreal rebelliousness—for it never gets beyond words, beyond fits and starts—to the meekest acquiescence, fascinates the reader from now on right to the end; and what is particularly striking is the magnificent and surprising flight of his fancy under the stimulus of those varying moods. The climax comes in the abdication scene, when the helpless King faces the cold, firm Bolingbroke, the victor, the usurper. Northumberland is hard, Bolingbroke somewhat pityingly contemptuous, and now the romantic Richard *acts* his misfortune, with the crown, with the mirror. When, at the last, he is murdered, he still, at the point of death, pronounces his royal blood to be something very particular, which will carry its shedder to hell; as for himself, his soul will mount to heaven.

Shakespeare does not polemize with that ultraroyalist view—that is not his way. Indeed, up to a point, as we know, he accepted it himself. In spite of the sanction of Parliament, Bolingbroke, now King Henry IV, felt the unlawfulness of his position as a heavy burden. Even Henry V was still conscious of the irregularity, and as a matter of fact, retribution was to come under Henry VI. And yet what the drama of Richard II most clearly conveys to our minds is that these highflying claims are untenable when advanced by so factitious a personality, at once weak and false. It is significant that Essex, on the eve of his rebellion against Queen Elizabeth, in 1601, had *Richard II* performed by his actors.[6] Shakespeare's play was certainly not intended to be revolutionary, but the idea that it made visible to contemporaries was nevertheless the possibility of a ruler, boastfully proclaiming his divine right, but hesitating, and given to listening to the promptings of evil councilors, being replaced, under the sanction of Parliament, by a more forceful figure.

And indeed, Shakespeare completely accepted Henry IV's kingship. As a matter of fact, and historically, he could not, as an Englishman, help doing so; his people's history had decided that issue. But poetically, too, we see Shakespeare making full use of the freedom thus given him, contrasting the born ruler in the usurper with the utter failure of the representative of the venerated hereditary monarchy. To Henry V particularly, still the product of rebellion, Shakespeare did homage as being the great and good King par excellence. It was only after Henry V, in whom rebellion seemed to blossom out so splendidly, that its poisonous fruit was brought forth, and I recall the fact that Shakespeare had begun by staging that awful example.

King Henry VI

In his trilogy of Henry VI Shakespeare had indeed given a shocking picture of confusion, hatred, bloodshed, treachery. Henry VI is a good and pious young man, but he is unworldy, more at home with his books than among men; the kingship weighs heavily upon him, and he sighs for the lot of the simple husbandman; and so under him the forces of evil have free play. Shakespeare judges his kings; and not only by their human qualities, but by their fitness for the exalted office, which makes demands of its own. It is not only, however, the personal failure of the youthful King which brings about disaster; it is, above all, the far-reaching effect of the subversion of order inherent in the deposition of Richard II. It is the struggle between Lancaster and York, all descendants of Edward III (Richard's grandfather), among whom Henry VI is not, after all, indisputably pre-eminent. It is the inner division of the dynasty itself. It is all that which leads to that terrible civil war and to the impending destruction of all human values and of law. The King himself was fated to hear a father, over the dead body of his son, bewailing this dissolution of society:

> O! pity, God, this miserable age.
> What stratagems, how fell, how butcherly,
> Erroneous, mutinous, and unnatural,

This deadly quarrel daily doth beget!
O boy! thy father gave thee life too soon,
And hath bereft thee of thy life too late.

To be born is in that juncture a misfortune, and to die, a blessing. . . .

King Richard III

The terrible time Shakespeare depicted in *King Henry VI* culminates in Richard III, the misshapen tyrant, the murderer of Henry VI's son, of the small sons of his own brother Edward IV, and of one after the other of his favorites and henchmen—the virtuoso of crime. The King, chuckling over the successes of his simulations and the gullibility of his victims, relishing a sense of power when the sister of the murdered boy princes, though shrinking from their assassin, consents to become his wife, is in many ways a figure of melodrama, and indeed the entire play, with its violent contrasts and hammering verse, vigorously proceeding on its headlong way, clearly belongs—however strikingly different in this respect from the rambling construction of the three parts of *Henry VI*—to Shakespeare's early period. Yet it is a powerful piece of work.

In the last act, on the night before the decisive battle, Richmond, the heir of both York and Lancaster, and destined to become Henry VII, is shown to us refreshed by the quiet sleep of a good conscience; Richard, on the contrary, who believed his royal dignity gave him, in the hour of crisis, a claim to God's support, is startled by the apparitions of all whose deaths he had compassed. Nevertheless, on the battlefield he behaves with courage, until defeat overtakes him. His horse is slain. "A horse! a horse! my kingdom for a horse!" In that last cry, so miraculously dramatic, is expressed Shakespeare's profound sense of the relative nature of all earthly power. After that career of reckless ambition Richard is ready to give its great object, his kingdom, for a horse to save his life.

King Henry V

Of the earlier play's final sense of relativity there is little trace in *King Henry V*. Glorification of the man of action as the ideal king is the dominant note. Many admirers of Shakespeare have felt some embarrassment with respect to this play. Shakespeare's detractors—for he, too, has detractors (there are Tolstoy and Shaw, the improvers of the world, who measure literature by ethical, or puritan, or practical-progressive, standards)—his detractors fasten upon *Henry V* with zest.

Taken by itself the sketch of the leader of men is masterly.

> Gloucester, 'tis true that we are in great danger;
> The greater therefore should our courage be.

The battle of Agincourt in the fourth act, which opens with these manly, clear-toned lines, constitutes the climax of the play, and Henry appears as a born ruler, a true commander, quick, firm, sure. A man who knows how to speak to his men to win them. Not a despot, not a despiser of his subjects; on the contrary, his influence, the impression he makes, proceed from his humanity. He can, when talking with the soldiers, joke about his kingship (the sense of relative values after all!). It is an anonymous conversation, in the dark of night, when he makes the round of the watches. He says: ". . . the king is but a man, as I am: the violet smells to him as it doth to me," etc.

But even in the light of day, when the Welshman Fluellen permits himself familiarly to express his delight that the King does not think it beneath him to wear the leek, he replies in homely fashion:

> I wear it for a memorable honour;
> For I am Welsh, you know, good countryman.

What a contrast when Shakespeare pictures the French! It is in itself an indication of a typically historical awareness that he found this contrast worth noting. After their defeat it is an added bitterness to the herald of the French to see nobles and commoners lying pell-mell on the field. Henry, on the contrary, in addressing the men before the battle (a rhetorical masterpiece, that little speech, to electrify an audience of solidiers—and of theatergoers!) had said:

> We few, we happy few, we band of brothers;
> For he to-day that sheds his blood with me
> Shall be my brother; be he ne'er so vile,
> This day shall gentle his condition:
> And gentlemen in England now a-bed,
> Shall think themselves accurs'd they were not here.

The *appearance*, then, is there, and it never misses its effect on the stage. But as for the *essence*, it leaves one cold, doubtful, irritated even. For what purpose all that energy and that eloquence? What do they signify? Shakespeare seems to want us to regard it all as something very high and noble, but in spite of the religious flavor with which he has permeated Henry's utterances, in spite of the insistence with which he pictures him as seeking what is good and right in the eyes of God, now with the help of the clergy, then in his personal prayers or in his communings with himself, one cannot help feeling that this war was no more than a reckless, frivolous, and fundamentally selfish undertaking.

That unctuous and would-be historical oration of the Archbishop of Canterbury in the first act, concluding with an assurance to the King's conscience that he is about to pursue a rightful claim, does not for a moment carry conviction. The impression of insincerity is thus created right from the beginning. It is strengthened by the incident of the traitors. Henry's behavior may look very fine—at once severe and mild, each quality accurately distributed; in short, a pattern of royal justice—but one cannot guard oneself against the suspicion of calculation, and the less so because the traitors have been touched off with too careless a brush; the poet is less than fair to them.

King Henry IV

The character of Henry V had been carefully prepared by Shakespeare in the two parts of *King Henry IV*. The Prince of Wales makes a prominent appearance in both plays. He is then the loose-living youth, a disappointment to his father. Only compare him with that other Harry, the ardent fighter Hotspur, son to the Earl of Northumberland (from the literary point of view a splendid character!), how sorry a figure does Prince Hal cut, drinking and gambling in Doll Tearsheet's inn with the gang of rakes and pickpockets of whom Falstaff is the chief.

But from the beginning Shakespeare had the conception (indeed he found it ready-made in the popular legend) of the gifted youth whose wildness is only evidence of his abundant vitality and who will prove completely equal to the responsibility of power.

I confess to a feeling that the contemptible quality of the young man's chosen companions is a bar to appreciation of his person. The critics have told us that in contemplating Falstaff we must suspend the working of our moral feelings. I am afraid the demand is too much for me. Falstaff, however amusing, however incredibly alive and in his wit at times profoundly wise, remains a swindler, a braggart, and a coward.[8]

However, I am now after data to define more closely Shakespeare's attitude toward kingship, and for this purpose his treatment of Prince Hal's association with that raffish fat man is certainly rewarding. It demonstrates his sure feeling for the human quality of the occupant of the high office.

The most priceless scene of all, in which at moments Shakespeare seems to make dangerously free with majesty, is the one in which Falstaff, his head covered with a cushion for the crown, acts the part of Henry IV and addresses his young friend in fatherly fashion; after which the roles are reversed and Hal, now the King, scolds Falstaff with much harsher fatherly authority. In fact, the dignity of the royal office comes out of this scene unscathed. Unexpectedly, and with inimitable tact, it is even brought out more clearly in this light-hearted fooling. The equilibrium is perfect.

In other passages, however, it seems to me that Shakespeare's freedom of mind as a creator of human beings was hampered by his respect for the office of king, and the damage done to the character of Henry is irreparable.

The first passage that I shall mention is an early one, where the Prince, having been shown for the first time in his familiarity with those scoundrelly companions, is made to reassure the public (for that is obviously what is intended by that monologue) and lets it be understood that he knows very well what he is doing. He compares himself to the sun, hiding behind clouds, but due soon to reappear to the greater delight of mankind.

> So, when this loose behaviour I throw off,
> And pay the debt I never promised,
> By how much better than my word I am
> By so much shall I falsify men's hopes;
> And like bright metal on a sullen ground,
> My reformation, glittering o'er my fault,
> Shall show more goodly and attract more eyes
> Than that which hath no foil to set it off.
> I'll so offend to make offence a skill;
> Redeeming time when men think least I will.

The second passage is that of the famous, or I may say, the notorious, "repudiation" of Falstaff. King Henry IV is dead. Prince Hal's boon companions are elated at the news and hurry toward London.

> God save thy grace, King Hal! my royal Hal! . . .
> God save thee, my sweet boy!

So cries Falstaff when the youthful king and his following, the

Lord Chief Justice among them, appear in "A public Place near Westminster Abbey."

K. Hen. V. My lord chief justice, speak to that vain man.
Ch. Just. Have you your wits? know you what 'tis you speak?
Fal. My king! my Jove! I speak to thee, my heart!
K. Hen. V. I know thee not, old man: fall to thy prayers;
How ill white hairs become a fool and jester!
I have long dream'd, of such a kind of man,
So surfeit-swell'd, so old, and so profane;
But being awak'd, I do despise my dream.

The scene is dramatically effective to a degree, but it sets on Henry an uneffaceable stamp of hypocrisy. Combined with the cold-blooded calculation implicit in the first-quoted passage—all the more repulsive because it concerns something so apparently spontaneous as the merrymaking of a lad loving a spree—this proceeding of the freshly-made king, too, casts on the conduct of the ripened man a most disagreeable light.

And throughout *King Henry V*, when we turn to that play again, we can now see a striving after effect, and the arts of the demagogue, where the poet invites us to admire greatness of soul and wisdom.

King Henry V (Once More)

In the third act of *King Henry V* the King summons the French governor of Harfleur to surrender the town. He dwells on his desire to save the citizenry from the horrors that would be the inevitable sequel to a capture of the town by storm. In advance he lays the responsibility upon the defenders. Now it is true enough that in the Middle Ages, and in Shakespeare's own day, the soldiery were not, in such a case, to be restrained. It might be said, therefore, that we are faced here by one of the hard facts of life as it was then, and that the realist Shakespeare did no more than accept it. Yet in the King's speech one is struck, as in the incident of the traitors in the second act—and this without the author having apparently intended or even noticed it—by an intolerable self-assurance, and what is worse, cleverness in casting himself for the generous role.[9]

How is it that Shakespeare, who elsewhere was able so impressively to make us accept a higher than worldly wisdom, did not here rise above an uncritical glorification of his practical-minded and self-confident man of action?

It should first of all be remembered that Shakespeare, whose powers of feeling and of creation covered so enormous an expanse, who, moreover, never ceased intellectually and sentimentally to develop, should not be judged by one play, or identified with the mood prevailing in one play. *King Henry V* was the last English history play he wrote—it was the last perhaps for the very reason that the culmination to which the genre had led left *him*, too, in his heart of hearts, unsatisfied. Perhaps it is his own criticism of the glorification of the active and triumphant victor, of the man whom the crowd hailed for his success, that soon afterward, in *Julius Caesar*, led him to present such a loving study of Brutus, of the unpractical idealist, great in spite of his incapacity to understand, or to get hold of, his fellow men, great in spite of his dismal failure. *Hamlet*, too, in which the chief character is ruined by the impotence of his superior mind, of his fecund imagination, of his oversensitive heart, in the face of the task imposed upon him by the stark and pitiless reality of life—*Hamlet*, too, was not far off.

SHAKESPEARE'S ACCEPTANCE OF SOCIAL ARRANGEMENTS (WAR AND PATRIOTISM)

The above considerations, I think, touch the core of the poet's being. But it is not on that account less necessary to observe that this peculiar quality of *Henry V* is at the same time connected with a profound and permanent feature of Shakespeare's attitude toward public affairs, toward the subject matter, in other words, that he has in common with the historian.

Shakespeare had nothing of the reformer. Tolstoy and Shaw, blind as they were to his greatness, did perceive *that* rightly enough. He accepted the world's order as constituted, and what he took to be its reflection in human society. In that order, as we know, the ruler's obligation had its appointed place, a moral obligation, an obligation with respect to God, but his authority nevertheless remained part of the unalterable order fixed of old. In *Henry V* Shakespeare pictured the social order with the help of yet another image than that of the firmament (employed in *Troilus and Cressida*).

Says the Archbishop of Canterbury:

> . . . heaven [doth] divide
> The state of man in divers functions,
> Setting endeavour in continual motion;
> To which is fixed, as an aim or butt,
> Obedience: for so work the honey-bees,
> Creatures that by a rule in nature teach
> The act of order to a peopled kingdom.

> They have a king and officers of sorts;
> Where some, like magistrates, correct at home,
> Others, like merchants, venture trade abroad,
> Others, like soldiers, armed in their stings,
> Make boot upon the summer's velvet buds;
> Which pillage they with merry march bring home
> To the tent-royal of their emperor:
> Who, busied in his majesty, surveys
> The singing masons building roofs of gold,
> The civil citizens kneading up the honey,
> The poor mechanic porters crowding in
> Their heavy burdens at his narrow gate,
> The sad-ey'd justice, with his surly hum,
> Delivering o'er to executors pale
> The lazy yawning drone.

This passage is not original. It follows Lyly's *Euphues and His England*, that too-famous book of 1580, whose ornate and hyper-ingenious style exerted so much influence over that generation, and over Shakespeare. But independently of Lyly (who was not himself, in fact, the first to use the comparison of the bees), Shakespeare's conception of human society was a static one; all thought of development or progress was alien to his mind, and so consequently was all desire for, all belief in, change. Thus Shakespeare accepted war, too, as a condition inherent in our humanity. No doubt he postulated a just war; but this justice was tested by the most conventional rules of the game of kings, laws of inheritance, honor, and such like; these rules satisfied, king and people could give themselves up wholeheartedly to the joys of conquest and glory. Throughout Shakespeare's work it is possible to trace that state of mind.

When we hear the business of war discussed slightingly, it is the sour Thersites speaking, the keen but crooked mind that likes to crab everything ("Good Thersites, come in and rail," Patroclus says laughingly).

> Here is such patchery, such juggling, and such knavery! all the argument is a cuckold and a whore [that is all Thersites leaves of that famed Trojan war]; a good quarrel to draw emulous factions and bleed to death upon. Now, the dry serpigo on the subject! and war and lechery confound all!

That concentrated bitterness, too, Shakespeare was able to feel with his imagination, but that he regarded it as a whisper of the Evil One appears from the fact that (even in this play of *Troilus and Cressida*, in which one senses his own mood must have been sorely troubled) he put those slighting words into the mouths of that most objectionable of plebeians. How differently does the noble Hamlet think of war and the glory of war! Nothing but envious admiration does he feel for "young Fortinbras," the Norwegian prince, who sets out with twenty thousand soldiers to wrench from the Polish King "a little patch of ground." Its very worthlessness adds to Hamlet's admiration.

Examples gross as earth exhort me:
Witness this army of such mass and charge
Led by a delicate and tender prince,
Whose spirit with divine ambition puff'd
Makes mouths at the invisible event,
Exposing what is mortal and unsure
To all that fortune, death and danger dare,
Even for an egg-shell.
. . . to my shame, I see
The imminent death of twenty thousand men,
That, for a fantasy and trick of fame,
Go to their graves like beds, fight for a plot
Whereon the numbers cannot try the cause,
Which is not tomb enough and continent
To hide the slain . . .

It is always necessary to guard against the all-too-insidious error of indiscriminately ascribing to Shakespeare the ideas voiced by his characters. Perhaps it is well to remember that the image of the beehive occurs in a speech of the Archbishop of Canterbury, and most certainly the excessive nature of the passage just quoted is to be accounted for by Hamlet's profoundly shaken mood, in which he attempts to whip himself up to "bloody" deeds. Yet I venture to maintain that both utterances generally agree with Shakespeare's attitude toward society.

In the English history plays he always regards foreign wars with a satisfaction unmarred by reflection. The glory of the battles in which the French are defeated is enjoyed without a scruple. This is the spirit that animates *King Henry V* and through which in times of heightened national consciousness this play has always made so powerful an appeal to the English public. The caricature of Joan of Arc served up in *King Henry VI, First Part*, is so repulsive that this is one of the reasons for which a later generation refused to accept the play as Shakespeare's work. And indeed it is hard to believe that Shakespeare in a later phase of his development could have repeated the crudity of that early effort. But the way in which at that early stage he simply followed the current English interpretation, the war propaganda of the evil-minded witch, is none the less typical of a certain feature of his personality. Of the French generally his sketches are always in tune with English prejudice, extraordinarily clever no doubt, done with a sure touch, but never rising above national bias. Characteristic is a sarcasm Joan of Arc herself is made to utter (most incongruously really):

> Done like a Frenchman: turn, and turn again!

But it is especially in *Henry V* that the French are depicted, in a masterly fashion, but always to make the manly and martial superiority of the English king come out the more brilliantly. Their boastings and at the same time their fears when they talk about him, their incorrigible frivolity, are irresistibly amusing, but for all that they remain within the bounds of a convention, and the poet, who at other times was able to look at life and at human beings with so free and penetrating an eye, here shows himself blinkered.

SHAKESPEARE AND THE PEOPLE

So far I have sketched the conservative, the assenting feature of Shakespeare's mind in relation to kingship, war, patriotism. It can be observed equally well in his attitude toward the lower classes. He does not merely indulge in generalities about the necessity of a stable social order.

It seems to me unnecessary (although it has frequently been done) to depict Shakespeare as a hardened aristocrat because in *Julius Caesar* he makes Caesar wrinkle his nose at the stench of the mob. It is true that the passage is not singular: Shakespeare's own sense of smell must have been keen. It is at any rate undeniable that he liked to show up men of the people in their stupidity and clumsiness. The ducal company in *Midsummer Night's Dream* makes mercilessly merry over the antics that Bottom and his fellow handicraftsmen perform in such deadly earnest. Audrey, the clumsy peasant girl in *As You Like It*, may have a touch of the pathetic in her callow innocence, but nobody, not even her creator, takes her seriously, and the last we hear about her is Touchstone's request to the Duke to be allowed to marry her—in this strain: ". . . an ill-favoured thing, sir, but mine own: a poor humour of mine, sir, to take that that no man else will."

The masterly little thumbnail sketch of the old nurse in *Romeo and Juliet* is strikingly unkind. True, over against these, characters of a different stamp can be placed. For instance, in *King Lear*, the servant who has the courage to protest when Cornwall is about to pull out Gloucester's eyes; or, in *As You Like It* once more, Adam, the old serving man, who sticks to Orlando in his misfortunes and offers him his savings; in his turn, when their journey proves too much for the feeble old man, Orlando carries him on his back. Here, of course, it should be remembered that the aristocratic code is always ready to acknowledge the virtue of faithfulness in a servant.

One hesitates what to conclude, but what must strike every reader of Shakespeare—and in my argument it has obvious significance—is his consistent lack of sympathy for popular movements or for any meddling with public affairs on the part of the multitude or even of the middle class. Anything in that line he treats with distaste and scorn.

In Dogberry and Verges, that precious pair of self-important but endlessly blundering constables of the civic guard in *Much Ado About Nothing*, ridicule is thrown not only on small-town middle-class men, but on the entire institution they represent. When, in *Richard III*, the King and his henchman Buckingham explain to the Lord Mayor of London how they were compelled to the killing of Hastings by the victim's (purely fictitious) attempts on their own lives, the crass stupidity with which the representative of burgherdom allows himself to be bamboozled is no less striking than the false scoundrelism of the highborn murderers.

The clearest evidence, however (although even this is not always interpreted alike in the countless speculations about Shakespeare's political sentiments by modern critics), is afforded by the set scenes of riotous, or at least politically excited, crowds in *Henry IV*, in *Julius Caesar*, and in *Coriolanus*. At every new reading one is amazed at the brilliant competence of those scenes. The arts of the popular orator, the reactions of the mob—how accurately have they been observed and with what faultless efficiency noted down. The historic sense is here very manifest. But to me there can be no doubt that observation and execution were inspired by hostility.

Jack Cade in King Henry VI

Hear the followers of Jack Cade. Says John: ". . . it was never merry world in England since gentlemen came up."

"O miserable age!" George echoes. "Virtue is not regarded in handicrafts-men."

And John once more: ". . . it is said, 'Labour in thy vocation,' which is as much to say as, let the magistrates be labouring men; and therefore should we be magistrates."

This sample of crooked logic sets the tone at once. Cade himself, who pretends to be of the royal blood, talks even more wildly: "There shall be in England," he promises his followers, "seven halfpenny loaves sold for a penny; the three-hooped pot shall have ten hoops; and I will make it a felony to drink small beer. All the realm shall be in common, and [he does not forget himself!] in Cheapside shall my palfrey go to grass." To death with all lawyers, cries one among the mob, and Cade, for his part, inveighs against the rule of parchment. "Away!" he commands a little later on, "burn all the records of the realm: my mouth shall be the parliament of England." This is indeed the revolution touched off in its deepest essence. Cade is also shown as the fanatic of equality when he sentences Chatham's clerk for being able to read and write and for possessing a book with red lettering. Lord Say is a traitor: doesn't he know French? The scene of his being convicted can serve for a satire on all brutal revolutionary trials, but it is especially the illiterate at whom the satire digs. And by what means does old Lord Clifford in the end succeed in detaching the people from the impostor? Not by rational argument, but by appealing to their feelings of loyalty to the veritable King, Henry VI, and above all by working on their hatred and fear of the French, against whom only the true blood can protect them (and, too, he offers them a chance of winning rank and spoils in France under his leadership).

It is not only, then, that Shakespeare condemns Jack Cade's rebellion; that he does so is only natural. But he does not evince the slightest sympathy for the groping aspirations that were behind it; he is silent about the distress that gave rise to it; he makes it, in all its manifestations, silly and foolish.

Julius Caesar

Everybody knows the crowd in *Julius Caesar* and remembers how it let itself be swept off its feet, first by Brutus, then by Mark Antony. Brutus impresses the people by his grave and noble personality, but so little do they understand the motives of the high-principled republican that in order to show their enthusiasm they wish to crown *him*. But now the unscrupulous Mark Antony manages to rouse them to the pitch of frenzy. Soon they are all impatience to wreak their fury on Brutus, whom they had cheered but a moment before; Caesar's avenger has to call them back in order to serve up to them the argument that is to bring them over to his side for good: he had begun with an allusion to Caesar's will, but they had forgotten all about it in their excitement. How they now love to hear that Caesar has left a large part of his fortune to the people! "Mischief, thou art afoot," Mark Antony exclaims as he remains behind by himself. And that too is brought before our eyes in the biting little scene wherein the raving citizens stop a gentleman to fire the maddest questions at him. When it appears, after some rather caustic answers, which have not exactly pacified the hotheads, that his name is Cinna, there is an outcry:

Second Citizen. Tear him to pieces; he's a conspirator.
Cinna. I am Cinna the poet, I am Cinna the poet.
Fourth Citizen. Tear him for his bad verses, tear him for his bad verses.
Cinna. I am not Cinna the conspirator.
Second Citizen. It is no matter, his name's Cinna; pluck but his name out of his heart, and turn him going.
Third Citizen. Tear him, tear him!

Coriolanus

There is one among the Roman plays, *Coriolanus*, in which the problem of aristocracy versus democracy is posed more directly—for what dominates the interest in *Julius Caesar* is, after all, the conflict between aristocracy and autocracy. *Julius Caesar* is perhaps the first of Shakespeare's works that can, without qualifications, be called great. It opens the poet's richest period. *Coriolanus* was written eight years later, after the great tragedies, to which it can be said in a sense still to belong. No other work supplies so much relevant material to the discussion of Shakespeare's feelings toward the people, about his aristocratic, or antidemocratic, attitude.

Caius Marcius, the son of the noble lady Volumnia, is a formidable warrior, and at the same time, a despiser of the plebs. A bitter social struggle is raging in Rome. The plebeians want to have corn at a lower price than that fixed by the Senate. Old Menenius, a wise man in spite of his somewhat wordy and jolly manner, tells them the parable of the stomach and the limbs—again a comparison in which the social order appears as a thing fixed forever and the poor are taught that they must have patience. The story makes a profound impression, until the hot-blooded Caius Marcius enters and starts inveighing against the plebeians' impudence in criticizing a decision of the Senate. Meanwhile the Senate, to the intense indignation of Caius Marcius, appoints two tribunes to look after the interests of the people; these men, Brutus and Sicinius, regard Marcius as the principal adversary.

Marcius, however, now wins new glory by conquering Corioli, the capital of the hereditary enemy, the Volsces, and the Senate, honoring him with the name of Coriolanus, elects him to be consul—an election, however, still to be confirmed by the people.

With the greatest reluctance, but encouraged by Volumnia, Menenius, and other friends, Coriolanus submits to ancient custom and goes to the market place to beg for votes. With thinly disguised contempt he assures the voters that it is only for the sake of their votes that he has exposed his life, and his begging cry: "Your voices . . . your voices," sounds like mockery. To bare his body in order to display his scars—that, too, required by custom—is a humiliation to which he cannot stoop. But his heroic deeds count, and the election is confirmed. Soon afterward, however, while Coriolanus is being installed in the Senate, the slow-thinking crowd is beginning to realize it has been insulted; the tribunes stir up the ill feeling; and on Coriolanus's return to the Forum, his right to the office is called into question. In spite of the attempts of Menenius and some others to hold him back, he replies with bitter taunts, carefully noted down by the tribunes. At last he draws his sword, a crime for which he is exiled from the city by the tribunes, in the name of the people. Coriolanus receives that sentence with heartfelt bitterness. "I banish you"! is the rejoinder he hurls at the crowd, with scathing remarks about the reek of their breaths.

> . . . Despising,
> For you, the city, thus I turn my back:
> There is a world elsewhere.

And indeed he makes his opponents feel it. He goes straight to the enemy. The chieftain of the Volsces, Aufidius, joyfully takes him in and entrusts to him the command of a fresh attack on Rome. Rome is shaken; people and tribunes tremble at the imminent danger. They humble themselves before Menenius, imploring him to go to Coriolanus and prevail upon him to forbear in his revenge. Coriolanus rejects his old friend's plea. When, however, Coriolanus's wife, and particularly, his mother, come to add their supplications, he cannot resist any longer.

> . . . O my mother! mother! O!
> You have won a happy victory to Rome;
> But, for your son, believe it, O! believe it,
> Most dangerously you have with him prevail'd,
> If not most mortal to him. But let it come.

His was true foresight. Aufidius turns against him, and he is killed by the Volsces.

The critics—as I hinted before—do not agree in their interpretations of this powerful tragedy. Coleridge says that it illustrates the wonderful philosophical impartiality of Shakespeare's political drama, and Hazlitt, in the same vein, argues that here all is said that can be said both for the aristocrat and for the democrat. Brandes, on the contrary, is struck by "the physical aversion to the people's atmosphere" and by "the absence of any humane attention for the oppression of the poor"; it all turns on the divine greatness of the hero Marcius. Brandes believes that Shakespeare did detest the latter's betrayal of Rome, but of criticism of his earlier behavior as the virulent hater of the people he finds not a trace. Shakespeare's view of life in this play is, according to Brandes, that "round the lonely great ones of this earth there is inevitably a conspiracy of envy and hatred, hatched by the base and common sort."

M. W. MacCallum,[10] overseeing these pronouncements in 1910, attempts to prove the truth of Coleridge's view. But when he admits that Shakespeare will always, in other works no less than in *Coriolanus*, picture the multitude as changeable, blind, and unfit to govern, he has practically given way to those who see in Shakespeare the aristocrat and antidemocrat. That this does not involve hatred, that Brandes is wrong when he ascribes to the poet the feelings of physical loathing expressed by his dramatic personages, may be true; I myself noted above that Shakespeare, to use MacCallum's words, "is kind enough to individual representatives" of the people and that "he certainly believes in the sacred obligation of governing them for their good"; even so, the question of what must be understood by this good that is to be promoted by the people's governors continues to present a complication of problems. And the mentality here sketched is in any case a typically aristocratic one. The effect of this on the historic truth of Shakespeare's picture of the plebs I shall indicate in a moment; my conclusion now is only, not that Brandes takes the right view, but that at least Shakespeare's politics are not so philosophically impartial as Coleridge would have us believe, and also that, if he says all that can be said on behalf of the aristocrats, he certainly does not—as Hazlitt asserts—say all on behalf of the democrats.

But indeed one has only to read the play. It is not that Shakespeare unreservedly exalts Coriolanus before he committed his high treason. Brandes commits a double error. The treason is, in Shakespeare's eyes, a much less heinous crime than we moderns would expect; but in any case the poet makes it proceed naturally from the defect of character shown from the beginning as the root of the tragic conflict: his hero's stubbornness and lack of self-restraint.

The conflict is not between two political attitudes, not between aristocrat and democrat. That struggle is no more than the occasion. In itself it did not interest Shakespeare overmuch, so confidently did he take his stand with one side. Volumnia, Menenius, the senators, all hold the same view, in no wise differing from Coriolanus's own, of the stupid people, the crafty and ignoble tribunes. Only, Volumnia and Menenius and the other friends deplore the reckless, the all too outspoken, the imprudent behavior of the man who seemed destined to become the soul of their party. Coriolanus is great; he is noble. His nature is too noble for the world.

This is what Menenius says of him. He cannot stoop to compromise. Allard Pierson, the great Dutch critic of the late nineteenth century, compared him, very aptly, with Alceste in Molière's *Misanthrope*. Coriolanus cannot conceal the contempt that he (with all of his class) feels for the plebeians. Before Corioli, cowards as they are, they had left him in the lurch: their stupidity is equaled only by their unreliability. Even more profound is the loathing he feels for the tribunes, who flatter the crowd the better to nurse their own ambitions. Even among the plebeians some seem to take this view. Two servants laying cushions in the Capitol discuss the situation. One thinks that Coriolanus goes too far: not only does he abstain from flattery of the people, he seems wilfully to seek their displeasure and hatred. The other cannot help feeling respect for a man whose claims rest on honorable deeds: ". . . his ascent is not by such easy degrees as those who, having been supple and courteous to the people, bonneted, without any further deed to have them at all into their estimation and report." When in the fatal dispute the tribune Brutus condescendingly admits that Coriolanus has served Rome well, the latter interjects cuttingly: "What do you prate of service?"

Shakespeare gives a most striking little sketch of the tribunes Brutus and Sicinius, a sketch charged with that active dislike which the true conservative is apt to feel for democratic politicians much more than for the people. Envious and given to intrigue, it is they who goad the hotheaded hero on to his ruin. "Put him to choler straight," is the advice of the one to the other before the fateful encounter, and Menenius's whispers to Coriolanus—"Nay, temperately; your promise!" and "Is this the promise that you made your mother?"—cannot save him from himself.

There is no lack of writers who delight in the picture of false, petty, and pushing demagogues drawn by Shakespeare in Sicinius and Brutus, maintaining at the same time that nothing can be deduced from this picture as to Shakespeare's feelings about true democracy. These writers only betray their own conservative prejudice. The tribunes in *Coriolanus* are most certainly instructive about Shakespeare's antidemocratic sentiments—not, of course, because Shakespeare detests demagogues. Everybody does! But because Shakespeare cannot view the advocates of the plebs as anything but abject demagogues.

Occasionally, nevertheless, the tribunes do say something of what they might have said for democracy, such as Hazlitt asserted Shakespeare made them do consistently. So Brutus snaps at Coriolanus:

> You speak o' the people,
> As if you were a god to punish, not
> A man of their infirmity.

One more word, and one that indeed cuts deeply, is spoken by Sicinius in reply to a senator who warned him that by undoing the election of Coriolanus to the consulate he risked overthrowing the city:

> What is the city but the people?

The citizens at once shout their assent:

> True,
> The people are the city.

But Coriolanus takes up the senator's warning and exclaims:

> That is the way to lay the city flat;
> To bring the roof to the foundation,
> And bury all, which yet distinctly ranges,
> In heaps and piles of ruin.

We can see in this exchange the contrast between a humanitarian, social, democratic ideal, in which pride of place gives way to the interest of the community, that is to say, of the human beings composing it; and a conservative and authoritarian ideal, in which the state, apart from its citizens and their needs and desires, is regarded as the primary interest. Here we get a glimpse of that complication of problems of which I spoke; and it is, at any rate, beyond all doubt that the second of the two alternatives is the one inspiring *Coriolanus*—insofar as the play can be said to be inspired by any political notion. The citizens had bluntly stated their needs at the outset, but neither Coriolanus nor Menenius and Volumnia give these the slightest attention, and the motif soon recedes from view. It is the state that is important, the well-being of Rome as an independent entity over against the Volsces. And just as in the case of Jack Cade's rebellion, it is the foreign danger that becomes, toward the end, the ruling factor, making even the plebeians change their minds.

So we see Shakespeare once again as a son of his country and of his age. Among the most influential and intellectual classes, newly awakened national consciousness, and pride in their own state and monarchy maintaining themselves against great Continental powers, were infinitely stronger considerations than those of social betterment or internal politics. It might be thought that one outcome of such an attitude must have been detestation of Coriolanus's treason. Naturally the deed is condemned: it is the last and worst result of the hero's defect of character, of his pride, his inability to observe measure, and it leads directly to his ruin. But it does not detract from his nobility, which is acknowledged even by the Volsces after they have killed him. To understand this it is essential, once more, to remember the many instances Shakespeare's age still offered to the observing eye of great noblemen deserting to their country's enemy out of wounded pride, or because they considered themselves wronged. It was an age of suddenly erupted national passion, but the code of honor of the great still admitted of a good deal of trifling with national solidarity.

I cannot take leave of *Coriolanus* without stating (although the remark is implied in what was said before) that it is a history play in a sense differing from the English dramas. *Julius Caesar* in this respect may be said to mark a transition. In the English history plays the *history* constitutes the real subject matter—this is true even of *Richard II* and *Richard III*, in which the persons of the kings occupy so striking a position. *Coriolanus* is more similar to the great tragedies Shakespeare had just written. Its real subject is the hero's ruin, due to the defects of his heroic personality. The history, however loving the care with which it has been treated, is an ornamental dressing.

The Tempest

He who would try to deduce Shakespeare's political philosophy from *The Tempest* must be sadly lacking in feeling for poetry; even some sense of humor should suffice to make one desist from the attempt. And yet it is impossible, when considering Shakespeare's attitude toward authority, toward the people, or toward social problems, to keep completely silent about that charming fantasy with which he concluded his literary career.

An unambiguous answer to our questions, a coherent system, we must not expect to find. What will be revealed to us is Shakespeare's mind playing with all sorts of ideas on these matters, and now and then we shall be able to surprise his involuntary reactions.

Among the varied company that, after the shipwreck caused by Prospero's magic, comes ashore on his bewitched island, the good Gonzalo is the most inclined to reflection. He expounds to his companions in the adventure how *he* would arrange matters were it given to him to rule over the island. A complete utopia, which Shakespeare had found in Montaigne: everything in common, no riches and no poverty, no contracts and no law of inheritance, neither field nor vineyard enclosed, no trade, no magistrates, no writings, neither trade nor handicraft.

> . . . all men idle, all;
> And women too, but innocent and pure;
> No sovereignty—

It does not mean much that the bad men, Sebastian and Antonio, scoff at these imaginings, or that King Alonzo, who has in the past plotted with Antonio against Prospero, does not think them worth more than a shrug. But the contrast pointed by reality, by the reality of the fantasy, by the island such as Prospero has made it, is striking.

For Prospero, the best and wisest of men, does not scruple to exercise authority (sovereignty, as the poet calls it), nor does he shrink from resorting to harsh methods. The monster Caliban, the slave used for the rougher kind of work, is driven with merciless imprecations and kept in order by his fear of the colics and bellyaches with which the potent magician will punish him in the event of disobedience; even Ariel, the graceful spirit of the air, who at Prospero's command directs the breezes and with their music attracts the shipwrecked men and soothes them to sleep, is forced to stay in Prospero's service only by the cruelest threats.

Prospero, like his creator, accepts the conditions of our humanity, or rather, of existing social arrangements. When his daughter, Miranda, expresses the horror she feels at the sight of the wicked and common Caliban, he replies with unmitigated matter-of-factness:

> But, as 'tis,
> We cannot miss him: he does make our fire,
> Fetch in our wood; and serves in offices
> That profit us—What ho! slave! Caliban!
> Thou earth, thou! speak.

Did Shakespeare mean Caliban to represent the people, the laboring classes? The passage quoted would almost persuade one to believe it. But in that case Caliban's evil nature, his coarse materialism, his vulgarity, which is such that he will use the human language learned from Prospero only to curse, his superstitiousness, his inaccessibility to arguments other than those of punishment or pain—all this would betray a particularly unpleasant attitude in the poet. Many commentators (and one is reminded of what happened in connection with *Coriolanus*) have done their best to clear "the gentle Shakespeare" from the suspicion.

The most interesting alternative explanation is that Caliban (anagram of Can[n]ibal) represents primitive man, the savage to whom voyages of exploration were just drawing the attention of the European public. As a matter of fact, Caliban is soon shown more particularly in relation to Stephano and Trinculo, the two vulgar types among the shipwrecked, the drunken sailor and the clown; and it is then possible to construct a contrast between the natural barbarian and the dregs of civilization, a contrast in which Caliban really does not come off worst. Even then, however, it is not exactly Shakespeare's "gentleness" that reveals itself. Kreyssig remarks that in presenting his natural man Shakespeare, as it were, by anticipation, rejected Rousseau's conception. Instead of giving way to an optimistic belief in man's innate goodness, which is corrupted only by civilization, Shakespeare drew a repulsive picture of man in his natural condition, his evil proclivities needing to be curbed by a civilized society, by order, by authority. Whether or not this conception actually guided Shakespeare's mind in the creation of Caliban, it is certainly in agreement with the entire spirit of his writings. That man's nature is beset by evil inclinations, which have to be carefully restrained, and that order and punishment are indispensable to that end—Shakespeare has expressed these views not once but countless times.

Nevertheless, Stephano and Trinculo are even more contemptible than Caliban. The monster at first pays divine honors to Stephano, who treats him to wine, but in the long run he turns out to have more common sense than that base pair of topers, and in fact forswears his veneration. Indeed Stephano and Trinculo are no very edifying samples of the society existing outside the bewitched island. Is that the sailor, this drunkard with his bottle, singing songs like "The master, the swabber, the boatswain and I . . ."?

But do not let us make the mistake of wanting to explain everything symbolically. Shakespeare knew well enough that there were better sailors and that "the people," if not portrayed in Caliban, was not fully represented in Stephano and Trinculo either.

One is struck, all the same, by the difference of the treatment Shakespeare meted out, in the denouement of his idyll, to the aristocratic and to the plebeian scoundrels. Both kinds are present. There are not only Caliban, Stephano, and Trinculo; there are also Sebastian and Antonio. In the past Antonio had thrust Prospero out of his lawful inheritance, the duchy of Milan, and now he incites Sebastian to kill his brother, Alonzo, in order to obtain the throne of Naples for himself. The crime is prevented by Ariel. Prospero, who now has them all in his power, does not think of revenge. Under the stress of the helpless condition into which he has maneuvered them, they show repentance, and this is sufficient for him to forgive them. But does the repentance go more than skin deep? Rather, Antonio and Sebastian, at the moment of punishment, behave defiantly, and once sure of their pardon, they are as breezy and arrogant as ever. Caliban, Stephano, and Trinculo, on the other hand, who also have misbehaved themselves, plotting and committing robberies, are let off less lightly in the hour of retribution. True, they are not punished again, but they are still writhing with the pains already inflicted upon them. While the gentlemen look on, and laugh, they slink away under a shower of hard words to take the loot back to where they found it. "Or stole it, rather," the unsuccessful murderer Sebastian has the impudence to add. Shakespeare clearly uses two measures: his plebeian monster is indeed treated very unfairly in comparison with his aristocratic evildoer.

The impression we already formed of Shakespeare's attitude toward state and society is confirmed. To Shakespeare, state and society were static entities, firmly settled in an order linked to the eternal cosmic order. Labor was the lot of the many, so that the few might be more complete human beings; the authority by which that order was to be protected belonged in the hands of those called to this high task by birth and culture; the task laid obligations on them, but to think that the multitude could call them to account was mere foolishness.

Attitude toward Social Reform

In Shakespeare's system the wretchedness of the poor had its place. Criticism of social conditions, in the sense of an indignant awareness of shortcomings allied to a desire to remedy them, is hardly to be found in the whole of his works. One may think of the starving apothecary in *Romeo and Juliet;* his misery is keenly observed, but it is coolly used to help Romeo to his poison. Or of Hamlet's soliloquy, in which he mentions "The slings and arrows of outrageous fortune":

> The oppressor's wrong, the proud man's contumely,
> . . . the law's delay,
> The insolence of office, and the spurns
> That patient merit of the unworthy takes.

An enumeration of social evils—and indeed Shakespeare was not blind, nor did he try to blind himself. But the thought that in a differently arranged state or society men might be spared these trials is utterly alien to his mind. To him they belong (if I may once more use that expression) to the conditions of our humanity, so much so that half way in his little list (where the dots indicate an excision in my quotation) he mentions the "pangs of dispriz'd love"—all in the same category of inevitability.

I can remember only one passage where a different note is struck. Listen to Lear, in the storm, on the heath:

> Poor naked wretches, wheresoe'er you are,
> That bide the pelting of this pitiless storm,
> How shall your houseless heads and unfed sides,
> Your loop'd and window'd raggedness, defend you
> From seasons such as these? O! I have ta'en
> Too little care of this. Take physic, pomp;
> Expose thyself to feel what wretches feel,
> That thou mayst shake the superflux to them,
> And show the heavens more just.

But if anywhere, then it is here necessary to remember that it is Lear who speaks like this, Lear in his misfortune. The expression of a feeling of kinship in suffering, including even those words "O! I have ta'en—Too little care of this," is as it were wrung from the dramatic situation. The poet's all-embracing imagination could comprehend this too. But it is no more than a cry of anguish, which leads to no consequences in the play and has no place in Shakespeare's philosophy of state and society.

It would be an error to think that the mentality here delineated was the only one possible for men of Shakespeare's age. It reigned supreme, no doubt, in political and social thinking, but not everybody accepted it as wholeheartedly as Shakespeare did; here and there not only blind sufferers but also clear-sighted thinkers contended with it. The utopias of the age should not, certainly, be regarded as programs of action, yet in the minds of their devisers they stood for more than Shakespeare was willing to see in that of Montaigne. More in particular intended a serious criticism. Erasmus, too, treated kings and their wars with a good deal less resignation than did Shakespeare. The contrast between the acquiescent conservative and the critical reformer is one of all times, and about Shakespeare's place in his generation there can be no doubt.

SHAKESPEARE AND THE PURITANS: HIS RELIGION

It is significant that Shakespeare had no use for the Puritans and liked to ridicule them. The Puritans, certainly, were not first and foremost reformers of state and society, but they regarded these with an independence that was enough to annoy Shakespeare and to rouse his scorn. That traditional order, which was to Shakespeare the immutable setting within which the human drama, the drama of good and evil, was enacted, that order which he respected and loved with all its shadings, its heights and its depths, the Puritans tested, if need be, by a command—to them, of a superior nature; but to Shakespeare, arbitrary, fantastical, arrogant. It is true that neither in *Twelfth Night* nor in *Measure for Measure* did he put the problem in those terms. He girded only against the rejection of joy of life and of natural enjoyment of the senses which struck him in Puritanism.

> Dost thou think, because thou art virtuous,
> there shall be no more cakes and ale?[11]

Of Malvolio, moreover, he made a coxcomb, and of Angelo a hypocrite. That the idealist, that is to say, the man who sets an abstraction above life, who wants to remodel the order in the image of his personal opinion, was not to Shakespeare's liking, so much is in any case clear from that scathing reaction.

It will be seen that I do not express the problem of Shakespeare's attitude to Puritanism in religious terms. And indeed I do not think that that was how it presented itself to him. Much has been written about Shakespeare's religion; attempts have been made to drag him in various directions.

Dowden saw in him a Protestant.[12] But what was Protestantism to Dowden? "Energy, devotion to the fact, self-government, tolerance, a disbelief in minute apparatus for the improvement of human character, an indifference to externals in comparison with that which is of the invisible life, and a resolution to judge all things from a purely human standpoint." For the Puritan, for the Calvinist, for the sixteenth-century Protestant, that definition would have been, in essential parts, unacceptable. What Dowden had in mind was the Protestantism of his own day, a bastard of the genuine brand and of the Renaissance. The Renaissance—is not that where we should look for Shakespeare's spiritual home? "The Renaissance," says Croce, "had made earthly life a reality, and that is where he belonged."[13]

In 1922 a Catholic author, Looten, of the Catholic University of Lille, published a little book on Shakespeare's religion. According to him Shakespeare was a Catholic for a good bit of his life; all the first half of his literary output, Looten says, bears witness to this. Not until the closing years of the sixteenth century did the humanistic and Machiavellic influences of the age reduce him to doubt, and it is this that explains the gloomy, the despairing mood of the great tragedies.

No more than the others does this view carry conviction. Familiarity with Catholic attitudes is no doubt unmistakable in Shakespeare's dramas, but this was not as yet anything singular. And the attacks on Catholicism that can be observed later do not denote skepticism; they are rather typically Protestant and are directed against the papacy and the Jesuits. But such attacks were conditioned by the national temper, and even though they were conducted with weapons taken from the Protestant armory, they were not necessarily inspired by any distinct religious conviction. That much discussed gloominess of the first years of the new century, moreover, cannot be so lightly equated to despair.

Bradley has made on all this the most penetrating and the most balanced comments. "It does not seem likely that outside his poetry he was a very simple-minded Catholic or Protestant or Atheist, as some have maintained; but we cannot be sure, as with poets like Milton, or Wordsworth, or Shelley we can, that in his works he expressed his deepest and most cherished convictions on ultimate questions, or even that he had any." And Bradley goes on to suggest that one must temporarily sharpen one's particular religious faith if one is to undergo to the full the tragic impression of the Shakespearean drama. This impression is made by the representation of human action within the framework of a moral cosmic order. The world is not governed by a blind and indifferent Fate: yet there is not, either, a just dispensation according to which merit is rewarded. By the morality of the cosmic order is meant that this order strives after good, exists through good, and reacts to evil by expelling and destroying it. The process of life nevertheless involves a disturbance of the order; it is attended by violence and entails the ruin and waste of much that is good and noble: this is its tragic aspect. The Shakespearean tragedy, however, is not therefore depressing. In the solution one will always observe the expulsion of evil, at the cost of however much suffering and waste; the assertion of a moral order.

In this view of Shakespeare's attitude toward religion the dogmatic contrasts within the Christian world recede into the background. And indeed it seems possible to me that here, too, Shakespeare's reactions to public life were simply conservative and national, that is to say, that he accepted the Church "as by law established" and detested the Puritans as fanatics and disturbers of the public peace.

PURITAN REACTIONS TO SHAKESPEARE, TOLSTOY, AND CROSBY

Nothing seems more natural, when the above observations have been made, than that modern puritans and radicals (I alluded to the fact before) are so often hostile to Shakespeare. I mentioned Tolstoy. His very shallow and insignificant little book (by the author of *The Kreutzer Sonata*, not by the author of *War and Peace*!) is inspired by the Shakespearean criticism of some nineteenth-century English writers, of Ernest Crosby more particularly, who himself quotes Edward Carpenter. Crosby does not go the lengths to which Tolstoy, who writes off the Shakespeare cult as a ridiculous and ephemeral phenomenon, goes, but he does feel that the poet's lack of understanding of humble folk, or his aversion to them, seriously detracts from his greatness. This judgment proceeds naturally from his conviction that democracy, liberalism, faith in progress, are requisites for the production of great literature; it is the task of the great writer to lead mankind toward emancipation. Edward Carpenter's indignation is roused by Prospero's remark (which I quoted above) on Caliban's usefulness in spite of his repulsive appearance: "Who are you," he exlaims indignantly, "pouring out sarcasm on him who gets you bread, who clothes you, who all day and all night slaves for you obscurely on the earth."

Shaw

The rejection of Shakespeare by Shaw has its place in this tradition. I must admit that I can read an early essay of Shaw's on *Henry IV* with a good deal of agreement. It deals particularly with the figure of Henry V, who, as we know, appears already in the plays called after his father, and who toward the end of the second, repudiates Falstaff. One can hardly quite forgive Shakespeare for the worldly phase in which he tried to thrust such a jingo hero as his Harry V down our throats.

After so much uncritical acceptance of the conventional and demagogic hero (even a generally very sensible German like Kreyssig allowed himself to be swept off his feet and envied the English for the possession of so patriotic a play; a sensible German, but one who was strongly moved by the spirit of 1870, so that he could not help thinking the cheap caricature of the French a wonderful bit), after streams of praise, Shaw's biting criticism is indeed refreshing.

But when he wrote it, at least he still acknowledged Shakespeare's greatness. Soon he was totally to reject him.

In the whole of Shakespeare not a single hero! Only one man in all those thirty-six big plays who believes in life, enjoys life, thinks life worth living, and has a sincere, unrhetorical tear dropped over his death-bed; and that man . . . Falstaff! What a crew they are, these Saturday-to-Monday athletic stockbroker Orlandos, these villains, fools, clowns, drunkards, cowards, intriguers, fighters, lovers, patriots, hypochondriacs who mistake themselves (and are mistaken by the author) for philosophers, princes without any sense of public duty, futile pessimists, who imagine they are confronting a barren and unmeaning world when they are only contemplating their own worthlessness, self-seekers of all kinds, keenly observed and masterfully drawn from the romantic-commercial point of view. . . . Search for statesmanship, or even citizenship, or any sense of the commonwealth, material or spiritual, and you will not find the making of a decent vestryman or curate in the whole horde. As for faith, hope, courage, conviction, or any of the true heroic qualities, you find nothing but death made stage-sublime, sex made romantic, and barrenness covered up by sentimentality and the mechanical lilt of blank verse.

After this wholehearted denunciation, of which the final words are hard to forgive (especially coming from a man who had elsewhere shown himself sensitive to the delight of the Shakespearean verse), Shaw points a contrast; and the man he dares to proclaim truly great, as against the hollow, romantic Shakespeare, is a Puritan among Puritans.

All that you miss in Shakespeare, you find in Bunyan, to whom the heroic came quite obviously and naturally. . . . "My sword give to him that shall succeed me in my pilgrimage, and my courage and skill to him that can get there." The heart vibrates like a bell to such an utterance as this. To turn from it to "Out, out, brief candle," and "The rest is silence," and "We are such stuff as dreams are made on, and our little life is rounded by a sleep," is to turn from life, strength, resolution, morning air and eternal youth, to the terrors of a drunken nightmare.

This is no more than letting off steam, I know. It is a scream of hate when understanding fails. Yet I have thought it worth quoting, because it helps to distinguish even more clearly this one aspect of Shakespeare: that his view of life has a repelling effect on the puritan, humorless mentality intent only on reform. To a sober, practical, progressive mind, to a man who regards life as a task to be fulfilled and the world as an ill-arranged muddle that he feels called upon to set right, to such a one Shakespeare is an objectionable, an antisocial, figure—like an artist who in a miserable slum thinks of the picturesque instead of falling to work with statistics and a stethoscope.

Indeed, a plan of improvement in accordance with Shaw's political or scientific principles will not be found in Shakespeare's works. Yet the picturesque effect is far from being all to him. He struggles with life after his own fashion, a purely personal struggle. The social problem does not exist, there is only the moral, and that is to say, the individual problem. The social environment certainly claims attention, for it is part of life. And life in all its forms is given, in its contrasts and unintelligibilities, in its sorrows and its joys, its love and sin, its hatred and its folly, in its light and its dark. Unceasingly changeful, this life is ever the same, glorious and terrible, repellent and beautiful. To every generation and to every human being it is set again to be lived through and to be struggled with, and whatever the puritan or the reformer may think, no wisdom, no faith, and no philosophy will ever succeed in solving its riddle.

A Dutch Marxist's View

In concluding this section I cannot refrain from offering a digression on the Shakespeare interpretation sprung from the brain of a fellow countryman of mine. Theun de Vries belongs, spiritually, to the small group of radical dogmatists, one or two of whom I have discussed already. He has tried to place Shakespeare in history. Shakespeare's rejection of the Puritans is to him a sign, not of conservative and nationalist feeling, nor of humanism and love of intellectual freedom, but of backwardness, of reactionary and unavailing resistance to the forces of the future. In that period of Shakespeare's, the period of transition from the Middle Ages, with their static conception of the world, to the age of modern capitalism, of cool, matter-of-fact and rational burgherdom—the latter represented by the Puritans and soon triumphant in Cromwell—he felt distracted. He could not let go of the poetry of the past, of the dream, the fancy, the fairy tale; yet with a large portion of his personality he was undoubtedly modern, critical, given to questioning.

Bold theories indeed! but from how distorted a view of English, and in fact of European, history do they proceed! The identification of Calvinism with middle-class capitalism is as completely unjustified as is that of both with rationalism and of the Middle Ages with poetry; and no less wrong is the opinion that Cromwell won for Calvinism and burgherdom more than a fruitless victory, a victory without a morrow. Yet these are the views, or I may say errors, that obliged Mr. de Vries, thinking on the lines of his historic-materialist philosophy, to posit Calvinism as a postulate for Shakespeare and his contemporaries. Calvinism, a critical sense, and capitalist burgherdom are one, and the future is theirs—no more need be said, for the future determines what is truth. But if, as a matter of historic reality, Calvinism was not so cool and matter-of-fact, and if its victory and the victory of the middle class represented by Cromwell was but a hollow victory undone by the Restoration and with little effect on the development of England—what remains of the argument?

Everything is error here. According to De Vries the gloom of Shakespeare's penultimate phase has to be explained by his growing awareness of the inevitable ruin of his world (even in our author's own train of thought it is surprising that a less gloomy last phase was still to come!). But apart from the fact that a poet's mood is not to be explained with greater probability by general, or social, circumstances than by personal experience, Shakespeare's world was not by any means in so bad a way; its self-confidence was far from being shaken. I do not admit that the connection of a poet's thought with the future is the only, let alone the principal, measure of his greatness, but even when that standard is applied Shakespeare will succeed. Not, however, in the way indicated by De Vries when, as an afterthought, he ascribes to Shakespeare "a premonition of a higher order more in accordance with justice, and an aspiration after such an order"; for of all that, as I have demonstrated at sufficient length, Shakespeare was completely innocent. But in his earthiness and in his humanity Shakespeare did have something strikingly modern. He has his place in a great intellectual movement that was to sweep on ever more powerfully in the succeeding centuries.

And in nothing does this modern quality of Shakespeare's mind appear more clearly than in his aversion from Puritanism. To De Vries this is nothing but the stage director's material interest, strengthened by hidebound traditionalism, loyalty to King and Church and all the established institutions. It should be observed, first of all, that this conservative attitude, far from being a spent force, was able to survive the shock of the Cromwell episode, and down to the present day has proved itself a factor to be reckoned with in English society and civilization. But besides, the aversion to Puritanism, to Calvinism, to the real (as distinguished from Dowden's imaginary) Protestantism, which Shakespeare shared with so many of the greatest minds of the Reformation period, was directed against a new dogmatism, in which there was nothing modern apart from its being new, which preached a scholastic, inexorable, inflexible morality, and which was hostile, not to the stage only, but to all free expansion of the human mind.

The one thing that De Vries has discerned in Puritanism is its doctrinaire revolutionary tendency. In his schematic view of the world and of history, that is the only progressive force, and apart from it, all that he can see is sluggish conservatism feeding on self-interest, however variously and attractively it may disguise itself. Now the doctrinaire revolutionary tendency is a permanent force in history, which has often powerfully contributed to its movement; I shall not dream of denying it. But in English history especially—not that this feature is unique in English history, but it is perhaps exceptionally marked—that force has never been able to work itself out. Has English history therefore stood still?

The fullness of life knows other contrasts. Over against the doctrinaire revolutionary spirit that De Vries unduly identifies with Calvinism, one can place the genuine devotion to religion that, although it was not the whole of sixteenth-century Calvinism, was undeniably present in it. But, above all, there is, opposed to revolutionary doctrinairism, comprehension, leading to acceptance, to toleration, to compromise—the recognition of the relativity of the merely social, and of the eternity of human values. Contrasts, let me add, that are not to be equated with periods. The one is as little medieval as the other is modern. There is a struggle here that is of the essence of the history of mankind, as old as is its past, as young as is the hour in which we draw breath.

B
Shakespeare's Historical Capacity

COMPARISONS WITH DUTCH AND FRENCH PLAYWRIGHTS

In what has preceded I have tried to define the general views that helped Shakespeare give form to his history plays, his attitudes toward some of the great problems that are bound to crop up in every historic presentation—kingship and authority; rank and class; war and, generally speaking, contest or strife; poverty; religion—and I have attempted to establish a relation between those attitudes and a general philosophy of life and of the world. It is indispensable to have some notion of Shakespeare's views on these points if the history plays are to be understood. Yet from the historiographical standpoint, when we ask, as I have set out to do, what Shakespeare's qualities as a historian are, these general opinions, though they did help to make of his *oeuvre* a considerable intellectual achievement, are not in themselves the most important matter.

It is not in his general outlook that Shakespeare shows the originality of his genius. The conceptions in which this outlook expresses itself were mostly borrowed from others. This aspect of his drama proves Elizabethan civilization to have been a noble and a rich civilization in which Shakespeare had his full share. That is much; but it is not the main thing, not for us, not, I should think, for the poet either. It is not why his plays were written; those general ideas were present in his mind, but they did not supply the real motive force to his interest. Nor is his dramatic presentation dominated by them to the extent that he attempts to force them upon the reader. The reader, or the spectator, can enjoy that work without even noticing them. The poet saw and felt and wished to communicate so many other things: human beings, and the events or mutual relationships in which human beings reveal their personalities. This, after all, is the miracle in Shakespeare's historical work: the power of historic presentation, the plastic power, the power of evocation, of character exposition.

Before I try to bring this out—and here I shall do it mainly by comparison with other playwrights—I want to make the remark that in a world view such as was described earlier resides the promise of a special aptitude for historic presentation. Perhaps not for the most penetrating form of historical understanding, at least not according to modern standards, which attach so preponderating an importance to the genetic principle applied to the social body. The Elizabethans were familiar with the idea of a concatenation of cause and effect,[14] nor does Shakespeare ever lose sight of it; we saw how it gave unity to his eight English history plays. But he sees it realizing itself in the moral sphere, and through persons: *there* lies, for him, the intimate connection of history and drama. In the social sphere, on the contrary, where the modern historian will try most of all to apply this concept, *he* never thought of development; his conception of the community life—I have emphasized this point—is a static one, and his attitude with respect to it in the present, quiescent. His mind is fascinated in watching the varied spectacle of history, but it is not tempted to reduce it to any rigid system nor to subject the men and the events of the past to a present aim. It is a mind that is open to life.

I am far from intending to suggest that Shakespeare was capable of absolute objectivity. His glorification of Henry V and belittling of the crowd (and of the French!) were proof of the reverse. Now ultrapatriotism, then aristocratic prejudice—and other biases might be mentioned. But there remains a vast sphere in which Shakespeare manifests a divine understanding, just because he does not look upon the society of men as an object of reform but simply accepts it as the arena where the eternal conflict is waged between good and evil.

HOOFT'S HISTORICAL DRAMAS

Shakespeare's amazing historiographical power, and its connection with the state of mind that has been indicated above, are suddenly illumined when Shakespeare's history plays are placed side by side with P. C. Hooft's *Geraard van Velzen* and *Baeto*.[15]

How frequently, says Mézières in his *Shakespeare et ses critiques* (1860), has it been deplored that the French seventeenth-century playwrights left unused the subject matter offered by their own medieval chronicles; see what Shakespeare managed to make of his dry Hall and Holinshed!

In Holland that complaint would be ill-founded! Hooft read Melis Stoke[16] for his *Geraard van Velzen;* he even incorporates an archaic-sounding sentence taken from the Middle Dutch text. Hooft's *Baeto*, too, and Vondel's *Gijsbreght van Aemstel* and *Batavische Gebroeders*, all deal with national subjects. Why is it that, compared with Shakespeare, the Dutch—Hooft, and Vondel, too, as I shall show later on—have made such a poor job of it?

In a certain sense their subject matter, compared with that of the English poet, although in innumerable details promising enough, must be said to have been ungrateful and refractory. There had been too sharp a break with the past; medieveal conditions had become too alien. To begin with, it could never be Netherlands, it had to be Holland, or even Amsterdam, matter. Besides, the seventeenth-century historians and antiquarians had their minds stuffed with confusing fallacies about the Middle Ages. A continuity was postulated that had no basis in reality. England had not had a similar break; the national kingship went back into the centuries and supplied a natural and close connection with the older history.

This is one explanation of the absence in Dutch literature of a living national drama such as Shakespeare was able to create. The explanation will not work for France, where, too, the kingship was rooted in a remote past and survived in the modern age; the even more complete absence of national history plays there is an indication that we must look elsewhere. For the moment I confine my attention to Hooft, and what I find first and foremost is a mental structure radically differing from Shakespeare's.

The theme of *Geraard van Velzen* is the deposition of a ruler (of the thirteenth-century Count Florent V of Holland), the theme, one might say, of *King Richard II*. The comparison will be instructive. Shakespeare was obviously gripped by his subject as such. His intention must have been, first, to bring to the stage that fragment of English history, next, to delve into the personality of the King—perhaps it is more correct to say he imagined a personality for him, and what a personality! a subtly shaded one, revealing unsuspected depths.

As for Hooft, he does not seem to care much for the piece (of history that he has chosen for his subject. It is disposed of very summarily. Shakespeare gives scene after scene, thrilling, immediate, full of life, in order to build up the crisis and place it before our eyes to see; the solution is made intelligible, and again, visible. The great noblemen, their grievances, their quarrels, it all receives color and character. In Hooft's play the course of events—Florent

V's misgovernment and crimes, the conspiracy of the nobles and their internal divisions, the people's loyalty to the Count, the resulting castastrophe—is indicated only very slightly, mostly in long monologues, or even in choruses (for that device was still employed by the Dutch playwrights, and it was the occasion for some of the finest poetry of both Hooft and Vondel). There is no question of any delineation or evocation of character. Machteld (Velzen's wife, dishonored by Florent) is mildness personified, superior to earthly passion, while Velzen is the worldling keen on honor, and breathing vengeance; but the contrast remains stark and simple, neither character is in any way individualized. Even Florent V, so rich in possibilities one would have thought, remains shadowy. Compared with Shakespeare's vivid and fascinating treatment of Richard II, there is a distressing poverty of invention here.

But indeed invention was not what Hooft was out for. His mind ran on an entirely different track. The difference here is not to be expressed in the contrast I shall draw later on between the French playwrights and Shakespeare, that is to say, between the classicist and the romantic-realist style. Hooft's dramatic work is not so severely classicist. That is to say, it is modeled on the example of Seneca rather than on the precepts of Aristotle—precepts, indeed, of which the French had made their own exceedingly inflexible system. Hooft could still permit himself realistic touches, for instance, the incident of the esquire and the soothsayer—elaborated, but in the result rather colorless and insignificant. Had he been so minded, he might have gone in for more scenes of that nature, but he preferred to use his stage time for allegoric characters like Strife, Violence, Deceit. No, what mattered to him were the constitutional and theological ideas that he expounded. The historical theme was no more than an excuse for speaking his mind on those.

I shall not maintain that no work of true literary significance can be written in that fashion. The poetic imagination can be fired in many ways. This much is certain, however: in *Geraard van Velzen* the miracle has not happened, and not in *Baeto* either. Both are completely cerebral performances. Sixty years ago the very able Dutch critic Koopmans wrote an essay in which he determined and analyzed the ideas running through these two plays. The impression created is of something very high-minded and pure. Criticism of that sort has its use, but it should be made clear that Hooft deserves this close attention from the literary critic only on the score of the totality of his work and of his remarkable and interesting personality. It is this that adds to the dramas of his youth an importance they would not otherwise possess. And in any case, that importance remains confined to the history of ideas of the period. Koopmans does not even try to test these plays on their aesthetic value, and as soon as aesthetic standards are applied (and it is by them that the true significance of a drama must be determined), it will be seen that the plays are completely impotent products, failures, nothing!

To me it seems certain that the method employed in *Geraard van Velzen* and *Baeto* cannot yield any historic perspective, any evocation of a civilization or sphere belonging to the past. Circumstances and events may differ ever so much from what Hooft in his own time was familiar with, but the personages of his dramas are exactly like those he saw around him, and they talk and argue about their problems in the same spirit and as much as possible in the same phraseology. But in fact the characters in *Geraard* and *Baeto* are hardly human beings. They are ventriloquist's puppet in fancy dress, who declaim a treatise by P. C. Hooft on authority and liberty, the right to rebel and its limitations, the importance of concord and peace, and the horrors of civil war; all in dialogues and under pretense of fighting out a dispute of the past.

What was the message of which Hooft felt he must unburden himself? He preaches a curious kind of political quietism. Before everything, he wants order and quiet to be ensured, and for this purpose he looks to a strong government. No doubt this government should be legitimate and conduct itself in accordance with the highest moral law, but if it does not, there is still nothing but submission. To pursue one's right at all costs can, like the desire for revenge, lead to nothing but misery.

Florent's misgovernment is not condoned in *Geraard van Velzen.* The poet thinks that there was much to be said for Florent's being put under restraint. Everything is, however, compromised when the conspiring noblemen definitely part with law and call in foreign (that is, English) help. The Lord of Aemstel, who represents the poet's own political wisdom, knows exactly what the law requires: to leave the matter to the assembly, the States (which was as a matter of historic fact far to seek in the year 1296). When his two comrades express doubts about whether the States will show sufficient vigor, he warns them that in that case acquiescence is the only course: to "overthrow" legality, "guarded by the best part of the people," means running the risk of getting rushed along by "the scum of citizens and of peasants."

This political creed—and the conviction that the priesthood should be kept firmly under the control of the secular authority forms an integral part of it (this is stated more particularly in *Baeto*)—is closely related to that of Shakespeare. He, too—we have seen it—was an upholder of authority and a despiser of the people, a believer in the aristocracy of the mind and of the blood. Shakespeare, too, believed that authority had to keep within the law—although, of course, with respect to the relation between aristocracy and monarchy, his position was different from that of the republican Hooft. Shakespeare, too, believed that he who resisted a tyrannical king loaded himself with a guilt that would have to be atoned for, albeit perhaps only in a succeeding generation. Bolingbroke, who deposed Richard II, remained, we know it, oppressed by the consciousness of his offense, and indeed, under his grandson Henry VI disaster came. The entire series of Shakespeare's English history plays was, as we saw, dominated by the idea that by contest about authority, by civil war, usurpation, disobedience, the eternal order is disturbed; and the moral that England can be great only through unanimity under a strong king is more than once impressively emphasized.

With respect to the church, too, Shakespeare's attitude did not differ greatly from Hooft's. This problem in fact is intimately connected with the general problem of authority, which contributed not a little, all over Europe, toward the readiness with which the intellectuals ranged themselves behind the secular power. They were fed up with religious strife and with the extremism of the sects as much as with the ambition and intolerance of the old priesthood. These were forces that in the last resort rested on the unreason of the crowd, and in order to keep that under control and protect freedom so that intellectual culture might flourish, they felt the aristocratic organization of society and royal power to be indispensable. No more than Hooft was Shakespeare a fervent Christian (this, too, I tried to demonstrate above). The theological controversy cannot have interested him much. He was no doubt satisfied, somewhat indifferently perhaps, with the settlement that had the support of the secular power and that was intended to suppress the extremes of subjection to a foreign papacy and of revolutionary puritanism (the latter, in fact, was not free from foreign attachments either, looking, as it did, longingly to Geneva).

So much for kinship; but at the same time how striking a difference! This difference was in the first place one of artistic temperament; only in the second place, although no doubt the two were connected, of politics, of opinion.

Shakespeare's attention is first and foremost for events and for human beings; these he wants to bring out individually, in their own rights. It is not only that the case for Bolingbroke is put with as much force as is that for Richard II; it is especially that the for or against does not hold the stage all the time. We are made to live with both sides; we are interested in the spectacle, in the conflict of passions and personalities. I wrote a moment ago that a moral was emphasized. Was that not putting it too strongly? At any rate, the moral is not (as is the case with Hooft) hammered in, commented upon at length, and illustrated, and in the end, triumphantly repeated. Generally it can at most be deduced. Perhaps a strong light will be cast upon it for a passing moment, but always men and events will hold the attention. This peculiarity of Shakespeare's art, a reflection of a leading quality of his nature, has its counterpart in his political views, insofar as it is possible to determine these with any certainty.

Hooft, regarding himself to be above the contest of theological dogmas, was himself a dogmatist. He had complete and finished theories about the relationships in state and society, about authority and freedom, about state and church, and into those he fitted, or forced, life; his history plays show life in those categories.

Take once more the passage in *Geraard van Velzen* from which I quoted before. (It is Amstel speaking.)

> If the best part of the people [i.e., the States]
> is willing to be oppressed by tyrants,
> Theirs is the judgment. So, if they acquiesce,
> let everybody
> Acquiesce with them, or depart for elsewhere.

I pass by the anachronistic argumentation by which this pronouncement was preceded and in which Amstel exhorts his friends to leave everything ("after the custom of the ancestors") to the States, that is, to "Nobility and Large Towns, to which the sovereignty has been committed"; at the absolute disposal of this assembly stands the decision between submission or resistance with respect to the Count. This is bodily transferring the seventeenth-century States into the thirteenth-century assembly! But does not so positive a prescription in itself transcend life? Does it not go against life? The play is a rhymed treatise of dogmatic constitutional law, not history.

And indeed where do we find life in it? We heard Amstel's warning that if the decision is not left unconditionally to "the best part of the people," "the scum of citizens and of peasants," the mob, will be roused and spoil everything. So it happens. The project to deliver up the captured Count to England leads to a commotion in which Velzen stabs him to death. And now there is a great deal of talk about the raging people, of song even about the blind people; the murder is described, though now the furious mob is not even mentioned. The sequence of rioting, too, is dispatched in a chorus; and that is all. Shakespeare, on the contrary —but have I not dealt with the mob scenes in *Henry VI*, in *Julius Caesar*, in *Coriolanus*? It may be said that he did not there maintain his high impartiality, but nevertheless those scenes pulsate with life and testify to his keen psychological and political insight; and above all, these men of the people are brought to the stage for their own sakes as well, with their humor, and in their trades.

Baeto does not in this respect differ from *Geraard van Velzen*. Baeto's submission to his father at the moment when he has the victory in his hands can hardly be called human; it is not, at all events, how one would expect the hero, or the prince, to behave; it is more suited to the saint, or to the martyr. But to Hooft it seems the acme of political wisdom, and in those terms he imagined himself able to give history and drama!

How much freer is Shakespeare's mind in its attitude toward the phenomena of life, how much broader therefore is his outlook, and how much more truly historical and at the same time dramatic his presentation! Richard II is the Lord's anointed. According to Shakespeare's English view he was a more exalted figure than was the medieval Count in Hooft's Holland aristocratic and republican system. The deposition could not, to Shakespeare, be anything but an unlawful act, yet he understands, and makes understandable, that life sometimes demands that the law shall be broken. He realizes that this must have its sequel of commotions; retribution will follow; but Henry IV, who has to atone for the transgression committed when he was still Bolingbroke, is not therefore any the less a true king and a man.

I am not writing about Hooft and his work in its entirety. Most certainly he succeeded in largely overcoming the system-bound rigidity of his historical outlook. When, later on, he undertakes his *Historiën*, it will be in a more truly historical spirit, with a broader and more human feeling for the spectacle as well as for the actors. In fact, if that enormous work still makes an appeal to the modern reader (as it does) and deserves to be numbered among the great achievements in historiography, it is on account of the close attention to the significant as well as colorful detail and of the plastic capacity of its sometimes labored but always vivid and personal style. What strikes us in the youthful Hooft of the history plays, however, is the a priori, the abstractness of the approach. The comparison helps us to discern in Shakespeare's work, glowing with life and gloriously concrete, the historic veracity that cannot exist without those qualities.

SHAKESPEARE'S AIM IN THE ENGLISH HISTORY PLAYS

Hooft wanted to illustrate with his history plays certain political tenets. What was Shakespeare's aim?

Above all, Shakespeare was concerned in his plays about the English kings to picture thrilling events—this is what he repeatedly says himself, in the prefaces to each of the acts of *King Henry V*. To none of his other history plays did he add comments of exactly this nature, but the *poetica* to be found here holds good for all, at least for all those on English subjects. What makes itself heard in these prefaces is the passionate desire to bring to the stage the variety and the fullness, the color and the life, of history. The poet feels overwhelmed by the rich abundance of history. The small compass of his stage is compared with the realms of England and of France, where the reality had been enacted; the poor trappings, with the grandeur and the luxury; the little company of actors he will show, with the armies that actually engaged in battle; the couple of hours the performance may take up, with the period of years embraced by the reign of his king.

> A kingdom for a stage, princes to act
> And monarchs to behold the swelling scene.
> Then should the war-like Harry, like himself,
> Assume the port of Mars; and at his heels,
> Leash'd in like hounds, should famine, sword, and fire
> Crouch for employment.
> . . . can this cockpit hold
> The vasty fields of France? or may we cram
> Within this wooden O the very casques
> That did affright the air at Agincourt?

The ambition is a superhuman one. Shakespeare is aware of it and calls on the spectator's imagination to assist him. "Let us . . . On your imaginary forces work."

> Piece out our imperfections with your thoughts:
> Into a thousand parts divide one man,
> And make imaginary puissance;
> Think when we talk of horses that you see them
> Printing their proud hoofs i' the receiving earth;
> For 'tis your thoughts that now must deck our kings,
> Carry them here and there, jumping o'er times,
> Turning the accomplishment of many years
> Into an hour-glass. . . .

That subject matter, that action, those events, on which the interest must turn in the English history plays, were to a certain extent known; they appealed to a vigorous sentiment that it was possible for the poet to suppose present in his public, that, in fact, he shared with it. I said something about this in the preceding part about Shakespeare's ideas on state and society. Let me again summarize it here, in the words of an English writer.[17] The points of interest, apart from the pure spectacle, that would be uppermost in the mind of the average Englishman watching these dramas based on his national history would be mainly these three:

> The unity of the country under the strong and orderly government of securely succeeding sovereigns, who should preserve it from the long remembered evils of Civil War;
>
> Its rejection of Papal domination, with which there might be, but more frequently among the play-going classes there was not, associated the desire for a more radical reconstruction of the Church;
>
> The power, safety, and prestige of England, which Englishmen believed to be the inevitable consequence of her unity and independence.

It is not that all this is expounded or argued in the plays. It was the advantage the English playwright had over the Dutch with respect to national subjects taken from the Middle Ages that these considerations were still so alive in people's consciousness that no argument was required. Of course I need hardly recall that Shakespeare went beyond both the spectacle and this touching of the chords of national feeling. He made human beings of his kings, of his noblemen, of all his personages. A few times, for example, in *King Richard II* and *King Richard III*, the figure of the leading character even took on a dominant interest. Yet, speaking generally, the prologues of *King Henry V* can be taken as an indication of Shakespeare's primary aim in the English plays.

In the English plays. For in the Roman plays it is a different matter. There the leading personage, or personages, and the inner conflicts in which they were involved, were always the main thing. More truly than any of the English history plays, these were tragedies. It goes without saying that the poet could not rely there upon comparable familiarity, or upon passionate participation, with the events staged. Yet, just as in the English plays he fashioned human beings and was at times fascinated by the development of a personality or by a purely individual conflict, so in the classical plays he was also interested by the events, by the spectacle. In fact, it was through the minor characters and the scenes outside the main line of the action that he came into the closest contact with history. Not only from the literary point of view of dramatic construction, but from the point of view that has here had my particular attention, that of the dramatic work as historiography, one notices a striking contrast presented in this respect by the classicist drama that was soon to achieve triumphs in France.

THE HISTORIC POWERS OF CORNEILLE AND RACINE

I have attempted to bring out the personality of Shakespeare by comparing him with Hooft. The contrast with the French tragedy writers of the seventeenth century is no less striking and will prove equally helpful in making us realize the unique, the distinctive, qualities of the English poet.

Shakespeare's ambition, which was noted a moment ago, to resuscitate on the stage the whole of life, never occurred to Racine, in whom the French style reached its pinnacle; or rather, Racine rejected it decisively. The feeling of insignificance and impotence which Shakespeare overcame with the aid of the imagination, the Frenchman, in proud self-restraint, denied. One has only to read the preface to *Britannicus*, in which Racine makes front against the activities of a more romantic school and against Corneille, his elder contemporary. Corneille, no doubt, accepted the Aristotelian precepts, and compared with Shakespeare's, even *his* work gives the impression of extreme classicism; yet he still permitted himself liberties that offended Racine's ideal of stark and rectilinear simplicity. What ought I to do—Racine asks scornfully—in order to please my critics?

> Instead of a simple action, containing little matter, such as must be an action that runs its course in one single day, an action that, step by step proceeding toward its conclusion, is sustained by nothing but the interests, the sentiments, and the passions of the characters, one would have to fill that same action with a quantity of accidents which could not happen in less than a month, with a large number of stage tricks the more surprising as they would be less probable.

A simple action, then, and perhaps it is even nearer the truth to say, a single action, an action reduced to a single motif, that is the French classicist ideal. It has been said—by a Frenchman, but a Frenchman who has commented on Shakespeare with both subtlety and good sense[18]—that it is this in which the high poetic quality of the French drama appears. According to Aristotle, as we know, the peculiar task of poetry is to express the general, while history remains stuck in the particular. We shall have occasion to observe in passing several things about the poetry of Shakespeare and of others, but in my argument it is history that matters. And this much is certain: history attempts to get to the truth of life in a way that cannot be simple, cannot be "single." *Simplex sigillum veri* is a saying without sense to the historian, he would rather make a thesis of the opposite. And is it not so, indeed, that Shakespeare's dramas owe their effectiveness as history largely to their not being "single," to their action being composite and varied?

This is not all, of course. There are other elements, and among them some that have a profounder significance than the stage technique that Shakespeare found existing in England or the authority of the Aristotelian rules that the French drama so universally accepted at the time of its highest development, a generation or two afterward. No doubt there was an organic connection between these rules and the "classical spirit," but even so, this spirit meant a good deal more than faithfulness to "the Aristotelian unities."

In reading Corneille, it does not matter which play, one notices first of all the logical construction and the cerebral method. Take *Horace*. The subject, typical for Corneille, is a conflict of loyalties; it is shown in five characters, moved by opposing sentiments of duty or affection, finely shaded, and in varying degrees of strength. At one end of the scale there is Horace, a man to whom country and honor are all and who considers himself obliged to sacrifice friendship and family relationships to them—and even makes these sacrifices with spontaneity and joy. The other characters all feel themselves more or less torn in different directions. As situations succeed each other, the entire register of their affections comes into play. The element of design is, in the composition and development of a case like this, somewhat disconcertingly obvious, and the execution proceeds in strict accordance with the rules of the analytical intellect. Every new turn in drama affords its personages an occasion to dilate subtly on their emotions, fears, and hopes, on their opinions and states of mind. As Camille puts it:

> Was ever a soul seen more affected in the course of one day
> By joy and by sorrow, by hope and by fear?[19]

It would be possible to compose a textbook out of the disquisitions, subdivisions, and conclusions of the characters in this play. Horace senior, for instance, at the moment when the fight between the twice three brothers (his sons for Rome, and Curiace and his brothers for Albe) is already on, delivers a lengthy speech to the two women, his daughter-in-law and daughter, Sabine (wife to Horace junior, sister to Curiace) and Camille (affianced to Curiace, sister to Horace). Both are naturally deeply moved, but father Horace, too, admits being near to tears. Yet, he says, my interest in the event is less close than yours.

> It is not that Albe has by its choice made me hate
> your brothers.
> All three are still very dear to me;
> But after all, friendship is not of the same rank,
> Nor has it the effect of love and blood relationship;
> I do not feel for them the sorrow that torments
> Sabine the sister or Camille the mistress.[20]

This amazing faculty of self-observation and conscious living is common to all the characters. And indeed what Corneille wants to present to us is, as motive force, a moral conviction becoming will, and, as directive, an intellectual awareness and sense of distinctions, allied to a devotion to duty which can overcome sentiment or passion. *Vertu*, *honneur*, *gloire*, *magnanimité*—these are magic words in his dramas. The personages—and the poet—react to them almost automatically. Pain may force cries from them, or at least, long speeches, but they do not seem to struggle with these behests laid upon them, as it were, from outside. It is the greatness of Horace's qualities that in the end makes him kill his sister. One would like to see the hollowness and falsity of a *vertu* that leads to such an effect argued, or rather, felt. Nothing would have been more natural for the poet, one thinks, than to have hinted at the question of whether Horace was not in reality betrayed by his vanity, whether his conception of duty to country and family honor did not rest on rickety foundations. But that is not Corneille's way. Unhesitatingly he sticks to the established social precepts and rules. He can dissect them down to a fine point; he can even show them in conflict one with the other. What he cannot do is to throw doubt on them; he is unable to reveal their emptiness or unreality by a lightning shaft of divine or human truth.

Moreover, the denouement of *Horace* supplies another instance —we came across one before this[21]—of how Corneille sacrifices higher moral feeling to social or state convenience. The solution through which Horace is safeguarded against punishment lacks all connection with the inner life, it is imposed by the King's command. With so many words the *raison d'état* is invoked:

Such servants make the strength of kings,
And such, too, are above the law.[22]

How sharp is the contrast with Shakespeare's sense of justice, which is not bounded by any external or conventional taboos! And how little can we expect, after having observed these features of Corneille's mental make-up, that he will tell us anything very profound or novel about historic conditions or historic personalities! Yet his outlook is at least compatible with interest in such conditions and personalities, an interest that is indeed much less pronounced with Racine.

Between Corneille and Racine there are profound differences. It is in the method of their dramatic presentations that they give the clearest sign of their close relationship in classicism. Like Corneille, Racine constructs his plays around a simple conflict that lets itself be unwound like a spool, ever displaying new situations, or new aspects of a given situation. The main characters, three or four at most, are systematically and ingeniously exposed to those changes so that they can show the entire register of moods of which they are capable. In this game, Racine shows himself a greater artist than Corneille, and the basic tone of his work is, moreover, utterly different. Instead of by the social virtues, by will, by a sense of duty or of honor, we see his characters moved by sentiment and passion. And so completely is the poet's attention concentrated thereon that to an even higher degree than is the case with Corneille the play is bared of all adventitious matter; secondary personages, for instance, are mere "confidants," without any strongly marked characteristics of their own that might stand in the light of the central figures.

The most typical of Racine's plays, and from this point of view the foremost achievement of his art, is *Bérénice*. It is a history play. The chief personages are the Emperor Titus and the Palestinian Queen Bérénice. At his accession to the government, Titus, to meet the prejudice of the Roman people, and in spite of the love they bear each other, sends Bérénice back to her native country. Five words from Tacitus—there Racine had his entire plot: *Titus Berenicem dimisit invitus invitam*. The action is resolutely reduced to variations on a single theme, a theme purely of sentiment. The play, in Racine's—for all its seeming monotony—sensitive verse, impresses like a piece of music—chamber music to Shakespeare's symphonies. Of its kind it is a triumph, but when one comes to it fresh from a reading of Shakespeare, how strongly does one feel the artificiality, the thinness, the overbred delicacy of the genre.

And does it need arguing that in such a treatment history cannot come by its due? The case, and its ramifications in the depths of the heart, that is what matters to the poet. He tracks them down without caring very greatly about personalities as such. Why is Titus worth more than Bérénice's unfortunate wooer, Antiochus? He is the Emperor; he has done glorious deeds. But about these we are merely informed, and this, in the usual conventional language. There is nothing distinctive. Nor do we *see* anything. We are not shown Titus acting as emperor, in his relations to his people, to the army, to the Senate; in such small scenes, in other words, as Shakespeare would have loved to devise, but which could not be allowed into the classical drama because they would have detracted from its "singleness." We see Titus as lover only. But now compare Mark Antony in *Antony and Cleopatra*! Him we come to know as a commander; we hear of the admiration and of the sorrowful impatience of his subordinates. We come to know him as a triumvir, in his relations to the cold, self-controlled Octavius and to the nincompoop Lepidus. And as a lover we see him in the grip of a passion that wrecks him. What a drawing-room lover does Titus seem, with his *larmes*, and his *flamme*, and his *chaînes*, and his *soupirs*. All that there is of true passion in the play is in Bérénice—once or twice, for brief moments; enough for the genre. It is just that which gives one the shock of surprise, the keen sense of beauty: the melodious stream of the alexandrines suddenly, as it were, held up by these very few, brief, vehement utterances.

There is in any case nothing specifically Roman in Titus, nothing Oriental in either Antiochus or Bérénice. And this holds good for the entire *oeuvre* of Racine. Whether it be Romans, or prehistoric Greeks, Asiatics before Christ, or contemporary Turks, it is really always Frenchmen, and even that very special brand of Frenchmen raised in the court of Louis XIV and in the drawing rooms of the nobility.

Taine, once, in a famous essay, proclaimed Racine as the finest product of that hothouse culture. A good many objections can be raised against his argument; as always with Taine, there is in his constructions a strong element of arbitrariness, of paradox almost, and he carries them to the point where they become impossible. His theory of "l'esprit classique" (of which Racine is made to be the representative par excellence) as the true expression of the French national character, for instance, seems incompatible with his other view of the close connection of that state of mind with the court life under Louis XIV, which was after all no more than an episode in French history. And the way in which Taine pictures that society, stressing its artificial and aristocratic and even bitterly antipopular character, should have made it clear to him that it could not possibly be *the*, *the true*, expression of the French mind. It was a temporary, an ephemeral phenomenon, and nothing is more absurd than to try to shut up French civilization in its entirety, and the intellectual and spiritual potentialities of the French nation, within the narrow bounds of that "esprit classique"—stiflingly narrow indeed as traced by Taine himself.

Moreover, Taine's aesthetic and moral appreciation of that seventeenth-century French civilization does err on the side of enthusiasm. He draws the picture with a master hand, and that there was much that was admirable and delightful can readily be granted. But undiluted enthusiasm hardly seems to accord with the emphasis, the almost exaggerated emphasis, with which he harps on the divorce from nature characteristic of that society. Especially when he compares—and he does so repeatedly, mainly with Shakespeare—he rouses to opposition. Taine feels at home with the courtly, delicate, mild, civilized, sensitve Racine; he shrinks at the touch of the savage, barbaric, unmeasured Shakespeare. He prefers, so he says, having to do with good manners rather than with unbridled passions, with a man raised in a hothouse than with one abandoned in the state of nature. As if the latter parts of these contrasts could be applied to Shakespeare! Taine has not proceeded beyond Voltaire's misapprehension. But more: as if the first parts gave a true image of Racine! For is not the secret of Racine's genius this, that through the veil of that decorous and artificial style which Taine describes so brilliantly—and so mistakenly identifies with the poet's innermost being—we can discern the man, who did not wholly belong to the court of Louis XIV?

The man, the human being, can supply the link needed by the historic sense. Yet that human factor reduced in Racine's way to its most general substance, although clothed in an outward shape so intimately connected with a particular period, does not offer much for our particular purpose. As an instance of what Racine can do as a historian, take the Nero he presents to us in *Britannicus*. Taine himself points out how different a Nero it is from the one portrayed by Tacitus. Racine's Nero is the perfect diplomat, and he could not possibly be more gracefully courteous to Junie; his falseness and wickedness only transpire in glints from behind the mask of the man of the world. In short, the bloodthirsty and insane despot has been transposed into the terms of Racine's own, all-too-narrow sphere of life.

This peculiarity of Racine's, which, with the concentration of his attention on the sentiments and the passions of love, so little fitted him to create a history drama, did not escape his contemporaries. Dryden poked fun at the delicacy of Racine's Hippolyte, who even in order to clear himself did not dare openly mention

Phèdre's crime to Thésée. Taine holds Dryden's criticism typical of the rude character of English as compared with French civilization. Though the contrast of "refined" and "rude," which Taine uses repeatedly—and especially to get at the core of Shakespeare—may be one, it is certainly not the most important, aspect of the difference. As to this particular point, Corneille, in France, made similar remarks about Racine. Of *Bajazet* the older writer said—quite rightly—"all the characters of that play have, underneath their Turkish dress, French sentiments." And he even spoke quite generally—the critical intention is umistakable—of "the ancient heroes recast to suit our fashion."[23]

Racine's son naturally considered this criticism unfair and maintains that "Mithridate, appearing with all his hatred for Rome, his dissimulation, and his cruel jealousy, showed the poet to be capable of giving to the ancient heroes their full likeness." The verdict cannot be accepted without demur. No doubt Racine made an attempt. Nevertheless, when Mithridate, on entering upon his dissimulation, tells himself that it is unworthy of him, when, in the final scene with Xipharès, his son, and Monime, his wife, from whom he has wrenched the secret of their love, he practically gives them, with his dying breath, his blessing, then one feels that the poet has remained blind to the barbaric—that is, to the really distinctive element on which true historic perception would have fastened.

Returning to Corneille, we must admit that his historic capacity does not after all very much surpass Racine's. I mentioned Corneille's *Horace* before. On close examination its ancient (almost prehistoric) Romans turn out, like Racine's characters, to be nothing but Frenchmen, of the age of Richelieu perhaps, rather than that of Louis XIV (and indeed, Corneille was born in 1606; Racine in 1639; Louis XIV in 1638). The objection that a Frenchman of Corneille's time can hardly be imagined killing his sister for the reason that seemed sufficient to the hero of Corneille's drama might cause a moment of embarrassment; it can, however, be disposed of by marking two points. First, the excesses of the play's action are situated in a line whose direction certainly runs parallel with that of French thinking of the period, and moreover, the prolongation of action into the excessive is typical for Corneille: it is his conception of heroism, of *vertu*. Nonetheless—and this is my second point—although it is undeniable that the deed is not in harmony with the general tone of the play, and also, that it met with disapproval on the part of the contemporary public, does not this, it might be argued in Corneille's defense, show how "ancient Roman," that is to say, how historic, it was? Of course Corneille had found the terrible act related in the legend. But his failure both as a poet and as a historian is that he did not succeed in preparing for it. He conceived the whole play as a dialectical treatise in casuistic morals in accordance with the ideas of his own time. His subtle and exact distinctions did not leave him any time or space (supposing that the Aristotelian unities would have permitted him, and his inclination and poetic powers would have run that way) to evoke in concrete incidents the profoundly different sphere of the ancient Roman age. Shakespeare excels in such background painting. Here it is practically absent.

Take *Le Cid*, which is set in eleventh-century Spain. Of a distinctive historic atmosphere, different from that in Corneille's other plays, there is no trace. No doubt the great motive force of the characters is honor, which may suggest Spain, although hardly the eleventh century; and there is much talk about the Moors. Similarly, in *Cinna* and *La Mort de Pompée* (about both of which plays more hereafter) the talk is about liberty, about Rome, about dignity and glory; and, while local color is not entirely lacking, it is always in the shape of definite facts supplied by the plot: Egypt, Roman conspirators. A different moral or spiritual atmosphere is not thereby constituted.

Of the feudalism, religious wars, barbarousness of the world to which the Cid belonged, nothing will be found in Corneille. Once more, he unfolds before his spectators a highly cultured, and in many respects artificial, society. It is not quite the same as that of Augustus or of Ptolemy, but much less is it the reality of eleventh-century Spain. It is the French court as Corneille knew it. The pugnacious and unruly noblemen have become courtiers; the King, who in reality was engaged in a daily struggle to maintain himself against them, an autocrat raised to an unattainable height. The political maxims are those of Corneille's own age. For instance:

> But this respect is due to absolute power,
> That nothing should be looked into when a king has
> willed it. . . .
> Whatever illustrious or considerable deeds one may do,
> A king never owes anything [any gratitude] to his
> subject.[24]

With all his veneration for royal authority, Shakespeare, whose English history plays were so largely intended to demonstrate the salutariness and the indispensability of the regal office, would not have overlooked the conflict between these slavish tenets and the higher moral law. And especially, he did not, for all his royalism, do violence to history in the way Corneille did. But indeed, we know already that Shakespeare, in addition to carrying through a certain general view of English history, desired to call up the spectacle of the past; whereas Corneille in *Le Cid* (to a lesser degree in *Cinna;* least of all in *La Mort de Pompée*, although here too) concentrated on the love interest and the conflicts of the heart.

It can be confidently affirmed that Corneille, like Racine, always staged the same sort of characters engaged in the same sort of inner conflicts (each of the two poets, as we saw, had his own sort)—in different settings, perhaps, but in settings that never had any profound connection with the theme. Nor were these sorts of characters and of conflicts anything like so universally human as has often been asserted; on the contrary, they were strictly determined by Corneille's—or Racine's—own age and culture, so that their appearances in other nations, surroundings, and periods always resemble fancy dress parties.

Corneille had, moreover, only one style for all his personages; again, like Racine for his. With inexorable regularity the alexandrines succeed each other from beginning to end. That style, steadily flowing, ever logically developed, the style of highly cultured drawing-room ladies and gentlemen trained in argument and analysis, remains more purely cerebral in Corneille's handling than in Racine's. It is a style full of clichés. Everything that comes up for treatment falls under the sway of the current moral code, of conventional or social conceptions of love, duty, honor, country, parental authority. The problems, too (leaving *Polyeucte*, which is a religious drama, aside), are, so to speak, given. History supplies the plot and the setting, but it has no independent existence. The dramatic effect must be obtained by means of a love interest, or one of the recognized, duly labeled conflicts. Even Caesar has, in *La Mort de Pompée*, to submit to that law. Corneille's characters are not individualized human beings; they are merely embodiments of the familiar stage types, the lover-hero, the lover-ambitious-politician, or for the women, the lover-dutiful-daughter, the lover-patriot. The conflicts in which these characters get involved, as in a complicated, but well-known and symmetrical, dance, supply them with abundant matter for ratiocination, carried on with amazing subtlety and quickness of wit. And they all raise their voices to the same pitch, and display the same kind of sensitiveness.

Rodrique, the hero of a hundred battles, sighs and whimpers about the sorrows of his love no less than does Cinna, the Roman conspirator, and Caesar himself would do the same if Cleopatra happened to have been "cruel." That "scourge of the Moors,"

Rodrigue, living before the year 1100 (in historic reality, by the way, he was not above occasionally making common cause with the Moors), this "Cid," holds forth about his *flamme* and his *âme* like everybody else, and about his despair, and about his having lost his all now that Chimène pursues him with her hatred.

I recall in passing that Shakespeare's heroes of the battlefield are presented to us as heroes of the battlefield indeed. Coriolanus, hard and proud, whose wife hardly counts in his life; Hotspur, loud-voiced and jovial, fond of his Kate no doubt, but easily, and without pretending that she comes before the all-important business of war; Henry V, whose love scenes with the French princess have no other purpose than to make the public laugh about the language problem, except insofar as they illustrate the triumph of the English conqueror. . . . How infinitely more richly shaded is the presentation of life, and how much better will a mind like Shakespeare's be able to comprehend the varied multiplicity of history!

CINNA AND *JULIUS CAESAR—LA MORT DE POMPÉE* AND *ANTONY AND CLEOPATRA*

Corneille's most ambitious attempts at history writing are *Cinna* and *La Mort de Pompée*.

Cinna, ou la clémence d'Auguste, was obviously written to glorify that magnanimity mentioned in the title. In Corneille's play the aristocratic-republican opposition to the establishment of the monarchy is more articulate than in Shakespeare's *Julius Caesar*. But that does not mean that the French poet shows a more profound understanding of it.

With *Julius Caesar*, Shakespeare ventured out into an entirely different political sphere from that which he knew in England. The theme is of a dictator who, leaning on the people, overthrows the aristocracy, and of the last, convulsive resistance of that aristocracy. Was the poet, with Plutarch for a guide, able to find his way through those unfamilar conditions?

The monologue in which Brutus tries to defend to himself the murder plan is, it must be admitted, very thin. Suppose Caesar succeeded in making himself king, how might he misuse his power! English criticism pointed out more than a century ago that the argument ill fits the traditional republicanism of the Roman, to whom the royal title was detestable as such. But apart from that passage it is surprising with how firm a hand Shakespeare brought out circumstances sharply different from any in the history of his own country. He is far from confounding the Roman patricians with the English feudal nobility, or Caesar's dictatorship, continued by the triumvirs, then by Octavius alone, with English monarchy. The Roman conspirators may wear hats and Caesar a "doublet," but they make a very different appearance indeed from the great noblemen in the English dramas, with their estates and their fighting ideals, and from the kings, trusting to their blood and their divine right. It may be true that Shakespeare failed to grasp the exact tenor of Brutus's republican theory, so foreign to his own experience of politics. He rejected it no doubt unhesitatingly, and he did put Caesar in the place of an English king to the extent that he saw him as dominating the situation even after his death ("O Julius Caesar! thou art mighty yet!"), and the opposition to him as a vain revolt against the only possible order. But after all, that view had sufficient roots in history to enable Shakespeare to evoke an entire world that gives us an impression of being un-English, and at the same time, authentically Roman. Touches supplied by the other conspirators—Casca's scorn for the mighty Caesar compelled to seek popular acclaim like any play actor; Cassius's devouring envy of the man who is after all no more than a man, and not, for that matter, a better man than he, but who is taken for the only man of the age—such touches, unthinkable in any of the English history plays, do effectively transfer us to ancient Rome.

But the greatest contribution toward that end is the complete sympathy with which Brutus is treated, even though an ingredient may be missing from a purely intellectual comprehension. Shakespeare pictures Brutus as the intractable, unworldly, unpractical idealist, but he has withal made him a human being of unmistakable goodness and greatness. It is that glorious liberty of his mind that makes it possible for him to recognize a good and a great man on a side that is not his. For it is Caesar's spirit that he makes us feel dominates it all. And in spite of the small foibles and pettinesses with which the poet shows him to us in his last days, it is Caesar's spirit that continues to dominate the drama when after the great man's death his power has fallen into the hands of that hardly impressive triumvirate. The little scene in which Shakespeare presents Mark Antony drawing up a proscription list is in itself a brilliant sample of his art. It is taken almost bodily from Plutarch, but in the few lines given it takes on fresh meaning, and we are made to see that bartering of lives in all its repulsiveness. In this, too, we are a long way from English history—not that there was a dearth of horrors there, but they were of a different kind.

Corneille, as I hinted, rendered the republican arguments of his conspirators more correctly than did Shakespeare in the Brutus monologue. But after all, Corneille only followed the Latin sources without probing underneath the words. Shakespeare, on the other hand, made of Brutus a living character and of the conspiracy a gripping reality. If this proved to be beyond Corneille's power, it was first of all because he was lacking in that comprehensive sympathy which enabled Shakespeare to approach the losing side, whose defeat he felt was required by the immutable order of things, with understanding, let it be intuitive rather than intellectual understanding. Corneille presents the exposition of the republican ideal, but only in order to dissent from it, to make it appear as nothing compared with Augustus's (calculated) magnanimity. The whole play ends in an apotheosis of the ruler, which was what was intended from the start.

And certainly, the poet here for a moment succeeds in infusing life into his handiwork. In the long speech in which, in the last act, Augustus addresses the discomfited conspirators, revealing his imperial dignity and his contained force—a force which could annihilate did it not let itself be dominated by higher considerations—one feels in contact with a poetic, which is at the same time a historic, reality.

But this in the final reckoning is all. The rest of the play, the secondary characters and preparatory scenes, lack all value. In the poet's mind, or heart, the play had no other significance than that it should contribute to this one leading motif. The consequence is that this conspiracy of Cinna and his comrades remains a thing of purely mechanical dramatics and never becomes true history. All republican tirades cannot make it appear less factitious. Aemilia seems to take the creed seriously, but Aemilia, too, collapses. Cinna and Maximus are stage lovers rather than republicans. This complication of politics with love is purely a matter of stage convention; we have to accept such love as a mere verbal affirmation, for it never communicates itself to us by touching our feeling; and it destroys historic truth. It is as in *La Mort de César*, in which Voltaire (who was still, two or three generations later, a faithful adherent of seventeenth-century poetics) imagined he could improve upon Shakespeare (and upon history!) by making Brutus Caesar's natural son. But in consequence, veracity has fled. In *Cinna* Corneille has devised a plot that gives him an opportunity to let his personages (or puppets) declaim on all the variations of the given theme; but a real conspiracy and real Romans we are never made to see.

La Mort de Pompée is different. Here, more than in any other play, the poet has set out to give history from beginning to end. He is not a little proud of his documentation. In his preface he writes:

If I were to do here what I have done in my earlier works and give the texts or summaries of the histories from which this play has been derived, . . . I should have to compose an introduction ten times longer than my poem, and entire books of almost all the authors on Roman history would have to be transcribed.

Good documentation does not by itself make a good work of history, much less a good history play. What did Corneille want to use his material for? Was he able, through imagination, to achieve contact with the life of antiquity? The underlying idea may be said to have been historic, albeit, in the proper classicist manner, generalizing and abstract. Corneille wanted to oppose the baseness, cowardice, weakness, and treachery of Egyptian royalty and the grandeur and nobility of the Romans. The ideal figure of the Roman, the dominator of the world, proud of his *vertu*, looking down on other nations and indeed inspired by a higher principle than any within their reach, is here embodied in Caesar; Cornelia, Pompey's widow, although Caesar's enemy, is in this respect his worthy compatriot, living even more completely as one dedicated to the ideal. The figure of Cleopatra is the play's great weakness. She has not been conceived historically, but was construed out of the logic of the poet's scheme. She is a ruler rather than a woman; and she wishes to show herself worthy of Caesar, her lover, by treating Ptolemy, his enemy, magnanimously, in the Roman fashion. When Charmian, her lady in waiting, does not know what to make of this, Cleopatra says, superbly:

> This is what rulers owe to their high birth:
> Their souls take from their blood impressions
> Which subordinate their passions to their virtue.
> Their generosity places everything beneath their glory.[25]

This is not the historic Cleopatra, nor could it be. Such boasting, in one breath, of high birth, *vertu*, generosity, and glory belongs indissolubly to Corneille's own time and nation. Stapfer, while clearly discerning this, wants nevertheless to praise the tragic playwright and his classical manner. "Thus does Corneille, a great poet rather than a great painter, ennoble all that he touches." But this distinction between poet and painter is senseless. It is the poet himself who fails when his imagination will not create a Cleopatra in whom we can believe. And it is the poet in Shakespeare that made him create a Cleopatra who not only *lives*, with all her indestructible charm and insatiable coquetry, but might *really* exist in history. Corneille, in his customary style, has been able to evolve only a puppet, and the result, with all the eloquent phrases and high-sounding words, is no more poetic than Shakespeare's, nor is it any nobler—for what is the good of a nobility that has not come to life?

But Corneille's Caesar, too, misses the tune of both life and history. I hinted before that Corneille does not dispense even Caesar from his rule that the drama depends on love interest. The enamored Caesar assures Cleopatra that it is in order to possess her that he has conquered the world. His assurance takes forty verses, and then another twenty-four, with a brief addition in conclusion, all in the insufferably repetitive language of convention, that which any courtier familiar with the knightly epic of the decadence might have used. In Shakespeare's *Antony and Cleopatra* the love for Cleopatra is pictured as a destroying element. Mark Antony, too, was a Roman and a dominator of the world; but because he was at the same time a lover, and a real one—not one only in protestations such as anyone in Corneille's age could reel off—he had to go to pieces. The distance between Corneille and Shakespeare is unmeasurable: as poets no less than in the capacity to get a grip on the past, in historic power. That these two qualities can be closely related, here becomes plain.

Racine's perception of Corneille's shortcomings was as keen as Corneille's perception of his. In the preface to *Britannicus*, from which I previously quoted his confession of faith in the single-motif drama, Racine added, as an instance of the senseless incidents and silly decoration with which others wished him to spoil his work, a caustic reference to this scene in *La Mort de Pompée* showing "a conqueror who would do nothing but descant on love." How could I dare, he exclaims, enter with such speeches as these into the presence of the great men of antiquity—for such he liked to imagine would be his readers and spectators. That his work is incomparably more harmonious than Corneille's, that it penetrates more profoundly into the human heart, and that in its own artificial world it exists triumphantly, everyone who is sensitive to poetry will admit. But in Racine's case it appears that the poetic imagination is not necessarily identical with the historic. Corneille manages occasionally to get hold of history; Racine, whatever he might think, remains divorced from it.[26]

SHAKESPEARE'S HISTORIC ATMOSPHERES, OR BACKGROUNDS

That the history dramas of Corneille and of Racine, albeit in different ways and to different degrees, are largely unhistoric, has been recognized long, and on all sides. But on Shakespeare there is, in this respect, much less agreement among the critics. In France especially the theory has been expounded (it was already adumbrated in the passages quoted from Stapfer) that history and poetry cannot really exist together; that the dramatic poet cannot do otherwise than bring to the stage men and conditions of his own time; and that history can only serve him for a poetic haze or by way of decoration. Already Goethe said that Shakespeare had turned both his Romans and his medieval barons into Elizabethans.

Before Stapfer, Taine, in the essay on Racine which I discussed before, had systematized this view:

> Racine has been blamed for having under ancient names portrayed courtiers of Louis XIV; but that is just where he deserves praise: the theater always represents contemporary morals. Euripides' mythological heroes are lawyers or philosophers like the youthful Athenians of his day. When Shakespeare wanted to paint Caesar, Brutus, Ajax, and Thersites, he made of them men of the sixteenth century. All Victor Hugo's young men are gloomy plebeians in revolt, the sons of René and of Childe Harold. In the last resort, an artist copies only what he sees, and cannot copy anything else; the remoteness and the perspective of history are of use to him only to add poetry to truth.

It is surprising that a theory which on critical analysis turns out to be completely untenable made such an impression on Stapfer. He closely follows Taine. The staging of a drama in the past or in a distant country, he says, has a poetic object: "The poet finds there the elevated generality that suits the inventions of poetry." So far his argument is less offensive than Taine's thesis of poetry (the past) superimposed upon truth (the poet's own civilization). Stapfer continues by saying that the illusion of remoteness in time and space is therefore all that is required, and that the antiquarian exactness of Ben Jonson imprisons the imagination in an inelastic reality. Here, too, I can assent. Ben Jonson, Shakespeare's contemporary, whom many scholars of the time placed above Shakespeare by virtue of his erudition, cannot base thereon any claim either as a poet or as a historian; no more than can Corneille on the wide reading of which he boasts in his preface to *La Mort de Pompée*. "The Turkey of the Turks," says Stapfer, "the China of the Chinese, is the object of erudition, not of poetry." I am not sure that I will agree, but now Stapfer jumps to a conclusion to which I most certainly cannot follow him. "The Turks, and also the Greeks and the Romans, staged by Racine, exhibited French and modern sentiments, but what to superficial criticism seemed a ridiculous error is at bottom the very law of art." Voltaire (it is still Stapfer speaking) was wrong in wanting to fix forever the particular style and the particular anachronism of the age of Louis XIV. "But the great poets of that age of Louis XIV had, in accordance with the law of art and of the theater, made their own anachronism: they had put Greeks and Romans on the stage, and through the mouths of those Greeks and Romans they had voiced the soul of their own epoch. They were right."

They were *right*? If this is meant to mean "It does not matter in Racine's case because, when all is said and done, he has, in whatever way, created imperishable works of art, perfect of their kind," I for one shall not demur. But if a "law of art and of the theater" is constructed and the historical drama told it must not be anything but anachronistic, or it will become unpoetic, then it is time to protest. I readily concede Victor Hugo to these system builders. Again like Taine, Stapfer adduces him triumphantly, remarking that he, who laughed at Racine's "Frenchified Greeks," did not, in *Hernani* and *Ruy Blas*, show Spaniards, but only "young men of 1830, their heads afire by the reading of Chateaubriand and Byron," a new anachronism in the place of an old. That may be—but is it not due to the egocentrism of that romantic school that nowadays its work sounds so unbearably hollow to our ears? And in any case, it denotes a curious blindness to put Shakespeare's work on one line with that of French classicist and romantic poets and to suggest that it, too, owes its beauty to the observance of that alleged law.

Stapfer admits that there are anachronisms in Racine that offend (that there are such in Corneille we have seen); such, for instance, are the presentations in the same play of barbaric customs of the past and modern delicate sentiments: in *Iphigénie*, the human sacrifice; in *Andromaque*, the vanquished reduced to slavery. As a matter of fact, it would be possible to extend that objection considerably and to observe in all these plays a lack of harmony between the setting and the temper, or tone. But I shall confine myself to pointing out how farfetched and how lame is the argument when it is invoked to prove that Shakespeare was saved from offending anachronisms only by the striking resemblance existing between the cruelty of ancient Rome and the rough manners of his England. The remark had already been made by Heine. Goethe and Heine, Voltaire and Taine,[27] and apparently Stapfer too—how little did they know of the England of their own day, let alone Elizabethan England! But one is tempted to add: how little did they understand Shakespeare, when, as against the uniformity of the backgrounds and characters in the French drama, they failed to observe the rich variety in his work; when they overlooked the miracle of his genius manifesting itself in the capacity to present mutually differing civilizations and the characters germane to each, and thus transcending mere observation (and "copying," to use Taine's word!) of the reality of his own day and surroundings.

No, if one reads Shakespeare without preconceived notions of what poetry should do or can do, it will be seen that the imagination opens up the past to him. He was aware of the difference of periods, and of the difference of civilizations. I think that this is the essential feature of his historic powers—which will always remain mysterious up to a point. His plays are not always set in the same stage-world, in what was really—in varying disguises—the poet's own drawing room. Each play has its particular background, its own historic ambience. Its history is not just a superimposed decoration; it makes itself felt in all parts, like the key in a piece of music.

Shakespeare's sensitivity to different spheres or states of society and his capacity to suggest each in its peculiarity—one of the great gifts for which the historian should pray—appears in the whole of his work, including the plays that cannot be counted among the history plays. Action never develops in the abstract, nor necessarily in Shakespeare's own English, Elizabethan society. The impression made by the setting cannot always be expressed in historic terms. Sometimes only vaguely sociological terms, or even terms indicative of a mood, will suggest themselves; then one will speak of primitive, or highly-civilized; of fresh and sound, or corrupt; of cheerful, or melancholy; of light, or dark.[28]

How masterly is the evocation, in *Romeo and Juliet*, of the character of the little Italian town torn by a noblemen's feud, and how very specifically historical is this evocation. The very first scene gives a little sketch (I allude to that of the quarrel between Capulet's *bravi* and the adherents of Montague), in itself irresistibly witty and alive; moreover, it "places" the whole drama—and places it outside Shakespeare's own England. The love story, the character of Juliet, the monk, all helps to keep up the Italian atmosphere. No doubt, Mercutio's rousing tirade about Queen Mab is, listened to with this idea in mind, out of tune, for both the fancy and the folklore are thoroughly Germanic and English.[29] But the poet must be allowed his liberty. In some of the comedies such mixing of ingredients has been done systematically. And even so, Shakespeare shows his mastery in the characterization of social atmospheres. This very thing is one of the delights of *A Midsummer Night's Dream:* the Athenian court and the regal air of Theseus and Hippolyta and the two pairs of lovers, contrasted with the lower-middle-class (and frankly English) appearance of Bottom and his companions, and behind or above these two groups the ethereal world of the fairies.

The scene of *Othello* is laid, and laid truly, in a Venetian, a Mediterranean surrounding, and one of a not very distant time. The play's vivid coloring and passionate temper agree with that setting. Against this, *King Lear* is a northerly piece, with gray and gloomy tints; in the storm and on the heath that tonality culminates, and withal there is—from the opening scene on—the distant in time, the primitive. Compare *Hamlet* and *Macbeth*. What a contrast! One will best realize this by trying mentally to transpose a character like Polonius from the one play to the other: he would be completely out of place. But the same is true for Horatio, for Osric and the duel, for the traveling players and their performance at court, and really for every character and for every scene. *Hamlet* may have nothing very typically Danish, but the world in which the action unfolds bears a modern, a sixteenth-century, character; the scene is laid at a highly-cultured Renaissance court. As against that, the world of *Macbeth* is, and not through the witches only, but in all its details, wild, barbaric, remote in time.

Need I remark that this transposing of minor characters from one play to another would not in Racine's dramatic *oeuvre* raise the same difficulty? Make, for instance, Phénice and Zatime exchange places, your only difficulty will be that you cannot picture to yourself either of these personages in any sharply marked delineation. Zatime, the slave woman of Roxane in *Bajazet*, has nothing Turkish but her name; while you will, I trust, take it from me that Phénice is Bérénice's "confidante."

VONDEL'S HISTORICAL DRAMAS

There is another poet whose work will yield interesting points of comparison: Joost van den Vondel (1587-1679), who, between 1620 and 1674, wrote a large number of plays, some of which are among the glories of Dutch literature.

Many of these plays were history plays, and Vondel, more than the French playwrights, more also than Hooft, plainly and principally intended, in several of them at least, to do justice to historic truth—to stage an episode of history, certified by the best authorities. In this respect there is a similarity between Vondel's history plays and Shakespeare's plays about the kings of England. Unfortunately, Vondel saddled himself with one crushing difficulty: the Aristotelian unities, which he obediently accepted, and which could not but hamper and stunt the execution of this task.[30] Local color had mostly to be supplied in the form of lengthy descriptions, or in relations of events that had happened before, or elsewhere.

This is one explanation of the appalling long-windedness and the deficiency of true dramatic power by which so much of Vondel's work for the stage is characterized. Another is in Vondel's propensity to casuistry, in which he betrays his relationship with the French, and especially, with Corneille. The intellectualism of the seventeenth-century classicist mind, which the personages of Vondel's plays can so tiresomely reveal in their finespun dialectics about moral problems, about the divine law, about social propriety, tends not only to lessen the dramatic tension but to blot the delineation of character. Must I in this connection make mention also of the alexandrine? The alexandrine was perhaps a disaster for French poetry and the French drama; that it was a disaster for Dutch poetry and the Dutch drama seems to me undeniable. The Dutch alexandrine, lacking the rapidity and the suppleness that the French still managed to impart to the cumbrous meter, was like a heavy cloak thrown round each of the characters in the drama, impeding natural movements with its stiff folds. Quick, witty, passionate, subtle touches could hardly be attempted; they would in any case be stifled under that oppressive decking. Shakespeare's pentameter, especially as he developed it in the course of time, eliminating rhyme altogether and freely using enjambments, afforded incomparably greater facilities for adaptation to various characters and to dramatic situations. And Shakespeare, moreover, did not scruple to drop into prose when he thought fit.

However, the purely historic intention can be observed in Vondel. It is even predominant, to such a degree that several of his plays are no more than dramatized historic events. True dramatic conception is lacking; there is no denouement, at least no tragic one, none that might shed significance on what the spectator had witnessed on the stage, that in his perception might elevate or ennoble the hero.

Take *Jozef in Dothan.* In the last act Joseph is sold into slavery by his brothers; the entire play before that consisted of their deliberations and of their disputes with the one among them who attempted to prevent the crime. At first they had intended to kill Joseph; the kindly brother had indeed thought, for an instant, that Joseph had been killed. This brother is enlightened, yet the play ends on a misunderstanding: the plotters trick their aged father, Jacob (whose preference for Joseph was the source of their hatred), to believe, by means of a coat dipped in goat's blood, that Joseph has been devoured by an evil beast. Since Jacob could not be shown on an Aristotelian stage, the kindly brother has perforce to portray his despair for the benefit of the audience. That Joseph still had a future, the spectator knew because he was familiar with the Bible, but Vondel could not realize this fact dramatically. The incident alone was what the poet sought. And, indeed, Vondel followed the play with another about an incident in Joseph's life, his involvement with Potiphar's wife. *Jozef in Egypte* ends equally undramatically, with Joseph's imprisonment. The guilt of the lying temptress remains hidden, and once again the perilous situation in which the hero is left is not in reality the last chapter of his life.

Nevertheless Vondel has most certainly, in *Jozef in Dothan* at least (for *Jozef in Egypte* is a much weaker play), caught something of the flavor of the Old Testament world. How heavy a handicap he imposed upon himself by submitting to the Aristotelian rules is most strikingly apparent in Jacob's absence from the stage. We are only told about him. The motif of the patriarch and his sons is, after all, the most characteristic, and the most historically as well as dramatically significant theme of the story—we would like to have *seen* it. Shakespeare, with the so much greater latitude afforded him by his dramatic style, would never have allowed it to escape him. But at any rate, Vondel, if only in the circumstantial accounts given by the conspiring and quarreling brothers, proves, not only that he has understood something of the relationships of their patriarchal society, but that it has moved him and that he has sought to communicate his interest. The play has more color and more historic background than the average French tragedy.

At times Vondel has been completely successful in such milieu painting, in such placing of a drama in a particular past.

Will it be permissible in this connection to mention *Lucifer* and *Adam in Ballingschap* ("Adam in Exile")? In any case, the beauty of these—the greatest of his plays—is to be found largely in the grandiose experience they have in store for us, the suggestion of actions occurring not simply on our everyday earth, not simply among human beings, but among angels and archangels, and between the first created couple and God. In characterization Vondel is never strong, but it is not only symbolism or theology with which his mind is occupied: he is an imaginative poet; his work has a strong plastic quality.

For purely historic presentation or description we must, of course, turn to other plays. The finest instance, truly poetic, that I know in the whole of Vondel, is the first act of *De Gebroeders* (*The Brethren*). The play itself, which in Vondel's *oeuvre* immediately precedes *Jozef in Dothan*, is not without dramatic power. The theme of the killing of Saul's seven sons by the reluctant King

David, at the bidding of a divine oracle and under popular pressure—a placatory sacrifice in the face of the destructive drought with which God is visiting Israel—that gruesome theme lends itself to dramatic treatment. It is true that Vondel gives free rein to all those peculiarities that so easily chill us: the case is *argued* with the greatest intellectual refinement; the tragic mother's despair is presented movingly enough, yet always conventionally as a tragic mother's despair, without any of those lightning or abysmal phrases that might make us feel in the presence of a human being struggling with the eternal mystery, or with fate; moreover, she proves herself, in a pages-long stichomythia, to be possessed of a dialectical readiness of wit that is indeed highly untragic. As for the seven unfortunate brothers, they remain completely devoid of individual features, and throughout they are made to speak in chorus.

However this may be, the first act is a splendid piece of poetic evocation. It portrays no more than the meeting between the High Priest of Geba, accompanied by his attending priests, and David, with his train of Levites. The misery caused by the drought is related, and it is decided to go and pray for God's counsel. The broad swell of the alexandrines, interrupted by some single lines at the moment of salutation, and concluded by a chorus, flows along with the action: Abiathar and his priests descending from the mountain, David and his followers coming up, their meeting, their going off together. The exalted status of the priesthood, and the majesty of the kingly office are expressed in that powerful rhythm. And meanwhile, from the exchange of speeches there has risen the spectacle of the parched land, of the desperate people, of the priest in his symbolically meaningful garnish, of the pious David chosen by God himself to take the place of the idolatrous Saul—and we feel that we are not in Amsterdam or in Holland, nor in the year 1639, but in the distant, foreign world of the Old Testament.

As a matter of fact, this Old Testament world lived particularly insistently in Vondel's imagination.[31] He has most convincingly succeeded in giving shape to it in *De Gebroeders*, but it may be said that generally, in all the plays dealing with this kind of subject, it makes itself felt to some extent. He was less successful with the earlier history of his own country.

Gijsbreght van Aemstel? It is obvious indeed that the poet set out in that play to sketch a society different from that of his own day. His loving treatment of Romish features was one contribution to that end (he was, indeed, soon to become a convert to Catholicism). The turmoil of war, too, must have given the quiet citizens who saw the play performed the feeling that they were transferred to older times. But in the play's characters there is nothing, either in behavior or in outlook, that is specifically medieval.

No doubt the poet has done his best, and he treats us to a good many historical particulars. These, however, strike us as interesting bits of knowledge and as evidence of erudition rather than as indispensable elements that set the play's historical atmosphere. This is partly due to the technique to which I alluded before: lengthy narrative speeches instead of action; characters who argue and deliver dissertations instead of speaking from the heart or just simply living in their own different ways. There are moments when we seem near to getting scenes such as those through which Shakespeare makes us breathe the historic atmosphere of a play, scenes that would be unthinkable in a French tragedy: when, for instance, the soldiers violently break into the monastery. Nobody will want a period piece, correct in all details, so long as life has been surprised in one of its universal manifestations. Yet, although there is the attempt, Vondel's strength does not lie here. One could more easily imagine that the great comic playwright Bredero (1585-1618) might have equaled Shakespeare in the achievement of this kind of effect, if only the classicist fashion had not made so rigid a separation between tragedy and comedy as to leave little more than the lower forms of life to the latter.

No play is so exclusively a piece of staged national history as *Batavische Gebroeders, of Onderdrukte Vrijheid* (*Batavian Brothers, or Freedom Oppressed*). One cannot without a certain hesitation undertake to test it on its poetic and historic value: it was a work of Vondel's extreme old age. Yet *Adam in Ballingschap* was still to come. Was not the weakness of *Batavische Gebroeders* the result of the impotence of Vondel's imagination in the face of this kind of subject matter, and does the play not therefore demand a relentless examination?

What strikes us in the first place, then, is the utterly undramatic character of *Batavische Gebroeders*. There is no action, there is no conflict, there are no living persons; the historic atmosphere is only related (and with the most startling anachronisms), it is never made visible.

One would expect any poet who intends to show us Claudius Civilis in opposition to Roman dominion in the country of the Batavians to place him, as the great leader of the revolt, squarely in the center. But when one has finished reading the *Batavian Brothers*, the revolt is still only in prospect. Vondel chose as his theme the oppression that went before (and he plainly expressed this in his subtitle). The unity of time, the compulsive prescription of the one day, which did not hinder Racine in the development of his purely inner conflicts, was a serious stumbling block for

Vondel. He could not treat together both oppression and revolt —in this he was less fortunate than Shakespeare, who would not have scrupled to cover a period of years if this was necessary for the purpose of making history live. Historically speaking, Claudius Civilis had not been the indisputable leader during the oppression, for he had shared that position with his brother; together they were arrested, and it was the brother who was put to death. What matters to Vondel is to display their innocence. This lends to their appearance something of timidity. The chorus and even their sister, who in the first act come to incite them to action, obtain nothing but dilatory and pacifying words. The brothers are, nevertheless, arrested, and sentenced—unjustly. Again, the brothers merely proclaim their innocence, and subsequently, stage a contest of magnanimity to determine which of them shall bear the (undeserved) blame. Martyrs, much more than heroes, are these two.

Typically Vondel? Indeed, even of Lucifer he—differing from Milton!—was not able to make a true rebel. But it is typical, too, of the spirit of a century in which there was a widespread feeling that submission to the established powers was the highest virtue. It is typical, moreover, of the then current historical view of the Batavians: in them and in their "constitution" Dutch intellectuals recognized (no less a person than Grotius had set the fashion) the prototypes of themselves and of their own constitution, and moreover, they idealized themselves and that constitution as the embodiment of the pattern of liberty consonant with order and respect for authority.

The observation I made with regard to Hooft can here be applied to Vondel as well. The poet's object is rather to offer a lesson or treatise on constitutional law than to evoke an image of the past; and the drama suffers. When the mother of the two brothers, exhorts them to fight to the death, it is for "the country's liberty" and for "the holy right of the States" (meaning the sovereign assembly of the province of Holland, which was, of course, far to seek in the days of the Romans). Claudius Civilis and his brother (who is called Nicolaas Burgerhart in Vondel's play) are therefore pictured as patrician gentlemen, averse to precipitate action and popular passion, fond of liberty no doubt, but above all dedicated to order and the rule of law.

This makes it understandable—although it does not make it any the less undramatic—that Vondel has neglected that splendid detail offered him by Tacitus, namely, that Civilis used to compare himself with Hannibal and Sertorius, both one-eyed like himself. In the play, Fonteius, the Roman governor, does mention those two dangerous enemies of Rome—in order to compare *both* the brothers to them. We are meant to note the injustice done to the brothers, who were—we are not allowed to forget it—loyal, and men of order; but meanwhile all difference between the two is obliterated, and there is not a word about that thrilling bodily defect of Civilis. The fire of opposition to an alien rule is expressed only at the very end of the play, in an explosive speech by Burgerhart. Five acts had apparently been needed to justify Burgerhart's outburst for Vondel's tender sense of legality.

And how much prolix argumentation has been involved. The play as a whole is almost intolerably wordy. The endless stichomythias are not more exhausting than are the lengthy speeches made by each character in turn. A feeble attempt has been made to characterize Fronto, the Roman director of the press gang: he is the lawless oppressor, the exponent of tyranny. But he is no less given to long speeches. When he has managed, for instance, with great difficulty, to load a number of Batavians aboard a ship, he describes the scene of woe thus:

> . . . all the river's bank was wet with the tears
> Of grandmother, mother, niece, daughter-in-law,
> sister, aunts.

No parody could surpass this!

As regards the historic background, here, although Vondel had Tacitus's *Germania* before him, he was not even remotely successful in visualizing that primitive society. When Fonteius describes the defeat of the Chats (of course, the rules prevented this being shown on the stage), for a fleeting moment we seem to be getting nearer; elsewhere, too, we hear of holy oaks and orgies in dark forests. But *mentioning*—and there is nothing else, never more than narration—will not do the trick. Besides, the characters talk just as fluently about streets and towngates, and about milkmaids with shining copper pails. And what is the important thing: these sentimental, tearful, softhearted Batavians, forever holding forth about their rights, resemble in nothing the Batavians as they were in reality, do not even resemble the idealized Germans Tacitus had sketched.

A moment ago, to explain Vondel's presentation I referred to the spirit of the time. Genius, of course, does not let itself be curbed by such a master. In Shakespeare's time the horror of rebellion was already making headway, and Shakespeare had his share of it. But that did not prevent him from understanding the great rebels and bringing them to life. The comparison that here thrusts itself upon one is, however, with Rembrandt. Just before

Vondel wrote his *Batavian Brothers*, Rembrandt had been commissioned to paint the "Conspiracy of Claudius Civilis" for one of the walls of the Amsterdam town hall. All that is lacking in Vondel's play is to be found in Rembrandt. The barbaric, the savage, the vigorous, the passionate—in the countenances and in the attitudes of the plotters who crowd about the table lighted up by torches in the vast dark room—it has all been grippingly evoked, and the effect is embodied in the mighty one-eyed figure, who, sturdily and fatefully seated, holds his sword aloft, while the others touch it with theirs. That blunt presentation of the first Dutch warrior for freedom apparently offended the chastened convention soon to be enshrined afresh by Vondel. At any rate, the burgomasters of Amsterdam refused Rembrandt's largest historical painting. Today only the central fragment survives—in the museum at Stockholm![32]

Modern historic, no less than artistic, awareness will unhesitatingly recognize the veracity of Rembrandt's fantasy as against the nerveless invention of Vondel. What does it matter that the oaths were taken in a forest rather than, as the painter saw it, in a room; or that not everything is accurate about the costumes and the swords of these Germanic warriors; or that Civilis wears a turban! Rembrandt knew how to render the primitive and the savage. Everyone can see at once that his are the authentically desperate conspirators and that they were moved by very different motives and acted under the stimulus of very different passions from those the poet or the painter might have observed around him in the erudite and decent burghers of Amsterdam, familiar with the pen and the account book and the law court.

As an illustration accompanying the *Batavian Brothers*, Rembrandt's "conspiracy" would be absurd. But Macbeth's banquet, at which Banquo's ghost horrifies Macbeth and Macbeth's terror disconcerts his guests, might have been painted by that same hand.

(*Cetera desunt.*) (1947)

II

FRENCH HISTORIANS FOR AND AGAINST THE REVOLUTION

Is the French Revolution still worth talking about? Is it more than a subject with which historical erudition will no doubt go on playing its sterile game, but which can hardly affect us in our actual problems, in our thinking about the world as it is today?

If I ask these questions, it is not because there are any doubts in my mind. But there is a school of thought in our Western countries, nowadays, vocal, animated by the consciousness of having a significant message to impart, according to which this preoccupation with strictly European subjects denotes our blindness to the changes the world has gone through.

Professor Barraclough, for instance, tells us that we should "disabuse our minds of the illusion that there is any special relevance, from the point of view of contemporary affairs, in studying those neolithic figures"—he means: Louis XIV, Napoleon,

Bismarck! Mr. Toynbee has made the word "parochial" a familiar one in this connection. One of our Dutch historians (Professor Presser) gave it as his opinion, a couple of years ago, that compared with the Russian and Chinese Revolutions the French Revolution was but a provincial affair; others in Holland exhort us to take a "universalist" view of history and denounce "the Eurocentric" attitude.

I shall not enter into a discussion of these views. But I want to state, somewhat apodictically, that such views seem to me to lead dangeroulsy close to a denial of history. Is not western Europe, much as it may have lost in power, the same western Europe? And is it not our own past that is so cavalierly pushed aside? Do our traditions and ingrained beliefs no longer count because we have lost our grip on Asia and on Africa?

The inspiration of our universalists often seems to be what I regard as a detestable defeatism with respect to the vitality and prospects of Western society and civilization. They are obsessed with the idea of change to the extent of not caring any longer to preserve our heritage. Their outlook is akin to that truly revolutionary mentality which Croce, twenty-five years ago, described under the name of "anti-historism"—"that feeling," as Croce defined it, "that true history is only about to begin, and that we are at last escaping from the bonds of false history and struggling into freedom and space." What strikes me as being a little pathetic is that the advocates of a universalist revision have not even the satisfaction, and the excitement, and the pride, that can go with making your revolution yourself. But in the meantime, the illusion of anti-historism, as Croce, faced by the new barbarisms of Fascism and National Socialism, pointed out, entails a frightful wastage of cultural riches. True history, by ensuring, not immobility, but continuity, is indispensable for the preservation of civilization.

If there is one subject that can enlighten us on this score, it is the French Revolution, in which the anti-historical mentality was so prominent. In itself a fascinating spectacle! But it is not less fascinating, and certainly not less instructive, to watch the gradual disillusionment when reality did not so readily and completely as the enthusiasts and the fanatics had hoped, yield to theorizing divorced from history and tradition.

In referring, then, to the French Revolution, what I mean is the action and the reaction, the reforming zeal and the stubborn resistance. Neither the one nor the other tendency is to be wholly accepted, nor is either to be wholly rejected. Revolutions, for all their being necessarily destructive and but a clumsy and costly means of achieving a sometimes scanty result, belong to the forms of the life of mankind which historians cannot simply condemn. To us at any rate, the French Revolution will always be, in its entirety, of the most immediate interest, for it can be said that our modern Western world is largely shaped by it. But it is shaped by the negation as well as by the assertion, by the example of the daring attempt, and also by the warning implied in the partial failure, by the striving and by the recognition of the bounds calling a halt to it; it is shaped not by the revolutionary doctrine so much as by the protracted struggle to which it gave rise, not by orthodox acceptance, but by the debate.

A debate that was carried on through several generations! The French Revolution, when viewed in this way, did not end in 1794, with the fall of Robespierre—as Michelet thought it did; nor in 1795, when Bonaparte dispersed the Paris mob by "a whiff of grapeshot"—with which Carlyle concludes his history; nor in 1799, when Bonaparte constituted himself a dictator—where Madelin and a host of others write *finis;* not even in 1814 and 1815, when the Bourbon monarchy was restored. The contrasts had not been resolved. France was to be shaken by one violent change of regime after another. If at last a conclusion has been reached (and can we say it has been, even now?), it is one of compromise, of equilibrium, of synthesis.

I propose, in this essay, to trace developments since the Bourbon restoration, especially as they were reflected in the ever-changing historical interpretation of the great initial crisis. I shall limit my observation to France, because nowhere else was the great clash of ideas more continuous and more vehement, and nowhere else did it center to the same extent round the issue of the acceptance or rejection of the principles and the doings of the men of 1789 and 1793. Moreover, just as the exceptionally profound social contrasts and the economic maladjustment in France had caused the outbreak to occur there, so the resentments and hatreds left behind by the upheaval—resentments and hatreds that hindered developments after the Restoration from taking a smooth course—were more implacable there than elsewhere. Extreme still stood against extreme. The Revolution was not really overcome.

1.
Mme de Staël

Stability would be possible in France only if the government took seriously the *Charte*, which had been granted by Louis XVIII shortly after his return. This was the view presented by Mme de Staël in the book she left upon her death in 1817, *Considérations sur la Révolution française*. And her conclusion was based on a reading of the history of the Revolution.

"Not to be wholly accepted, nor to be wholly rejected"—this is indeed what had been said at once by those reacting from the extreme course of the Terror,[1] and it was repeated on innumerable occasions by their successors, by Napoleon himself. The idea that the Revolution must be terminated, and that it could be terminated only by a compromise safeguarding its beneficient achievements, had been a commonplace of French political thinking ever since the fall of Robespierre. Only, the compromises attempted had not worked. What *were* its beneficient achievements? What were its unfulfilled aspirations worth reviving? Those questions admitted of widely differing answers.

Equality was a principle commanding wide assent, but in practice no advance had been made beyond an equality restricted to legal or civil rights, an equality that did not hamper the propertied classes in enjoying their property, and adding to it. The aspirations toward social reform stirring wildly and blindly in 1793 and 1794 had been defeated, but they had not been really disposed of. The time was to come when this antinomy between bourgeois complacency about civil equality and the economic and social inequality that in fact it favored was once more to cause the most dangerous discontent.

Yet this was not at first the chief difficulty. For a generation after the defeat of the sans-culottes the most acute tensions were created by purely political problems, all coming under the head of distribution or implementation of power. The decentralization and the division of power that had marked the constitution of the year III (1795), the constitution of the Directorate—a reaction against the frightful despotism of the *Comité de salut public*—had resulted in the most hopeless confusion, accompanied by shocking dilapidation and corruption; the strong government soon afterwards established by Bonaparte had resulted, on the contrary, in enslavement to the will and to the ambitions of a master.

The lesson that Mme de Staël, true to her lifelong faith, now extracted from history, was that of liberalism. She writes enthusiastically about the beginning, about 1789. The *ancien régime*, the monarchy, had made the Revolution inevitable by misgovernment, by the arbitrary use of power. Liberty had the older rights; it was despotism that had been the disturbing innovation.

In sounding that note, which was eagerly caught up by liberal writers—of historians, I mention only Thierry and Guizot—Mme de Staël may seem to have merely revived the tradition of the appeals to history made by clergy, nobility, and *parlements* in their opposition to royal policy in the days of Louis XV and XVI. These representatives of the privileged classes had been accustomed to decorate their captious protests against attempts to make them submit to taxation or to the needs of unified administration with references to Louis IX or even to Charlemagne and his March Fields. In fact they had contributed not a little to the creation of the revolutionary atmosphere; but as soon as—even in the preparation of the election of the States-General in 1788 and and 1789—liberty was made to mean liberty for the people, or for the bourgeoisie, the vocal leaders of the antiabsolutist movement were disconcerted; put on the defensive, they were finally swept into perdition as the Revolution took its course. But as a matter of fact, Mme de Staël's interpretation of liberty in French history and of liberty as the goal now to be striven for had a wider scope. And as she read the events of 1789, too, these, and the States-General turned National Assembly, had offered the golden promise of liberty securely based on reason.

All the more horrifying had been the spectacle of the Terror and of the sanguinary reign of the small band of Jacobins who suddenly usurped the power that was to have been invested in the enlightened people, in the people as far as they were enlightened. Political fanaticism proved to be as reckless and inhuman as religious fanaticism had ever been. Bonaparte, who had been hailed as the restorer of order and moderation, soon abused power in a less barbarous, but no less insufferable and disastrous manner.

Parliamentary government, therefore, was Mme de Staël's prescription, but always allied to respect for enlightenment and for property, and guarded by a wise monarchy accepting the limitations set by the constitution.

In actual fact constitutional monarchy and parliamentary government did not work any more than had the other compromises. Because, Mme de Staël maintained, the government did not keep faith with the *Charte*. She was quite prepared to accept a monarch of the ancient line and praised Louis XVIII's good intentions. But in practice the tone was set by the reactionary temper of his faithful adherents. And it was not very likely that they should take to heart the admonitions of this bluestocking who lauded the mischief-makers of 1789 to the skies and was, moreover, always holding up the example of the English constitution to her French public. Her constant reminders that "they order these things better in England" could only rouse their impatience. "Anglomania" had long been, and was to be throughout the nineteenth century, the term of reproach with which the sermonizing of French liberals was met by their counterrevolutionary compatriots. In fact the reproach rose as readily to the lips of full-blooded revolutionaries, of those to whom the *Contrat social* was gospel and the years 1793 and 1794 the culminating point of the glorious liberating movement. But these voices were hardly heard in the first years after the restoration of the monarchy. The danger that Mme de Staël saw as immediately threatening was that of a reaction against the great principles of 1789 under the shelter of absolutism.

The air resounded with the clamors of the ultraroyalists. To these men, to take a detached view of the upheaval from which they or their fathers had suffered so cruelly, seemed little less than treason. Benjamin Constant (and I quote him from among many who continued in the same strain when the voice of the great prophet of liberalism was silenced) asked them not to confuse the Terror with what was admirable in the Revolution.[2] But in their view the Terror *was* the Revolution, and the Restoration ought to be a restoration in the full sense of the word. As an instinctive reaction this mood was natural enough, but it also found expression in the works of a few great theorists. One might say that it was rationalized by them, however incongruous the word may sound in connection with these despisers of reason. For distrust of reason as a guide in human affairs was a prominent feature of all these counterrevolutionary theories.

De Maistre and De Bonald

Of the writers, De Maistre and De Bonald were already past middle age and had testified to their detestation of the Revolution and all its works long before, while in exile. The Abbé Lamennais was a younger man, and with him the religious sentiment, which now made him reject the Revolution, was so much the dominant motive that it soon led him into conflict with a church relying on the restored State, to the detriment, as he saw it, of the church's spiritual freedom. De Maistre, too, made Catholicism the center of his system, but it was a Catholicism of a very different quality. One cannot help feeling that to him the primary motive was a horror of the insecurity and change threatening the social order, a fear that made him exalt authority; and while he duly honored the monarchy, the highest authority that he could think of, and from which the monarchy, too, should therefore derive its power to do good, was that of the Pope.

As for trusting to reason, or to liberty, De Maistre derided the notion in a famous passage:

We have seen a great and powerful nation making the most tremendous effort toward liberty that has ever been made in the world's history; and what has it attained? It has covered itself with ridicule and shame in order to place upon the throne an italic *b* [a Bonaparte] where there had been a capital B [a Bourbon king]; and for the people it has substituted servitude for obedience.

So much for the achievements of the Revolution! And indeed, how could there be any constructive achievements, since the Revolution, according to De Maistre, proceeded from "a satanic principle"!

But did not the reality patently contradict this negative valuation?

The Revolution and the "italic *b*," who had consolidated so many of its novelties in a more respectable manner, left behind them reforms that the royal regime did not dream of touching: the centralized administration, for instance, which was, as a matter of fact, no more than the completion of what had been prepared under the monarchy; the Concordat also, which incorporated much of the old Gallican tendencies. Above all they left behind them a personnel of Bonapartist high officials and dignitaries co-operating quite smoothly with the restored monarchy—a token of the hidden but profound solidarity between some of the tendencies of the Revolution and the interests of that monarchy. And was not even the church caught in a similar ambivalence? The bishops were not likely to welcome De Maistre's extreme ultramontanism—let alone Lamennais's ecclesiastical libertarianism. They were quite happy with the Concordat, to which, moreover, Rome itself continued to adhere. They might agree as to the satanic character of the Revolution, but they found it only in certain tendencies of the Revolution. They had compacted, and so had Rome, with the Revolution as regards other tendencies. They were now ready to preach obedience to the King, as they had until lately preached obedience to the Emperor. One is a little startled by the fervent servility toward the Bourbon king displayed by the Bishop of Troyes in a pastoral letter in which he exhorted the faithful to imitate this, and one is especially shocked when one learns that he had been Napoleon's great-almoner. But indeed, as Mme de Staël remarks with scathing sarcasm, he had learned how to bow in a good school.

The Revolution could not be so easily wiped out. Of the counterrevolutionary theorists, it was De Bonald who made the most genuine attempt to think historically; he has the most affinity with Burke. But in practice his view of the Revolution as a mere interruption of the historical process could not but land him in insuperable difficulties. How was one to link up the restored monarchy with the state of affairs prevailing before 1789? De Bonald became a member of the Chamber; he took an oath on the *Charte*—

it is true that he accepted it as having been freely granted by the King, not as a compact. Yet in fact he became a party to the Restoration compromise.

These ultraroyalists had a particular aversion to the well-to-do middle-class upon which the regime actually came to rest. De Bonald and many of his friends wanted to have the suffrage extended, for the primary assemblies at least, to a numerous class of small taxpayers. The majority of the members of the Chamber clung to their narrow *pays légal*—ninety thousand voters out of twenty-five million. But the aristocrats who listened to De Bonald still believed in the ability of their own class to lead. They still believed that their prestige, that gratitude or fear, that religion and the assistance of the priests, could win them the support of the farmers and of the lower middle-class. The ideal, in short, of Disraeli's Young England. But in France this ideal was vastly more remote from the possibilities of reality. When Mme de Staël, with all her respect for property, described the suffrage clause as the principal blot on the *Charte*, she was not thinking of a submissive class led by noblemen and parish priests and to which the suffrage ought to be extended. Was such a class still in being? For a long time before the Revolution the French aristocracy had neglected its task of leadership in local affairs. The Revolution itself had created a gulf between it and the people, and had left behind unappeasable resentments and distrust on both sides.

Courier

If one wishes to get an idea of the bitterness animating the class of small men, especially small farmers, against the leading class clustering round the government, there is no better way than to read the pamphlets of Paul Louis Courier. One must not expect in them any comprehensive views of the significance of the Revolution or of the problems raised by the restoration. But they are a startling revelation—even if the concentrated venom of these witty productions is very much the writer's own—of the suspicion tinged with hatred with which the inhabitants of his village in Touraine regarded noblemen and priests, and above all, the arbitrary and grasping Paris government and its instruments, the police, the judges, the *maire*, and all the government's officials. Reminiscences of the time when a nobleman could kill a villain for a fine of five sous lead Courier to the reflection that nowadays a *maire* had to spend seven and a half sous for a sealed paper to have a man arrested; the judge would see to the rest. Once upon a time, Courier observed, *corvéable, taillable et tuable à merci;* now only *incarcérable:*[3] we progress; this is what five or six centuries have produced—who knows but what in another five or six centuries it will be possible to sue the *maire* for money if he owes it to us, without being thrown into prison for our pains. Even the royal family was not safe from Courier's barbed witticisms, and when he was tried for libel, he had a gorgeous time describing the trial and making fun—always mordant and with undertones of subversive intent—at the expense of the public prosecutor.

The Revolution was never far from people's thoughts. In the political discussion liberals and royalists were constantly belaboring each other with interpretations of that great episode or of the causes that had led to it, with diametrically opposed arguments suited to each side's particular case. The Revolution, a wicked break with a beneficent past; or the Revolution, the culmination of an age-long striving after liberty which the monarchy had tried, to its own undoing, to impede.[4]

But the history of the crucial years from 1789 on was not at first examined at all closely. The politicians and the journalists dealt mostly in generalities, while the historians participating in the debate dwelt on earlier periods to bring out the trends that seemed to prove either the one or the other of the two opposing theses. The conservative or reactionary writers I discussed above took their views, so to speak, for granted and went on to elaborate their theoretical conclusions. If Mme de Staël's book created a sensation it was not only because it discussed events of the revolutionary period sympathetically—as far, at least, as the first phase went—but because it discussed them at all and in some detail. Under Napoleon silence had been the order of the day. The revolutionary tradition had lingered on, almost inarticulately, among the generation that had been active in the crisis. The younger generation was raised in the tradition of abhorrence. But just when, after the assassination of the Duc de Berry in 1820, ultraroyalism as well as ultra-Catholicism became more aggressive and opposition to the regime consequently more determined and more vocal, there appeared, in 1823 and 1824, the first two real histories: the first volume of the many that were to compose Thiers's *History*, and Mignet's two small volumes.

2.
Thiers and Mignet

It is with Thiers and Mignet that the historiography of the Revolution really begins, and it is worth noting that it begins with authors who had very definite political aims.

Thiers and Mignet, young men, were intimate friends, both hailing from Provence. They intended their accounts of the Revolution to be contributions to the opposition against the absolutist and clerical tendencies of the Bourbon regime. In essentials they followed the line traced by Mme de Staël. They, too, were liberals; they shared the ideal, so characteristically middle class and intellectual, of liberty through enlightenment and a parliamentary monarchy.

It is perfectly natural, then, that they explain the Revolution by the abuses of the *ancien régime* and by the errors committed by the monarchy before and during the crisis, and that they wholeheartedly accept the early phase, the phase of the National Assembly, and even, a little less wholeheartedly, the phase of the Legislative Assembly. It is also natural that they, like Mme Staël, deplore the dictatorship of the *Comité de salut public* and the excesses of the Terror. And yet here one notices a marked difference. There is in their comments nothing like that profound moral distress into which these developments threw Mme Staël; nothing like her straightforward condemnation. They deplore; but in the end they condone.

In order to show their style of treatment in some particular instances, let me confine myself to Mignet, whose rapid sketch brings out the main points with such admirable lucidity.

The sale of the church lands, while antagonizing the clergy, was, so Mignet argues, necessary to save the Revolution. The *constitution civile* may have been an injudicious measure, for it served the clergy as a "plausible pretext" to indulge in hostility to the Revolution, but, Mignet insists, the Revolution was not opposed to religion. The anticlerical tone can be heard throughout his book. Anticlericalism constitutes a major strand in the bond by which he (and the same is true for Thiers) feels himself united to the triumphant majority of the National Assembly.

The constitution of 1791 is to him the zenith of political wisdom. If it failed, it was not the fault of the Assembly, but of the factions: "attacked by the aristocracy, invaded by the multitude," the Assembly was thrown off its course.

The middle position of the bourgeois becomes very clear. Mignet does not waste a word about the census clause in that constitution he admires so much. The curious arrangement by which members of the Assembly were debarred from becoming ministers to the King; the folly of vesting executive power in a King who was only too patently out of tune with the Revolution—he passes all that by in silence. But the ever-more-violent action of the clubs, the terrible schemes of the Commune of Paris—this he notes with disapproval. The Girondins are the men after his heart, and their extermination is in his eyes a disaster.

He does, it is true, shake his head over the bellicose speeches delivered by some of the leading Girondin spokesmen in the Legislative Assembly, which contributed so much to the outbreak of the war in 1792. And the war, he does admit, opened "the dictatorial and arbitrary phase of the Revolution. . . . The energy roused by the war made the dominance of the lower class restless, oppressive, and cruel." But—and now there follows the twist in the argument which enabled Mignet, and has since enabled countless French historians and politicians, writers and orators, to accept without further qualms the *Comité de salut public* and its sanguinary exploits as part of the glorious tradition of the Revolution—*but*:

> The issue was no longer liberty, it was *salut public*. The Revolution became absorbed in a protracted struggle against Europe and against the parties. Was anything else possible?

To answer this question Mignet quotes an extraordinary passage from a book written as long ago as 1796, by De Maistre, the prophet of legitimacy and of ultramontanism. De Maistre was at that time already an implacable opponent of the Revolution, and his book had been published outside France.

> The Revolution once established [so he had written], France and the monarchy could not be saved but by Jacobinism. . . . Our descendants, who will care very little for our sufferings and who will dance on our graves, will laugh at our present lack of perspicacity; they will easily console themselves over the excesses that we have witnessed and that will prove to have preserved the integrity of the finest kingdom on earth.

The passage contains several points of interest. But let us only ask ourselves why Mignet thought it worth his while to quote. The answer is indeed obvious. What good fortune for the apologist of the Revolution to be able to extract this reflection from the writings of the royalist, for it clearly implied the simple statement: The dictatorship and the Terror were necessary to preserve the integrity of the French state. Mignet, of course, adds: "and to save the Revolution." Also: "it could not have gone otherwise."

The addiction of Mignet—and for that matter also of Thiers, for the two are remarkably like in these fundamental respects—the addiction to the doctrine of the inevitability, of the fatality, of the course of history has often been remarked upon. I do not know whether it has been sufficiently observed that this doctrine served the very useful purpose of glossing over the less sightly aspects of the Revolution and of French policy in those terrible years.

A host of questions seem to clamor for answers. To what extent was the bellicose policy of Brissot and Isnard—of the Girondins—responsible for the war? If to some extent it was, can the war be used as a sufficient excuse for the excesses that followed? Did not the Revolution carry within itself the principle that made both the war and the excesses difficult to avert? And when a man strove to avert both by preaching moderation, is it right to reproach him (as Mignet does Lafayette, although on the whole he had the greatest respect for Lafayette) with overlooking the extraordinary circumstances in which France found herself? For here another question arises, one that ought not to be evaded: is it so certain that the Revolution could only be saved by the war, and the war won only by the dictatorship? More, *was* it saved by the war and by the dictatorship? Was it not, on the contrary, ruined or frustrated by these wild courses?

For the advocate of the revolutionary tradition, and also for the French patriot to whom France must always have been in the right, the most convenient way of putting an end to a somewhat uncomfortable discussion is to say: It had to be so.

It would be difficult to determine which was, in the case of Mignet or of Thiers, the strongest incentive, the desire to whitewash the Revolution, or the desire to whitewash France. It is a difficulty that will repeatedly recur when one reads later French historians, indeed, down to the present day. For Mignet's method had a long career before it, and the blending together of worship of the Revolution and worship of the French fatherland became an enduring feature of French thinking. It should not, indeed, be forgotten that at the height of the crisis in the seventeen-nineties this double cult had already obliterated the original devotion to mankind. The combination of revolutionary and of patriotic ardor was, therefore, itself a legacy of the heroic years of the Revolution.

Mignet, to be fair to him, was perhaps too balanced, at times too critical and willing to make reservations, for the words *worship* and *cult* to fit his work. But he and Thiers pointed a way that was soon crowded by a rush of writers, neither balanced nor critical, but gifted in other ways, fervently preaching the revolutionary tradition as the true national religion. The two friends had had the satisfaction, almost immediately, of seeing the regime against which they had helped to mobilize the Revolution topple, making room for one that they could hail as being more in agreement with the revolutionary principles, with those worth retaining at least, with the principles of 1789. But they lived on, for something like half a century, to see the legend they had created flourishing almost too luxuriously and indeed bearing fruit that was not always to their taste.

Before long the bourgeois monarchy of Louis Philippe, too, ran into troubled waters. The working class began to make its voice heard. As a matter of fact, it had contributed not a little to the turn of affairs in 1830, only it had been the middle class that had benefited. Soon afterward, however, the restricted suffrage for the Chamber became a burning grievance. At the same time the Church attempted to regain its hold over education. Many bourgeois, Voltairians as they might be, or "enlightened" as they would describe themselves, were prepared to accept the help of the Church in keeping the people submissive and preserving the social order. But others were roused to fierce resentment, especially by the activities of the Jesuits. The compromise of 1830 was not to be the end of the journey. In the late forties revolution was again in the air—not in France only, it is well to remember, but in France that mood again fed on recollections of the events of fifty years earlier.

Buchez

The discussion now had more material to go upon, owing not only to the circumstantial accounts of Mignet and Thiers, but to the labors of Buchez and his associate Roux, who had between 1834 and 1838 published, in forty volumes of some four hundred fifty pages each, that invaluable collection of extracts from the debates in the revolutionary assemblies, from pamphlets, newspapers, memoirs, decrees, treaties, the *Histoire parlementaire de la Révolution française*. That this enormous series could be let loose on the public in so short a space of time and prove an immense publishing success shows the avid interest that the Revolution now evoked.

Buchez's prefaces are in themselves absorbingly interesting. Nearly every one of the forty volumes opens with a lively disquisition of a few pages in which he often takes issue with reviewers. The very first sentence of the first preface strikes the note that was to dominate all the rest of them; it is a note well suited to rouse the attention:

> The French Revolution is the last and most advanced consequence of modern civilization, and modern civilization has in its entirety sprung from the Gospel.

Liberty, equality, fraternity: these words summarize the aim of the Revolution. And what can be more in keeping with the teaching of Jesus?

We see at once how different is the state of mind in which Buchez will judge the Revolution from that which we observed in the liberal school of Mme de Staël. Buchez speaks for the people, which Mignet regarded with so much distrust; the Assembly, whose moderation and wisdom were extolled by the liberals, can find no grace in the eyes of a "Christian Socialist" like Buchez.

According to him there was unanimity in France before the meeting of the States-General. The *cahiers* prove it, all breathing the spirit of Rousseau. The Revolution's high design to realize Christian principles was the outcome of fourteen centuries of French history. Buchez reviews that period in a lengthy introduction, bringing out the great historic task of France, France the champion of European civilization.

The entire past of Europe can be comprised in two words: France and the Church. All the temporal work was, in the Christian era, done by the French; the spiritual achievement was the Church's.

Unfortunately, by the end of the eighteenth century, the rich, the nobility, part of the intelligentsia, had been fashioned by the exclusively critical spirit of Voltaire rather than by Rousseau, and immediately after the Fourteenth of July the bourgeoisie made themselves masters of the Assembly. The Declaration of Rights, instead of reorganizing society, asserted only the rights of property and other individual rights. If disturbances occurred, it was due to the fact that the new order, like the old, neglected its duty. The National Assembly was responsible for the insurrections that marked the course of the Revolution. "When men are blind, or prejudiced, or interested, must society therefore halt in the conquest of its aim?"

For the Revolution *had* an aim, and if in its own day so many of its leaders did not discern it, he, Buchez, knew: it was to cast out individualism and to realize the fraternity and sovereignty of the people.

Faced with the September massacre (1792), the Christian thinker does not falter. Other apologists of the Revolution, when Catholic writers denounced that horror, were to cast the memory of the Massacre of St. Bartholomew in their teeth. But Buchez boldly justifies both. The victims of September were to be commiserated, but they were guilty. Like the victims of St. Bartholomew's Day, they had conspired with the enemy and were attempting to "federalize" France.[5] It was to be regretted that they were not put through a regular trial, but even so, it should be remembered that it was the Assembly that by its culpable moderation, or rather inaction, had thrust the Revolution into the fatal sequence of disorder. As for the murders in themselves, they, like the murders of St. Bartholomew's Day, should be regarded as: "une mesure de salut public."

There is a strong element of monomania in this reasoning. Buchez was impervious to the evidence of the facts he so industriously collected. Instead of deducing from careful observation what this extraordinarily complicated phenomenon, the Revolution, really was, he began by dogmatically equating it with Christianity in action. He sees history ruled by purpose: "A nation is an association of men united to practice and to act for the same purpose." And he admits of no doubt as to what was the purpose of the Revolution. France was chosen, and had been prepared by the centuries, to accomplish the great task of leading Europe on the way of social reorganization in accordance with the principles of the Gospel. And after having exulted in the unanimity displayed at the start of that great undertaking, Buchez proceeds to quarrel with the actual doings of the men elected to carry it out, explaining their mistakes as the result of private interest and faulty philosophy—Voltairean, and also Protestant, a term that is to Buchez as opprobrious an epithet for individualism and selfish egoism as it had been to De Maistre. If it went badly with many of the obstructionists and the bunglers, their fate was not to be judged by any other consideration than that of the public interest as it had been revealed to him, Buchez. And in the end, after all his philosophizing, surveying the scene of the France of his own day encumbered with the remains of old abuses, he still exhorts his compatriots to complete the great work of the Revolution and to reconstruct French society, and at the same time, to resume the leadership of Europe, by placing themselves on the firm ground of Catholicism. Thus will society realize the morality of Jesus Christ.

The importance of Buchez's forty volumes lies, of course, in the material they made available.[6] His prefaces will not find many readers nowadays. At the time of their publication they were already received with head shakes—if not with ridicule—more often than with approval. And yet they were more than the lucubrations of a solitary eccentric. The absolutist thinking of Rousseau and his disciples, the Terrorists of 1794, was closely allied to certain religious states of mind, although, normally,

Catholics and Protestants alike, even if they recognize the affinity, will abhor such manifestations as perversions of true religiosity. At any rate, we shall see in a moment that even this most surprising aspect of Buchez's interpretation of the Revolution—his regarding it as the culmination of Christianity—was eagerly fastened upon by Lamartine, a writer of infinitely greater literary power, who enjoyed, as a matter of fact, a great popular success by his presentation of it.

It was much less singular and farfetched, of course, to represent the socialistic proclivities that dominated the scene in the violent years from 1792 to 1794 as constituting the real significance of the Revolution. Mignet, and indeed Mme de Staël, had already made this distinction between the early bourgeois phase of the Revolution and the later rise of proletarian influence. Their sympathies, however, had been with the Assembly and its respect for property; and the invasion of the scene by the hungry and impatient populace had seemed to them an unmitigated disaster. It was only natural—and from the point of view of the strictly historical discussion, it was useful—that the roles of the villains and the heroes should for a change be reversed. The time, moreover, as I already hinted, was propitious for this particular view. And so, here again, the suggestions contained in Buchez's prefaces were to be elaborated by an abler writer. The work of Louis Blanc, a bitter enemy of the triumphant bourgeoisie, although lacking in the romantic and poetic appeal exercised by Lamartine's immensely more popular *Histoire des Girondins* (which appeared about the same time as Blanc's first volume), did demonstrate some grasp of the reality of history.

Christianity, Socialism—but apart from any particular ideology or political conviction, Buchez represented a method of thinking that strongly appealed to the men of his generation. Its effect on the historiography of the Revolution was to survive him. To approach the confusion and multiplicity of reality with the presumptuous claim of knowing the one and only answer to its riddles, of knowing what History or Fate or Providence intended—how tempting it must be! Buchez's method allows one to walk in the light of an infallible revelation, ignoring or explaining away inconvenient features of the past; more than that, to feel able to censure or indict the men who had actually struggled with the problems as they arose; to censure or indict them for being unaware of the true significance of the events, and consequently, of their duty, and in the face of their insufficiency, of their gropings and fumblings; to maintain intact one's own preconceived idea of the Revolution and its predestined course.

Buchez's principal disciple in this devotion to an idealized

Revolution was, as we shall see, Lamartine. But Michelet, too, the greatest of the three writers (Louis Blanc being the third) who undertook large-scale histories of the Revolution just before the Orleans regime was overthrown in 1848, Michelet, although neither a Christian nor a Socialist, proved himself a kindred spirit.

3.

In the late forties revolution was again in the air. In 1844, Michelet and his friend Quinet, both professors at the *Collège de France*, lectured to excited crowds of students on the iniquities of the Jesuits and on the noble and eternal principles of the Revolution. They were dismissed by the government, but the atmosphere of Paris remained thick with forebodings and with hope. The young men in Flaubert's *Education sentimentale* (the novel appeared in 1874, but these scenes are laid in the years immediately preceding the Revolution of February 1848) dream of that glorious time, when "people *lived*, when they could assert themselves, prove their force." One modeled himself, or his future self, on Saint-Just, another on Danton, or on Marat, or Robespierre. And they loved to hear Barthélemy's poem recited: "Elle reparaîtra, la terrible Assemblée. . . ."

All three of the great histories that appeared, or began to appear, in 1847 were affected by that spirit. Widely as they differed among themselves in their interpretation of the action or of the actors on the stage of the great Revolution, their authors (and this, of course, can be said for Buchez as well) had in common a far more radical temper than had animated Thiers and Mignet. The influence of Mme de Staël seemed for the moment to have lost its power. That the Revolution and monarchy, albeit constitutional monarchy, were compatible seemed an outworn creed to all; some, as we saw, broke decisively with the bourgeois tradition in its entirety. And each, in exploring the inexhaustible story of the Revolution, brought out the aspects and the meanings that seemed to point his own particular moral.

Lamartine

Everybody agrees that Lamartine's *Histoire des Girondins* has no value as history. Particularly scathing was Tocqueville, who says (in his *Souvenirs*) that Lamartine not only made light with historical truth, but had no idea of what truth meant. It was, in fact, as a poet that he had suddenly, more than twenty-five years before, achieved fame. I do not mean to imply that the poet "has no idea of what truth means"; but Lamartine was a typically romantic poet, who could not imagine truth but in the unsubstantial and otherworldly regions of the imagination. As a politician, too (he had become a member of the Chamber after 1830), he only dealt in vague nobilities, in well-meaning generalities of a somewhat indeterminately democratic trend. If his historical work deserves our attention, it is because of the enormous influence it had at the time of its appearance—an influence that, in spite of the work's underlying chauvinism, was not confined to France.

Lamartine's is purely legendary, almost fictional, history. The spirit animating it is that of the growing opposition to the uninspired bourgeois conservatism of the Guizot regime, although Lamartine does not as directly and consistently preach socialism as did Buchez. He is nevertheless obviously inspired by Buchez's prefaces when, in his Introduction, he derives the Revolution from Christianity. Christianity had prepared men's minds for fraternity and equality, and French eighteenth-century philosophy had helped to carry them to that further stage where the Revolution could realize the application of these principles. A gospel of social rights and duties (it was Buchez's grievance against the Declaration of Rights that it had failed to state any duties); a charter of humanity—and France the apostle of this creed. "When Providence desires that an idea shall enflame the world, it kindles it in the soul of a Frenchman."

Again we see French chauvinism and revolutionary messianism walking hand in hand—as indeed they did in the great years of the Revolution itself. We noticed this self-intoxication in Buchez; we shall notice it in others. As a matter of fact, something very like it was already observable in Mignet and Thiers, although their general attitude was more sober, and in this particular aspect, more plainly and simply nationalistic.

When he comes to tell his story, Lamartine, every now and again, represents the Revolution as a living thing, with a character and aims of its own, independent almost of men and of events. It is the reversal—and we noticed it already in Buchez—of the truly historical approach. A subordination of the entire historical process to an abstract ideal, to a subjective a-priori. He writes, for instance: "The Revolution was not at first understood, except perhaps by Robespierre. All were blind, except the Revolution itself."

One is reminded of Hegel. The Idea compelling men to realize it in spite of themselves. Lamartine is even more extreme in practicing this personification than was Buchez, although the absurdity of his system occasionally led him to inconsistencies—by which he does not seem in the least troubled. What made him cling to these grandiloquent and philosophical-sounding pronouncements about the Revolution living its own life apart from the struggles of men was that they supplied a subtle way of apologizing for the Terror. Indeed, this and the other concepts with which he worked—the sophisms, or tricks, one might say—suited the public temper and certain idiosyncrasies of the French admirably well and helped to make the memory of the Revolution into an even more potent force in the politics of the present. "The shocks and the crimes," Lamartine says explicitly, "do not detract from the holiness of the Revolution: they were due to the imperfections of men. The holiest, most just and virtuous thought, when it passes through the medium of imperfect humanity, comes out in rags and blood."

Lamartine is full of admiration for the National Assembly—in which, of course, he sharply differs from Buchez and betrays a lingering kinship with Mignet and the bourgeois liberals. His exaltation in praising it, however, is peculiarly his own: "It was the most impressive body of men that had ever represented, not only France, but the human race. . . . Its members were not Frenchmen, but universal men. . . . They were the workmen of God."

This wonderful Assembly wanted peace. If war came, it was the doing of the party men and the ambitious. Lamartine even admits—it is one of those moments when he slips into forgetting his own system—that the Revolution had degenerated. He then proceeds as if nothing had happened and uses all the superlatives at his command to laud the Girondins, those great souls, whose delight in the triumphant moment of the deposition of Louis XVI he shares unconditionally—parting company with Mignet again, to whom the establishment of the Republic ushered in the "arbitrary and dictatorial" phase of the Revolution.

It is more surprising that when the dictatorship of the extremists comes along and the Girondins, his heroes, are the first to suffer, Lamartine, who had firmly rejected all palliation of the September massacres (differing this time from Buchez), submits. He admits necessity—Christianity and high morality now seem to be forgotten—and his explanations become as frankly realistic as were those of Mignet and Thiers. The *raison d'état* is invoked. The revered Girondins failed because they proved to be insufficiently energetic. The Revolution could not but rise against them and escape from their control.

Did the people act illegally? It believed that in acting as it did it made use of its supreme right, the right of survival. . . . In times of extremity, authority [*le gouvernement*] is, not legally but actually, wherever it can be made good. The centralization in Paris was necessary. The law had been violated too frequently already. And after all: the law was the Revolution itself. . . . The law was the instinct of self-preservation of a great nation.

Later on, he is horrified at the Terror, as he had been at the September murders. But in fact he had, by condoning everything beforehand, placed it beyond the reach of moral reproval—witness the passage I quoted. So, again, he is free to picture the Revolution as an all-powerful, suprahuman, indeed divine, being: "The social laws of the Committee of Public Safety emanated from its dogma; the Terror from its wrath."

Nevertheless, once more Lamartine takes the Revolution itself to task. It had become untrue to itself. The demolition of Lyons, for instance, was "a crime against the nation." But we also find him speaking as follows: "The anger of the Revolution had attained the power of a divine scourge." He thus magnifies and embellishes the excesses of that gruesome band of maniacs thrust into their short-lived position of power through the demented fight of the factions. Lamartine's favorite method, however, is to talk of *necessity*. In the execution of Danton, for instance, he sees "the cruel necessity of politics."

Like Buchez, Lamartine intended his book as an exhortation to the French public to prepare for a new revolution, but at the same time "to purify the doctrine, so that next time the Girondin spirit will not be assailed by Jacobin excesses." His recognition of these excesses did not, however, prevent him from extending in his conclusion a general pardon to the chief actors in the drama. After attaching to each the word indicating his characteristic quality—*liberty*, *energy*, etc., and also *crime*—Lamartine continues: "All [and Robespierre was among them] deserve the funereal description: *Died for the future, and workman of mankind.* Everything, the whole story, means imperishable glory for France."

Let me note, in fairness to the eloquent rhetor, that a number of years later he admitted, in an appendix to a new edition of his book (published in 1861), the falseness of this kind of argument. The disappointments of 1848 and the following years had created a different climate of opinion from what had prevailed before the crisis; we shall see this when we come to Tocqueville, Lanfrey, Quinet, Renan, Flaubert. To Lamartine personally, too, the experience of revolution in action had brought some unpleasant shocks. So now he rejects emphatically "the detestable theory" that the Terror had saved *la patrie*, and he blames himself for having written as if that were so. The indulgence and justification implied in the passage just quoted from the conclusion of the work of 1846 he now repudiates. The passage, he says, sounds "more like an ode than like a verdict."

It seems to hover over the entire scene of action like a glorious amnesty and to justify deeds and doers alike by casting a halo round them. . . . I was angry with myself when this morning I reread that lyrical last page of *Les Girondins*.

This is very fine as far as it goes. But even here, Lamartine's critical judgment is in default: he rejects only a few all-too-blatant passages, but all of his *Histoire des Girondins* is permeated with these sentiments.

Blanc

Louis Blanc's twelve volumes appeared for the most part after he had had to flee to England in 1848, when the reaction to the revolutionary spirit that had triumphed in February 1848 had set in in earnest. The change in the political atmosphere in France did not, however, affect his outlook, and his residence in England seems to have influenced his work only in that it enabled him to make use of the large collection of pamphlets that Croker left to the British Museum. Blanc differs from both Lamartine and the Buchez of the prefaces in that documents and facts did mean something to him; he could make, therefore, a more serious contribution to the socialistic interpretation of the Revolution than Buchez had done. For it was as a convinced socialist that Blanc came to the problem. But he did not, as had Buchez, identify socialism and the Revolution with Christianity. Indeed he was a Voltairean, anticlerical, even skeptical about religion.

Like Mignet, Blanc made a distinction between the Revolution of 1789 and the Revolution of 1792, 1793, and 1794. But while Mignet was wholly satisfied with the bourgeois Revolution, Blanc associated himself completely with the Revolution's second phase. Mignet was not interested in the social aims that were then voiced; he accepted the second Revolution only because he assumed it was necessary in order to save French territory (and also the initial achievements of the Revolution) from the assault of foreign invaders. When it collapsed in 1794, it had, in his view, done its service. Nothing came of its social aims, and so little does Mignet regret this that he acclaims the typically bourgeois constitution of 1795 as the best constitution France had ever had. To Blanc 1794 meant the end of the true Revolution and the disappointment (for the time being) of the hopes of humanity.

Blanc starts off with a bold survey of world history, which he sees developing in three movements, each of which is defined by one dominant characteristic. (The method is strongly reminiscent of that of Comte.)

The Middle Ages, the period when Catholicism reigned supreme, was the period of *Authority*. The Protestant Reformation introduced the principle of *Individualism*, which was extended by the Enlightenment. Both De Maistre and Mme de Staël likewise connected Reformation and Enlightenment in this, in itself, debatable way, De Maistre using "individualism" to damn both movements, Mme de Staël to applaud both. Louis Blanc, however, proceeds to subordinate these imperfect and inadequate efforts of the spirit, Authority and Individualism, to the final stage toward which he saw them tending: *Fraternity*.

And this is how he applies the vision of fraternity to the Revolution:

> There are contained in what it is customary to call the French Revolution, two revolutions, entirely distinct, although both directed against the ancient principle of *Authority*. One was carried out in favor of individualism; it can be dated 1789. The other was only attempted in a tumultuous manner, in the name of fraternity; it came to grief on the ninth of Thermidor (1794). . . . Montesquieu, Voltaire, Turgot, were the pioneers of *Individualism*; Rousseau at the same time prepared men's minds for *Fraternity*.

His heart being so much set on "the second Revolution," Blanc naturally is given, no less than was Buchez, to extenuating its excesses. The first test case is, of course, the September massacres. Nobody will be surprised when Blanc, too, recalls St. Bartholomew's Day, but while Buchez considered the victims in both cases equally guilty, Blanc uses the parallel simply to level a *tu quoque* at the Catholics, who raised their hands in horror at the second outrage only. "Souviens-toi de la Barthélemy!"

Robespierre, Blanc defends even more wholeheartedly than did Buchez. A tyrant? "A strange tyrant indeed, this man who never disposed of either treasure or soldiery, and who for his alleged tyrannizing had to rely on the effect produced by his eloquence allied to the belief he had established in his virtue."

The most general defense of the Terror, and indeed the most obvious—down to the present day it has been resorted to in various ways by all historians favorable to the Revolution—is the following:

> Whose fault was it if the Revolution in the end flew into a rage? It was what the Counterrevolution had been asking for. This was the answer it got.

In his last volume Blanc describes the *Terreur blanche* of 1814, and the comparison with 1793 and 1794 is entirely to the advantage of the earlier episode.

> There had at least been judges on that occasion. The promoters of the Red Terror were men of ferocious convictions, fanatics of the public weal, violent souls and grim; but at least they spoke the language fitting their actions. They did not offer the spectacle of trying to impersonate humanity while clasping a bloodstained knife and mounted on a pile of dead bodies; they were not seen daubing themselves with perfume and paint before entering the slaughterhouse.

But there is more in Blanc's book than mere rhetoric and special pleading. His point of view led him to direct his attention to problems that had thus far, as he put it himself, been "ignored to an unbelievable extent." The lower-class revolt against the exclusive bourgeois regime instituted in 1789 was reflected in certain measures taken by the Committee of Public Safety. There was, for instance, the attempt to control prices.

> Until today the historians of the Revolution [so Blanc writes] have failed—and the neglect is hardly conceivable—to write the history of *le maximum*. I shall attempt to fill that gap. . . . The subject is undoubtedly one of the most interesting as well as the most comprehensive on which the thoughts of the philosopher or of the statesman can be focused.

The execution that followed was less important than was this posing of the problem. By it Blanc pointed into the future, to Jaurès and Mathiez and later specialists by whom the social-economic history of the period of the Commune and the Committee of Public Safety was to be examined very closely.

Blanc had another brain wave when he noticed another omission—"a strange gap," as he says himself—in all the histories of the Revolution: "One would think that the historians, dazzled and fascinated by the spectacle of this France in transformation, never saw, never knew, anything of what went on around her."

Indeed, take Mignet and Thiers, Buchez and Lamartine, Michelet—international relations are disposed of very lightly and irresponsibly by all of them. The outbreak of the war in 1792, the declaration of Pillnitz, the bellicose speeches of the Girondin leaders, are all left without any background and judged from a narrow national or partisan point of view. The first historian to try to penetrate the secret of the relations between revolutionary France and the rest of Europe was Sybel, a German, writing in the fifties; Albert Sorel's classic work was not to appear until a generation later.

As for Blanc, the brain wave was all. His state of mind was hardly such as to fit him for the required task of scholarly investigation. He, too, was subject to the usual chauvinistic and messianic temper, which made him regard France as chosen among nations to be the agent of progress, and to suffer for it.

If France is tormented by a perpetual changeability, if her life is made up of the alternation of successes and reverses, if she is fated to astonish the world by so many different and unexpected vicissitudes, it is because the initiative of moral progress resides in her, because she runs an adventurous course for the benefit of the entire human race.

There is a torch in the light of which all peoples march toward justice, with unequal steps it is true, and since it is carried through storms, we should not be surprised to see it flutter occasionally and be near to extinction. It is France who carries it, that torch.

Michelet

But Michelet, the greatest writer of them all, and in spite of his unbridled emotionalism, the greatest historian, is the one who, in the long run, exercised the most profound influence and the only one who is still read today.

Michelet, who was born in 1798, had in his youth adhered to Catholicism.[7] His father, a Paris printer, had taken his small part in the Revolution, but the family tradition was dormant. The revolution of 1830 had made a tremendous impression on Michelet, but it was not until the forties that, under the influence of the rising excitement all around him, he was converted to the full doctrine. He did nothing by halves. He abjured the work he had written on the Middle Ages. He now saw that Christianity, preaching original sin, sacrificial death, and grace, meant arbitrariness; only the Revolution meant justice. No compromise between the two was possible: the Revolution must conquer. How different from Buchez! Henceforth the spirit of the Revolution was to be Michelet's teacher. "It knows, and the others do not know. *It* possesses the secret of all the preceding ages." The epic of the liberation of the French people, nay of the human mind, that was what his history of the Revolution was to be. Michelet's first volume appeared in 1847.

The past was forgotten in the dazzling light of a new day. Forgotten, denied, abolished. One is again irresistibly reminded of Croce's description of anti-historism. But no less remarkable is Michelet's terminology—*the Revolution, the spirit of the Revolution*—and in its absolutism and simplism no less unhistorical. To distinguish between phases when the Revolution was on the right track and when it went astray, and between beneficent and harmful tendencies; to accept and to reject—Michelet considered all that to be no better than juggling with truth. Truth was: there was but one Revolution. It came to a tragic collapse in 1794, with Thermidor, with the downfall of the *Comité de salut public* and the death of Robespierre. Our salvation can only be in the resuscitation of the great enthusiasm and faith of those unique five years, handed down to us by an unbroken chain of fidelity and hope.

Was Michelet, then, a worshipper of Robespierre and of the Jacobins? No: he was less of a partisan than were Buchez and Louis Blanc. To Michelet the first Assembly, the Girondins and the Jacobins, were all admirable, because in any case the true hero of the story was the French people. It is the French people he reveres, whose soul is all goodness, and who thirst after justice; their immense labors and sufferings in the heroic years of the Revolution were their sacrifice on the altar of the love of mankind.

It must be difficult, one cannot help reflecting, to write that terrible story and to retain this faith untouched. How could a man who admitted that the September massacres were "a crime," and who described (with shuddering emotion even) the Terror and Robespierre without extenuating its horrors and the man's insane egotism—how could this man lament the breakup of that system and the elimination of that agent as a catastrophe for Justice, Liberty, Democracy, Humanity? But moreover—and this, one should think, is a question, not of morality but of fact—*was* the Revolution in all its stages the work of the people? What, then, about the resisters? What about the civil war? What about the undeniable fact that the Revolution, after a while, fell into the hands of the Jacobin minority, an exiguous minority, but well organized, and ruling ruthlessly and dictatorially?

It all turns on the meaning attached to the term *the people*. Michelet excludes from the people all those who opposed the Revolution. The nobility, the priests, the Anglomane liberals, to begin with. But also the multitude of ignorant, simple souls who were led astray by them. The crimes, too, were committed not by the people, but by ruffians—or under the unbearable provocation of the foreign enemy, of Austria, of England, the personification of evil. The war, too. You say that the Belgians were plundered and oppressed by their French conquerors? That was no more than they deserved for being so blind as not to see that these conquerors were fighting a life-and-death struggle to make them happy, and indeed to spread liberty and democracy over all Europe and the world. The French people were good, the Revolution was beneficent. How can bad spring from the good and the beneficent? If the bad was there, it must have been in spite of the French people and in spite of the Revolution.

More than any of the writers discussed earlier, Michelet had made his own the spirit that had come to reign at the height of the Revolution. The others, as we saw, were all much affected by it, but each of them had a marked preference for one tendency, or was devoted to one rigid ideal of his own, to which he attempted to make the history of the fascinating episode conform, not scrupling to express disapproval when it too patently departed from the pet doctrine—be it liberalism, or Christianity, or socialism. Michelet wanted the Revolution itself to be his one and only guide. The philosophers' transposition of the Christian ideal of a Heavenly City[8] into secular terms, and from the indeterminate future to the immediate moment, was what had inspired both the courage and the follies of the enthusiasts and extremists. To Michelet this was the unique and elevating quality of the ever memorable spectacle. To justify their high-handed actions nothing had been more useful to the men of the Revolution than Rousseau's doctrine of the *Volonté générale*, that is, the well-informed wish of the people for its own well-being. The well-informed wish, the ideal wish, is a mystic and unchangeable entity, and if the majority do not understand their own interest, it may be carried through, it *must* be carried through, by the minority of well-thinking men. For our generation, this kind of reasoning has a familiar ring. It is in this way that the modern minority dictatorships justify themselves. They may not know the *Contrat social*, but they have their own prophets who knew it. And Michelet had drunk from the source.

What dominates his work more completely than it does that of his contemporaries, is this conception; or let me rather say, this state of mind. I called it absolutistic, simplistic. It is a state of mind that is impervious to criticism or to argument, that triumphs over contradiction and confusion, and over the contradiction and confusion of the facts themselves, by an act of will, by a faith. It enabled Michelet to glorify the Revolution and the French people with unshaken ardor, yearning for the new revolution, or rather for the resurrection of the old.

One can imagine Michelet's exultation when the Orleans dynasty was overthrown and the Second Republic founded. But how grievous, once more, his sorrow when the new revolution, too, was soon seen not to have introduced the reign of Justice and Universal Happiness! Liberty and democracy had appeared on the scene only to be tragically and ignominiously defeated, and in 1851 the dictatorship of Louis Napoleon began. Was, then, the Bonapartist tradition all that was to survive of the Revolution? Michelet sorrowed, but he did not despair. His volume on the Terror, in which he testified to his faith as ardently as ever, was written when the enchanting prospects of February 1848 had already been hopelessly compromised.

4.

And indeed, although the enthusiasm of 1848 (the "folly" of 1848, as others termed it) led to a staggering anticlimax when, once more, the well-to-do middle-class, sheltering itself behind the dictatorship of a Bonaparte, roped in the gains, it was more than the outburst of a moment. The messianic illusion—a mixture of idealism and national conceit—the feeling that the Heavenly City was round the corner and that it was the high mission of the French nation to lead mankind toward it, had been roused to a pitch by these eloquent revivers of the revolutionary legend, and although cast down by unforeseen developments, it continued to lie ready in the depths of the French mind.

It found encouragement, on the one hand, in the confident positivism of Auguste Comte, in the doctrine that by means of his reasoning powers man could shape his own future. Comte's voluminous and often obscure writings were made accessible to a large public by that many-sided scholar, Littré, the "Apostle of Positivism," as he came to be called. His *Conservation, Révolution, Positivisme*, published in 1852, enjoyed an enormous vogue. In it the Revolution was described as a national movement that would infallibly lead to a final stabilization of society.

On the other hand there was the romantic temper of the time. At first sight this would seem almost incompatible with the solemn asseveration of the omnipotence of science which was the message of positivism, but as a matter of fact the exorbitance of the scientific pretension was not itself free from the romantic impulse. As an instance of how unadulterated romanticism could act as a lasting influence, even while the political situation was adverse, take Victor Hugo. Hugo had long venerated Napoleon the Great as the chosen instrument to propagate the revolutionary gospel in the world—this, too, was a much more than individual variety of the messianic faith—but Hugo became, during his exile after 1851, the high priest of a more popular cult. In his famous diatribe against "Napoléon le Petit," who had overthrown democracy in France, Hugo professed his unshaken confidence in the glorious future, and the great role that France was to play in its consummation. "This century," he wrote, "proclaims the sovereignty of the citizen and the inviolability of life; it crowns the people and it hallows man." The ideas were at hand; the actual liberation was about to be realized. "The Chinese Wall around thought is crumbling. The fanaticisms are dying, oppression has become impossible," etc. As for France, in her present state of humiliation, brought about by a contemptible adventurer, "not a word against France. . . . It is the nineteenth century itself which is lying there prostrate with France." But do you believe that God will halt in his march before this ludicrous plebiscite?

And certainly the Bonapartist dictatorship was not to be the last word. Already in 1848 the clash between the middle class and the proletariat, following hard upon the successful *coup* of February, had been far more violent than in 1830. The proletariat had again been frustrated. Louis Napoleon reigned as a result of universal suffrage plebiscites. It was the groups that were frightened at the prospect of a real revolution which had rallied round the heaven-sent preserver of the social order and made these plebiscites possible: the bourgeoisie, the farmers, the Church. Whether that made the plebiscites "ludicrous," as Hugo said, is another matter. The essential thing is that among the urban masses the revolutionary tradition could at any moment spring to vigorous life again. When bourgeois and intellectual opposition became bolder, as it did in Napoleon III's later years, the revolutionary specter, too, reared its head.

Was French history, then, doomed endlessly to repeat itself? Was the Revolution, violent as ever, and this time more decidedly proletarian, again to be the answer to despotism and social privilege?

The historians of the French Revolution I have so far mentioned were all sympathizers. As a matter of fact, the Counterrevolution produced theories and systems, but in the first half of the nineteenth century it founded no important school of Revolution history-writing. This was to be different now. At least, attempts were to be made to question the historical legend that had been growing up and that seemed to many, by no means exclusively Catholics, royalists, or Bonapartists, a danger to the sanity and stability of French public life.

This will be discussed now, but later on the vitality and persistence of the legend will still form part of my theme.

The legend of the Revolution had been cast in historical form by Mignet and Thiers. A succeeding generation of historical writers had transposed it into a higher key of enthusiasm and radicalism; and among these writers it was Michelet who presented it most brilliantly and probably did most, even after the discomfiture of the radicals in 1848, to impress it upon the public mind. But simultaneously a reaction was setting in. The well-to-do classes had had a bad fright. The disappointment of fervent expectations had shaken many of the revolutionaries.

Tocqueville

Of the historical works that reflect the change in the public atmosphere the first that I shall consider is the Vicomte de Tocqueville's *L'Ancien Régime et la Révolution*, which appeared in 1856.

Although its incentive was undoubtedly Tocqueville's deep concern over the present state of affairs in his country, *L'Ancien Régime* was first and foremost a work of scholarship, based on patient research,[9] and one of the world's great masterpieces of historical interpretation.

The first thesis of this single volume (Tocqueville's death in 1859 prevented the work from being completed as planned) was that the Revolution had been long prepared by the monarchy—by its reforms, which left the feudal system an empty shell, and also by its failure to evolve a coherent and workable system to replace it. "The Revolution was no fortuitous event. It was but the completion of a long effort, the sudden and violent termination of a task on which generations had been engaged." And in which, in the end, the monarchy had failed to provide a consistent or effective lead.

It will be seen at once that Tocqueville was far from being actuated by counterrevolutionary motives. He knew that no return to the past was possible and also that the past was not worth returning to. But at the same time, in the place of the exaltation of the Revolution as an entirely new departure, as the beginning of a new era owing nothing to a past entirely evil, we receive a view in which it appears merely as the outcome of that past—of its shortcomings, but also of its constructive powers.

In his second thesis, too, when he attempts to evaluate the achievement of the Revolution, Tocqueville speaks neither in counterrevolutionary nor in revolutionary terms. The Revolution's original aspirations were, he says, toward liberty, but they were largely frustrated. One explanation he finds in the large part played by men of letters in the elaboration of political schemes and systems, a phenomenon due really to the fact that the monarchical regime had left no room for the development of responsibility on either a national or a local scale. Without a competent aristocracy, or effective leadership at various levels of society, there can be, according to Tocqueville, no liberty securely grounded in reality. A further explanation was the growing anarchy consequent upon wild popular outbursts. For these, too, the royal government was to some extent accountable. Promises had been made, and never executed (Tocqueville quotes the proclamation in which Turgot, then the King's minister, had spoken of the right to employment); they amounted to a "revolutionary education" of the people.

And so, in its dire need, the Revolution borrowed or copied from the regime it had displaced its pernicious tendencies toward despotism and arbitrariness; indeed, in the person of Napoleon, the Revolution, anxious as it was only to safeguard the equality for which it had also found the preparatory conditions laid down and which now had only to be developed and consolidated, practically restored the monarchy.

Tocqueville's conclusion is a gloomy one. As a result of that extraordinary episode, the desire for liberty, although by fits and starts manifesting itself, is, to his view, still weak in France. It is stifled by the strong tradition of *raison d'état*, by the cult of unity, and by the mania for equality.

Neither revolutionary nor counterrevolutionary, but not therefore free from bias. Tocqueville was a liberal and a professing Catholic, too. He had studied democracy in the United States and been struck by its leveling and illiberal tendencies. He had witnessed the revolution of 1848, and after shuddering at the vulgarity and harebrained optimism (so it had seemed to him) of its short-lived first period, had served the Second Republic as minister of foreign affairs. He was, after these experiences, oppressed by one great fear, that of the rise of the masses. He knew it was impossible to check this rise, and moreover, he accepted it and was willing to try to direct it into safe channels; nevertheless he saw in it a danger to the highest values of civilization. Let me add that he would never stoop to encourage despotism as a curb upon that tendency, nor did he indulge in contempt for the human species. On the contrary, he held fast to the hope that men would prove amenable to reason.[10]

So much for Tocqueville's bias. When we remember that pure, objective, historical truth is hardly within the reach of man, we shall marvel at the serenity of vision manifested in a book on the Revolution written in the disturbed and feverish atmosphere of France. If anything could break through, or bypass, the fatal conflict between revolutionary and counterrevolutionary, this lucid and dispassionate treatise should have succeeded. Fustel de

Coulanges must have, for a moment, forgotten Tocqueville when later, in the eighties, he wrote:

> For the last fifty years our historians have been party men. However sincere they may have been, however impartial they thought they were, they were subject to one of the political opinions that keep us divided. . . . The writing of history was one way of working for a party or assailing an adversary.[11]

Fustel's comment might indeed serve as an epitome of the story that I have been telling—up until the moment that Tocqueville appeared in it. Moreover, Fustel's words may be taken as evidence that Tocqueville's intervention did not really change the state of affairs. Not that Tocqueville's book did not influence, and deeply—at once and to this day—the historical treatment of the Revolution. Yet it will be curious to see how, on both sides, passion now ignored and then for its own purposes distorted Tocqueville's argument.

Lanfrey

The influence of Tocqueville is patent in an essay published in 1857 (the year after the appearance of *L'Ancien Régime*) by Pierre Lanfrey, a journalist of liberal principles, and a determined opponent of the empire. Later, Lanfrey was to strike the empire a keen blow by his *Histoire de Napoléon Ier*, in which he tried, often with great ingenuity, to expose as a disastrous fraud the great career from which Napoleon III derived his own.[12] In his essay on the Revolution, however, Lanfrey shows a closer attachment to its principles and slogans—always of the first phase—than does Tocqueville. Lanfrey's line is really that of Mme de Staël and Mignet; he attacks Louis Blanc (who was still, in his London exile, continuing his *History*, extolling Robespierre, and writing off the Girondins). But typically Tocqueville is Lanfrey's preoccupation with the contrast that had somehow grown up between the desire for liberty and the desire for equality. He duly reveres Rousseau, but he abhors the doctrine of the *Contrat social*, which seems bound to lead to the complete extinction of the individual and the individual's rights in the community. "Absolute democracy, as conceived by Rousseau, amounts to the most unlimited despotism." And it was that doctrine that triumphed under Robespierre, after whom the despotism of the multitude was countered only by the dictatorship of an adventurer. That is the depressing dilemma into which, more than sixty years before

Lanfrey wrote, the derailment of the Revolution seemed to have landed France.

Many French intellectuals, while chafing at the restraints put upon French life by the thinly veiled dictatorship of the Second Empire, were depressed by the thought of the alternative that the future might hold in store. Lanfrey was more alive than Mignet had been to the inconsistency with the principles of the Revolution offered by the limitation of the suffrage in the constitution of 1791. He tried to defend the bourgeois revolutionaries of that time against the charge that they had pursued a mere policy of abstention from interference with the social and economic process. But if the imperial regime, which for its part did its best to win the masses by material benefits, was overthrown, would the passion for equality again lead to another, and a worse, despotism?

Renan

Reflections like these passed through the mind of Ernest Renan, and they led him to a much more resolute rejection of the revolutionary tradition than was suggested by Lanfrey, or even by Tocqueville. In 1859 Renan added to his *Essais de critique et de morale* a preface, which struck a note then startlingly novel, coming as it did from a man who had renounced Catholicism, whose God was science, and who even now extolled liberalism as the "formula of the highest development of humanity."

"At the beginning of 1851," so Renan confesses, "I still had, regarding the Revolution and the form of society which issued from it, the prejudices current in France." He had believed that the Revolution was synonymous with liberalism. He now saw that it contained

> . . . a hidden virus: violence, a wholly materialistic conception of property, contempt for personal rights, attention for the individual only, and the individual considered as a being unconnected with yesterday or tomorrow and without any moral ties. If this is what the principles of 1789 mean, as they have too often meant in practice, let us renounce them. Nothing is more fatal to a nation than this fetishism, which makes it place its pride in certain words, with which one has only to cover oneself in order to lead it to the last limits of servitude and abasement.

What we can gather indirectly from this passage is that the strength of the legend of the Revolution was unbroken. The situation was indeed full of complications and contradictions. The Bonapartist regime was, after not very many years, to be swept away by a movement of opinion covering itself (to use Renan's phrase) with the great revolutionary words and indeed glowing with revolutionary ardor. All the time, however, Bonapartism had felt its own position to be grounded in the same legend, a legend it had therefore never been able wholeheartedly to oppose.

Another writer testified a little later, in 1865, to his disillusionment: no other than Quinet, who had in the turbulent forties been the comrade in arms of Michelet against the Jesuits and in defense of the Revolution, the champion of the eternal principles of liberty and democracy. He now, as he put it himself in a letter to a friend, "dared to break the holy seals of the book of the Revolution in order to put it to the test of the spirit of criticism." "Liberty," he wrote in his book, "is to be found at no epoch of our history. Do not let us look back for it."

Renan, meanwhile, was on a track much more definitely hostile to the Revolution, and events were to push him to its extreme limit.

In the late sixties, the position of the imperial regime was shaken. Its weakened prestige, resulting from setbacks to the Emperor's foreign policy, encouraged opposition on the home front. The newly founded First International had its branch in Paris and was agitating among the working population. The close alliance between the Church and the government, and the Church's zealous concern for the social order, that is to say, for the socially privileged, roused the latent but ever-present anticlericalism to renewed activity. "Be atheists first, you will be revolutionists next," said an orator at one of the innumerable meetings that were now being held in the less fashionable quarters of the great city.[13] The memory of the Revolution, and especially of the great years of the sans-culottes, 1792 and 1793, was constantly invoked. When in a discussion a speaker ventured to express his horror at the September massacres, the chairman interrupted him: "I shall not permit any of our great revolutionary dates to be insulted." The unrest was not confined to the popular masses. Nor were only isolated intellectuals affected by it. Freemasonry provided an organization, especially for the anticlerical tendencies of the movement. A regular opposition of journalists, lawyers, politicians was clamoring for the attention of the public, seemingly confident that its hour was soon to strike.

The Emperor himself was no longer spared. Hugo's *Châtiments*, those great poems of invective and moral indignation, were declaimed at students' meetings. In leaflets and obscure little periodicals Badinguet (the nickname by which his adversaries called the Emperor) was assailed; even a great boulevard paper allowed Rochefort to ridicule him in articles cleverly designed to evade the censorship, and for that, all the more intriguing and amusing. In 1868 a demonstration was organized, by men of extreme views who knew very well what they were doing (Delescluze was one of them), to honor the memory of one of the victims of the *coup d'état* of 1851—a painful date from the official point of view, but one that was now suddenly exposed to the glare of what almost seemed like concerted publicity. The organizers of the demonstration were prosecuted, but their views could not have received more sensational support than they found, at the trial, in the powerful speech made by Gambetta, a young, and till then unknown lawyer, but who now suddenly sprang to fame. Delivering a scathing denunciation of the man who, with his crew of fortune hunters and adventurers, had made himself master of France by brute force and unscrupulous deceit, Gambetta extolled Delescluze for having "throughout his life striven to have the French Revolution radically carried into effect."

This is the background against which an article of Renan, published in 1869, should be read.[14]

The situation, Renan affirms, is dominated by the Revolution. France was the prime mover of that world event: it was her glory, an epic unsurpassed in history. But that is what now counts against her. Just as Israel had to pay for messianism with extinction as a national state, so France is now torn asunder. (The parallel occurred quite naturally to the man who was later to write the *Histoire du peuple d'Israël*, but we have seen that the idea of France suffering for what she had done for mankind was a commonplace.) Only a liberalized empire (so Renan continues) can ward off the dual menace of despotism and anarchy.

In advocating the liberalization of the regime, Renan was not indulging in opposition, for he was, in his fashion, supporting a policy that Napoleon III had just adopted. Only, what did Renan mean by liberalism?

Equality, the abstraction of the Revolution, which, instead of allowing itself to be carried away by abstractions, ought to have set to work historically, he now resolutely attacked. "Society is a great providential fact." It cannot exist—civilization, humanity, cannot exist, "unless it is admitted that entire classes must live on the glory and the felicity of other classes." So it had been in the old days.

When Gubbio or Assisi saw their young lord careering by in his splendor, nobody was jealous. At that time all participated in the life of all. The poor man took delight in the wealth of the wealthy, the monk in the joys of the worldling, the worldling in the prayers of the monk. For all, there was art, there was poetry, there was religion. . . . Nature wills that the life of mankind shall be conducted on several planes. The rawness of many makes the education of one. The sweat of many makes possible the noble life of a small number.

It is clear that Renan has come to espouse a frankly counterrevolutionary position. The picture that he sketches of the *ancien regime* cannot be surpassed for idyllic loveliness. It is true that he does not advocate a restoration of the Bourbons: that tradition, so recklessly uprooted by the Revolution, cannot be revived. Rather, a liberalized empire and "a policy of contrition." Hardly an inspiring program! "Our task is not to continue the Revolution, but to criticize it and to repair the errors it has committed."

But what about the ticklish problem of religion? It is painful to see the famous philosopher and advocate of free thought hedging on this point. He blames the Revolution for having been irreligious and atheistic. Religion has a purpose to serve in society—not for him, Renan, but "to explain to those who are sacrificed on earth to social necessities the mysteries of the divine dispensation that holds out to them abundant consolation in an ideal world."

During the following year, 1870, the liberal empire was confirmed by an overwhelming vote of confidence (in Paris and all the large towns, however, the noes were in a considerable majority); almost immediately afterward, it was overtaken by the catastrophe of war and defeat, and collapsed.

It was the old story all over again. In Paris the spirit of the Revolution rose exultingly. The provinces showed a much more conservative temper. The great wish of all quiet men and of all who had any property to lose was to have an immediate end to the war, even at a price, and they frowned upon Gambetta, who, flaming with patriotic and republican zeal, tried, while Paris was desperately resisting its besiegers, to organize a *levée en masse*—the magic words of 1792 and 1793. The attempt was bound to fail. Paris had to capitulate. An armistice was concluded in January 1871 and a national assembly elected, which met at Bordeaux. It was dominated by conservatives, royalists numerous among them. Thiers, an old man now, had already, as head of the provisional government, negotiated a treaty by which Alsace and Lorraine were to be ceded. The treaty was laid before the Assembly for its approval. Both Louis Blanc and Victor Hugo, two more old men, back from exile, made speeches against peace on such conditions—speeches, it must be said, revealing two very different revolutionary temperaments, the one as bitter and dogmatic as the other was pathetic, prophetic, and high-flown; they spoke of the example of the Convention, of the undying glory of the Revolution, of the part that it behooved France still to play for the liberation and fraternization of the world. The Assembly refused to listen to them and voted overwhelmingly in favor of the treaty.

Paris now rose in revolt. The Commune—another word handed down from the heroic years—established itself. Among its leading members was Delescluze; most of the others were obscure men, working men, professional agitators. A *Comité de salut public* was instituted. It was to be 1793 all over again. The army of the Assembly forced its way into Paris. Terrible revenge was taken. Shootings, deportations. The red revolution had again been quashed.

The majority of the Assembly now wanted to restore the monarchy. It was only as a result of the refusal of the two rival monarchist parties, the adherents of Bourbon and those of Orleans, to give way one to the other, that in the end the Third Republic emerged. By then the public temper had changed. Royalism, closely allied to clericalism, no longer commanded a majority. Republicanism, strongly tinged with anticlericalism, could stand on its own feet. And again it had sucked strength from the revolutionary tradition, which it now cultivated with jealous gratitude as the ideology indispensable to the safety of the Republic and the greatness of France.

But before I come to that, I must say more about the reaction against the legend of the Revolution which we saw in full spate before 1870, and which of course received a further impetus from the events of that year and especially from the terrifying episode of the Commune in 1871.

In that same year, 1871, Renan published another essay,[15] "La Réforme intellectuelle et morale de la France." It is, in the main, a repetition of the argument of the earlier essay from which I quoted. Only, the contempt for the people, and the impotent despair of the intellectual at the way things have been going and are likely to continue going, is expressed even more crudely. "France beheaded herself when Louis XVI was executed." Leadership should again be based on birth: "the risk of birth as a criterion is less than the risk of the ballot box." "The people is much less capable than are the higher or enlightened classes of resisting the easy pleasures." (When I remember the wretched conditions in which the working classes had to live, this strikes me as a particularly heartless remark.) "It is well that the superior races should rule the lower." "The origin of property is conquest. Let the love of adventure and war, characteristic of the European, be used for colonial expeditions, and the Negro will work for a master as he was born to do."

Prussia, victorious Prussia, is now the example that Renan holds up for France.[16] "There, the *ancien régime* is continued in a corrected form. There, respect for property and subordination rule, and while France and England are, like America, worshipping the false gods of material prosperity, Prussia cultivates the military virtues."

He puts forward a plan for conservative reform. Almost comical in its mixture of cynicism and lack of a sense of the practicable is the proposal he makes to the Roman Catholic Church:

> At a certain degree of rational culture a belief in the supernatural becomes for many impossible. Don't compel us to wear a coat of lead. Don't interfere with what we teach or write, and we shall not grudge you the people; leave us in possession of the University, of the Academy; and we shall abandon to you the village schools in their entirety.

More extraordinary than the whole of this extraordinary production (which gives one but a low opinion of Renan's character) is that, for all his defiant gestures, Renan has not succeeded in really freeing his mind from the fascination of the Revolution. The preface is here and there in complete contradiction to the book. He who proclaimed conquest to be the basis of property complains that Germany, in retaining Alsace and Lorraine, is abusing the right of the strongest. With all her great qualities, "Germany is incapable of disinterested actions for the rest of the world." German philosophy has nobility, certainly; "but the rights of man are also worth something. It is our eighteenth-century philosophy, it is our Revolution that has established them." Has Germany a poet like Hugo, a prose writer like Madame Sand, a man of the imagination of Michelet? It is a little surprising to find these names included in Renan's list of honor. And now he returns to his idea that the great creative acts of history are visited on the peoples who performed them: Greece, Israel, the Italy of the Renaissance, the Germany of the Reformation—and so France now atones for the Revolution.

It may be a tragic greatness, but greatness is after all what France owes to the Revolution, in the estimation of Renan as of Michelet; or should I say, the Revolution is evidence of the greatness of France? Renan had a very similar passage in the concluding part of his essay of 1869, and it is, again, curious to note that, while his exhortations all wear an air of disenchantment and lassitude, he seeks comfort in a reflection, from which De Gaulle, too, in our own day, draws inspiration (for a very different policy): "La France peut tout, excepté être mediocre."[17]

Flaubert

But, after all, the indictment of the basic principles of the Revolution remains the significance of Renan's message. Many minds were long prepared to accept it. Flaubert, for instance, who had described with caustic skepticism the romantic young revolutionaries of the forties (I quoted from the passage above), expressed in 1871, in a letter to George Sand, his fervent agreement with Renan.

The people, so he wrote, is an eternal minor, and in the hierarchy of social elements it will always occupy the lowest rank. It is numbers, mass, the unlimited. What does it matter if many peasants are able to read and no longer listen to their parish priests? But it matters a great deal that men like Renan and Littré shall live and be listened to. (Note how variously the political lesson of positivism could be interpreted!) The French Revolution should cease being a dogma and submit to scientific examination. If people had really *known* history, we should have been spared Gambetta, and the Prussian occupation, and the Commune. "The Catholics did nothing but cross themselves" (for Flaubert was as bitterly anti-Catholic as he was anti-Revolution), "while the progressives cried *Vive la République*, evoked the men of 1792, and wanted to rush off to the Argonne—not that the Prussians were there now, but such is the tradition. They imagined that they could stop a modern army by fabricating *piques*."

"The crowd, the herd," reflected Flaubert in a more general strain, "will always be hateful. Let us be ruled by mandarins, by the *Académie des Sciences*. Universal suffrage is a disgrace to the human mind. So, actually, we plod in the aftermath of the Revolution, which has been an abortion, a dismal failure. . . ." The Commune attempting to regulate rents infuriates him. A throwback to the Middle Ages is what it seems to him. The government interfering with contracts between private persons, folly! ineptitude! . . . The idea of equality, which is the whole of modern democracy, proceeds from Christianity and is opposed to justice.[18]

(Michelet, it will be remembered, loved the Revolution because it promoted justice, while the essence of Christianity was arbitrariness. Buchez, like Flaubert, admitted the affinity of the two creeds, but drew a conclusion opposite to his. Similarly, two generations later, Péguy revered both Joan of Arc and the Revolution as the highest expression of the spiritual life of France. But this is passing.)

What strikes me particularly about these utterances of Renan and Flaubert is the hatred and contempt with which they regarded the people, the multitude. The problem of the masses and their rising importance was one that oppressed the minds of many of the great liberal intellectuals of the middle and second half of the nineteenth century. This was, as we say, the case with Tocqueville. John Stuart Mill, too, his correspondent and friend, struggled to find a solution for the conflict, which filled him with misgivings, between a mass society and civilization, between the new democracy and liberty. Burckhardt took a gloomy view of the future on this account. But not one of these allowed his feelings to be poisoned by fear as did Renan and Flaubert, and as did a third Frenchman, to whom I am now coming, Taine.[19]

Taine

Hippolyte Taine's *Origines de la France contemporaine* began to appear in 1871 with a volume on *L'Ancien Régime*; in 1878, 1881, and 1884, there followed three volumes on the Revolution; Taine died in 1892 after having completed only one volume (dealing with Napoleon) of *Le Régime moderne*.

As much as any of the works so far discussed, the volumes of the *Origines* owed their inception as well as their tone and spirit directly to the impression made on the author by his contemporary political environment. The war, and even more so the Commune, had been shocks from which Taine never recovered. He had not until then done any historical work in the strict sense of the word. He had made a name—and a great name—as a philosopher and a historian of art and literature. His brilliant books were all marked by an excessive inclination toward systematizing and generalizing. He was a positivist, proud of having his mind freed from the shackles of religion. Science was his idol, as it was Renan's. In the preface to his *Littérature anglaise* he had developed his theory that moral facts should not, any more than physical facts, move the historian either to sympathy or to disgust, for like physical facts, they are determined by causes that it is the historian's task simply to establish. "Le vice et la vertu sont des produits comme le vitriol et le sucre."[20] A primary cause, in Taine's view, was race: all the English writers, though differing among themselves and seemingly highly individual in their qualities, he explained by that dubious agency, about which he, however, never had any doubts.

As for his political opinions, his career had suffered, at its outset, from his refusal, however tactfully presented, to give an explicit approval to the *coup d'état* of 1851; next (as long as the *Université* was ruled by the clerical Fortoul), from his positivism.

In 1863 the Bishop of Orléans, Dupanloup, had in a solemn "Warning to Young People and Their Fathers Concerning the Attacks Against Religion by Certain Writers of the Present Day" bracketed Taine with Renan and Littré as a particularly dangerous influence.

Indeed all this time Taine accepted the view of the Revolution current in France since the twenties—"the willful illusion in which we live since the book of M. Thiers," as he put it much later[21] (and he might have added the name of Mignet). As late as 1864, when, as we saw, Renan was already in open revolt, Taine still vigorously defended the current view against Carlyle's presentation of the Revolution as nothing but an outburst of destructive fury.

> You should [he addresses Carlyle] not overlook the good beside the evil, nor the virtues beside the vices. Those skeptics believed in proved truth and wanted no other master. Those logicians founded society on justice only and risked their lives rather than renounce an established theory. Those Epicurians [all these terms of opprobrium, of course, had been used by Carlyle] embraced within their sympathies the whole of mankind. Those raging lunatics, those workingmen, those needy and naked beggars, fought at the frontiers for humanitarian interests and abstract principles. [Taine then attributed to the men of the Revolution qualities equivalent to those Carlyle admired in the Puritans, but moreover:] Their heroism transformed Europe while yours served only yourselves.[22]

Looking more closely at Taine's political opinions, however, it will be seen that this "liberalism" was of a kind with that of Renan and Flaubert. It was heavily laden with bourgeois class-consciousness. The socialist tendencies that came to the fore in the popular commotions of 1848 he regarded with detestation. To him "the right to property is an absolute one." The democrats seemed to him thieves organizing civil war in order to be able to lay their hands on the possessions of the rich. If he still accepted the revolutionary legend, it was because the semidictatorial rule of the Emperor, which in itself he did not like, had relegated the immediate danger to the background. When the shocking outburst of the Commune revived his fears, not only did his views of the politics needed for the present acquire a sharper edge—"what matters is that the enlightened and well-to-do classes should govern the ignorant and those who live from hand to mouth"; "speaking generally, it is wrong for the State to go beyond seeing to the safety of persons and of property"—but he woke up to the dangers inherent in those doctrines he had until then accepted because they seemed to form part of the glorious heritage of his country.

From now on he is out to demolish that "willful illusion" about the true significance of the Revolution, which he has come to see lies at the root of all the evils from which France is suffering. It takes one's breath away to see him repeating in his preface all the cant about science and to read that he will approach his subject as dispassionately as the naturalist watches the metamorphosis of an insect. One has only to look at his letters written in 1871 to see how he was driven into the camp of the conservatives and reactionaries by fear, fear mingled with rage and contempt, fear of the mob broken loose, which could be contained only by strong government.

These letters do not make pleasant reading. As early as November 1870 Taine had seen no salvation other than in peace. If only Paris will not spoil its chances and show some common sense! In January he admits that the resistance of Paris has saved the honor of France; in March, when the Commune has been proclaimed, he takes back even that praise: the resistance had "*appeared* heroic." The Commune is to him a shattering spectacle. "Fanatics, foreigners, and rogues planning a universal *jacquerie*." He sees "the reds" dominating the councils of Lyon and other towns, "fools and tub thumpers who have inherited the style, the violence, and the stupidity of the old Jacobins." "Away with universal suffrage, the lair of the demagogic monster," he says. I am not an admirer either of the old Jacobins or of the Commune, but what one sadly misses in Taine's letters is one word of sympathy with the people in their amazement and confusion, in their distress, infinitely worse than the difficulties of the comfortable bourgeois.

Yet that is the mood in which Taine now sets to work on the history of the Revolution. "The harm the Revolution has done France is that it has left no medium between despotism and anarchy." For despotism is not what Taine wants, even now; he still calls himself "a liberal." This, of course, is pure Tocqueville; or rather, it is Tocqueville carried one stage further toward absolute despair; it is Tocqueville without his moderation, without his love of the human species.

Taine does not idealize the *ancien régime* (except at moments when he forgets what he has written elsewhere, for his work is not without contradictions). He has indeed read Tocqueville and follows him in this most important of that clear-sighted man's perceptions: that the Revolution was not a fortuitous outburst, that it was not occasioned by immediate grievances or by sufferings either, but that the entire trend of the old monarchical government, including its reforming tendencies, had created the situation and the spirit from which the Revolution naturally proceeded. Unfortunately, Taine concentrates on one of the suggestions thrown out by Tocqueville and gives to it a prominence that throws the whole picture out of balance. It will be remembered what Tocqueville said about the part played in French political thinking by men of letters. Taine was a man of letters himself. He eagerly took hold of Tocqueville's idea and made of this factor the center of his interpretation.

The real cause of the overthrow of the old order, with all its terrible consequences, was a way of thinking: it was the philosophy of the French eighteenth century, the supremacy accorded to the *raison raisonnante*, a fashion to which the privileged classes succumbed; it was what Taine called *l'esprit classique* (a most confusing phrase really).

A society, a state (so Taine says), in order to exist or to survive, needs a submission and a loyalty that reason cannot supply. French philosophy, by calling everything into question, had ended by destroying everything. "En fait d'histoire, il vaut mieux continuer que recommencer,"[23] a phrase that might have been translated from Burke. For the old order, philosophy had substituted one principle, that of popular sovereignty. Rousseau was the architect of the doctrine that inevitably, through 1789 to 1793 and on to 1799, led the French nation from disaster to disaster: anarchy, despotism of the fanatics, anarchy again, despotism of the military adventurer.

When Taine represents the men of 1789 as impregnated with the dogma of the *Volonté générale* as taught by the *Contrat social*, he neglects differences of undeniable historic significance. His disposal of the Assembly as a crowd of mere theorists blind to reality cannot be justified.[24] As he describes it, the situation during the early years of the Revolution was one of complete anarchy. Here the objection is not so much that he charges the picture. On the contrary these chapters on "the spontaneous anarchy" are a most useful corrective of the rosy and unrealistic accounts current in the pro-Revolution literature of his predecessors. A historian of a later generation, Albert Mathiez, who was as firmly pro- as Taine was anti-Revolution, accepted that description. Only, Mathiez asks, Why this disorder? and he goes on to lay the blame on the bourgeois Assembly, which did nothing to meet the crying needs of the people. To Mathiez (as to Louis Blanc) the real Revolution was only the second phase, the social Revolution. One may well doubt whether indeed the aspirations of the second team of revolutionists are fully covered by that word "social," and especially whether everything these revolutionists did is thereby justified. But certainly Taine is a good deal more simplistic and unrealistic when he offers as the only explanation, hammering it in at every turn of the story, the state of mind brought about by the generalities of the philosophers, by the *Contrat social*.

Two large sections of the third of Taine's volumes on the Revolution are devoted to an analysis and characterization of the men who dominated the culminating years of that horror, the Jacobins, program and personnel. One may on good grounds object to the method of fixing into set lines a mentality so composite and so continually exposed to the multiple influence of events. Yet here the picture undoubtedly has an awful reality, and so has Taine's last volume, in which he considers the dictatorial regime of Napoleon.

Taking it altogether, the *Origines* remains impressive. It has the logic of Taine's particular nightmare.

> Our society has been rebuilt upon a false principle, in a narrow and superficial spirit, *l'esprit classique*. And from the first to the last sentence of my book, that spirit is my only and principal subject.

So he wrote to a friend.[25] The old order broken up, that is, society and civilization, protected by age-long custom and traditional authority, menaced, crippled, destroyed; that is, the lower orders, with their savage and barbaric instincts, set free to do their worst; that is, the fanatics coming into power and doing worse still. Taine revels in relating disturbances, violent incidents, murders, massacres, and the follies and downright crimes of the extremists. All caused by the inexorable working out of the primary principle. As a reader of Shakespeare he might have remembered Jack Cade and his followers, behaving exactly like French Jacobins. But indeed, he seems to have cleared his mind of all recollection of popular outbursts in centuries that knew not Rousseau. All follows from the *Contrat social*, until at last, in the preface to the volume on the Terror, he reveals the secret of the inner sanctum of the temple and shows the Revolution worshipping a Crocodile. The generous elation of the first phase moves him to scorn—"to pity," he says in the letter from which I quoted a moment ago; but there is not really any pity in his work, or at least, he reserves it for what in one place he calls "l'élite aimable et confiante." At any rate, it was all a huge mistake, for from the beginning, the vaunted principles of 1789 bore the poison within them.

I said "impressive." Yet I confess that I do not always find

Taine's famous work easy to read, and this in spite of its ever-vivid and colorful style. The cumulation of incidents ("petits faits significatifs," as Taine used to say), the endless repetition of comments of vituperation and loathing for "the gorilla, the immense brute, the human herd, the exasperated brute, *l'animal primitif, le signe grimaçant, sanguinaire et lubrique*," unchained by the *Contrat social*—this sort of thing does not, quite apart from any independent knowledge that we may bring to the text, seem true to life. The bias is too obtrusive. But the work *has* enormous power, and French opinion in the eighties, and for decades afterward, reacted strongly. The *Origines* was greeted with delight by the Catholics, who now preferred to have Monseigneur Dupanloup's denunciation of 1863 forgotten; it also excited the indignation of staunch upholders of the tradition of the Revolution.

5.

The latter were, as I hinted before, by no means driven from the field. On the contrary, in the actual course of French politics, the protracted attempt of the royalists after 1871 to bring about a restoration had caused the republicans to hoist the colors of the Revolution more defiantly than ever, and when the Third Republic was definitely established, it was they who controlled education. Anticlericalism allied with veneration of the sacred principles of 1789, or even of the Revolution in its entirety, seemed to them a requisite for reliable citizenship.

In the early nineties the Pope, Leo XIII, encouraged among French Catholics a movement of reconciliation with the Republic. Léon Bourgeois, a leading politician on the left and by no means an extremist, said in a speech—pretending to address the Catholics of the *ralliement* (as the movement was called): "You accept the Republic? Well and good. But do you accept the Revolution?"

In 1897 a play of Sardou's, entitled *Thermidor*, was performed at the *Comédie française*. It was not anti-Revolution, at least the principles of 1789 received a respectful tribute. But it was anti-Terror, anti-*Comité de salut public*, anti-Robespierre. One performance after another became the occasion for demonstrations and counterdemonstrations. An interpellation in the Chamber followed: the *Comédie française* is, after all, a state institution. In the heated debate, Clemenceau, who in his younger years had belonged to the small group in the Bordeaux Assembly of protesters against the cession of Alsace-Lorraine, spoke the memorable words: "La Révolution est un bloc, dont on ne peut rien distraire."[26] His conclusion is no less worth noticing. Why all this excitement? he asks.

It is because that revolution is still going on, it is because always the same men are facing the same enemies. Yes, *you* [addressing the right] have remained the same, nor have *we* changed. The struggle will continue until one of the two parties is victorious.

In 1899, when the Dreyfus affair had exacerbated the (already sufficiently bitter) conflict, Ranc, a friend of Gambetta (who had died years before), wrote: "La France? . . . Oui, la France grande et la République forte, mais la France de la Révolution, et la République représentant dans le monde le Droit et la Justice."[27]

By then Charles Maurras had risen to notoriety on the right, a man who with his *Action française* was to do what he could to inflame feeling still more. He commented, sarcastically: "La France mais . . . La France si . . . La France à condition que. . . ." And he exclaimed: "Français avant tout, et sans conditions."[28] But one of his friends, the highly cultivated literary critic Jules Lemaître, who had after long hesitations entered the ranks of the *Action française*, once wrote to him from a holiday in Switzerland: "I hate much more cordially a certain number of my compatriots than any group of foreigners." And this was really truer for Maurras, too, and for the whole of his movement, than was his own virtuous rejoinder to Ranc.

The above has been no more than a glimpse of the political background that illuminates the significance of the appointment, as early as 1885, of Alphonse Aulard to the newly established chair of Revolution History (endowed by the municipality of Paris) at the Sorbonne.

Aulard

Alphonse Aulard was to study the history of the Revolution, but he was to study it in the right spirit. And this he did in a long and active scholarly life. His influence in the all-embracing *Université* was immense. In spite of the acrimonious dispute in which he was later involved with his disciple, then rival, Mathiez, and although many scholars followed Mathiez's line rather than his, it may be said that it was Aulard who inspired a new school of Revolution historiography, closely related in spirit to the pre-1848 phase. The grandeur of the Revolution was to him an article of faith. However far removed from Michelet in his style and general address—characterized by academic dullness and pomposity—in his wholesale acceptance of the Revolution he was nearer to him than to any other of the earlier writers. Danton was his hero. Indeed, his difference of opinion with Mathiez was brought to a head when the latter, whose hero was Robespierre, exposed Danton as an unprincipled and corrupt opportunist.

There was, of course, much more involved than a dispute about persons. The approach of Aulard was primarily political, while Mathiez, under the influence of Jaurès, whose voluminous *Histoire socialiste de la Révolution française* appeared in the opening years of the twentieth century, and Louis Blanc, who stood behind both, came more and more to look for social and economic aims and factors—with results, it should be added, that have proved illuminating even for those who discerned, and balked at, his bias.

But I cannot go into any detail about the complications and refinements of modern scholarship. From the point of view that I am taking, the broad interpretation of the Revolution and the conflict between acceptance and rejection is what matters. In that connection Aulard's famous attack on Taine and its sequel must now claim our attention.

Aulard's *Taine: Historien de la Révolution française* appeared in 1907, fourteen years after Taine's death. In it Aulard questioned Taine's documentation, method, premises, conclusions—everything. It had, as might be expected, a very mixed reception. It is not an engaging book, and reviewers—I am thinking now particularly of two Dutch historians, leading men in their time[29]—were apt to say that it was a miserable spectacle to see a small mind carping at a great one. There is something in that. Aulard meant to destroy Taine once and for all. He even said that a candidate for a history degree at the Sorbonne would not make a good impression if he quoted Taine as an authority.

To destroy Taine, of course, was more than Aulard could do. The animosity he displays, the deadly seriousness with which he accumulates the charges of inaccuracy, of incompleteness of documentation, elicited a reaction of sympathy. Even Mathiez, who had written about Taine with infinitely greater comprehension, for all that he, too, detested the great man's reactionary mentality, ended a very damaging review of Aulard's book[30] with a sarcastic warning to "naïve readers" that they should not imagine one is a great historian simply because one never makes a mistake about references to archival files.

One important point Aulard no doubt does make, but indeed it had been made by many others before him, by Seignobos, a colleague and fellow radical, even by Albert Sorel, a man with an unmistakably conservative type of mind and an admirer of Taine, but one who could not for all that accept a purely negative view of the Revolution—one important point, namely, that Taine, in explaining the developments taking place during the years from 1794 to 1799 as the natural consequence of a mistaken philosophy, as the progress of a mental malady, isolates purely psychological or spiritual aspects in a truly unhistorical manner. The leading idea of Sorel's great work was related to that of Tocqueville's. Rejecting the view of the enthusiasts of the Revolution as an entirely new beginning, he brought out, on the contrary, the continuity of the Revolution's foreign policy—as Tocqueville had done for its domestic reforms—with that of the monarchy; a sobering view, but one that could imperceptibly change into apology. In any case, both Aulard and Sorel agreed that external circumstances—the resistance, the court intrigues, the plotting of the *émigrés*, the threats, and at last, the interference of foreign rulers—cannot be overlooked as Taine had overlooked them.

Aulard, however, is inclined unduly to emphasize the factor of external circumstances, to present it as the all-sufficient explanation, and at the same time the justification, of the September massacres, of the overthrow and extermination of the Girondins by the Jacobins, of the dictatorial rule of the *Comité de salut public*, of all the excesses of the Revolution. It was always the court, and the *émigrés*, and the foreign powers. Aulard was here in the tradition set by Mignet, and followed by countless others. But Aulard was the first, in his great *Histoire politique de la Révolution française* (1901), to erect this argument into an imposing system based on the statements and apologies of the revolutionary leaders and bodies themselves: Assemblies, Committees, Paris Commune, etc. One will find in his book against Taine lucid and uncompromising summaries of the system as set out in his larger work, summaries that are very helpful for anyone wishing to understand his "philosophy of the Revolution" (to use a phrase that he would have indignantly rejected). It is in this "philosophy" that Aulard laid himself open to counterattack.

Cochin

In 1909 an essay, "La crise de l'histoire révolutionnaire," written by a young Catholic historian Augustin Cochin,[31] provided a formidable counterattack to M. Aulard, whose history, says Cochin, is but the history of the professions made by the revolutionaries themselves. As a result his *Histoire politique de la Révolution française* is impeccably orthodox; it is the legend in its pure form. But *la thèse des circonstances* will not do; no more than *la thèse du complot*, by which more moderate revolutionaries had tried to establish their alibi, imputing the crimes and the horrors of the Revolution to the deliberate and conspiratory actions of a small number of evil-minded men.

Taine, so Cochin continues, whose book Aulard imagined that

he had disposed of, brought out realities that the legend had obscured. First, he enabled us to see that the Revolution was a progressive, and more and more oppressive, subjection of the people by the self-styled right-minded people, of the real people by the revolutionary minority, of *la grande cité* by *la petite cité*. Second, by going outside the official circles and their high-sounding and often exculpatory statements, he reminded us of the ordinary men and of what actually happened in the street; not the phrases, not the idealization and the apology, but the stark reality. Third, he showed the connection of all this, or at least that there was a connection, with the revolutionary ideology, which had dissolving and demoralizing, at least as much as it had constructive, effects.

So far, I think Cochin's comments are most illuminating. When he uses the last point to bring out the insufficiency of the thesis of a plot, I can still applaud. Now, however, he goes on to argue that the process revealed by Taine was an automatic process, governed by a social law discovered quite recently by the great sociologist Durkheim, a law that offers "the solution," while Taine, for all his clear-sightedness was prevented by his individualistic psychological method (and he should not be blamed, for he had not yet been able to read Durkheim) from giving a satisfactory "explanation."

The idea is certainly one to stimulate thought, but developed in this way it may lead to a dangerously simplistic doctrinalism. The "law" is the law of mechanical selection and acceleration ("entraînement"), which operates quite independently of "intention" or individual wickedness (no "plot" therefore), and brings, when the dogma of direct sovereignty has once been launched, ever-more-extreme elements to the fore and makes ever-more-fanatical methods prevail, *automatically*.[32]

Twentieth-century French Historians of the Revolution

Taine, as I said, was not destroyed by Aulard. His influence continued to be considerable, but it made itself felt almost exclusively outside the *Université*.

Indirectly, no doubt, the work affected even those who were antagonistic to its general tendency by turning their attention to those realities that Taine had dealt with, in a partisan spirit no doubt, but that he had at any rate dragged into the light of day. Not, of course, that French scholarship was not already trying to free itself from the generalities and emotional engagements that characterized so much of the earlier work. I spoke of the new school to which Aulard's appointment in 1885 gave rise. The work on divers aspects of the Revolution produced by scholars formed in the *Université* assumed ever larger proportions. To mention a few names—only of those who wrote more comprehensive accounts—there was Seignobos, born in 1854, who was only a few years younger than Aulard; there were Sagnac and Pariset, who supplied the first volumes to the large *Histoire de la France contemporaine* published shortly after the first world war under the editorship of the great Lavisse, who was seven years older than Aulard; and of course, there was Mathiez, whose short history of the Revolution appeared in 1922. Among the scholars he influfluenced there stands pre-eminently Georges Lefebvre.[33] These men did not all think alike. The clash between Aulard and Mathiez is an extreme instance of what may be regarded as a normal and healthy phenomenon: differences of opinion, which helped to elucidate what had really happened, and what it signified.

Nevertheless practically all of them started from an assumption that they did not even recognize as such: it seemed to them as self-evident as the fact that they were Frenchmen. They began by accepting the revolutionary epoch as the formative period of the republican regime under which they lived. The concomitants of this acceptance were that national pride in the Revolution, that impatience with opponents whether at home or abroad, and an addiction to those various methods of apology for the excesses of the Terror which we observed in Mignet (even in De Maistre!) and in Michelet. The signs of it will every now and again emerge to strike the attentive reader from beneath the smooth surface of the well-documented accounts composed by the men I have mentioned, and by other modern professional historians.

I cannot try to show this in any detail by a systematic examination of twentieth-century work. I shall give one single instance of the sort of thing I have in mind.

I take it from Georges Lefebvre's volume on the Revolution in the well-known *Peuples et civilisations* series. Lefebvre's repute as a scholar is richly deserved. His critical powers are unmistakable, his tone is restrained and balanced, in several monographs he made a large contribution to the better understanding of the period. I was surprised, some years ago, on reading his *Notions d'historiographie moderne*,[34] to see how he extolled Michelet as "our greatest national historian," and this on the strength of the volumes on the Revolution and without apparently being put out by Michelet's worship of the Revolution, by his emotionalism and chauvinism. But now this is what Lefebvre himself has to say about the Terror,[35] and it will be enough to show that he did indeed follow the tradition of what Renan termed "the prejudices current in France," and Taine, "the willful illusion in which we live since the book of M. Thiers." After noting that the Committee of Public Safety at one moment tried to limit the scope of the Terror, he goes on:

Do without it, however, the Committee could not, for it was indispensable for breaking down passive resistance, silencing personal interests, and crushing particularism. The majority of Frenchmen no doubt were devoted to the Revolution and detested the foreign intervention, but they were lacking in a "civic culture" sufficiently comprehensive to enable them to submit to discipline voluntarily. The Terror compelled them to do so and thus contributed mightily toward developing the habit of, and consequently the feeling for, national solidarity.

The counterrevolutionary tradition, which had been given such an impetus by Taine's work, was not, meanwhile, brought to a halt. It continued on its course, crying defiance to the Revolution, to the modern age, to the Republic itself, but, as I said, outside the *Université*. The influence of Taine's book was reinforced by the spirit of the *Action française* which, although it never managed to come into actual power, in the early decades of the twentieth century obtained a remarkable hold over the French intellect.

Maurras was far from being a disciple of Taine. Instead of denouncing *l'esprit classique* as the source of the Revolution and of all France's troubles, he held up a return to the classic spirit as the only way to salvation. It is true that the two men used the phrase in entirely different senses. I hinted already that Taine's use of it was very arbitrary and confusing. By *l'esprit classique* he meant the passion for arguing in the abstract, *la raison raisonnante*, indifferent to the realities of history and of life. The classicism that Maurras preached was the spirit of order, of subordination to, or respect for, the conventions and the proprieties; order as it had reigned in the seventeenth century, *le grand siècle*, under Louis XIV, *le grand roi*. National unity and strength. "La France seule!" Renouncing all her history before 1789 would not make France strong; on the contrary. The enemies to Maurras were Romanticism, Individualism, Protestantism, Judaism; these it were that had triumphed in the Revolution. We seem to be nearer here to De Maistre or to De Bonald than to Taine. Yet Taine's denunciations of the Revolution and all its works were grist to the mill of the *Action française*.

One of the ablest books produced by the movement was *Le Romantisme français* (1907), by Pierre Lasserre. It opens with a merciless attack on Rousseau and later on disposes of Michelet and his messianism as baneful products of Romanticism. Presented as a thesis for the doctor's degree at the Sorbonne, it gave rise to an acrimonious discussion between the candidate and Professor Aulard.

A few years later, in 1912, Lasserre published a book in which he boldly challenged the *Université* as a whole: *La doctrine officielle de l'Université.*

The state's educational policy was a hotly debated issue in those years. The radical Combes government, emerging victoriously from the Dreyfus affair, had ruthlessly declericalized the elementary schools (it will be remembered that Renan had offered to leave these to the priests, if only they would not meddle with higher education; a very different climate had come to prevail since). In secondary education the clergy still maintained a position, but in the state secondary schools the program had been revised in 1902 to the detriment of the traditional classical humanities. This gave rise to protracted and bitter debates, and it was the immediate occasion for Lasserre's book.

Lasserre charged the *Université* with being a fighting machine and attacked the leading men of the Sorbonne, especially Lavisse, Seignobos, and the historian of literature Lanson, for making education serve political ends. What is behind the dead set made against the humanities? They are looked upon as an obstacle to the desired equality. They belong, so Lavisse said, to a stage of society when "the family, the corporation, the order, surrounded and classed the individual." All the more reason to preserve them, Lasserre exclaims. And history, too, he notes, is being badly treated by the men of the regime, treated so as to bring into contempt the "stupid" religiosity of the Middle Ages or to cry down the glorious seventeenth century: Lavisse's (famous!) volumes on the age of Louis XIV amount to a systematic detraction of the great king; Seignobos, in a textbook for schools, characterizes the policy of the Church by an illustration showing a heretic at the stake, and the *ancien régime* by one of a peasant on the gallows.

A special chapter on history as taught and written in the Sorbonne was contributed to Lasserre's book by a young man, René de Marans. He shows us Seignobos priding himself on the share he had taken in the reform of 1902 and from the height of his position in the Sorbonne telling the secondary-school teachers how to carry out their task: "Our pupils will be electors. It is the duty of the history masters to look after the political instruction of future citizens." They must, comments De Marans, fashion electors who will vote Radical Socialist. Less attention, according to Seignobos, should be given to periods of stability (as, for instance, the seventeenth century!); the critical periods, on the contrary, the periods of change, should be placed in the forefront. The concept of change itself, of evolution, should be impressed on the minds of these budding members of our democracy; and from that point of view the eighteenth and nineteenth centuries, "the period in the history of mankind when evolution has been fastest," are the most interesting.

I have been familiar for many years with the work of Lavisse, of Seignobos, of Lanson, and the affectionate regard I have for them can withstand these attacks. Lasserre's book is, moreover, disfigured in places (this does not apply to the part due to De Marans) by the reactionary idiosyncracies and fanaticism of the *Action française*. I was nevertheless impressed by this book when I got hold of a copy a few years ago (it is so little known that not one of the university libraries in Holland, or the Royal Library either, possessed it). The political preoccupations of the French historians of the period are indeed made unmistakably clear.

The insistence of Seignobos and Langlois in their well-known *Introduction aux études historiques* on the most depersonalized scientific method is shown by De Marans not in the least to provide a remedy against the fashionable partiality. Indeed this talk of objectivity and of sticking to the documents, in which especially Langlois indulges (I used the book in question in my undergraduate days, and my recollection of Langlois is not an "affectionate" one), seems only to serve as an excuse for the most outrageously unhistoric pronouncements: "en marge de ses travaux scientifiques."[36] De Marans remarks acutely that once the connection between the fact-finding and the historic judgment gets lost, opinions proceeding straight from present-day preoccupations will obtain a free rein. To look in the past for nothing but what led up to the Revolution and the actual republican regime that issued from the Revolution is debasing history. The invaluable importance of history for our civilization lies in the fact that history maintains a disinterested understanding of the past, remote and "stable" periods included.[37]

I have, then, found it instructive to listen to the criticism leveled at the "official" historians by the conservatives. (Let me remark in passing that I know of no later work by De Marans, who I suppose was killed in the first world war, as was Cochin; and that Lasserre later on seceded from the *Action française*, a convert to liberalism.) The historical work produced by the conservatives themselves, however, for the most part sinned from bias as badly or worse.

One of the most popular of modern brief histories of the Revolution was Louis Madelin's volume, which appeared in 1911 ("ouvrage couronné par l'Académie française"), in the *Histoire de France raconteé a tous*. Extreme bias is not the reproach one can level against this book. *Was* the writer a conservative? In the sense of viewing things from a bourgeois and chauvinistic point of view, yes; but not in the sense of rejecting the Revolution *in toto*. He says expressly that he does not want to range himself among either the Guelphs or the Ghibellins. He is only a Frenchman, "adoring" his country "under whichever flag it may triumph or succumb." In fact, of course, he was deluding himself when he thought this pronouncement was a guarantee that his appreciation of events would not be governed by any definite political philosophy.

The Revolution was, Madelin considers, inevitable. But the reforms that "the nation" wanted were all comprised in the *cahiers* of 1789. In other words, Madelin regards the second Revolution, of 1792 to 1794—the real Revolution in the eyes of Mathiez—as an aberration that could not lead to enduring results. What enables Madelin to approach even the extremists without the detestation that might go with this position is his chauvinism: they were Frenchmen engaged in a life-and-death struggle with the foreigner. It is also the conviction he expresses in one place that the Revolution was "the explosion and the assertion [*revanche*] of the noblest sentiment that, to my view, distinguishes man: I mean *Energy*." A conviction on so different a plane from all ideology or moral sentiment that it not only guards the man who holds it against giving way to blinding indignation, but also debars him from profound understanding.

Madelin devoted the rest of his life to a many-volumed work on Napoleon[38]—the admirer of "Energy" had found his subject. He may be regarded as a professional historian, although with him we are not really, any more than with Lasserre and De Marans, in the sphere of the *Université*.

Of more definitely counterrevolutionary writers, I mention Bainville and Gaxotte, both members of the *Action française*, both elected into the *Académie française*, as indeed was Maurras himself. In my *Napoleon For and Against* I drew attention to the contrast between the conservative *Académie* being for, and the radical *Université* against the dictator. With respect to the Revolution it was the reverse: the *Université* was for, the *Académie* against.[39]

One quotation from Gaxotte's book, which appeared in 1928 and went through innumerable editions, must serve to indicate the sort of French nationalism that went down with the public, as well as the incredible, almost childish simplification of history that did not prevent the "Immortals" from voting for a "well-thinking" candidate.

The seventeenth century had been, for the French genius, an epoch full of efflorescence. The Frenchman, such as one loves to picture him then, is a being conscious and reflective, capable of silencing his instincts and his passions in order to submit himself to a superior rule of order and harmony. He is on his guard against individual fantasies.

In the early eighteenth century, Gaxotte goes on, slight movements of impatience may be observed. But the imposing good sense of the admirable Louis XIV easily had the better of them. The Germans, always individualistic (did not the Reformation have its origin in Germany?), the English, given to rebellion against their kings, go on indulging in the most reckless speculations. In France there were at most little sparks, here and there, which did not kindle any fire. Until? . . .

Until Montesquieu and Voltaire went to stay in England for a while. Then, and this time in real earnest, the individualistic and revolutionary preaching was revived.

6.

I must try to come to a conclusion. Or *is* there no conclusion? Is the story that I have been telling just going on endlessly repeating itself?

I cannot help recalling a personal experience here, one that is not of any importance in itself, but that has stuck in my mind because I found it so revealing on this very point.

It happened in 1948, when I attended the last sitting—only the last—of the great international congress held in Paris and devoted to the history of the revolutions of 1948. Professor Labrousse delivered the final lecture. Then, in the discussion, up rose from a back row an old gentleman, bearded all over his face and rather shabbily dressed, who sounded a note that apparently, after a full week of talk, impressed the assembled members as altogether novel. He said that what had struck him in the proceedings was that everybody seemed to have started from the assumption that revolution was "a good thing." As for him, he ventured to question this and to urge his hearers to ask themselves whether really revolution was the best method for promoting reform and progress, whether it was not on the contrary an extraordinarily wasteful and risky method, a method always leading to unforeseeable complications and unhappy aftereffects. "*Taine*," he said, and at that name the audience of distinguished French historians, which had turned round to look at the speaker with slightly bored amusement, positively broke into a ripple of laughter. Imagine mentioning Taine, who was a mere interloper, and to mention whom seriously (as Aulard had actually written) would almost cause a candidate for a history degree to be ploughed! I particularly noticed the broad smile and the expressive shrug of the excellent and deservedly famous old Professor Lefebvre.

The speaker was Daniel Halévy, and I confess that my sympathy at that moment was with him. Later on I read his *Histoire d'une histoire* (1939), an essay in which he made his contribution to the one hundred fiftieth anniversary of 1789 by attacking the cult of the revolutionary tradition as he saw it observed in the official world of French historians (exactly as Lasserre and De Marans had seen it twenty-seven years earlier), and I found the little work very stimulating and instructive. At the same time, how one-sided was the view taken by this same M. Halévy. How blindly he revered, not either Danton or Robespierre, not Mignet or Michelet, but Renan and Taine. And still later on I discovered that M. Halévy had, during the war, been an ardent supporter of Marshal Pétain.

Isn't it clear, not only that the Revolution still is an issue in present-day French politics, but also that the attitude of French historians toward it is still connected with their political convictions? I believe that this is indeed so, but at the same time I see plenty of evidence for the statement that, compared with the situation in the nineteenth century, the tension has slackened.

This is partly due to the passage of time. So much has happened since the end of the eighteenth century! And while 1848 and even 1871 could still with some show of reason be connected with the great Revolution, there have since been shattering events of a tendency and an origin patently different. The effect has been to draw dividing lines right across the traditional one separating radicals upholding the revolutionary legend from conservatives rejecting it. Take the Communists. How embarrassing must it be to some of the older devotees to see them posing as the true and only heirs of Robespierre's greatness and ideals![40]

But men of a different type altogether on occasion invoke the glorious epic, thereby upsetting the original pattern of for and against. In 1956, for instance, Jean Dutourd, exasperated by the slackness and lack of spirit that were responsible for the collapse of French military resistance in 1940, and even more by the complacency with which the humiliation of that terrible episode was now on all sides glossed over or forgotten, and wanting to goad his fellow countrymen to a proper appreciation of their plight and to the courage required to overcome it, wrote in that bitter book, *Les Taxis de la Marne:* "The Revolution of 1789 and the Terror convey a solemn warning"—to the Republic, which, according to the writer, had sunk almost to the degree of stupidity at which the old monarchy had been overtaken by disaster. "It was not so much the aristocrats as stupidity which then [in 1793 and 1794] had its head cut off."[41]

But the passage of time and the intrusion of extraneous events is not all. Modern historical scholarship has undoubtedly made a contribution of its own toward softening the all-too-rigid contrast. In the foregoing I have mainly brought out the weaknesses of the application of it by the French in dealing with their great Revolution. I have shown that the historians on both sides of the traditional controversy had in many cases succeeded but imperfectly in freeing their minds from the domination of the legend—of the legend of either for or against. To bring out the positive effects resulting from indefatigable research and from incessant questioning and trying out new approaches, I should have had to review dozens of writers and to enter into subtle and complicated arguments. By avoiding doing so, I am afraid I must have created an impression that does not do full justice to French historiography.

Let me now state emphatically, however generally, that modern historical scholarship in France, taking it as a whole, *has* helped to free men's minds from easy generalizations and from tendentious exaggerations. Modern historical scholarship is from its very nature inimical to simplistic views like the Revolution being "a block," to be religiously accepted or to be rejected *in toto*.[42] It tends to complicate the image of the past to such an extent that the legend, and for that matter the counterlegend, more and more comes to wear an air of unreality. This, as Fustel de Coulanges realized with such clarity of vision, is the great service that the study of history, if rightly practiced, can render to the community. And to some extent undoubtedly French historiography, in spite of the shortcomings that it is easier for the foreigner to detect than for the Frenchman to avoid, has succeeded in doing so.

(1956)

III

NETHERLANDS HISTORY

1
MOTLEY AND HIS "RISE OF THE DUTCH REPUBLIC"

A hundred years ago John Lothrop Motley published his famous history of the revolt of the Netherlands against Spanish rule. Generations of English and American readers since have gathered from its pages all their notions of that famous episode and even of Dutch history.

A work that conquered the world in the way *The Rise of the Dutch Republic* did must have qualities. They are not the qualities that appeal to professional historians, and some reserve was apparent in the reception the work received in their circles, especially in Holland. Indeed it was a little hard on the small band of devoted workers in the field of history, men whose names are still honored in Holland among scholars, and are not unknown to the general public (let me mention only Fruin); it was a little hard on them that, while they were laying the foundations for a truer understanding of the great events of the second half of the sixteenth century, along came this unknown American from Boston and set the world (including the Dutch public) reading about the wicked Philip II and the noble William the Silent, about the struggle between the tiny Netherlands and the mighty empire of Spain.

Fruin, in a review expanded into an essay of two hundred pages, in effect rewrote all Motley's chapters on the preliminaries of the revolt, down to the arrival of the Duke of Alva in 1567, and, while he never departed from the tone of courtesy and respect, the impression Fruin left with the reader was that Motley had not really understood the events about which he wrote with such fervor and in such glowing colors; that he had used all his art to heighten the effects of the drama by representing one side as villains or fools and the other as Virtue, Wisdom, and Heroism personified; that he had not probed behind the appearance of events. The truth, as shown by Fruin, was less dramatic; the rights and the wrongs, the virtues and the vices, were more equally divided. The actors prominent on the stage of events were not the masters of the action either; history was not decided by their personal aims and qualities so much as by large tendencies, general European developments of which they were the exponents.

Fruin's work could never attain the popularity that Motley enjoyed for so long, but it has stood the test of time infinitely better. His interpretation has been found to be faulty in more than one respect, but it is still a matter of debate among historians. No historian, however, can take Motley's interpretation seriously any longer, and scholars carry out their investigations and conduct their discussions without referring to him or to his views.

Nevertheless, when, after I don't know how many years, I read *The Rise of the Dutch Republic* again, I could understand how it came to make such an impression. It is admirably told. The characters are sketched in bold outline. There are about the book a vigor and a conviction that sweep the reader along. One is not invited to pause and consider subtleties or contradictions. A sense of drama is conveyed by clear-cut contrasts, and the plot and the solutions all seem perfectly obvious.

Yet even the general reader of today—more than the general reader of the nineteenth century—will instinctively doubt whether life can have been as dramatic, and especially, as clear, as all that. The positiveness, the absence of half-shades, will arouse his distrust. As for the historian, who comes to the book with some independent knowledge, what amazes him is how it has been possible to miss the realities to such an extent and yet to create an illusion of pulsating life.

To Motley—and this explains both the weakness of his history and the fascination it exercised over readers of the Age of Liberalism—the story of the revolt was an epic in the eternal struggle waged by Liberty and Enlightenment with Despotism and Darkness.

Motley sees Philip and his servants (above all, that unspeakable man of blood, the Duke of Alva) as the forces of Evil. He admits no redeeming features. He cannot accept that they honestly believed themselves to be doing their duty, and instead of explaining their harsh policy as conditioned by the prevailing sentiments of their time, or as the outcome of all-too-human shortsightedness or stupidity, he can see nothing but the crimes of cruelty or of sycophancy. It is not only Philip who is to him the Prince of Wickedness: from Charlemagne on, that is how he regards all emperors and kings. In the Netherlands he sees the rulers, throughout the centuries preceding the revolt, trying to fasten lawless domination and oppression upon a brave, innocent, and liberty-loving people, a people as brave, innocent, and liberty-loving as were the English who rose against the Stuarts, and the Americans who rose against George III and his ministry. This, to him, is the true meaning of history: the struggle between Despotism and Liberty resulting in the glorious victory of the latter. The Netherlands and the English revolts had been important contributions to this victory, until it was finally consummated in the American Revolution.

I hold no brief for despotism, nor do I wish to decry liberty. But the simplistic view of Motley is a denial of history. History is not made up of struggles between God and the Devil. The Good Cause is inevitably and treacherously attended by tendencies less good. The Bad Cause has its connections with what is wholesome and indispensable. Fallible man, on whichever side of the struggle he is engaged, is not sanctified, nor is he entirely given over to evil. The absolute rulers of the sixteenth century, and indeed their predecessors, tyrannical as they were at times, do represent a beneficent principle: they were the builders of states in which order prevailed; order, not of subjection only, but of law.

On the other hand, the cry of "liberty" covered a multitude of selfish interests, local narrowness, class privilege. In the Netherlands especially, the national unity that was to shake off the aline monarchy so dramatically had had the way prepared for it by the centuries-long action of this same power acquiring or conquering one after another of the separate counties and duchies that were to become the seventeen provinces. The republic born from the violent reaction against the authoritarian tendencies of the monarchy is unreservedly hailed by Motley as a great achievement of wisdom and true statesmanship, and no doubt it did make a striking appearance in a Europe in which absolutism continued to prevail for another two centuries and more. The principle of liberty proved a fruitful one in many areas of life. The seventeenth century became Holland's golden age in power, in art, and in literature. That burgher society teemed with energy.

But it was a major disaster in Netherlands history that in the process north and south were disrupted. The Dutch Republic consisted of only seven of the seventeen provinces. Moreover, interprovincial relations were regulated by the Union of Utrecht on the basis of provincial sovereignty. The problem of unity, in other words, remained unsolved, and this was a constant source of weakness and of trouble, to which in the end the Republic succumbed. Another revolution, under the aegis of the great French Revolution this time, was needed to bring about that national state to which Netherlands history had been tending—but this state was achieved only on the basis of the seven provinces, all situated north of the river barrier, that had been able to hold out against the Duke of Parma's campaigns of reconquest. In the later stages of the protracted war (the Eighty Years' War!), some forty or fifty years after the southern provinces had been reduced to obedience and at the same time purged of Protestantism, the northern Republic (as it now was) had been able to launch out south of the rivers and occupy portions of the provinces of Flanders and Brabant, which, completely re-Catholicized as they were, were held as "Generality Lands."

There are questions involved here which belong to the very heart of the story and to which Motley gave only scant attention—questions, one may say, which he never understood. The most fundamental problem, the problem of Protestantism and of its role in the opposition and the revolt, was entirely beyond him. In Motley's account the fight for liberty and the fight for Protestantism seem one. In reality the two were not only distinct, but, although in some ways and at some moments they coincided and reinforced each other, they were also liable to lock in disastrous conflict.

"All this we do for liberty," or "all this we do for religion": these tags formulated two opposing views of the aims of the rebellion. The first: to put a stop to the centralizing policy and its highhanded methods; to safeguard the old liberties and privileges of towns, provinces, and classes; to ward off the arbitrary interference of an alien ruler served by alien ministers and soldiers. The second: to break the monopoly of the Roman Catholic Church and to make the country into a preserve for the elect, a temple for the true word of God, cleansed from superstition and priestly tricks; in short, something entirely different. The first program may be described as the national one. Insofar as the revolt was dominated by it, the parallel, on which Motley insists so much, with the English Revolution of 1688 and the American Revolution of 1775, is justified. But the second, the program of the Calvinists, which appealed to no more than a minority, a tiny minority even, of the nation, introduced into the situation a more violently revolutionary element.

What Motley never seems to realize clearly is that the Protestants *were* but a minority—and the Calvinists were but a section of the Protestants. The Calvinists, naturally, pricked up their ears when the nobility began to oppose the King, and they became the most energetic and determined supporters of the struggle when it developed into a rebellion. But from the first their coming out into the open tended to frighten Catholics back into the royal fold. I am thinking now of what happened in 1566, as a result of the famous outbreak known as the "Breaking of the Images."

Radical minorities, no doubt, often manage to impose themselves in revolutions. That they could do so in Holland, however, they owed entirely to geographical circumstances and even to help from outside. In the first real act of rebellion, in 1572, when the two seaboard provinces of Holland and Zeeland declared for the Prince of Orange, their stadholder, now in exile, the determining factor had come from overseas. It was the Sea Beggars—the Calvinist exiles of 1567, drawn from all the provinces, who had taken to the seas, forming an irregular fighting force for the displaced Prince—it was they who now invaded the two coastal provinces and by their unforeseen intervention brought their coreligionists into positions of power.

This is how Motley opens his chapter on this really crucial moment in the revolt: "The example thus set by Brill was rapidly followed." But look a little more closely and it will be seen that Brill, the little seaport where the Beggar fleet first put in an appearance, did not do anything so active as setting an example. The magistrates fled in fear of their lives, followed by most of the inhabitants. It was an almost empty town in which the Beggar chief effected a landing. Motley, however, goes on to describe the subsequent events in the province as "a spontaneous movement": "With one fierce bound of enthusiasm the nation shook off its chains."

Again, how different was the reality! With one single and still somewhat doubtful exception, not a town declared for the Prince of its own accord. All waited until a Beggar chief with his armed band appeared before the gates. Generally he was only reluctantly admitted, after a long parley, and after articles of capitulation had been agreed upon. Chief among these there was always a stipulation that the exercise of the Catholic religion and the persons and goods of the clergy should be left undisturbed. Hardly were the Beggars inside when, in most cases, returning exiles, with the help of secret sympathizers in the town and backed by the presence of the armed invaders, made themselves masters of the town hall, reconstituted the town government, and seized one or more churches for the Protestant service.

Once matters had come to that pass, there was no holding them. The States of Holland, representing the revolutionized town magistracies, which began by proclaiming the Prince of Orange, soon forbade the exercise of the Catholic religion. And when the Spanish army, which had easily overawed the provinces south and east, entered Holland and Zeeland to put down the rebellion, it found an established government, headed now by William the Silent and provided with a fighting force determined to stick it out. It was this that stiffened the resistance of Holland and Zeeland through those heroic years from 1572 to 1576. And when, in the latter year, by the Pacification of Ghent, the other provinces joined in, spontaneously this time, under their traditional and unchanged magistrates and assemblies, it was still the fixed point acquired by Calvinism in 1572 in Holland and Zeeland which determined the course of events in the Netherlands as a whole—which determined, in particular, that the rebellion was to be wedded indissolubly to Calvinism. Note that the part played by the two provinces was due, not to the exceptional enterprise of their populations, or to any more than average inclination toward the new religion, but to the descent, at an opportune moment, of the Sea Beggar forces, which were drawn from the more radical elements of all the provinces.

It is at first sight extraordinary that Motley praised the revolt as a triumph of Liberalism, of Enlightenment, of Democracy. That it was carried through by a minority dictatorship, using the customary methods of violence and suppression, seems to have escaped his attention. Revolutions do not work by the rules of liberalism; enlightenment and democracy do not fare well by them. We of our generation have had our memory refreshed on that score. At the same time it is also true that one must not paint all revolutions with the same brush. In the case of the Netherlands revolt the excesses of minority dictatorship were soon mitigated by the new regent class, which, while dutifully conforming to the new dominant church, was in truth more concerned about freedom than about religion. Its members were, in fact, regents before they were Calvinists, and they were very determined not to allow themselves to be dictated to by the Calvinist ministers. The Dutch Republic was certainly very far from being a model of either a liberal or a democratic state, yet it was much more liberal and democratic than its origins would lead one to expect.

This no doubt was one of the factors that led Motley into his interpretation of the revolt. And he was, in fact, far from being singular. Among Dutch historians, too, the myth that suited the interests of the newly dominant group of Protestants has long ruled supreme. Today one will not look in Motley's work for a faithful presentation of sixteenth-century men and conditions. But one can still enjoy it as an eloquent and sincere testimony of nineteenth-century liberal idealism.

(1956)

2
ORANGE AND STUART: 1641-1650

A
Frederick Henry of Orange and King Charles I

The interests of Orange and Stuart first became entangled through the marriage of Frederick Henry's only son, William, to Mary, the eldest daughter of Charles I, which took place in May 1641 in the chapel of the palace at Whitehall. It is not difficult to indicate the reasons that led Frederick Henry to seek this alliance. He was actuated by purely dynastic considerations. He hoped that if he could link the name of Orange with a royal line, it would mean an accession not only of prestige, but of power in the Republic. The prerogatives of the stadholder were ill-defined, and in the struggle with the burgher-oligarchy of Holland, high titles, military fame, and the splendor of court life played no small part.

When, in 1625, Frederick Henry had succeeded his brother Maurice, he had had to proceed very carefully. It was a serious time for the Republic. From its renewal in 1621, the war with Spain had gone badly, adding fresh dangers to those left by the bitter quarrels between strict Calvinists and Arminians for which the Twelve Years' Truce is memorable. The new stadholder, whose sympathies had been with the vanquished party rather than with his brother, was cautious in openly displaying his leanings. At one moment it seemed as though the stadholderate would spontaneously adapt itself to the supremacy of the States. Frederick was not only courteous and affable; he was subservient. He adopted a genial tone with the patricians of Holland, declaring that he had "no taste for German pomp," but that he was a Hollander like themselves, "born at Delft."[1]

With the first successes on the battlefield the position changed. Little by little Frederick Henry's authority in the state increased, and soon it appeared that he was far more intent on making his power felt than Maurice had been before him. Maurice had seized power, which lay ready to his hand, only when his passions were roused by a violent political crisis, and then only to let it slip almost heedlessly from his grasp again as soon as he had gained his end.

Not so Frederick Henry. He worked consciously and steadily, albeit patiently and cautiously, toward the strengthening of his position, and, again unlike Maurice, he had a son; he worked not for himself alone, but for his house. He made use of all the resources offered him by the peculiar constitution of the Republic. By the distribution of offices he won for himself partisans in every quarter. The permanent committees that played such an important part in the administration of the Dutch Republic were devoted to his interests, and in more than one province he had his confidants, who at his will and through his protection could sway their respective provincial States assemblies.

In particular, Frederick Henry turned his earnest attention to the composition of the States-General. The deputies were usually appointed for long periods, and it was an easy matter for him to exercise considerable influence, at least upon the representatives of the inland provinces, most of whom were nobles and depended on his favor for the military careers of their sons and near relations. Far removed from their principals, who, moreover, were in session only for a few weeks in the year, they were able to follow their own, or rather, the Prince's, will much more easily than could the Hollanders, who, as the States-General met in The

Hague, were always under the eyes of their masters, the States of Holland. When in the course of time, for the sake of speed and secrecy, the custom had crept in of allowing the stadholder to decide important questions of foreign policy with a committee of the States-General, Frederick Henry had little difficulty in finding men for this body who were ready to follow his lead. Indeed, as a rule he was even permitted to co-opt personally one deputy of his own choice from each province.[2] In this way he came near to being possessed of supreme power.

In June 1634 this Secret Committee (*Secreet Besogne*), which had until then borne a purely informal character, was placed on a somewhat firmer basis. A resolution was passed authorizing the Prince to have minutes of the decisions arrived at in the Committee kept by the greffier of the States-General and laying it down that these decisions would be as forceful as if they had been taken in the full assembly. The States-General did not, naturally, completely relinquish their control of foreign policy: it rested with them to "defer," or not to "defer," a question to the Committee. It must have been difficult, however, for it to resume a matter once "deferred" because the secrecy applied also—indeed that was what mattered—to the principals.[3] So far did the Prince's influence reach already that the States often allowed him to select (to "assume" was the current term) deputies for the Committee himself.

For a number of years there had been very little difference of opinion concerning the lines of national policy, so that the Stadholder could be regarded as the natural leader. This had enabled him quietly to pave the way for his advancement to a position of real power. Curiously enough, at the moment of this important step, when the Secret Committee was established more firmly and at the same time largely fell under the Prince's control, there was already growing dissension over the plan of an alliance with France, the object of which was to be the final conquest of the Spanish Netherlands, which were then to be partitioned between the two powers. There were many who considered this a dangerous policy. *Gallum amicum non vicinum* was the cry raised at Amsterdam. Peace with Spain, leaving the Spanish Netherlands as a buffer between the Republic and France, seemed to these men preferable. But Frederick Henry managed to get the policy of war in conjunction with France adopted: the Secret Committee, just established, proved an efficient tool in his hands, and the decision, which was one of great consequence, in itself again strengthened, for the time being, his position. Richelieu's gratitude expressed itself by his addressing Frederick Henry by the title of "Highness," whereas hitherto, like his brother and father, he had had to be content with "Excellency." This, too, was an important step, without which the next, the royal marriage, would probably have been impossible. Moreover, the confidential understanding with the French ambassadors strengthened the Prince's position in foreign politics.

Thus, from the moment when this question came to the fore, a renewal of the opposition to the Stadholder can be observed, but it was of an entirely different character from the movement in the days of Maurice. It was not directed merely against some definite policy; it was inspired no less by concern over the growth of stadholderly power as such. All over Europe sovereign rulers were struggling for absolute power with assemblies that held fast to their ancient privileges. In France Richelieu did the work for his king with marked success—Richelieu, who in 1635 had entered into such close relations with Frederick Henry, and who, doubtless of set purpose, did all in his power to reinforce the monarchical principle in the Republic. In England Charles I had been carrying on an arbitrary regime without a parliament, and when at length he was obliged to summon one, it was only to enter into bitter conflict with it. And it was with Charles I—a prince so much a monarchist that, speaking to a Dutch ambassador, he described the Dutch government, quite calmly and without a thought of discourtesy, as "a populace without discretion"[4]—it was with Charles that Frederick Henry was now seeking an intimate connection, one that was still further to increase the prestige of Orange; by many at the English court it was even regarded as preliminary to a *coup d'état* whereby the Stadholder would be transformed from a servant of the States to sovereign of the country.[5]

No more is needed to account for the fact that the regent class of the Netherlands, and especially of the wealthy trading province of Holland, did not take kindly to the English marriage plans. This royal connection did far more than had the French alliance to loose a storm of opposition against the Stadholder in his latter years; and what made it the more serious for him was the fact that the intimacy with the Stuarts was palpably at variance with national interests: it was so obviously a purely dynastic move. Neither Frederick Henry nor William II after him could in pursuing this policy count absolutely on that popularity with the Calvinist middle-class which was since the days of Maurice among the greatest assets of the Princes of Orange in their struggles with the States of Holland. The army, of course, never failed to support them, nor the nobility, especially the poor gentry of the inland provinces, who were closely connected with the army and who moreover looked to the Stadholder for help against the ambitions of the towns represented in their States assemblies.

It was through them that Frederick Henry, for his part, had so great a hold over the States-General. If in that assembly the smaller provinces generally stood by the Stadholder's policy and the center of gravity of the opposition against him was always to be found in Holland, it is by no means necessary to assume that the interests of these provinces really were best served by the Stadholder's policy, which meant first, war with Spain, and soon after, as we shall see, war with England. It meant only that Holland, the wealthiest province by far, with the strongest and most self-confident burgher-class, represented that element in the Republic that was sufficiently independent to stand up against the encroachments of the Stadholder's power.

At the time when Frederick Henry on behalf of his son made overtures to Charles I for the hand of one of his daughters, Charles's leanings were much more toward Spain than toward Spain's enemies, France and the United Netherlands. In 1635 the plans of these two countries to divide the Southern Netherlands between themselves had had a very disquieting effect at the English court, and in 1637 the King declared to the Comte d'Estrades that he would do all in his power to oppose the conquest of the Flemish coast. True, as a result of the growing internal dissensions in England and the revolt brewing in Scotland, his power appeared to be extremely limited. He certainly had, with the help of the levy of ship money, equipped a fleet, but in 1639 it proved beyond his power to avenge the disgrace of the Downs, when the Dutch admiral Tromp had fallen upon the Spanish expeditionary fleet in English waters where it had expected to be safe. The attitude of the English government about this affair had been so ambiguous that in Holland it was at first suspected and afterward generally believed that England had undertaken to support the Spanish enterprise.[6] The suspicion was in fact groundless, but Charles I was certainly anxious to curry favor with Spain. His favorite project in those days—it had been his father's before him—was to negotiate Spanish marriages for his children. Above all his wife, Henrietta Maria, a sister of the reigning king of France, strengthened him in this resolve, and her friend, the Duchesse de Chevreuse, who was a sworn enemy of Richelieu, acted as go-between. Under these circumstances, the French government could hardly regard the English court as anything but hostile. There is no conclusive proof that Richelieu actually supported the Scottish rising of 1639, but he certainly did maintain friendly relations[7] with the English parliamentary opposition when, in the following year, it was able to make itself felt again and still further paralyzed Charles I's capacity for action.

It was in these days that the idea of a marriage between Frederick Henry's son and one of the daughters of Charles I was mooted once more. The subject had been first discussed with the queen's mother, Marie de Médicis,[8] the queen mother of France—no friend of Richelieu's either—during her stay in Holland in 1638. In the following year Jan van der Kerckhoven, lord of Heenvliet, who happened to have been presented to Marie de Médicis, was sent to England as the Prince's private envoy, with secret instructions[9] to enter into negotiations about the project. He had made little progress when, in February 1640, Frederick Henry requested Aerssens van Sommelsdijk, who was then in England on a special mission on the part of the States-General, to come to an understanding with Heenvliet and to try to further the matter.[10]

It was Sommelsdijk's official mission to explain the motives that had led to the action of the States-General at the Downs; at the same time he was to investigate the possibilities of a treaty with England. What he had had to report concerning the attitude of the court was not, however, very encouraging, and when Frederick Henry's request reached him he had just, in exasperation, begged the Stadholder insistently to arrange for his recall, as he suspected that his presence in England and the proposals he had to make were merely being used to force the hand of Spain, whose help was looked for against the Scots. Sommelsdijk was enough of a statesman to have protested vigorously, in a letter to Frederick Henry himself, when it appeared that it had been hinted to the King (apparently by Heenvliet in his zeal for the matrimonial plan)[11] that the Dutch ambassador was not merely to justify the battle of the Downs, as was prescribed in his instructions from the States-General, but also to apologize for it. At the same time he was too much of a courtier not to accede with zeal, even with gratitude, to the request to take over the marriage negotiations. (The regular ambassador from the States-General, Joachimi, who had been in England for many years and was by now a very old man, hardly took part in these matters. He was a refugee from Flanders and a States of Holland man rather than an Orangist.)

One might imagine that a Dutch statesman, especially one who belonged to the Orange party, that is to say, the party that believed in war *à outrance* with Spain, would try to use the marriage plan for an attempt to divert England from Spain. This was how the Orangist people regarded the matter.[12] Sommelsdijk himself did in fact express this point of view on a number of occasions.[13] But could he seriously have supposed, after the experience he had just had of the temper prevailing at the English court, that this could possibly be the result? The suggested connection would involve, not the conferring of a favor on the King by the Stadholder, but the reverse.[14] As early as January, when Sommelsdijk, although he had not then been asked to do so, was already doing his best to further Frederick Henry's design, he had with striking lucidity pointed out this fact to Charles I himself:

> By this marriage you will gain for yourself a first claim on the affections and interests of His Highness and the United Provinces, while if you seek kinship with a house of greater power than your own [Spain], you can expect nothing from their ambitions, but will only lose your daughter, whom you will force into wedding interests opposed to your own.[15]

The questionable character, from the Dutch national point of view, of a dynastic relationship between Stuart and Orange could not be better expressed. Again and again in generations to come the danger was to arise that this relationship might place the lesser of the two united houses in a position of dependence. Heenvliet in fact had been instructed to assure the King in the most respectful manner that the Prince, his consort, and his son would never forget the great favor of this connection, but that he, Frederick Henry, would on the contrary "acknowledge it by his services whenever it might please His Majesty to let him know his commands."[16]

But Sommelsdijk at least wished to make one stipulation. He wished that only the eldest daughter should be accepted. That would at any rate rule out the possibility of a Spanish marriage, for Spain would certainly not condescend to take the second daughter if the eldest had been allotted to the Prince of Orange. But, no doubt for the same reason, the English court was only prepared to enter into negotiations involving the second daughter. Sommelsdijk saw in this the design of the two queens, whose plan was to pave the way for a Spanish marriage for the eldest by means of a Protestant alliance for the second daughter.[17] He even feared, as he had done about the political treaty, that the whole negotiation was meant only to put pressure upon Spain.[18] If it was only possible to get a second daughter, he said finally, then he was for a marriage with a French princess.[19] Certainly a French connection was much more in keeping with the policy represented by Orange at that juncture, but Frederick Henry had set his heart on a marriage with a king's daughter and decided to take the second daughter if the eldest was not available.

Thus when the matter was settled in principle at the end of 1640, it was the second daughter of Charles I, Elizabeth, a child only five years old, who was designated as the future bride of William II. The final negotiations were carried on by a formal embassy from the States-General, which had been officially informed by Frederick Henry in December 1640: the position of the Stadholder approached nearly enough to that of a monarch for the marriage of his son to be regarded as a matter of state. So Sommelsdijk, who was a member of this new mission also, could now give even more positive assurances that the friendship of the Prince of Orange meant the friendship of the Republic. Yet Frederick Henry at the same time sent Beverweert to France, where the English marriage project was naturally causing uneasiness, to explain that it was a private matter and had nothing to do with the policy of the Republic.

If the ambassadors, in January 1641, listened to English proposals for a treaty between the two countries, that was not really in conflict with the view expressed to France. The ambassadors were expressly instructed to do what they could to separate England from Spain, and it was the popular interpretation of the marriage plan that it would serve that very purpose. The question is only, how far did the royal negotiators actually represent the King's intention? or even, how sincere was the King himself when he assured his Parliament that he meant to go in that direction?[20] The prevailing opinion in the House no doubt was all for that policy. But was it not Charles's intention merely to use the name of Orange as a sop to irritated Protestant opinion, and this without loosening his contact with Spain?

Domestic difficulties were beginning to overwhelm the King. Shortly before the arrival of the Dutch ambassadors, after over eleven years during which he had ruled without a parliament (except for the so-called Short Parliament of April and May 1640) he had had to summon another parliament, and this assembly (the Long Parliament as it was later to be called), using to the full the King's impotence as shown against the Scottish Covenant army in the north of England, had at once opened a deliberate attack upon the monarchical regime. Charles's advisers, Strafford and Laud had already been arrested; Windebank and Finch had fled. Yet Charles did not for a moment think of adopting a Protestant, anti-Spanish policy, which would have swelled the pride of his new parliamentary advisers. On the contrary, to him the marriage still was what Sommelsdijk had led him to hope it would be: a way to gain the good offices of the Prince of Orange. And as things then were, this was a prospect not to be despised.

Great as it was, Charles I had certainly an exaggerated idea of the power of the Stadholder.[21] He thought, and Sommelsdijk did nothing to disabuse him, that the Prince could manipulate the foreign policy of the Republic at his will, and that he would be in a position to give effective help in the English domestic troubles. Charles was now willing to give his eldest daughter to the young Prince of Orange.[22]

Thus, even before it took place, the significance of the marriage was entirely changed; but Frederick Henry was in no wise daunted by that. At the very moment when Sommelsdijk was beginning to realize that the upheavals and divisions in England were too serious to allow a political treaty to be thought of, the marriage united the stadholderly power in the Republic, not with England as a whole, but with one of the parties contending for power, and with that which was for long to fare the worst. On February 12 the contract was signed.[23]

When young William of Orange came over and the marriage with Mary took place (early in May 1641), the royal family was going through the deep humiliation of Strafford's trial. Mary herself, in spite of her youth, had been present with her parents during the tragic proceedings in Parliament.[24] A few days before the marriage ceremony the Lower House had passed the bill of attainder against Strafford; a few days after, it passed the Upper House. Even before William (who had to leave his bride behind for the time being) had left the country, the King had given his assent to the bill. It was indeed a far from propitious moment for a union with the Stuarts. The English people, who not so long before would have welcomed the Protestant marriage with enthusiasm as a sign that the King was turning away from Spain, now regarded it with suspicion, fearing that Charles had stipulated for help against his subjects.[25]

Sommelsdijk felt by no means sure that the marriage between the children would not in due time be annulled by the English, seeing the obstinate resistance to all requests that the nine-year-old Mary accompany her husband to Holland. Others, too, regarded this as suspicious. As long as "the bride is not aboard,"[26] ran the opinion of Reigersberch, the brother-in-law of Grotius, it was useless to hope for anything from the marriage; and that, he argued, was to the advantage of England, which would be able to extort still further benefits. When, in October, the question of a new embassy to England arose, one ostensibly to negotiate an alliance but in reality to bring about the *domiductio*, Reigersberch feared that the English would want to "make use of this goad a little longer,"[27] and he expressed anxiety that negotiations carried on in such circumstances would not be very favorable to the interests of his country. But as regards the country where the girl wife was to reside, at any rate, there soon was to be no question any more. The course of events was such that Charles had no choice in the matter. In 1641 his cause went from bad to worse. Finally, at the beginning of 1642, civil war came. Charles had to leave London, and he sent his wife, Henrietta Maria, with the Princess Royal to their new friends in Holland.

In announcing the intended journey to the States-General Charles's resident, Sir William Boswell, said that Charles was sending his daughter over as a token of his friendship for the Netherlands and that her mother was coming to bear her company. As a matter of fact, fear for the safety of his wife, a Roman Catholic whose strong personality had made her the soul of the antiparliamentary party, was the main motive of Charles's decision. The journey was a flight. Yet at the same time Henrietta Maria meant, as we shall see, to seek help in the Netherlands.

Instead of bringing the dowry stipulated in the marriage contract, she carried with her the crown jewels, which she hoped to pawn in Holland. She was moreover to try to get war material shipped from the Netherlands to England and to obtain leave for English officers and men in the States' service to return for action under the King's standard.

The two royal ladies who landed in the Netherlands under such unhappy circumstances were received with great display. All that they now brought to the House of Orange was their royal blood. Frederick Henry was all the more zealous in seeing that this should receive due homage. If we are to believe a royalist writer of the period, he himself never entered the presence of his daughter-in-law, then a child of ten, "but with a reverence more like a subject towards his sovereign than the freedom of a father towards his son's wife."[28] In fact, he arranged in every detail the formalities with which the Princess Royal was to be treated now that she was delivered into the hands of the Orange family, and these were all calculated to lay continual stress on her rank.[29] On the English side too, great care had been taken that her rank should be maintained.

It was by no means a small household that was considered necessary for the King's daughter. It had been stipulated in the marriage contract that she was to be allowed forty English servants, in the appointment of whom the House of Orange had no say, although it had to bear the cost. At the head of her household, it is true, Charles I, acting on the powers he had under the contract, had placed a Dutchman,[30] that same Heenvliet who had been used by Frederick Henry in the negotiations for the marriage. But the ambitious Heenvliet—he was the son of a Leyden professor of theology and had himself bought the manor of Heenvliet—had given a pledge of his attachment to the English royal family. Shortly before—his first wife having died in March 1640[31]—he had married an English widow of position, Lady Stanhope, and his ambitions were now centered in English titles and English property. Lady Stanhope (she continued to bear that name after her second marriage) was appointed governess to the young bride.

The retinue of eighty persons which Mary brought with her from England was modest compared with the three hundred followers by whom, according to Aitzema, her mother was attended. Frederick Henry paid for the upkeep of her court with resignation—for it practically all fell on him. The States occasionally chafed at their share, especially when the Queen "for her amusement" traveled through the province "at the country's expense, with a retinue of 600 persons."[32] (Such is the number given, but this probably included the Stadholder's court.)

The people were dazzled by the splendor of English royalty. In particular, the ceremonial reception at Amsterdam made an impression. To that town the Princess, accompanied by the Stadholder and his son, paid a visit in May. In the allegorical scenes that, according to the taste of the day, formed part of the celebrations, reference was made to marriages of counts of Holland and Gelderland with English princesses; and thus already the Prince of Orange was ranked with the former sovereigns of the country. Vondel's voice, too, is heard in heartfelt jubilation; in one breath he speaks of the children of kings and those of princes as

> . . . those who by God to Godhead are ordained
> To serve the common weal.[33]

Even Hooft—the scion of an Amsterdam regent family—who in that year dedicated his *Historiën* to the Prince, not, of course, omitting a reference to the "royal bridegroom," refers to himself as the Prince's "subject," as though he had for the moment forgotten the sovereignty of the States.

All this was just what Frederick Henry had intended. But the situation was not without its ugly aspects. Not only did the royal child prove a far-from-docile member of the Orange household—before the year 1642 was out, there are reports of a violent scene in which she showed her mother-in-law her "contempt, hatred, and dissatisfaction"[34]—but the effect on the public, too, was far from being unmixed. The people might revel in the display, but that did not alter the fact that the papist Queen was far from popular. Events in England were followed with interest,[35] and sympathies were almost universally on the side of the Parliament.

The religious factor alone was enough to account for that. Even Dr. Rivet, William II's tutor, had been unable, during his stay in England in connection with his pupil's marriage, to disguise his sympathies with the parliamentary party.[36] It is true that he never dared to give open expression to them,[37] but clerics less closely connected with the court were not so scrupulous. In particular the Synod of Zeeland expressed itself more than once, and its letters were very welcome to the Presbyterian party in its struggle both with Episcopalians and Independents. They were in fact inspired by the minister of the Scottish Staple at Middelburg (Spang was his name),[38] by means of whom the Scottish Presbyterians kept in touch with the Dutch Reformed Church. And, indeed, the Synod of South Holland, too, learned "with joy" that the Synod of Westminster had put before Parliament "a certain project of church government, agreeing practically on most points with the government of the Reformed churches in this country."[39] Nor did the Dutch Reformed in those years, 1644 and 1645, confine their sympathy for the cause of their foreign coreligionists to words. The Dutch church sanctioned a collection for "the oppressed Protestants in Ireland," which brought in 300,000 guilders.[40] Later, when enthusiasm had cooled under the influence of the rise of the Independents and of the war with the English Commonwealth (in 1652), one pamphleteer recalls with bitterness that "we prayed for them in the churches," and he reproaches the rebels because "they had used the money collected for them in our country in the struggle against their lawful sovereign."[41] Whether the generous donors in the years 1644 and 1645 would have minded that so much is a matter of doubt.

In any case it is natural that the bishops and their ceremonial should appear hateful to the Dutch Calvinists, and the papist Henrietta Maria was not the ambassador best fitted to make them acceptable. Thus it came about that it was especially the members of the ministry, in other respects the most loyal adherents of the House of Orange,[42] who shook their heads over the Stuart connection. In England the religious factor was bound up with the political issue in much the same way as had been the case in the Dutch war of liberation. Reference to this resemblance was one of the favorite forms of propaganda of the parliamentary party in the Netherlands,[43] propaganda that was certainly the more effectual in that it was known how Charles had looked to Spain as long as he felt sufficiently independent.

But this traditional Calvinist and democratic aversion to despotism was now linked with the republican sentiment of the regent class, which before long expressed itself in an unwillingness to make the liberal donations to the young couple upon which the Orangists had counted,[44] and which is reflected in the caustic observations of Aitzema on the pretensions of the English, their greed for money, etc. Their "High Mightinesses" bowed down to the Queen, they kissed the hem of her garment,[45] but nonetheless they felt uneasy about the royalist invasion, and this feeling was not lessened by the suspicion, soon to be confirmed, that it was not merely a harmless, if annoying, exhibition, but a move in the Prince of Orange's game.[46]

On the very day of the royal personages' arrival a dispute is said to have arisen; the story is too characteristic not to insert it here.[47] A supper was held, attended by a number of the English visitors as well as by States' officers and Holland regents. The Prince's health was drunk before that of the States-General, an irregular proceeding at which the regents present showed their displeasure: the Prince, so they said, was their servant and stood in their pay. A French captain of horse retorted that a Prince who had just married his son to "a daughter of England, granddaughter of France" should be ashamed to pass for the servant of brewers, bakers, and feltmakers. Judicial proceedings were said to have resulted. The contrast between Orange and the oligarchy is seen to be taking on a sharper edge!

The royal alliance certainly gave birth to a universal suspicion that the Stadholder was aiming at sovereign power.[48] All the more closely was his foreign policy watched. And here the oligarchy and the Calvinist commonalty—a rare occurrence in Dutch history—found common ground in their disapproval of his policy. Under the peculiar conditions of government in the Republic, only the States of Holland, as I have already pointed out, could offer any effective resistance. But on this occasion they could count upon much more moral support than in most of their conflicts with the Princes of Orange. Thus among the first fruits of Frederick Henry's dynastic triumph must be counted not only the fact that new life was infused into the opposition of the States of Holland to the stadholderate,[49] but also the fact that they appeared against him as the defenders of a national policy.

The issue was one of no small importance: it was whether, in the struggle between the King of England and the Parliament, which broke out openly in August 1642, the Netherlands should remain neutral or should range themselves on the King's side, at least to the extent of giving him secret support. Holland was powerful enough to secure the acknowledgement of neutrality as the official policy of the States;[50] it was, indeed, unmistakably in the national interest. But Frederick Henry, on his part, was sufficiently powerful, supported as he was by most of the smaller provinces and by some officials and even colleges of the generality, constantly to obstruct or evade the official policy. The result was that, although it was impossible to give the King the effective aid on which he had counted, so that in the end his ruin was not prevented,[51] the Parliament was nevertheless given abundant cause for violent resentment.[52]

The chief care of Henrietta Maria and her advisers during their stay in the Netherlands was to put the King in a position to defend himself, to help him with money, troops, and munitions. The support given by Frederick Henry was certainly valuable. He was the only man of any power on the Continent prepared to exert himself on behalf of the King's cause—Henrietta Maria knew full well that she could expect nothing from her brother, the King of France, and his government. Without Frederick's help Charles I could not have held out so long. Indeed, Frederick Henry's services were far from small. Not only did he bear the burden of Henrietta Maria's retinue, but he took immediate steps to borrow for her on his own credit a sum of 300,000 guilders, and this at a time when his own income was no longer adequate for his standard of living.[53] As captain general of the States' army, moreover, he could render the King great service by allowing English officers serving under him to join the royalist army.[54] Thus it was that in August 1642 Charles's nephew Prince Rupert left the Republic with his brother Maurice and a following of some hundred officers. Frederick Henry even placed one of the country's warships at their disposal when it proved difficult to find a means of transport.[55] Moreover, in spite of the scruples of the responsible official,[56] he allowed guns from the country's arsenal to be sold to the royalists.

This was not enough. One of the main things the Queen had to do in the Netherlands was to raise a loan on the crown jewels, which were valued[57] at a sum of 1,265,300 guilders. It was no easy undertaking. The bankers thought the stones too large, and they did not in general care to do business with princes; but the greatest difficulty was that the Parliament had made a serious protest to Joachimi that the Queen had no authority to dispose of the jewels. Heenvliet, who represented the Prince with the Queen in Holland (the Prince himself had been with the army in the field since June), did all he could by interceding with men of experience and influence, but it soon became clear that the transaction was impossible unless the Prince was willing to raise a loan on the jewels in Amsterdam in his own name, and thus run directly counter to a protest of the Parliament. Heenvliet had once declared to the Queen[58] that it would not do openly to provide arms from the arsenals while preparations were being made for mediation between the contending parties in England, that this would be "procéder contre la foy publique et tout honneur." Whether it was any more loyal or honorable to do it in an underhand way is a moot point; but the raising of a loan on the crown jewels in Amsterdam in the Prince's name—for Frederick Henry succumbed to the entreaties of the Queen, faithfully repeated to him by Heenvliet—was done more or less publicly.

Was Frederick Henry won over by the power of her pathetic entreaties, or was he moved by the reproaches that Henrietta Maria, proud and passionate, did not spare him? The promise of fresh favors carried more persuasive power than the reference to those already granted, now that the little Princess had been delivered up irrevocably to the house of Orange,[59] and undoubtedly more also than the pressure the child herself had at times to exert at the instance of her despairing parents.[60] If Frederick Henry and Amalia of Solms (for express mention is frequently made of her zeal,[61] and it is well known how ambitious she was) took so much trouble to satisfy the Queen, if they suffered her vehemence and her threats, if they led the Republic again and again to the brink of a breach with the Parliament and were ready to bear the brunt of a bitter contest with the States of Holland, it was above all because the prospect was held out to them of a second marriage, a marriage between the Prince of Wales and their daughter, Louise Henrietta.

Their daughter to be Queen of England—even in the perilous circumstances in which the Stuarts found themselves, this seemed to the Prince and Princess well worth all that unpleasantness and even the lowering of the prestige of Orange with the Calvinists at home. While still in England, Henrietta Maria had broached the idea with Heenvliet. Now, in conjunction with the Queen's councilors, Goring and Jermyn, they worked together continuously to win over the Prince. Jermyn, wrote Heenvliet, was urging the affair of the jewels and the permission for officers and soldiers: "il mesle tousjours parmy son discours l'affaire que V.A. sçait."[62] He did not do it very delicately either, but said quite bluntly, as Heenvliet reported, "that the one thing would be done in return for the other and not for nothing." This was why

Heenvliet was always anxious lest the Queen should be displeased (at least if for a moment his personal interests are left out of account),[63] and this it was that led him to "make excuses" for the States of Holland[64] and to speak so highly of the good disposition of the Prince. And this also was why the Prince, as he himself expressed it, did "the impossible" in order to please her.[65]

The most important question during the Queen's stay in Holland (she returned in March 1643, after the loan on the jewels)—the question, too, that led to the first serious clash of the Prince of Orange and his adherents with the States of Holland—was in connection with the export of the arms and munitions that had been bought for the King in the Netherlands, and with that question was bound up the question of the attitude to be adopted toward Strickland, the envoy whom the Parliament had sent to the Netherlands in September 1642 expressly to prevail upon the States to forbid the traffic. Heenvliet was taken aback by the Queen's excitement at the appearance of "this person"—an excitement that grew to a pitch when the States-General received him, not, it is true, in a full assembly, but through a deputation from all the provinces—and listened to his message. The crucial item in this was a complaint that a number of ships laden with munitions for the King's army had been equipped in Dutch harbors; several were at that very moment lying ready for departure. The majority of the States-General had only reluctantly decided to receive the envoy. They had at first tried to escape from the necessity by raising all sorts of pretexts, and immediately after having given way, in order to soften the impression of their actions, they had given a ceremonious reception to one of the King's ambassadors who was passing through the country.[66]

It is not surprising that the States-General dared not offer an affront to the Parliament. Its dominance was now assured over the greater, or at least, the more important, part of England, and above all, it was powerful at sea—and the Parliament men were at least as anxious as had been the kings to watch over the trading and colonial interests of England. In Joachimi's correspondence, for all that he avoided contacts with the Parliament as much as he could, there are repeated reports of complaints and threats laid before him by the new officeholders in connection with such matters. The Prince and his supporters, who were not in ordinary circumstances primarily concerned about the interests of Holland trade, did not now miss an occasion to point out how detrimental it would be to allow the English Parliament to come out on top. The Hollanders retorted that the Parliament's irritability over such issues was in reality due to the unfair and offensive treatment it received at the hands of the Orangist States-General. They insisted therefore that attention be paid to the complaints of Strickland, and knowing well that no determined action on the part of the States-General was to be expected in this matter, the States of Holland took the matter into their own hands and themselves ordered the detention of the ships to which Strickland had referred, all of which were making ready in Holland ports.

This roused the Queen to fury, and she was in no wise to be soothed by the circumstance that the Hollanders, once they had embarked on investigations, discovered also ships destined for the Parliament, and ordered that these should be detained with the others, because, they said, they wished to observe neutrality.[67] It was precisely this equality of treatment which she felt to be insulting. She called Frederick Henry to her assistance with the loudest complaints and reproaches. "The States," she declared to Heenvliet, "had promised that the marriage alliance should not be the concern merely of His Highness but also of the state; but they are not acting up to this."[68] The Prince, reminded in this way of the ambiguous assurances of Sommelsdijk, could hardly do less than admit that the Hollanders had been mistaken in their action,[69] but all the same, he could not change the policy of neutrality. Theoretically there might be something to be said for the view that it was only to the King that the Republic was bound by treaties,[70] but actually it was impossible to identify the King with England any longer now that the power of the Parliament had become so great and tangible a reality.

Small wonder, then, that throughout this affair Holland enjoyed the support of Zeeland, although in the States of this province the Stadholder, in his capacity of first noble and lord of the two towns of Veere and Flushing, had an exceptionally strong position. So high did the resentment run over the way in which the States-General allowed themselves to be managed by the Prince, that there was some talk of a closer association between the two seaboard provinces, and even of secession. The Grand Pensionary of Zeeland and the First Noble's representative, De Kruyt, exchanged acrimonious words in the provincial States assembly. But all things considered, the Prince's policy was so impossible that he could not maintain it in the States-General.

On November 1, 1642, Their High Mightinesses issued a general proclamation forbidding the export of arms to either of the contending parties. Thus the principle maintained by Holland was definitely accepted as an article of federal policy, and Strickland had gained an important success.[71]

Yet the Prince continued to work against it in an underhand

way, and as several of the smaller provinces and some of the administrative colleges of the generality were devoted to him, he was able to do so with no little effect. The greffier of the States-General, the notorious Cornelis Musch, a great friend of Heenvliet according to the latter's own statement,[72] was invaluable as an agent for invalidating the resolutions ordering the detention of munitions ships which his masters, to keep up appearances, were every now and again obliged to issue. Strickland felt greatly aggrieved by his attitude.[73] He took to heart even more the treatment he was to receive, in the beginning of December at the hands of Renswoude, one of the gentlemen, be it noted, who shortly before had been appointed to take part in a mediatory embassy (about which more hereafter).[74] Strickland went to him on one occasion when he happened to be "President of the Week" (of the States-General) to talk to him about some ships at Medemblik which were to transport officers and two to three hundred men besides twenty guns. Without even looking at the note that Strickland had handed to him, Renswoude declared that Strickland could not prove the facts of his complaint and demanded the name of his informant. But, writes Strickland, no English or Dutch merchant would have cared to be mentioned as informant for fear of the displeasure of "great ones." So angry was he that he told his government he could be of no use in the Netherlands unless it was made clear that there must be an end of such treatment. Probably with a view to mollifying him, the Prince himself received Strickland when the latter came to him shortly after this incident with a letter from the Parliament.[75] But this roused the anger of Henrietta Maria—to such an extent that the Prince instructed his confidants to declare that Strickland had taken him by surprise and that he should not be received again.

Soon after this a far more serious clash took place between the Parliament's envoy and the States-General. The Queen had at last taken her leave—to the relief of the States-General, says the Venetian ambassador in England, and we can well believe him! But even her departure was accompanied by dissonance and friction. With the ship in which on February 28, 1643, she crossed to England, there sailed another, crammed full with arms and soldiers. Parliament men-of-war had intended to intercept her at the mouth of the river Maas. But she was escorted by a Dutch fleet under Tromp, who had to defend her, even after her landing, against a bombardment by a Parliament squadron.[76] Shortly afterward Strickland approached the States-General with the complaint that there were twenty-four ships lying at Dunkirk (in the Spanish Netherlands) all ready to sail out against the Parliament, and that the Prince of Orange had already given passports to two of them to enable them to get through the Dutch blockade. The Prince's attitude in the face of the danger that Spain might use Dunkirk as a base from which to help Charles I by sending support to the Catholic revolt in Ireland had for a long time past given rise to suspicion. But the Prince explicitly denied the imputation now made against him, and the States-General, packed with his supporters, resented so greatly the insult offered to the Stadholder that it looked for a time as though the incident would lead to a rupture of relations between the Republic and the Parliament. Once more, however, matters were smoothed over. The Parliament (where Tromp's statement that he had let the two ships pass on the strength of a letter of the Queen was met with skepticism: he must at least have had oral instructions from the Prince, so it was thought there) allowed itself to be pacified by "letters from Holland." Soon the Orange party tried to bring about the breach in another way.

Attempts to mediate between the contending parties seemed to offer an opportunity. As early as January 1642, Joachimi as the Republic's ambassador in England had been instructed to make an offer of mediation. But Joachimi was not the man the royalists wanted. The States-General would have liked to give him the support of Heenvliet, who was at that moment still at the English court in the capacity of envoy from the Prince of Orange. Holland, however, refused to agree to this because mediation through Heenvliet would have been tantamount to choosing sides. The Prince of Orange endeavored nevertheless to induce Joachimi to submit to the co-operation of Heenvliet "either in my name or otherwise," [77] but the States of Holland had taken the precaution of informing Joachimi of their objection,[78] and so nothing came of the Prince's efforts. And in truth, when one sees what Heenvliet's conception of the task of a mediator was, it is difficult to do otherwise than applaud the Hollanders' discernment. Heenvliet objected to Joachimi's way of carrying out his work as mediator in the open. He, Heenvliet, would have begun with secret attempts, in consultation with the King, to lure certain gentlemen from the parliamentary party by offers of titles, offices, and other favors.[79] Joachimi never got a chance, because soon he had to report that the parliamentary party would not hear of mediation at all.

Yet, when Henrietta Maria arrived at The Hague, a plan had immediately been mooted to send a special embassy for this very purpose. Holland alone, basing its policy on reports from Joachimi "that no mediator from this country would be pleasing to the Parliament,"[80] held up the proposal in the States-General, but in May the province had to come into line—not, however, without making reservations.[81] One of these, namely, that the ambassadors should not attempt to sow dissensions among the members of the Parliament, shows that there were apprehensions that Heenvliet's methods might still be adopted. In fact, the gentlemen delegated for the embassy, William Boreel and Reede van Renswoude, both Orangists, notoriously inclined toward the royalist cause.[82]

But it was a long time before they set out on their mission. At first the English royalists in Holland, much to the annoyance of the Prince of Orange, would have nothing to do with the peace mission.[83] Later it was once more Holland that obstructed it. It was hinted in the States-General that Holland thought the continuation of the civil war would be advantageous to its trade;[84] and Boswell, Charles's resident at The Hague, in the bitterness of his heart, made the same observation.[85] But it is not probable that it was this conviction that led the States of Holland to sabotage the mediation. Their principal objection was, without doubt, that an embassy over which the Prince of Orange had so much influence would inevitably get too closely involved with the royalist party and would lead the Netherlands into difficulties with the Parliament.

These were questions of great consequence. The English marriage and the resulting complications had placed the Stadholder in sharp contrast to a broad public opinion on issues of vital interest to the state as a whole. As always, it was first of all the States of Holland who disposed of the political power needed to switch over from disapproval to opposition, and inevitably they directed their attack against the personal authority over foreign policy which the Prince had been building up before he had discredited his person by indulging in dynastic ambitions. Holland could no longer leave any of the hotly contested issues concerning England to the decision of the Secret Committee, in which its deputy could be voted down by the Prince's other "gentlemen of the cabinet" while remaining bound to secrecy with regard to his own "principals." We saw above that already in 1642 the province had ventured privately to warn the States-General's ambassador, Joachimi, not to accept Heenvliet as joint mediator. This was rather a strong step for the province to take. But it was inevitable that in the face of the English entanglement Holland should try all means to wrest the lead of national affairs from the Stadholder. His abuse of generality powers—"abuse" because of his dynastic aim as well as because of the methods of pressure and corruption applied to the deputies of the smaller provinces—could be most readily countered by Holland taking its stand on the principle of provincial sovereignty. This is what the States of Holland now did, with shattering effect on the Prince's policy. The private warning to Joachimi had been applauded by that staunch republican Van Reigersberch as a welcome "sign of public vigor." Yet he had gone on to speak slightingly of "particular views" as the motive force behind that action and to deplore that this vigor "was nowhere to be found in matters of greater importance and weight."[86] In the next year he had nothing to complain of any more.

In August 1643, in fact, the States of Holland drew up a new instruction for their deputies in the States-General, upon which these gentlemen were to take an oath. It was intended to tie them more strictly than before to the directives of their States. In particular they were instructed not to act on a number of points without such directives, in the assembly of Their High Mightinesses *or elsewhere*. Among the points specified were: "peace or truce, war, negotiations with other potentates about alliance or aid, lands or cities, . . . also the sending abroad of ambassadors or any notable deputation." All the eighteen towns voted in favor, without any reservations; only the "member of the nobility" (a committee of some five or six men representing the entire order and casting one vote of the total of nineteen) made difficulties. Aitzema takes care to point out in passing that the "member"—meaning the entire delegation—of the nobility "depended entirely upon the Prince." The States of Holland overrode that opposition. It is clear that by means of this instruction they killed the Secret Committee instituted nine years before, and that this is what they meant to do. The lord of Mathenes, the nobleman in the Holland delegation in the States-General, had objected that "it is necessary sometimes to secrete matters among a few." "But that," Aitzema comments, "was the very reason why those of Holland wanted the instruction, because under that pretext, as they said, the most important matters were settled by the Prince with some gentlemen 'assumed' by him."[87]

It is idle in this connection to blame the Holland States party for having sacrificed a promising unitary institution to provincial particularism. Too often, unfortunately, the States-General, and especially this otherwise so useful Secret Committee, had appeared to the Hollanders not as the true representatives of Union interests, but as the tools of an ambitious stadholder. How generally concern was felt over Frederick Henry's policy is shown by the fact that in nearly all the provinces attempts were made to follow the example set by the Holland instruction, but only in Gelderland was something similar brought off; everywhere else the Orange party managed to block the way.[88] This does not necessarily mean (to repeat the caution) that in those provinces there was any real sympathy with Frederick Henry's foreign policy. Aitzema tells a story that gives plain evidence of the contrary for the province of Overijsel. A man who went there in October 1643 to apply for the office of Bailiff of Salland, and who carried with him letters of recommendation from the Prince, discovered "that the Overijsel towns, both on account of the English marriage and because they did not like His Highness favoring the King of England more than the Parliament, would not be much impressed by this recommendation and that it might do him harm rather than advance his cause. For which reason he kept the letters by him."[89]

The fact remained, nevertheless, that the Prince could still count on the deputies of most of the provinces in the States-General, and the struggle therefore continued with increasing bitterness. To begin with, Holland could not prevent the mission of Boreel and Renswoude. The province endeavored to obtain that a third man of less pronounced Orangist proclivities should be added to the delegation.[90] But nothing came of this, and it was difficult for Holland to persist in its opposition when, in 1643, the position in England seemed to have altered so much to the disadvantage of the Parliament that Joachimi declared that the embassy would be able to accomplish something, while Strickland refused to make any pronouncement. Thus in October 1643 Holland agreed to the departure of the envoys, and early in the following year they at last set out.

It is no more than natural that the leaders of the parliamentary party received the envoys with suspicion. The war was suddenly taking a turn in their favor again: they had concluded an alliance with Scotland; Charles was in grave danger. In the beginning of December 1643 a letter was intercepted, in which one of Charles's councilors wrote to a royalist at The Hague to urge the necessity of sending the mediators.[91] Even before this, however, it was well known in England that the mediation emanated from the Orangist States-General, and that both the envoys extraordinary were declared adherents of the Prince of Orange and had already shown themselves inimical to the Parliament. Also, it can hardly have been a secret that Renswoude carried on a regular correspondence with the Stadholder's court.[92] Thus, when the ambassadors were at Oxford, where the King had his court, we find the Scotsman Baillie writing that they would be able to accomplish nothing, "for they are taken here [in London] for the Prince of Orange's creatures."[93]

It is not surprising that the envoys met with a better reception in Oxford than in London, where the parliamentary leaders had done their best to isolate them.[94] Baillie complains loudly that, taking advantage of a moment of discouragement after the disaster of Newark, Renswoude and Boreel created dissension in the Parliament, and between England and Scotland,[95] and the ambassadors themselves admit in their report—which, however, as Holland was sure to examine it closely, can only have been written with a minimum of frankness—that they were persuaded to stay a little longer in London so that the "good" people, i.e., the peace lovers, might not lose hope of some arrangement.[96] After another journey to Oxford they came back to London and stayed there for months, but all they got was empty compliments, and they were treated at times with a good deal of impatience. Among the people wild rumors were afloat concerning the evil intentions of the principals of the so-called mediators, who felt themselves to be in so false a position that they begged to be recalled. The States-General, however, instructed them to make one more attempt. Without doubt the Prince of Orange and his royalist friends had come to think that they would yet be able to do service to the King's cause.[97] So they went—it was now 1645—for the third time from London to Oxford and back again. On this occasion the suspicions of the parliamentary party[98] led to an unpleasant incident, which was taken very much to heart by the ambassadors, and it was in a very bad humor that, in April 1645, they delivered their farewell speech to the Parliament, a speech that added fuel to the flames. In it they made it very clear that they held the parliamentary party to blame for their failure, and in London the conclusion was drawn that the States-General had at last decided to range themselves openly with the King.

Certainly the report that the ambassadors presented to the States-General on their return seemed to point to that conclusion,[99] and it is difficult to escape the impression that in this they were faithful to the intention the Orange party had from the first attached to their mission. At any rate, we know from letters that have been preserved by chance[100] that in April, while the envoys were still in England, the Prince of Orange was already discussing with an emissary of the King, one Dr. Goffe, how to make the best use of their return in order to get the States on the side of the King,[101] and that after their return they were working, in close touch with the Stadholder's court and with the same Dr. Goffe, to overcome the opposition of Holland to their war policy. Goffe was delighted at their zeal. The Prince of Orange himself spoke of them in the highest terms to the Englishman: "Ils se crèveront," said he, if they do not succeed in accomplishing some good.[102] And Goffe declared that their report was so clearly in favor of the King, that no better plea could have been made for his case by one of his own subjects.[103] As for Boreel, his "mind was set on serving the King," and he was determined to do something in the States "which shall be very high and bold."[104]

But the bold plan did not succeed. What no doubt paralyzed Frederick Henry's action was that he could not, as he would have done a few years before, deal with the report in his "cabinet," with some "assumed gentlemen." Everything came before "the full assembly" of the States-General, and it was not so easy there to dispose of Holland's neutrality policy, with which most of the deputies at heart sympathized. The Prince, however, had not given up hope of reaching his goal by devious paths. As late as June he was still assuring Goffe that everything would come right:

> Hee [Goffe writes] had given Sir William Boswell his taske, to propose the liberty of their Havens and hiring of ships, and the Ambassadors theirs to urge the necessity of granting of Letters of Reprisall to the many complaints received in England from their owne people, and then he added: Croyés-moy, par ce moyen ils seront menés insensiblement dans une guerre.[105] [The word "insensiblement" speaks volumes.]

But this was equally unsuccessful. The King's envoy had already tried, in "poincten van consideratie," to draw attention to the harm caused to trade by the Parliament's supremacy at sea.[106] But the Hollanders, who must have smiled to themselves at the ardor of the Stadholder's party for their trade interests, managed to get the States-General to refer these matters, too, to the provinces and thus to postpone them. However, the Orangist deputies in the States-General certainly succeeded in making the Parliament suffer a few pinpricks. When, for instance, Strickland came forward to clear his masters from blame for the lack of respect shown to the ambassadors during their stay in London—a great deal was made of the "insults" offered them by the Parliament—he was, at the instance of Boswell, denied a hearing. Whereupon, however, the States of Holland received him, and he was able to express himself freely to this body over the partiality with which the ambassadors had conducted themselves in England. Holland was not so easily intimidated as Dr. Goffe and the Prince had anticipated, and still less so since several other provinces, somewhat hesitatingly to be sure, ventured to join in the opposition to the unpopular Stuart policy of the court.[107]

Even apart from the general question of war or peace with Spain, which began to be acute again in 1645, this was not the only point of foreign politics on which the Prince and the States differed. In 1644 and 1645 a war raged in the Baltic, in which Holland, almost dragging the States-General along, threw the weight of its powerful influence on the side of Sweden. That Holland's trade interests required this policy leaps to the eye. Denmark controlled the Sound and took advantage of this position to exact tolls that no country felt so heavily as did the Netherlands. Added to this was the fact that in the wider European policy Denmark had for a long time been inclining toward the Hapsburg party. But the King of Denmark was an uncle of Charles I, and in the plans made untiringly by the latter's friends for his relief, an important part was assigned to Denmark.

The outbreak of the northern war was a disappointment to the royalists, who had all through 1643 and 1644 been counting on help from Danish troops.[108] Especially when the war turned to the advantage of Sweden, Frederick Henry thought it his business to save Denmark, but the States of Holland were not to be restrained. The Prince's warning that his plans against Antwerp would be endangered by a new war—and this was the only argument of which he could make open use[109]—had little or no influence on Holland, which did not particularly desire the conquest of the great commercial town on the Schelde. On the contrary, at the beginning of 1645 the Hollanders threatened to withhold all contributions to the campaign in the Southern Netherlands, if they were not allowed to carry out their northern policy. Frederick Henry, burdened with the odium of his dynastic policy, could not prevail against the powerful public opinion that was with the States of Holland in this matter too. However, with the help of Zeeland, which was more dependent on him than any other province, he obstructed Holland's policy as much as was possible, and his attitude so embittered the Hollanders that one man felt called upon to warn him "not to strain this rope too much lest greater ill arise therefrom."[110]

The public of that day had its suspicions, which were to be confirmed in the following year,[111] as to the incentive for this new outburst of zeal for the Stuart cause. At the beginning of 1644, when the two mediators were on the point of crossing to England, a French diplomat at The Hague wrote[112] that a number of people were of the opinion that Renswoude had a commission to open fresh negotiations with a view to a marriage between the Prince of Wales and Louise Henrietta of Orange. There is no evidence that this was so: no trace of it is to be found in the archives of the House of Orange; in Renswoude's own letters the subject is not mentioned, and in the correspondence with the English his name does not occur. But the first letter of Renswoude which has been preserved is not until April 7,[113] and it is apparent from what he writes to Huygens on more than one occasion that he had other channels for keeping in touch with the Prince while he was in England. In any case, it is a fact that he and his colleagues had hardly arrived in Oxford, when the subject of the marriage, which had been allowed to lapse[114] in 1643, when the King's prospects seemed more cheerful, was again broached in a letter from Jermyn to Heenvliet.[115] And so while the Netherlands envoys were "mediating" under an instruction which expressly forbade them to listen to proposals for an alliance until the contending parties were reconciled,[116] Charles I and Frederick Henry were busily negotiating not only about the second marriage scheme, but, in close connection with this, also about a political alliance. In 1641 the English court had been content with a marriage alone, relying on the assurances of Sommelsdijk that in this way the royalists would win the friendship of the States. Now, with the wisdom of experience, the English wanted to make a formal alliance with the Dutch Republic the price of the marriage.

The plan in the form in which it was presented to Frederick Henry in June 1644 by Dr. Goffe contained two alternatives:[117] if France was willing to participate, it was to be a triple alliance, whereby the Republic would provide ships for the transport of French troops to England; if France was not willing to participate, the Republic was to conclude a truce with Spain, in order to have its hands free, and to send the English troops in Dutch service over to England by whole regiments. Frederick Henry replied immediately that a truce with Spain was impossible without France, in view of the treaties with the latter country. Indeed, a month or two before this date, the French plenipotentiaries for the congress at Munster had written from The Hague, that the Prince of Orange was too conscious to the unpopularity he had brought upon himself by the English connection to risk a peace that would make it easier to get on without a captain general.[118] To conclude peace or a truce without France, which would thus become alienated, with the express purpose of forging a still closer bond with the Stuarts, would be too hazardous. But it did not seem at all impossible that France would participate. Since the death of Richelieu in 1642, a more favorable attitude toward the Stuarts had grown up in that country, and Charles was not without hopes in his negotiations with Mazarin.[119] Thus it was that in 1645 the Prince of Orange had accepted the English conditions that he should try to induce the States to declare against the Parliament, and that he should have a force of three thousand fighting men raised and sent to England; but only in conjunction with France.[120]

But we have already seen that the danger spurred the States

of Holland to a successful resistance. The triple alliance between France, the Republic, and Charles I, on which the English royalists had set their hopes, came to nothing. Yet another member of the Stuart combination, Denmark, as we have already seen, was put out of action by Holland, despite the endeavors of Frederick Henry. Circumstances, moreover, favored Holland. France's co-operation was often lukewarm. If Frederick Henry did not always display sufficient energy in the struggle with the States of Holland in May and June 1645, this was attributed by the mediators then back from England to "private discouragements" he had suffered at the hands of France. They advised, therefore, that the Queen of England should try to use her influence with the Queen Regent and Cardinal Mazarin.[121] But fate was against the whole scheme. The Stuart cause itself went down with a rush. On June 24, 1645 the army of Charles was routed at Naseby. From papers captured on that occasion the Parliament was able to prove, as it had indeed suspected for a long time, that the King had been negotiating with the Catholic Irish rebels—thus robbing him of the last remaining vestige of honor in Protestant eyes.[122] During the period that Charles wandered about before the final surrender to the Scottish army in May 1648, he had practically no army any more, only irregular bands, of which the principal was after a while the one commanded by the most romantic of all Cavaliers, Montrose.

Frederick Henry became only the more eager to offer help, but it could now be nothing but the old policy of unauthorized actions and obstructions pursued as far as he dared.[123] It was a curious position. Not only did the Stadholder consider himself justified in making use of the envoys, supposed to be mediating in England in the name of the States, for intrigues with the royalists, and in making plans, without any reference to the States, with the ambassadors of Charles I and with France, he even presumed to withdraw a few ships from the blockade of the Flemish coast and to place them at the disposal of the Queen of England.[124] But his real concern at the end of 1645 and the beginning of 1646 was the equipment in Holland or Zeeland of a considerable fleet for the transport of troops, French troops or such as the Duke of Lorraine[125] was prepared to provide. At first it was hoped that the peace in the Baltic (September 1645), which brought a stream of ships back to Dutch harbors, would provide a good opportunity. Particularly in Zeeland, where the Prince's servant (his representative as First Noble) De Knuyt, was lending his help, the English agents hoped to get a good fleet together.[126] Again, nothing came of the Prince's efforts. In the early months of 1646 some ten ships were being equipped in Amsterdam at French expense and were doubtless intended for the English adventure. The States of Holland, acting upon complaints from England, induced the States-General, which had been long inactive, to put an end to this undertaking.

All Frederick Henry's great plans were linked together. The support that was to be given to Charles I must be based on the alliance with France. France in its turn must help Frederick Henry to win a share of the Southern Netherlands, either by war or by peace with Spain, for early in 1646 there was talk of a reconciliation between France and Spain with the Southern Netherlands as a prize to be paid for by the evacuation of Catalonia. The French obtained the Prince's agreement to this scheme not only by holding out the prospect of an independent position for him outside the dominion of the States[127] (preferably in Antwerp), but also by hinting that, if only they had their hands free in relation to Spain, stronger co-operation might be expected from them in the restoration of Charles I.[128] To the States these plans were not only objectionable in themselves, but they were particularly disturbing because they so clearly tended to increase the power of the Stadholder. Allied to two great monarchs, one of whom, the French King, would have become an immediate neighbor of the Republic, master of a new and important territory, the States could no longer have stood up to Frederick Henry.

But the Spanish-French plan for peace on the basis of an exchange, too, was exploded, for suddenly it became clear that it had never been more than a feint by which the Spaniards intended to create dissension between the States and France. The States were indeed greatly alarmed by the rumors that the Spaniards let purposely transpire, while the Prince, for his part, when he found that he had been taken in, could do nothing but hurry to the States-General and deny all knowledge of the transaction. This did not really clear him in their eyes.[129]

This proved the final failure. Frederick Henry could not carry through his policy. In April 1646 the negotiations for a marriage between the Prince of Wales and the Stadholder's daughter were definitely broken off.[130] In May, as we saw above, Charles I had to surrender. About this time the piquant details of Frederick Henry's secret negotiations with the Stuarts, which had come into the possession of the Parliament with the papers of Lord Digby, became known in the Netherlands. Dr. Goffe's reports about his conversations with the Stadholder—some details of which I mentioned already—appeared in a Dutch translation.

The Holland regents, in studying this most confidential correspondence about their Stadholder's foreign intrigues, must have found their own thoughts expressed in the prayer of thanks with which the English Puritans introduced the publication. "God's blessings," so they could read there, "appear in the discovery of the enemy's counsels as well as in the dispersal of his hosts." The self-confidence of the leading province was considerably strengthened. Holland could now only with difficulty be persuaded to provide a meager sum for the new campaign in the Southern Netherlands. The great scheme, so much was clear, was doomed to fail in every detail. The Prince, discouraged, old before his time, felt his authority totter.

All through those years the storm of opposition against Frederick Henry's dynastic policy had been gaining force. Annoyance at the involvement with the unfortunate Stuart family, a settled suspicion that every suggestion made by Frederick Henry was inspired by his determination to acquire sovereign power—these were the sentiments that gave impetus to the anti-Stadholder movement. In 1646 matters had gone so far that three members of the States of Holland dared to tell the Stadholder to his face that in his dealings with France his sole object was to oppress Holland, and when the Prince refused to take them seriously, their principals came and repeated the accusation.[131] The French plenipotentiaries at Münster, who were trying to keep the Republic from engaging in serious negotiations with Spain for which the Hollanders thought the time had come, and who in 1646 were continually traveling back and forth between Münster and The Hague, noticed with the greatest displeasure that the reality of power now rested with the States of Holland.[132] Already in April[133] they feared that Frederick Henry, anxious for the future of his House, would prefer to give way and allow the States to conclude a separate peace with Spain in direct contravention of the treaty of alliance with France (of 1635) by which the contracting parties had undertaken to make peace only jointly.

And so in fact it turned out. Amalia of Solms saw greater advantage[134] in accepting the proposals of Spain, which would bring to the family, according to the French ambassadors, "3 ou 400,000 livres de rente." Considering how little chance there was of a return of the sums advanced to the Stuarts, the temptation must have been very great. The increasing helplessness of the old Prince certainly explains in some degree Amalia's choice as well as his. Young William, his son, soon his successor, did not think the game lost yet; he resisted the change of policy as much as he could, and was furious with De Knuyt, who had arranged the bargain with Spain (empowered thereto by the Princess, although he did not forget to line his own pocket in the transaction).

The truth of the matter was that Frederick Henry's dynastic policy in conjunction with Stuart and France had called into being forces that he could not control. At the end of his life the whole edifice of his great scheme was crumbling, while the States of Holland stood triumphant.

B
William II and the Stuarts

William II had not wanted to give way as his parents had, and when his father died, in March 1647, it might have been supposed that he would still manage to accomplish something, for peace with Spain had not yet been concluded. He had in fact, while his father was still alive, been in close communication with the French ambassadors, who did not fail to appeal to his ambition, giving him to understand that his greatness depended on France, and that France was prepared to do everything to maintain, nay even to advance, his interests.[135] When he became stadholder this relationship naturally became even more intimate, and the French vigorously urged him to prevent the treaty of 1635 from being broken.[136]

But although the young Prince made a few attempts proving that he still cherished the plans his father had abandoned in despair and was anxious to avert a peace that would mean their complete breakdown, his French friends soon evinced their bitter disappointment in him. It was clear that "ce bon petit Prince," as De la Thuillerie scornfully calls the twenty-one-year-old youth,[137] could not stand up against the States of Holland. "Neither determination nor prudence"—in these terms does Servien characterize William's conduct in the critical conflict with the States in this first phase of his stadholdership. In May 1648 the Count d'Estrades writes bluntly that he has received a most unfavorable impression of the young Prince: he does not seem to care about the inroads made on his authority by the States, lost as he is in frivolity and debauchery; advice is wasted on him, for all his time is spent on hunting and playing ball. And so about this very time the peace with Spain was made.

But strangely enough, no sooner was the separate peace an accomplished fact than William II seemed to throw off his indifference. Brasset records, on July 13, 1648, a firm resolution made by the Prince two days previously, to apply himself seriously to business from that day on,[138] and although at first sight one is inclined to smile at a promise of amendment announced so emphatically beforehand, it is certain that during the two years of life that still remained to him William II cut a very different figure. Although there are reports of wine and women even in this latter period, there is no further mention of indifference, of lack of ambition or of courage. On the contrary, from that time forward William II threw himself with youthful impetuosity and rashness into the task of undoing the peace and resuming with France, not only the plans for partitioning the Southern Netherlands, but also the scheme for the restoration of the Stuarts.

There appeared to be more hope for the Stuarts in 1648 than there had been in the years immediately preceding. The increasing power of the party of the Independents, who had the disposal of the army under Cromwell and Fairfax and opposed the introduction of a stiff-necked and intolerant Calvinist theocracy by the Presbyterian Parliament, seemed to offer a good chance to Charles I in his captivity. After having in the first place made advances to the Independents, he unexpectedly attached himself to the Presbyterians, and a new civil war broke out in which Presbyterians and royalists joined forces. Their main hopes were centered in a Scottish army under the Duke of Hamilton, but there were serious disturbances in the south of England as well. In the beginning of June, a number of ships belonging to the parliamentary navy declared for the King, and sought a refuge on the roadstead of Helvoetsluis. At first the young Duke of York, who had lately fled from England, tried to secure the command of this fleet, but the lack of unity among his counselors caused such confusion that the Prince of Wales was called to the rescue. He arrived at Helvoetsluis on July 21, and to his brother's great indignation deprived him of his command.

The Prince of Wales had spent two years in France, where his mother was still continuing her vain efforts to induce Mazarin's government to render some effectual aid. Mazarin's main idea was to prevent any party in England from achieving a complete victory which by restoring unity might renew England's power, and for this reason he was inclined to encourage resistance to the Independent army, which he feared most of all. But just at this time, owing partly to the defection of the Dutch Republic, partly to the domestic disturbances of the *Fronde*, France was in no position to spare money or troops for an English expedition. Once more all the hopes of the royalists were centered in a Prince of Orange.

An envoy from the Scottish Committee of Estates, dominated at that time by the royalist Presbyterian party of Hamilton, had just had to report from Amsterdam that the States would not hear of an alliance with Scotland against the English Independents—no wonder when it is remembered that even loyal adherents of the Prince of Orange, as we shall see presently, placed no faith (and rightly) in the power of the Hamilton party—and that William II himself was not equal to his position.[139] This was about the time of the Prince's resolve to begin a new life. It soon became clear, in spite of the pessimism of the Scot, that William was indeed ready to render all the help that lay in his power. It is true that he could not move the States of Holland. He even frankly admitted this to his brother-in-law, warning him not to expect any action that would be too directly opposed to the declaration of neutrality, and also not to count on financial support from the States.[140] All that could be expected was the kind of help his father had always given—whereby he had almost ruined himself without averting the fall of the luckless Stuart family. Together with that same somewhat incalculable Duke of Lorraine on whom hopes had been set even in Frederick Henry's day, the Prince raised troops, which were encamped for the time being at Borcum, and for whose use he chartered a couple of ships in Amsterdam. This transaction took place in consultation with the English royalists.[141] At the same time the Prince arranged for the purchase of munitions for the Scottish army,[142] up to a sum of 30,000 francs.

This was the first business into which William II threw himself heart and soul after his resolve to improve his manner of life, and his own servants observed it with profound concern. A man like Heenvliet, to be sure, served without offering criticism and was content if he won the gratitude of the Stuarts.[143] But the letters in which De Wilhem, the member of "His Highness's Council" who was commissioned to carry out the work, describes his activities to his brother-in-law, Huygens, are one long lamentation. De Wilhem ventured to warn his master against "getting more deeply involved in the English labyrinth," but no attention was paid to him.

In particular De Wilhem complained most bitterly of the incapacity and intractability of the servants of the Prince of Wales and of the infinite confusion prevailing among his counselors.[144] Culpepper was the man who had the most influence with the Prince of Wales in those days, and predominance on the whole was with the party that, following the lead of the Queen and her confidant, Jermyn, placed all its hopes in the Presbyterians. True Episcopalians, such as Sir Edward Hyde and Sir Edward Nicholas, had already been attached by the King to his son, but they were not yet making their influence felt. It is certainly remarkable that De Wilhem, as strict a Calvinist as any of the Prince of

Orange's followers, was so little impressed by the policy of working with the Presbyterians. In any case, his judgment was right. He realized that little reliance could be placed in the Hamilton party, which was losing ground even in Scotland, and he shook his head over the imprudence of exposing the Prince of Wales in such a hopeless enterprise. For after fruitlessly cruising about the English coast for a week or two with his ill-disciplined fleet,[145] young Charles—he was eighteen at the time—did indeed make preparations to go and place himself at the head of the Scottish army. But he was still in The Hague when the news came that there was no longer a Scottish army: Cromwell had annihilated it at Preston (end of August 1648). The 30,000 francs worth of munitions too, which had just been dispatched, would now, says De Wilhem, probably fall into the enemy's hands; the troops at Borcum were disbanded, and the Prince of Wales with his ill-assorted retinue—Catholics, Episcopalians, and Presbyterians; English, Irish, and Scots—lingered on at The Hague at the expense of his brother-in-law of Orange,[146] his fleet blockaded at Brill by a parliamentary fleet under Warwick, and gradually disintegrating through lack of funds.

William II was himself of too active a nature not to be impatient at the ease with which the English Prince accommodated himself to his idleness. [147] As for the States of Holland, they would not have been sorry to see the parliamentary Admiral seize the opportunity and destroy the weaker royalist fleet at one bold stroke,[148] but when he neglected the opportunity, they could hardly do otherwise than observe neutrality. Soon afterward Rupert Prince Palatine was placed at the head of this fleet, and he with his indomitable energy succeeded in preventing further decay, even though there was the greatest difficulty in finding money and making the fleet seaworthy again. All sorts of ambitious plans were built on the possession of this force—the last almost on which the royalists could completely rely—but practically the only way in which Prince Rupert was ever able to use it, after he had set his course for Ireland early in 1649, was for privateering expeditions against English merchantmen, and this soon became the only source of income for young Charles in his exile.

The disaster at Preston had sealed the fate of Charles I. Scotland still maintained its independence: now that those Presbyterians who under Hamilton had thrown in their lot with the Stuart cause were beaten, power was in the hands of the implacable Presbyterians under Argyll. This party for the time being worked with the Independents although it did not really have any more in common with them than had the Hamilton Presbyterians. But in England there was now no longer any power capable of withstanding Cromwell. In December "Pride's Purge" expelled all oppositional elements from the Parliament, and in January the King appeared before his judges.

The Prince of Wales, who at the pleasure-loving court at The Hague, with his brilliant Palatine-Bohemian cousins and the beautiful sisters of his brother-in-law of Orange, had forgotten his political troubles amid gaieties, now had a rude awakening. On January 22, 1649 he received reports from which it became clear that his father's life was in jeopardy. The next day he appeared in the States-General, where Boswell spoke for him, saying: "J'ai horreur de dire, qu'un prince d'Angleterre vient requérir intercession pour la vie du Roi son pere." At the proposal of Holland it was resolved to send across without delay Joachimi, who was on leave in the country, and Pauw van Heemstede. Everybody realized that adherents of Orange would not be the best advocates to soften the hearts of the Independents. Without heeding storm and ice the envoys sped to London. It needed some insistence, although they were treated with due courtesy, to obtain access to the Parliament, which listened to their plea for the King's life in silence. The next day, January 30, 1649, O.S. (February 9, N.S.), Charles I was beheaded at Whitehall. A few hours later the Parliament issued a solemn warning that no man was to presume to claim the title of King of England.

The deed made a profound impression in the Netherlands. The nation, its own revolution already but a memory stored in the glorified annals of the past, saw with horror "the hosts of hell" building "their throne in England's realm," as Vondel expressed it. Even those who hitherto had been on the side of the Parliament, be it on grounds of freedom or of religion, expressed detestation. Such is the testimony of Aitzema,[149] the chronicler, and there is no doubt that it deserves every credence. Strickland, so it is said, dared not show his face in the streets.[150] The ministers of religion were vehement in their condemnation of "the atrocious deed." No doubt they had little sympathy with the Episcopalian doctrines, and even Catholic leanings, of the Prince of Wales and his counselors, but for a long time past they had looked on the looming specter of Independentism with the greatest uneasiness. The Zeeland ministry, under the influence of Spang, and Voetius himself, the "Pope of the Dutch Reformed Church," as he was sometimes called, were no less vigorous in their protests against Independentism, that is against freedom of worship (at least for Protestants), than against Episcopalianism. The religious sympathies of the Netherlands Calvinists were entirely with the Presbyterians, who had now suffered defeat in England. The *odium theologicum* is clearly seen in the address in which four Hague clerics felt it their immediate duty to offer condolence and comfort to the son of the King who had been deprived of his life. After vigorous manifestations of horror at "this unheard of parricide, that accursed destruction of the holy, anointed head, and that never sufficiently to be deplored murder of this one King of the Reformed Faith," the reverend gentlemen declare that from this can be seen "what it is to be an Independent."[151] But they were reprimanded very sharply by the temporal powers for their interference in politics. The States of Holland told them in unmistakable terms that they were not in future to address *en corps* foreign potentates, that they were not to discuss the affairs of Great Britain from the pulpit, and that they were not to carry on correspondence across the sea.

For in the midst of the general excitement, the States of Holland were unyielding in their adherence to their guiding principle, that it was essential to keep on friendly terms with the parliamentary party, and all the more now that this party had the whole country at its feet. Aitzema remarks caustically that the States party was absolutely determined to keep in with the winning side. Indeed it was the wordly-wise maxim, one that we have already seen the French government establish as the unshakable *raison d'état*,[152] and one that was so obviously in the interest of the Netherlands that the other commercial province, Zeeland, in spite of the Prince of Orange's influence there, continued in these days to go hand in hand with Holland. All the other European powers too—with the exception of Sweden, where the somewhat unbalanced Queen Christina indulged in a short-lived outburst of noble indignation—took it as their guiding principle. As for France, with which the Prince of Orange would so gladly have allied himself in order to set things right in England, that country was entirely powerless just at this time on account of its own *Fronde* risings.

However, it was certainly not only their inclination to *Realpolitik* that ruled with the States. These men, who did not really sympathize with the religious aims of the Presbyterians any more than with those of their own Calvinist clergy, must have cherished a certain secret admiration for the bold republicanism of the Independents. Aitzema himself cannot refrain from remarking on the folly of the public, who were now all "full of compassion over the death of the King, *one* person—and had looked on with dry eyes while thousands had lost their lives in England, Ireland, and Scotland, during the English disturbances."[153] And he refers to "Libertinists" who put awkward questions about the consistency of people like the Calvinist ministers, who were now so indignant, although their predecessors, too, had, after all, offered armed resistance to their lawful king. No doubt, so he goes on, it was objected that the English republic was only established by a small section of the House of Commons. But in the United Netherlands the revolution was not even begun by any States assembly or by a section of any parliament, but by some rabble at Flushing in Zeeland and at Enkhuizen in Holland. . . .

That there were freethinkers who dared to say such things, and not under their breath either, we need not assume only on the authority of Aitzema. A student of the University of Utrecht published a refutation of Professor Boxhorn's *Dissertatio de successione et jure primogenitorum*, in which it was argued that innocent sons of kings possess a right to succeed to the throne which cannot be invalidated by the deposition of their fathers, whether guilty or not. How does the professor—so the Utrechter would like to know—rhyme this with his loyalty to the state from which he draws his salary and which would not be an independent state if Philip III's right had not been invalidated by the abjuration (or deposition) of his father. He goes on to state as a general proposition that kings do not rule by the grace of God, a phrase without a meaning, but by the grace of the people—which the writer assumes to be acting through a States assembly, for he is clearly a regents man. And he is not a little surprised to see that in free states and republics there still are men who think so highly of royal authority.[154]

When the well-known lawyer Dirk Graswinckel published a little book, or rather, when an older book of his was reprinted for the occasion, the ultraroyalist views expressed in it drew further opposition. A pamphlet appeared in which a cultivated and well-read man pleaded in temperate terms for the principle—indeed a typically Netherlands principle, as he does not fail to remind his readers—of royal power limited by the interests of the people. And he concluded very sensibly that those who meant well by the King ought now to wish that he had listened more to his people and less to his court.[155]

One can be certain that views like these were pretty generally current in regent circles.

All this does not alter the fact that the rise of the Independents, and their impressive judgment on the King, did more than anything else to bring about a great revulsion of public opinion in the Netherlands in regard to English affairs. The Calvinists, who had been in sympathy with the Parliament in its struggle with the King, were distinctly inimical toward the English Commonwealth. William II might well think that a policy of interference with the domestic affairs of Great Britain, although even now there were certainly no signs of any active desire for it, would be less unpopular than it had been in the days of his father, particularly as the Scottish Calvinists or Presbyterians, too, seemed at that very moment to be reverting to the monarchy.

Yet here a serious complication presented itself. The Presbyterians, frightened by the danger of Independentism, were reverting to the monarchy, but Charles II was by no means eager to meet them. He would no doubt have been ready to join the Hamilton party, although even that was not at all to the taste of the majority of his English advisers. But the Marquis of Argyll's party, which had come into power after the fall of Hamilton, was considerably more obnoxious. It consisted of the most rigid Presbyterians, unwilling to make the slightest concession to the policy of the Stuarts, or even to put an end to the persecution of those who had formerly served them, or were tainted with Episcopalian leanings. It is true that the execution of Charles I had aroused great and universal indignation in Scotland also. The Scottish Parliament moreover, immediately after the receipt of the news from London, had proclaimed his son King of Scotland. It did, however, attach conditions to its proclamation, which in the main came down to this, that Charles II was to give certain personal assurances in the matter of religion, and that he was to swear to both the National Covenant of 1638, which established the Presbyterian church order for that realm and required severe persecution of men of different persuasions, and the Solemn League and Covenant of 1643, which was intended to introduce Presbyterianism into the King's other realms as well. In other words, it was demanded of Charles II that he should embrace the policy that had been so unacceptable to his father and all his father's faithful followers that they had preferred to face civil war. Small wonder that in the King's English council there was strong opposition to acceptance of the Scottish demands. The unfortunate result of the naval expedition in August of the previous year had weakened much the influence of Culpepper and the other Presbyterians. It was now the turn of the strict Episcopalians, such as Hyde and Cottington. Charles II indeed, who, so far as his nature allowed him to believe in anything, believed in the full royalist program and in the Episcopalian Church, did not relish the prospect of submitting to the Presbyterian yoke and entrusting himself to the people who, as it was said in the terms of party feeling, had sold his father to his executioners. Particularly so long as there was an alternative course open to him.

In Ireland the Lord Lieutenant, the Marquis of Ormonde, had not only managed to stand his ground, but he had just concluded a peace with the Catholic insurgents; he was confident that he would soon be able to restore to their allegiance to the King the towns that were in the hands of the Parliament, and that he would then have at his disposal an army to make an attempt on England itself. In February he sent an envoy to The Hague to invite Charles to come to Ireland, and one can imagine what a temptation this idea must have been to the young King. It was really a resumption of the old plan of Charles I and Strafford to establish the royal power in England with the help of Catholic Ireland. In case of success, young Charles, instead of being, under the royal title, bound in religion and in politics by the Covenants, would become the autocrat his father had dreamed of being. The greatest obstacle was that, in spite of the assurances of Ormonde, the position in Ireland still appeared very uncertain, and consequently several English councilors preferred Scotland. There were, moreover, in The Hague, Scots of various shades of opinion who advised an acceptance of the Scottish conditions, among them even several nobles of the Hamilton party who had been banished by the present government. Of the Scots it was only Montrose—the representative of absolute royalism, the man who had fainted on hearing of the execution of his King—who unhesitatingly urged the choice of Ireland, and there was no one to whose urgings Charles gave way so easily, however fiercely the Presbyterians might hate this man. It was not until April that the envoys of the Scottish government arrived to negotiate with "the proclaimed King" about his reception.

One cannot wonder that in these circumstances the Prince of Orange must have greatly preferred to see his brother-in-law depart for Scotland than for Ireland. For anyone who was trying to make the King's cause palatable to the people of the Netherlands that plan had all the advantages. It was one thing to recommend an alliance with the free Presbyterian kingdom of Scotland, but a very different matter to plead for support for an Episcopalian Stuart, dependent on Catholic Ireland and aiming at autocracy. The chaplains of whom the Scots wanted Charles II to rid himself were equally repugnant to the Netherlanders; one of them, for instance, used to preach vigorously against the Calvinists in general.[156] The Scots themselves counted on William II's advocating their cause with the King and used all possible influence with him.

The fullest and most authentic account in this connection is that of the Scottish minister, Spang, whom we met before.[157] He went from Veere to The Hague in March, at the request of his friends in Scotland, and had a personal interview of over an hour with the Prince.[158] It appears from Spang's detailed report that the Prince was very well informed as to the confused state of affairs in England and Scotland, and that, although he naturally gave a sympathetic reception to the Presbyterian spokesman, he was well posted in the arguments of Charles's English counselors and gave a fair exposition of them. Above all he saw clearly the dangers of the fierce intolerance of the party in power, and he feared, too—surely not without ground—that to embrace the Solemn League and Covenant would damage the King's cause by alienating the Catholics and Episcopalians in England. Yet he concluded by promising that he would advise the King to accept both covenants, and he assured Spang on the following day that he had done so.[159] When the envoys of the Scottish government themselves arrived at the beginning of April, they were able to report immediately that they hoped to get their demands accepted with the help of the Prince of Orange.[160]

Lord Byron, Ormonde's envoy, was of the opinion that the Scottish sympathies of the Prince of Orange and his mother were to be ascribed in the first place to the renewed suggestion of a marriage between the King and one of Frederick Henry's daughters.[161] No positive evidence that this was so can be found. But there is no doubt that Amalia of Solms actually gave open support to the Scottish envoys,[162] while Sophia of Bohemia, afterward Electress of Hanover, declares in her *Mémoires* (a doubtful source, however, for the years she spent at The Hague) that the old Princess about the same time, 1650, threw suspicions on her, Sophia's, orthodoxy, in order to make the Scots the more readily conclude to the suitability of her, Amalia's, daughter for the dignity of Queen of Scotland.[163] And of course we know only too well how very largely Amalia's policy was decided by the matrimonial prospects of her children. Byron, however, somewhat later commits himself to the rather surprising statement[164] that William II by no means allowed himself to be talked round by the Scottish lords, but that he had a higher opinion of his, Byron's, principal, Ormonde, than of any of them and desired to maintain friendly relations with him. This probably means simply that the Prince, who wanted to take up a propitiatory and mediatory attitude, thought it worth his while to cultivate the Irish party as he did the others, and was prodigal at least in protestations.

Meanwhile it is very probable that William did not always follow a consistent course in this difficult question. Even Henrietta Maria and Jermyn, of whose advice William II always thought very highly, considered that the Scots were too exacting. And the Queen of Bohemia and her daughters, too, were opposed heart and soul to the policy of submission to the covenants, a policy that was loathed by the most famous of her sons, Rupert, who at this time was at sea with the royalist fleet. How much more attractive to chivalrous minds was the idealistic royalism of Montrose or even the unbending Episcopalianism of Hyde. In November the Queen of Bohemia writes to Montrose that her niece, the Princess Royal, "still keeps steadfastly to our side." All the English influences in his cosmopolitan court and in his cosmopolitan family acted on the Prince to the detriment of the Scots. Nevertheless it is certain that in June, when Charles was already in Breda and on the point of setting out for Ireland, the Prince once more brought serious pressure to bear on him to induce him to accept the Scottish demands.

And indeed, however much one may sympathize with the point of view of the English royalists, who not only felt deeply wronged by the negotiations with the Presbyterians, but the noblest of whom abhorred them as a line of action both insincere and humiliating, it is natural enough, and it speaks something for his independence, that William II took into account in the first place not English but Dutch conditions. That the States-General wanted an arrangement between the King and Scotland is most positively asserted in all the contemporary sources.[165] Strickland hits the nail on the head when he observes that the Prince is doing his best to bring the King and Scotland together, "hopeing by that means to carrie all heere."[166]

In 1649, however, when there was still a possibility of a choice between Scotland and Ireland, William II, for all the obligations under which he had laid the King, did not succeed in keeping him back from Ireland. Nor did the Scots by any means make things easy for Charles. Compliance with their demand to introduce the Presbyterian religion into England and Ireland would cost the King the support of the only true friends he had. In Scotland, moreover, the persecution of the real royalists was being relentlessly pursued; above all, the execution of the Marquis of Huntly in the beginning of April was extraordinarily painful to the King. During this same period the Scottish envoys arrived at The Hague, and the first demand they put forward (and in the most offensive manner) was that the King should banish Montrose from his entourage.

It is not to be supposed that the States of Holland could have been prevailed upon to give any practical help if Charles had chosen the Presbyterian path. *They* were not in the Netherlands the admirers of that ecclesiastical system. But in any case, when the King applied to the States-General for transport ships and a loan of £200,000 to further his expedition to Ireland,[167] at the same time explaining exhaustively why he could not give ear to Scotland's call, the request fell on deaf ears. The Prince of Orange had supported the request even though he had advocated the alternative course, but a policy that was to cost money could not easily be carried out against the wishes of Holland, and Holland would not hear of it.[168] When at last, in June, the King set out on his Irish expedition, William II had once again to put his hand in his own pocket to prevent Charles from being retained by his creditors.[169]

Yet all this trouble was for nought. It went ill with Charles's cause in Ireland from the moment that Cromwell set about subduing the island. The King himself, after long delay in France, never got any farther than Jersey, where he waited for months in the most straitened circumstances, and where eventually in September and October the news of Cromwell's complete triumph reached him. "It is obvious," writes De Wilhem to Huygens,[170] "that God wishes to make him understand that Scotland is the only way to his restoration." In fact there was nothing else left. But the Scots had not become more tractable. It is true they were ready to renew negotiations—they had even sent envoys to the King in Jersey—but always on the same conditions. It was now agreed that the negotiations should be resumed at Breda through the mediation of the Prince of Orange.[171]

The King accepted the proposal of these negotiations on January 21, 1650, N.S. On the following day he wrote to his trusted Montrose that he nonetheless wished him to proceed with his proposed expedition against the Scottish government. Montrose, the unconditional royalist, now represented Charles's only alternative, but the way in which Charles sent him out against the Scottish Presbyterians at the moment he himself was entering into negotiations with them is a striking example of his duplicity.

The position of the mediator in these negotiations was clearly no easy one. After consultation with his mother in France, Charles arrived at Breda with his destitute retinue early in April. Feelings between his English adherents and the Scots had not improved since 1649. The English were in a suspicious mood even regarding the Prince of Orange. They knew that the Scots were counting on his support and that some of their spokesmen had spent the whole winter in The Hague in order to bring their influence to bear on the Prince.[172] According to an English Republican, who had wormed his way into the retinue of Charles II and who from there wrote vivid reports to the government in London,[173] the King's followers comforted themselves with the thought that he would after all feel fairly independent with respect to his brother-in-law, for William had so completely ruined himself in the service of the Stuarts that little more financial support could be expected of him; besides, in his own country he had serious difficulties to contend with, and his position was hardly secure.[174]

There is no doubt that, just as in 1649, the Prince did his best to induce the Scots to be more reasonable. Even the English royalists, for all their malicious talk, recognized that fact. According to the Republican spy, William made use in these efforts of the services of the Dutch Calvinists, of Dr. Rivet (who was at that time rector of the university founded by Frederick Henry at Breda), and of Voetius himself. The Dutch Calvinists were, as the Englishman says, "nothing so rigid" as the Scottish, and Voetius was expected to lend his name out of complaisance toward the Prince.[175] But the Prince's overriding desire was that an agreement should be arrived at, he cared not on what terms. The English Republican, who watched the doings at Breda with a strong sense of their humorous aspects, perpetually alleges that the Prince's chief motive was determined by the fact that the upkeep of the King and his retinue fell entirely on him and his already overburdened fortune—that therefore he wanted to be rid of Charles at any cost.[176] It is not improbable that this consideration counted (although just at this time the Prince obtained the use of a very large sum),[177] but as has already been explained, an agreement between Charles and the Scots fitted in with William's general policy, in which an alliance of the States-General with the Stuarts against the English Commonwealth formed so important a part. In any case, it is certain that the Prince urged his brother-in-law to an acceptance of the most important demands of the Scots: one or two documents have been preserved[178] in which he puts before the King his ideas on a possible answer to the Scottish delegates, and according to these Charles was to take his oath upon the National Covenant, as well as upon the general Solemn League and Covenant, and personally to conform to the Presbyterian form of worship all the time he was in Scotland.

And so, to the bitter disappointment of Charles's English followers, the negotiations ended by his giving in. He still made a few reservations, but the main points he accepted. Montrose and Ormonde were repudiated, and with them Episcopalianism. In the beginning of May Charles signed the agreement. Dr. Rivet, who also took counsel with the Scottish ministers as to the manner in which, in accordance with the treaty, the Anglican chaplains were to be removed from the King's entourage, was present at the signature.[179] Loyal royalists learned with indescribable bitterness that the King had adopted for himself and his subjects a religion in which he had no faith, and that he had undertaken to cast off all those who had ruined themselves for him and for Episcopalianism in order to be received as the mock king of the hated Scottish rebels. His mother herself repudiated the suspicion that she had "urged him to sacrifice his honour and his conscience." Royalists in England were discouraged.

And even before he left the Netherlands, Charles received news that was to bring home to him acutely the false position in which he had placed himself. Montrose had fallen into the hands of the Scottish government. It is not improbable that his expedition might have had a better chance of success if Charles himself had not by his negotiations with the Covenants smothered the desire of wavering Scots to join Montrose's ranks. In any case, no mercy was shown to the captured hero. Despite the King's commission, he was hanged and quartered as a traitor. No greater ignominy could have been shown to Charles. The news reached him while he was staying with his sister and brother-in-law Orange at Honselaarsdijk,[180] immediately before he was to embark. For one moment it caused him to hesitate.[181] What would his own life be worth if he put himself into the power of these inexorable fanatics? But it was too late to turn back. Toward the middle of June he embarked on a Dutch man-of-war, commandeered for the purpose, with a couple of others, by his brother-in-law. With him sailed a party of English Presbyterians and moderate Scots, whom the true Presbyterians regarded as nothing short of "prophane," and whom on his arrival (still further concessions having been wrung from him en route) he was forced immediately to dismiss. He was irretrievably delivered into the hands of the unbending clerical party, and it was to spare him no humiliation.

And Charles had not the Scots alone to reckon with. There was the English Commonwealth. The English spy to whom I have so often referred wrote to his principals as soon as he knew of the conclusion of the agreement, to warn them that the royalists would now move heaven and earth to get foreign troops into Scotland in order to use that country as the back door for an attack on England. "Therefore if you be wise, shut the back door this summer, and then you will be safer next"[182]—advice that Cromwell was to follow in less time than Charles needed to get hold of foreign auxiliaries. For although his brother-in-law Orange, in whom, as ever, his main hopes were centered, still managed to help him to get some more funds,[183] he had his own opposition to reckon with before he could think of mobilizing the resources of the Netherlands on behalf of the Stuarts.

The history of the last year and a half had proved that the opposition of Holland was enough to cripple all political action on the part of the Stadholder. In order to grasp that fact, we must go back to the moment when the news of the execution of Charles I reached The Hague. From that moment, the middle of

February 1649, there was as violent an onslaught on the policy of neutrality established in 1642 as there had been in 1645, and from that moment, too, the States of Holland, with the same success as before, had put up an obstinate resistance. The Hollanders did not allow themselves to be upset for one moment by all the excitement about "the regicide." From beginning to end they made it their business to keep on good terms with the actual rulers in England. It was not in the first place a feeling of spiritual kinship with the Republican party that prompted their attitude. It was above all a dispassionate appreciation of the interests of their own province. True, it might be argued that those interests would be endangered rather than helped by the conquest of Scotland by the English revolutionaries. The French, as has been observed already, realized quite clearly that the disunion of the island kingdom fitted in best with their interests, and events were soon to prove how dangerous for the Netherlands particularly a strong and united Great Britain, be it under Cromwell or under the Stuarts, could be. In fact, the commercial interests of the moment played an important part in the political considerations of the Holland party—as they always did—and that meant, of course, avoiding irritating the Commonwealth, which was powerful at sea. There was, moreover, the fact that it must have been difficult for the States of Holland, realistic as they might try to be, to take an unprejudiced view of a question that, owing to the dynastic policy of the House of Orange, had become so essentially a party question. Had the States of Holland and Orange been of one mind they might perhaps have played off the Stuarts against the Commonwealth—it would have been a dangerous policy at any time!—but the Hollanders naturally preferred not to have any dealings with a Stuart whom Orange when it suited him might play off against them.[184]

In the meantime the Orange party had immediately attempted to make the proclamation of the Commonwealth the opportunity for a break. Naturally it hoped to be able to carry the States-General with it in its dangerous policy. The Lord of Renswoude, the Utrecht Orangist whose performance as "mediator" in England will be remembered, happened to be "President" for that week, while the greffier, Musch, whose duty it was to "extend" —that is, to resume and formulate—"resolutions," could always be counted on. Together these gentlemen did their best to push through a resolution that Charles II should be acknowledged formally as King of Great Britain. Holland and Zeeland—urgent commercial considerations again made this latter province shake itself free from Orange control—opposed this proposal tooth and nail, and succeeded at length in modifying it so far that Charles was to be addressed merely by the general title of King, a title to which, of course, since his proclamation by the Scottish Parliament, he had an unquestionable right. The two provinces also succeeded in preventing the éclat of an ostentatious recall from England of the ambassadors who had been sent in a vain effort to save the King's life. Pauw van Heemstede, who had to return for private reasons, gave great offense to the Orange party by reporting that he had been treated with the utmost consideration by the new rulers in England. But he had been merely an envoy extraordinary; the great point was that Joachimi was allowed to stay. And, in fact, why should he not stay? The ambassadors of France, Portugal, Spain, were not recalled either, even though for the time being the English Commonwealth was not recognized by any other state.

But the Dutch Republic was a house divided against itself. Each party succeeded in making it impossible for the other side to carry out its policy, and the result was a grievous lack of cohesion in the conduct of foreign affairs. The States-General could not recall Joachimi against the wish of Holland, but it could prevent his being accredited to the new government. To all the ambassador's urgent requests for more definite instructions no other reply was made than that he must observe—and not enter into any negotiations. This attitude naturally roused ill feeling in the new rulers of England.

Then a sensational event took place in The Hague. In May, Doreslaer, a Hollander in English service, was appointed by the Parliament as ambassador to the States in addition to Strickland. A few days after his arrival he was murdered in cold blood by some Scottish royalists from Montrose's following. The States of Holland did what they could to bring the perpetrators of the deed, which had taken place in their territory, to justice, but without success, and the occurrence naturally made a profound impression in England. The Parliament addressed a very sharp note to Joachimi, who replied by expressing in writing his horror at the event. This roused the indignation of the States-General against him, because it implied a recognition of the Republican government. The ambassador, consequently, could not move a finger, and at the same time the States-General persisted in their refusal to receive Strickland, who now presented himself again with new credentials on behalf of the English Commonwealth. Here again the opposition of two forces resulted in a negative policy, although in maneuvering as they did the Orangists were keeping their aim in view. Their idea was that in this way, simply by doing nothing, it would still be possible so to poison relations with England that a conflict would become inevitable.

In fact, this question of recognition grew to be the most dangerous of all. Holland could easily enough, as we have seen, prevent any help being given to Charles II on his expedition to Ireland. But although Holland could obstruct, it could not compel. And so Strickland, in spite of all his importunities, eventually even by using the threat that he would have to leave the country, could not obtain admittance to the States-General. This was taken very much amiss in England. Strickland himself, as far as can be gathered from his letters in the well-known *Thurloe State Papers*,[185] was inclined to be satisfied with the deference shown him by the States of Holland, which had received him as Resident of the Commonwealth of England as soon as he turned to them.[186] He was perpetually urging his masters, the Council of State, to encourage the Hollanders in their line of action by giving them satisfaction on the blockade questions that were always cropping up. In this respect the English government was at times willing enough to be accommodating, but the threat to recall Strickland, in other words, definitely to break off diplomatic relations, was nonetheless seriously meant. The States of Holland, therefore, who were no doubt impressed by Cromwell's victories in Ireland just at that time, proceeded to act in a way that bitterly offended the Orange party, but was all the more enthusiastically welcomed by Strickland.

So far the Hollanders had been trying to bring the States-General to view things in their way by long arguments presented by extra-numerous delegations, but now the Holland deputies requested the "recording" of a formal and vigorous protest. What makes this document so interesting is that it contains an accusation against the deputies of the other provinces which one will rarely find expressed so pointedly. The protest is directed, not against these other provinces, but against their "deputies" who were holding up the admission of Strickland "*under pretext of* having no instructions."[187] The deputies of the other provinces (with the exception of Zeeland, which was still acting in harmony with Holland in all these matters) felt not a little aggrieved at thus being regarded as "such agents who, knowing the wishes of their honorable principals in matters of state of this importance, would delay the effect of them instead of reporting and acting upon them in due time and place." This was perhaps more than the Hollanders had meant to hint. Strickland indicates more exactly what was in their minds. The important thing to them was that the attention of the provincial States assemblies to which the protest would have to be sent should be directed to the question. Those States, he explains, "who live remote and know noe more then their deputyes informe them," did not see through "the mystery of iniquitye" that was enacted in The Hague. This is the view that I have set out already: that the deputies of the landward provinces let themselves be used by the Stadholder for the purposes of his personal policy, perhaps not exactly against the intentions of their respective States assemblies, but in the comfortable knowledge that these lived too "remote" to check their doings very accurately. And we have here proof that the Hollanders believed firmly enough that this was the case to expect their protest to have the effect that these gentlemen would for once be called to order by their principals. As a matter of fact, both Aitzema and Strickland testify that the protest created a good deal of uneasiness among the deputies attacked. But the power of the Prince, the dispenser of countless jobs, not only in the army, let itself be felt sufficiently by their principals as well to see that the deputies were not disavowed.[188] Holland's protest did not in the end result in anything. It appeared convincingly that the Prince of Orange could influence the States-General to carry through a policy that served no single Dutch interest, that indeed most obviously ran counter to Dutch interests.

Under these circumstances, then, the States of Holland decided on a step of incalculable import. In the beginning of December 1649 it was proposed in the Holland assembly[189] to send a "commissioner" to England on behalf of the province, and in fact, on May 21, 1650, Mr. Gerard Schaep of Amsterdam crossed to England in that capacity with an instruction dated May 5.[190] The aim of this mission, which is indeed clearly stated in the instruction, must have been twofold. In the first place, Holland, whose inhabitants had so many interests to be looked after in England, wanted to have an agent there who could accomplish more than the regular Union envoy, Joachimi, who now was nearly ninety years of age, and whose hands, as we have seen, were tied by the States-General. Then, Holland wanted also, particularly now that there was the danger of Strickland being recalled, a channel through which to keep in touch with the Commonwealth administration in England and to mitigate somewhat the ill feeling caused by the attitude of the Orange party. Thus, to look after commercial interests and to counteract the war policy of William II was to be the task of Gerard Schaep. If Holland was not meekly to submit to the dynasticism of the Stadholder's policy and allow the country to be plunged into a senseless war, a step of this kind was inevitable, but that it might have a serious effect on the unity of the Republic, even though it was not a violation of the Union of Utrecht,[191] needs no arguing. The Prince of Orange spoke with the greatest concern about it to the French ambassador, describing it as a maneuver that if it were not thwarted, would result in the complete disruption of the Union.[192]

Solicitude for the Union was always the fine-sounding shibboleth by which the Princes of Orange, who could do what they liked with the States-General, tried to impress public opinion. In reality, it was the opposition Holland offered to his English policy which William II could not brook. It is of course incontestable that in those days the Union was tottering on its foundations. The conflict between Holland and the Orange party was almost more than the defective constitution could bear. But I trust I have made it clear that it was the Prince's action in the English question, together with the unrepresentative, even corrupt, character of the States-General, which was the main cause of the crisis; Holland's attitude was fundamentally a defensive one. The constitutional slogans were not the issue of the struggle; they were the weapons with which it was fought.

At this very time the conflict was beginning to concentrate round the question of the disbanding of the troops. Now that there was peace, Holland wanted to diminish the military charges so as to be able to set about clearing off the public debt. Far from negligible in itself, this question became one of crucial importance mainly because of its connection with the great conflict of opinion over foreign policy and who was to have the deciding of it.

Here the English question, which under Frederick Henry already had been the principal factor in causing the revival of the States' opposition to the Stadholder, was still the most prominent. Aitzema, after having spoken about the difficulties in connection with the reception of Strickland, says: "This in time caused a difference between Holland and the Prince, which was increased by the questions of economy and reduction of the army." It is to be noted that Aitzema, too, regards the English question as the main cause of the breach. An even more definite expression of opinion in this sense came from the Spanish Ambassador, Brun, who watched with anxiety the course of the party struggle that for his King, too, would result in war or peace. "It appears," he wrote a few weeks after matters had worked up to the crisis of the famous attempt on Amsterdam (about which more soon),[193] "that the event in Holland has occurred in retaliation for the action of the States in sending a resident to England, and not on account of the troops."

It is true that the English question was not the only one in the realm of foreign politics, but it was indissolubly bound up with the others. In the mind of the Prince it had long been connected especially with the question of the peace with Spain and with the attitude toward France. The plan that occupied his mind (as we already know) was to undo the work of Münster, to renew the alliance with France for the partition of the Southern Netherlands and for the restoration of the Stuarts to the throne of England.[194] In this he followed the tradition of his father, but without the latter's caution. In itself already his scheming with France behind the back of the States with a view to breaking the freshly made peace was much worse than anything Frederick Henry had ever done. But moreover, William's secret negotiations had the highly objectionable purpose of drawing France into the Dutch domestic quarrel.

In October 1648 he had already made an opening through the instrumentality of Aerssens van Sommelsdijk the son, but Mazarin had his hands full with his own *Fronde* difficulties and the whole year 1649 passed by without anything being achieved. In the next year matters at first wore a more promising look—not for long, in fact—and now William came with positive proposals. Probably there is no document in the archives of the House of Orange that redounds so little to its credit as does that of February 1649,[195] in which William II, in his own imperfect French, wrote down his ideas on the subject of his co-operation with France as an instruction for an envoy of his own to the French government. France was to be assured that he had sufficient influence in the six small provinces to venture to count on their support for his war policy against Spain. Without mincing words he calls on the support of France against the opposition of Holland. He reckons with the possibility that a schism might break out in the Republic, in which he and the six provinces would find themselves opposed to Holland—and not even a united Holland. If France then should be willing to recognize the six provinces as a state and come to their assistance with money, he would be able to quell Holland with the army and lead the whole Republic into the war.

Of course the States of Holland had no knowledge of this startling document, but the Hollanders must have had a suspicion of what was going on. In more than one case the Prince's intentions came to light clearly enough. In December 1649, for instance, he had managed to prevail upon France not to call back its troops in the service of the Republic, as it was entitled to do under the treaty of 1630. Why was he so anxious to retain them? Because for his plans against Holland he could rely on French troops more than on Dutch.[196] For that same reason the States of Holland would have acceded eagerly to the first request for a recall, but the French government supported the Prince against Holland. Indeed the whole dispute about disbandment turned largely on the foreign troops, which the Prince, with a view to his dynastic and antinational policy, would not have on any account dismissed.

Compared with the almost treasonable relations with France into which William II had entered, the mission of Schaep, the boldest step that the States of Holland permitted themselves, was innocent enough. If this act of his adversaries nevertheless more than anything else moved William II to undertake his *coup d'état* of July and August 1650, it was, therefore, on account not so much of its constitutional impropriety as of its political tendency. Naturally the Orange party made grateful use of the Hollanders' straying into diplomacy to reconcile public opinion with the Prince's resort to force of arms, but for that purpose the Orangists had badly to distort its significance. Although the French Ambassador immediately on hearing the news was ready to declare[197] that the task of the "commissary" was to bring about an alliance between the province of Holland and the Commonwealth of England, there is no single indication that this actually was the case. The Gelderland Orangist Van der Capellen gives an account of a rumor[198] to the effect that "Bicker, De Witt, and others," through the medium of Schaep, had carried on "a secret correspondence with the Parliament in England," but he is obliged to add that there is "no evidence of it." As a matter of fact, such stories were circulated of set purpose. About the time of the attempt on Amsterdam a pamphlet was published in which a letter from Schaep is printed, dated July 14, 1650, with a complete draft-treaty between Amsterdam (not even Holland!) and the English Commonwealth, which undertook to furnish troops. This was a barefaced fabrication. It was part of the plot against the great city. It made some impression at first,[199] but soon people began saying that the Prince ought to lay proofs on the table.

Of course, with their opponents in so close a bond, a working alliance between the Republican parties in England and the Netherlands would have been quite natural. Nor is there any doubt, as has already been indicated, that the Hollanders wished Cromwell every success in his military enterprises both against the Scots and the Irish.[200] Their desire to keep on good terms with England went so far that the States of Holland did their best to suppress the writings of Salmasius and Graswinckel against Milton's *Pro populo Anglicano defensio*.[201] The correspondent of the *Briefe Relation*[202] even gives an account of somewhat reckless utterances he has heard from Hollanders: "If the rest of the provinces will be slaves, they will not. If the bundle of arrows must be unbound, they of Holland know into what quiver to put their arrows with safety and advantage."[203] Remarkable language certainly, but obviously more an expression of irritation and fear than the reflection of a responsible political plan. A main characteristic of the regents of Holland was their caution. Their tactics had all the weakness that is usually the accompaniment of a defensive attitude. In order to act offensively they would have had to be better organized under a universally recognized leader. Men like the Bickers of Amsterdam and De Witt of Dort certainly made their weight felt in the States of Holland, but the only position that offered an opportunity to a real leader to develop himself to the full—the position of grand-pensionary—was held by the timid, pliant Cats.[204] The States generally left the initiative to its opponents, who, whatever else they lacked, had the advantage of being subject to a strong personal leadership.

Thus it happened that at the end of July 1650 the crisis took the States party unawares with an act of aggression on the part of the Prince. He had, after all, to risk the *coup* without French aid, of which, as the *Fronde* troubles were still continuing, there was no likelihood. It is not necessary to repeat here all those familiar happenings, the capture of the six members of the States of Holland, the attempt on Amsterdam, all undertaken on the authority of a most irregular and very vaguely worded resolution of the States-General. It is enough to observe that in none of the struggles between the House of Orange and the regent party was the sympathy of the people so little on the side of Orange. The German captain of horse who snapped at one of the arrested gentlemen, "whoever has the army on his side is master,"[205] was not unfair to William II's cause. It was military force that decided the issue.

It is true that the Calvinist clergy on the whole worked for the Prince,[206] and probably the agreement that the Prince had brought about between Charles II and Presbyterian Scotland at Breda had still further strengthened the Calvinists' zeal. The Reverend Maximilian Teellinck, for instance, a Zeelander, expresses himself quite vehemently in the dedication to the Prince of a little book by his father Willem Teellinck, *Den Polityken Christen*, which he published just about this time. After having glorified Maurice and Frederick Henry and anathematized their adversaries, he extols William because in him was *the wisdom of God* (I Kings 3: 28) and because he opposed the peace (of Münster), *a girdle marred, profitable for nothing* (Jer. 13: 7), finally to explode: "It cannot be denied, there are only too many *sons of Belial* [Judg. 19: 22], Papists, Arminians, enemies of religion and of the state, in our midst who dare *bring a railing accusation against* [Jude 9] Your Highness . . . as if Your Highness, who have in all this proved yourself to be *wise in heart, and mighty in strength* [Job 9: 4], would have had no other aim than to make your own authority *increase* and the authority of the state *decrease* [John 3: 30]. . . . *The Lord God of Gods, he knoweth, and Israel he shall know* [Josh. 22: 22], with all true patriots, your *witness is in heaven*, your *record is on high* [Job 16: 19], that suchlike never occurred to your princely heart."[207] No less instructive than the ecstatic praise is the defensive tone.

The commercial classes in any case can hardly have looked forward but with the greatest uneasiness to the Prince of Orange's being able to carry out his military plans. We have seen how Zeeland, where the Prince had great personal influence, but where at the same time the commercial interest was almost as predominant as in Holland, had ventured to make a stand against his English policy in 1649. That was no longer so in 1650. Zeeland was again obeying the demands of the court. As Aitzema puts it, in his most unflattering manner: some of the "principaelste" of the Zeeland delegates "tried as usual to comply as much as possible with the Prince's wishes to serve their private interests and intrigues."[208] Particularly significant is the unanimity with which the inhabitants of Amsterdam stood by their regents during the siege.[209]

One might have thought that the failure of the attack on Amsterdam would have offered a splendid opportunity to the States party once and for all to square accounts with the ambitious Stadholder. But here the party's lack of organization told. Van der Capellen says scornfully that he "had expected more wisdom and courage from these gallant spirits.[210] Indeed, particularly the lack of unity among the Amsterdam magistrates, some of whom used the opportunity to oust the Bickers from power,[211] makes a pitiable impression.

Thus in spite of his initial defeat William II managed not only to find a way out of the impasse, but also decidedly to strengthen his position, and he made use of it with more talent perhaps than he had displayed hitherto. There are signs more than enough that his *coup d'état* instilled feelings of fear in his opponents: for some time they left him a free hand. The small provinces swallowed their objections to his action[212] and vied with one another in offering him resolutions of thanks. Aitzema relates that the States of Groningen had passed a resolution to the effect that the envoy of the English Commonwealth ought to be received, and that their delegates dared not now table this proposition in the States-General.[213] The English Republican whom I have so frequently quoted observed it all with the greatest annoyance. Writing in the beginning of September,[214] he refers to "the miserable base business of Amsterdam, whereby hath been discovered the baseness of som Provinces, and the weakness of other, and by both their ripeness for slaverie, and readiness to succumb; certainly that gallant spirit, which possest those people when they bravely (to their hitherto lasting honor) vindicated that libertie from the oppressions of the most potent Prince of Europe, which they have now tamely given up into the hands of their own servants, hath made a transmigration into our Nation." Indeed the records that are left of the conduct even of the Hollanders in the hour of crisis do not impress one with respect for their strength of character. The imprisoned gentlemen were left in the lurch without much opposition. Several of them addressed humble letters to the Prince which are far from edifying.[215] Gerard Schaep, too, wrote from London to the secretary of the Frisian Stadholder, William's cousin, in the hope that "sinistre opinies" that were cherished about him at the court would be given up.[216]

Nevertheless it would be very wrong to believe that the crisis had led William II into an unassailable position of power. It is certain that he was preparing himself for a vigorous attempt to carry out his foreign plans when death took him by surprise. But it is equally certain that Holland immediately thwarted him again when, as early as August, the question of war was brought up once more.[217] The States had bent under the force of the storm, but they were by no means broken. They were probably still as little fitted as ever to take an energetic initiative against the Prince, but under their new leaders, now that the old ones had been forcibly removed, they were no less adept in the tactics of parrying and checking.[218] The English Republican in Leyden anticipated that the Prince would succeed in moving the States-General to a war with the English Commonwealth if Cromwell was not successful in Scotland.[219] There was a close relation between the development of events there and in the Netherlands. The Scots themselves expected much from William II.[220] MacDowell, as resident of the King of Scotland, made tremendous efforts, and the Hollanders hardly dared protest against the vehemence with which he expressed himself against the English Republic in official documents.[221]

The battle of Dunbar, however, where the Scottish army suffered a crushing defeat (September 13, N.S.), was a fresh setback to the English policy of William II. The position certainly became more perilous than ever when, in October, the English government, which now felt itself to be stronger, turned Joachimi out of the country to avenge the refusal to receive Strickland. An actual break in the diplomatic relations between the two states had taken place. But without doubt Dunbar renewed the courage of the Prince's opponents in Holland as well. On September 24 Sir Edward Nicholas, one of the most eminent of royalist exiles, writes from The Hague that party feeling against the Stadholder is increasing daily.[222] William II had by no means done with the opposition in Holland. The actual battle would yet have to be fought when he decided the moment had come to press for a decision on the all-important point of foreign policy.

Nobody can tell what the outcome of that battle would have been. On November 6 the Prince, but twenty-four years old, died of smallpox, and the States of Holland, led by the staunchest Republicans, suddenly found themselves masters of the field, not only in their own province, but in the Republic.

(1923)

3 HISTORICAL APPRECIATIONS OF THE HOLLAND REGENT REGIME

The struggle between the Holland "regents"[1] and Orange—the Holland regents acting from their bulwark, the States of Holland, based securely on the Amsterdam town hall—presents one of the most spectacular aspects of the history of the Republic of the United Netherlands in the seventeenth and eighteenth centuries.

In the first decades of the Republic's existence these two powers had not been at variance. The crisis that opens the contest is the famous one occurring during the Twelve Years' Truce (1609-1621), culminating in the execution of the old "Advocate" of the States of Holland,[2] Oldenbarnevelt, in 1619. After that there still were periods of harmonious, or tolerably harmonious, co-operation, but rivalry and suspiciousness were never completely overcome. In 1650, 1672, 1683, 1747, and 1780 they gave rise to new crises, until in 1795 regent sovereignty and Orange eminence together were brushed aside by the Revolution.

The history of the Republic presents itself stiffly framed within unshakable constitutional forms. From start to finish the towns in Holland (to speak only of that province; the other provinces each knew different arrangements, but all alike were wedded to them immovably) were administered (or "governed," as it was put at the time) by corporations (*vroedschappen*), consisting of from twenty-four to forty gentlemen who sat for life, filled vacancies through co-optation, and every year appointed burgomasters and aldermen. The citizens had no say in the election of their rulers or in the conduct of affairs. Order was maintained by civic guards drawn largely from the lower middle-class, but officered by members of the regent class. In 1581 the States of Holland passed a decree forbidding the town governments (that is, its own component members) to consult the guilds about matters on which the town delegates would have to pronounce in the assembly.

The States of each province exercised the rights of sovereignty in that province. In Holland it consisted of eighteen town delegations, appointed and instructed by the town governments, and the committee of noblemen (so that nineteen votes were cast). The conduct of foreign affairs rested with the States-General, which was no more than an assembly of the deputies of the sovereign provinces, bound by the instructions given them by the respective provincial States. The stadholder was a minister of the provincial States, although reminiscences of the royal period, when he was the representative of the common sovereign, continued to cling to the office: he had, for instance, a say in the election of town councilors and magistrates, that is, ultimately, in the appointment of his masters, the delegations composing the States of the province. From 1650 to 1672 and again from 1702 to 1747 Holland managed without a stadholder, but when there was one, his function was always essentially the same.

This immobility, which to the modern observer seems astonishing, made it possible for a legend to grow up in which the party struggle, the antithesis between regent class and Orange, was reduced to the simplest terms and all the successive conflicts were explained thereby.

I should have said: *two* legends, for each of the parties, the Orangists and the Statists, had its own legend. The political contest was largely waged with the aid of arguments drawn from history. This is one of the characteristics of public life in the seventeenth and eighteenth-century Dutch Republic, and a phenomenon to which I have devoted a good deal of attention.[3] Each party cultivated a view of the past in which the great men of the rival party cut sorry figures: the stadholders were maltreated in the history of the Statists; and so were the great grand-pensionaries, the States of Holland, Amsterdam, in the history of the Orangists. Each side used these self-constructed bogies in order to cast ignominy on its contemporaries of the other persuasion. In those impassioned controversies cool historical criticism did occasionally make itself heard, but this—not exclusively, yet mainly and more effectively—on the side of the Statists.

Take what was called the "Wittian War," an eruption, in 1757, of pamphlets attacking and defending "the character of the Lord Grand-Pensionary Johan de Witt." The protagonists on the opposing sides were Jan Wagenaar and Elie Luzac, and when I studied their writings I was struck to notice how much stronger was the legendary element in the history presented by the Orangist Luzac than in the expositions of the Statist Wagenaar. The whole of Luzac's method consisted in deducing conclusions from dogmatically advanced constitutional (or one might say, party) premises, while Wagenaar at least attempted to discern the facts and place them in a context of their own.

The Orangist legend, so prevalent in the historic consciousness of the Dutch people, owes its vitality largely to the connection with religious sentiment. The fact comes out very clearly, after the downfall of the Republic and after the miserable episode of the gradually increasing dependence on France, in the opening decade of the kingdom established in 1813 to 1815. The legend was then reanimated and given a new lease of life by that great counter-revolutionary eccentric, the protester against the spirit of the age, Bilderdijk. As far as the period after the sixteenth-century separation of the Netherlands is concerned, Bilderdijk's *Geschiedenis des Vaderlands* is no more than a highly seasoned rehash of the Orangist party stuff dished up by eighteenth-century writers like Blomhert and Arnoldus Rotterdam, Elie Luzac and R. M. van Goens. The twelve volumes of Bilderdijk's work are indeed one protracted pamphlet, and one of unprecedented virulence. The pathological bitterness of that dynamic personality exercised, not a wide, but a profound influence. Soon it was canalized, and purged of its worst excesses, in the work of a younger man, Groen van Prinsterer, who, when a student at Leyden, had followed the master's unauthorized lessons. Groen used to emphasize his independence with respect to "the acrimonious Bilderdijk," and not without justification; yet in a way he acted as the apostle of the older man's message.

Groen's *Handboek der Geschiedenis van het Vaderland* appeared in

1846. It is free from the vehemence, from the wild fantasticalities and scurrilous invective, by which Bilderdijk's work is disfigured. There is infinitely more genuine research behind it. But it follows the same party line, while even more exclusively interpreting events from the religious point of view. It is a religious epic of the chosen North Netherlands Republic, chosen in order, under the leadership of the providential House of Orange, to provide a shining example of God's mercy showered on a Reformed people. By his indefatigable resistance to dominant liberal thinking, Groen van Prinsterer, the political free lance, was a potent force in helping his coreligionaries, later in the nineteenth century, to constitute once more a strong, coherent political group. The historian's authority with them was enormous. His *Handboek* was reprinted again and again. Even today countless teachers at orthodox Protestant schools[4] will swear by it.

Contemporary liberal historians had protested from the first. Yet they too, and especially Fruin, absorbed more of Groen's leading ideas than they were aware of. The influence of Groen's version of our history went, in any case, far beyond his own circle. The specifically religious motivation can, it is true, have its full value for the like-minded only; that is, for the orthodox section of the old Netherlands Reformed Church and for those who, dissatisfied with the liberalist watering down of the religious life within its precincts, seceded from that church to set up orthodox churches of their own (there were secessions in 1834 and 1886, resulting in what is now called *Gereformeerde kerk*).[5] Yet Groen's views found sufficient support in general Protestant (as distinct from specific Calvinist) sentiment, which in the nineteenth century still dominated public opinion.

But the Orangist tendency in the interpretation of Dutch history appealed to entirely different sentiments as well, sentiments that could in part still be connected with the ecclesiastical motif, but partly were completely free from it. Otherwise it could not have shown such tenacious vitality.

There were unreasoning feelings of loyalty toward the reigning family, or more generally, a kind of snobbism, an inclination to assume that the regents, being shortsighted merchants and moved by self-interest, could not but compare unfavorably, on the score of political wisdom, with princely personages like the stadholders. One reproach leveled at the States was that of blindness to the dangers threatening from France. This, curiously enough, although nobody could deny that Frederick Henry (stadholder, 1625-1647) and his son William II (1647-1650) had based their entire policy on co-operation with France, and that it was Amsterdam and Holland that had raised the cry "Gallum amicum non vicinum" against the Franco-Dutch alliance of 1635 aiming at a partition of the Spanish Netherlands.

An important factor, too, was the satisfaction with which the men of the nineteenth century regarded the unitary state that had at last been achieved in the closing years of the century before. The liberals set at least as much store by this acquisition as did the conservatives, and in historic appreciation it was the stadholders who benefited, for it was taken as an axiom that they had, in the days of the Republic, been the bearers of the idea of unity. Again, however, the current view was not quite in accord with the facts. At times, certainly, the Orange party had made much of the principle of Generality before Provincial Sovereignty, but long before the end of the Republic the stadholders had become the supporters of things as they were, of the constitution as it had been inherited from the glorious forefathers, and unity had to be realized by the Revolution and against Orange.

Then there was—this, too, a point of great importance—the modern aversion to oligarchy. The stadholders had indeed been the only power that under the Republic constituted a counterpoise to the regents. In order to represent them on that account as the protectors of the people's interests, historic truth had nevertheless to be drastically simplified, even distorted.

All these elements, without the qualifications, will be found in Groen's history, and the whole system can actually be traced back to writers like Luzac, to the party propaganda of the stadholders' own days. And however much the liberal writers of history of following generations may have revised the picture, correcting the obvious errors and toning down the more extreme partialities—the grand-pensionaries, for example, they treated on the whole with respect—traces of these old tenets of the Orangist legend will frequently obtrude themselves. This is true of the work of Fruin, of Fruin's contemporary Jorissen, and of Fruin's disciple Colenbrander, of the work of Japikse, of Elias—to mention only a few. A considerable part of my own work, *Willem IV en Engeland* (1924), some of the essays in *Kernproblemen van onze geschiedenis* (1937), *Oranje en Stuart* (1939), also my studies of seventeenth- and eighteenth-century party literature (1947, 1950, 1953), has been devoted to this problem. By means of an exact investigation of the events and an analysis of the expressed opinions I have attempted to substitute for the legend the much more complicated, sometimes radically different, reality of history.

Let me now consider separately each of the points enumerated. I shall do this in connection with the great crises I mentioned before—or rather, in order not to take up too much time, I shall confine myself to those of the seventeenth century, that is, those of 1618 and 1650 and the long-drawn-out one under De Witt which was violently resolved in 1672.

Only in the first crisis did the church question stand in the forefront, and I want to emphasize at once the fact that each of those conflicts bore a character of its own. To think that one fixed opinion concerning those two powers, the stadholders with their adherents and the States of Holland with its, will supply the key to the reading of them all, is to begin with a serious error of historical method. Each conflict should be studied in its own circumstances. But I need hardly say that I am not here propounding a novel principle.

Only in 1618, then, did the dispute turn—in outward appearance at least—on the relationship between church and state. There was not yet at that time any tradition of antagonism between the Holland regents and the House of Orange. Friction with Calvinist ministers had been of frequent occurrence from the beginning, but William the Silent himself had been at loggerheads with zealots as well as had certain Holland town governments. His relations with the regents, on the other hand, had on the whole been harmonious. Young Maurice[6] had originally been entirely the man of the States of Holland. Oldenbarnevelt, the States' powerful "Advocate," gave Maurice all the support in his power to acquire the stadholderly dignity in other provinces. As late as 1610, Grotius, still a young man at that time, but a typical representative of Holland regent circles, had, in his famous little book *De antiquitate reipublicae Batavae*, praised the constitution of the youthful Republic for being a mixture of the three forms enumerated by Aristotle; democracy, aristocracy, monarchy. His identification of the democratic element is done somewhat perfunctorily, but monarchy he wholeheartedly admitted was represented by the stadholder's powers and position. Later, when the antithesis had become traditional, Orangist polemicists never missed an opportunity to remind the Statists of these words of Oldenbarnevelt's theoretician, who had become so great a saint in their calendar. When Grotius wrote them down, in 1610, a tiny cloud was already appearing in the political sky. Maurice, who was by now a great figure, an internationally famous army commander, had opposed the conclusion of the truce[7] with all his might, and now that Oldenbarnevelt had succeeded in forcing it through, was still grumbling.

But the occasion for the crisis was the dispute about the powers of the church. The Reformed Church was the only one officially recognized in a country where there was still a great variety of religious convictions. The problem now was whether that church might through its own organs purge itself from ministers inclined (under the influence of the teaching of Arminius) to gloss over some of the severer aspects of the Calvinist doctrine and whether at the same time it might impose that doctrine (as maintained by Gomarus) on public life in its entirety; or should not the state have a say in the matter to see that comprehension, and tolerance, were enforced? The attempts of the States of Holland to act in the latter sense gave rise to a storm of protest. From having been a mere dispute between theologians, the quarrel took on national dimensions. The passions of the people were roused—of the Reformed people, that is, and it should never be forgotten that, even though these constituted no more than a fraction of the nation, the Catholics, the Baptists, and other Protestant dissenters were too timid, or too cowed, to count for much in the great political contests.

What brought Oldenbarnevelt to the block and Grotius, now his most intimate adviser, to imprisonment in the Castle of Loevestein, was not, however, the church question alone. The small provinces championed in the States-General the cause of orthodoxy, but not only because they were orthodox. And likewise, if the Prince of Orange, Maurice, who had for so long followed Oldenbarnevelt's lead in political matters, now declared against him (and Maurice's choice of sides was more than anything else to prove the decisive factor), it was principally the difference of opinion on the great question of war or peace that moved him. Maurice, the stadholder-captain-general, and the Calvinists were at one in their irreconcilable hostility to Spain. But the consequence was that from now on the combination of Orange and the Calvinist small middle-class with its ministers in opposition to the regent class, which was inclined to be more opportunist in religious matters and generally speaking more worldly, came to constitute an almost constant feature in the political life of the country. It may at times have been crossed by other contrasts, or have for a while lost some of its distinctness in the public mind. But down in the end of the Republic it could be revived to sudden potency. The aftereffects made themselves felt by fits and starts all through the nineteenth century, and even in our day the pale reflection can still be observed.

The cry of the seventeenth-century church was for liberty. The most serious charge against the States of Holland, in the hectic years that led to the decapitation of Oldenbarnevelt and the imprisonment of Grotius, was that by supervision and interference (intended to protect and maintain the minority of Arminian, or Remonstrant, ministers) it was in fact reducing the church to a position of slavery, that its pretended tolerance amounted in reality to spiritual tyranny. The charge was repeated on many occasions in the succeeding generations, and in the nineteenth century Groen and his school made the most of it, but even in the hearts of many Dutch liberals these bitter complaints of the Calvinists raised an echo. It was the liberals who had, in 1848, in the new constitution, proclaimed the freedom of churches and of schools. "The claim [of the Contraremonstrants in 1617] was justified," Fruin, who was far from being a Calvinist, wrote in 1858: "without freedom the church cannot develop."[8]

Now I, too, find it a repulsive spectacle when the States of Holland in their "resolutions" lay down (as they did in the years preceding their spectacular defeat in 1618) exactly what may be demanded of a new minister's orthodoxy as being indispensable for salvation; when they prohibit dealing from the pulpit with the points in dispute, threatening the preacher who transgresses the order with suspension or dismissal and dispelling by main force congregations assembling elsewhere to hear him in their despite. But must not the historian remember that the problem as it presented itself in the seventeenth century was different from what it is in the nineteenth or twentieth?[9] The church for whose freedom the seventeenth-century Calvinists contended was a state church that took it upon itself to supervise the government in the matter of orthodoxy. It claimed freedom to expel whoever deviated from the right doctrine; but expulsion from the church meant expulsion from the state, from political life. The church wanted to be free in order to dominate the state.

This was an ambition every government was bound to resist. It was out of the question for the States of Holland, even after, in consequence of Maurice's *coup d'état*, they had been purged of Oldenbarneveltians and filled with "Contraremonstrants," docilely to hand over the reins to the ministers. The Synod of Dort was (in 1619) left free to draw up the *confession of faith*, but in the "church arrangement," laying down rules for *the relations between church and state*, the gentlemen saw to it that secular authority prevailed. They proved to be regents before they were Contraremonstrants. The zealous Calvinists were far from content. It was seen that the crisis had not really, or at least far from exclusively, been about the church question. What had been uppermost in the minds of Maurice, of Holland, and of the other provinces was the desire to get rid of Oldenbarnevelt.

Maurice's successor, his younger brother Frederick Henry, was not a true Contraremonstrant at all. If, after some years, he in his turn fell out with the States of Holland (which, after the purge effected by Maurice, was for quite a while much more concerned about Calvinist orthodoxy than he was), it was about foreign policy. Frederick Henry obtained Charles I's eldest daughter as wife for his son William, and when this young man had become stadholder, it was not long before another crisis of the first magnitude broke out. In 1650, some prominent members of the States of Holland were arrested and sent (again!) to Loevestein, while the Stadholder-Captain-General tried with the army of the States-General to surprise Amsterdam. And the real issue of the conflict still was nothing but foreign policy.

At least, that is my view of the case as I have expounded it in my *Oranje en Stuart.*[10] The current interpretation was that young William II, who had indeed procured a vague commission from the States-General, was forced to bring the province of Holland to reason because it had, of its own authority, disbanded certain regiments, for the pay of which the province was responsible, but which nonetheless resorted under the States-General. The conflict, in other words, was one, on that view, between Holland particularism, resulting in nothing less than a breach of the Union, and the Captain-General, protecting the Union's rights. Looking a little more closely, however, one will observe that William II, continuing along lines started by his father, had succeeded in making the States-General a tool of his purely personal, or dynastic, policy. The deputies from the smaller provinces were for the most part dependents of his. The States-General had become (as I put it years ago, to the indignation of Dr. Japikse) "a corrupt body." To see the Stadholder as the avenger of the Union is to let oneself be misled by the outward appearance. Naturally this was the propaganda reading advanced by his party in 1650, but the reality was that he used the Union slogan to mask his private war schemes: a renewal of the war with Spain (he had been unable to prevent peace from being concluded at Münster in 1648), prepared in secret confabulations with Mazarin, and simultaneously a war on behalf of his relatives by marriage, the Stuarts, directed against the newly established Commonwealth of England. In order to oppose that adventurous policy the Hollanders had no other possible tactics than to fall back on the entrenchment of provincial sovereignty; the disbanding of the regiments no doubt was irregular, but it was a desperate measure to prevent a war that might well have proved disastrous. "The constitutional slogans," so I wrote in *Oranje en Stuart*, "were not the issue of the struggle; they were the weapons with which it was fought."[11]

Religion at any rate did not come into the conflict, at least not in the way assumed to be normal in the legend: it was not possible on this occasion to mobilize Calvinist opinion against the Holland regents; William II had, on the contrary, antagonized it by entering into a connection with the Anglican and Romanist Stuarts. Nor can it be said that the Stadholder had the backing of any strong popular opinion. When he appeared before the walls of Amsterdam with his army (the army of the States-General, rather), the town government had no reason to feel worried over the attitude of the citizenry. The civic guards manned the walls without showing any sign of disaffection to the burgomasters.

The surprise failed, and the undertaking ended in a compromise that left both parties in their old positions. But a few months afterward William II died quite unexpectedly, and now the States of Holland, controlled by his adversaries, the Loevesteiners (after the repeated residence of their leading men in that castle, that is how the thoroughgoing Statists were beginning to be called), decided to manage without a stadholder. A son was born a few weeks after his father's death, and when he grew up, and especially when in 1660 his uncle Charles II was restored to the English throne, young William III constituted an anxious problem for the States and its new grand-pensionary, in effect its leader, De Witt.

De Witt and his political friends, who easily dominated the States of the province down to 1672, were determined to see to it that the new Orange would never combine the high military and civil offices traditional in his family. The danger of the combination of the stadholdership with the captain-generalship had become sufficiently clear under Maurice, Frederick Henry, and William II. The attempt on Amsterdam in 1650, especially, was not easily forgotten, and there now sprang into existence what had hardly existed before—a sharply anti-Orangist doctrine, consistently and intolerantly Republican. Fruin admits:

> It was not only love of power and partisanship if after 1650 we notice this ardent opposition to the idea of appointing a stadholder who would at the same time be captain-general. An all-too-natural anxiety for the threatened liberty, a well-founded fear for an arbitrary and adventurous policy contributed to this feeling.[12]

It is surprising, however, when he continues:

> I strongly blame the repression of the House of Orange, especially because it was done against the ardent desire of the nation and exclusively in the interest of an egoistical and dishonest aristocracy.

It is surprising, because he had just admitted that the States' suspicions were based on valid reasons of public interest. But it is in itself extraordinary that Fruin in this passage does not seem willing to ascribe to the regent class any qualities except those of self-interest and dishonesty.

The "ardent desire of the nation," moreover. It is a fact that the lower middle-class, which filled the civic guards and from which were drawn the most devoted followers of the Calvinist ministers, in moments of danger, even during this "stadholder-less" period, thought of Orange.

In 1653 for instance: De Witt had only just taken up his office of grand-pensionary, at a moment when the first war with England was on and was going very badly indeed. De Witt and the States of Holland had looked upon that war as a mistake from the start. As a matter of fact, the Orangists had contributed not a little toward its breaking out. Among the deputies from the land provinces on the States-General the clients of Frederick Henry and William II were still numerous. The public, even in Holland, naïvely included in its affection for Orange the unfortunate Stuarts, who were now wandering in exile on the Continent. When in 1651 special ambassadors had come to The Hague on the part of the Commonwealth of England to discuss the points of friction, the States-General had not been co-operative and The Hague mob had insulted the regicides in the streets. No wonder that the States of Holland were anxious, in 1653, to make an end of this disastrous war. The multitude, too, wanted peace: the effects of the blockade were felt grievously enough. But the measure for which the multitude clamored, the elevation of the baby prince to the dignities of his ancestors, with his cousin the Stadholder of Friesland as his deputy, could only have the effect of making Cromwell intractable, for to him the connection of Orange with the deposed Stuarts was a sore point. De Witt felt it to be his duty to remain firm against the popular demand, and from his point of view he was perfectly justified.

After 1660, with Charles II reigning in England, the Orange-Stuart problem took on an even more serious aspect. The dangers came to light during the second war with England (1664-1667) in the Buat conspiracy. Colonel Buat, who had been a page to the young prince, entered into a correspondence with the English government and collected a number of Orangist regents with a view to overthrowing the Statist regime and arranging for a peace on English terms. It was an ominous symptom of the direction in which Orangist partisanship had been developing that this man Buat, after his execution, was venerated by many as a martyr of loyalty to Orange and of the Calvinist faith.

The outcome of this war, after the glorious raid on Chatham, placed De Witt and the regime for a short while beyond the reach of criticism. The Triple Alliance (Dutch Republic, England, Sweden) to make a front against French northward expansion seemed an impressive success. When, however, soon afterward Charles profited from Louis XIV's resentment, which was directed against the Republic alone, to enter into an agreement with him (Dover, 1670), and the concerted attack of the two kings brought the Republic within an inch of its ruin, De Witt and the dominant faction in the States were held responsible. In panic and fury the people gave clear evidence once more of inability to grasp the realities of the situation.

William III had already been appointed stadholder by the distracted States of Holland, and De Witt had resigned his office (his murder was to come later), when a little party of English gentlemen on their way to Utrecht, where Louis XIV was now residing, came ashore at Helvoetsluis. The object of their mission was to arrange with Louis the details of the projected partition of the Republic, but first they called at William III's headquaters on the Holland "Water Line," in order to offer to their King's nephew the sovereignty, under the protectorship of the two kings, over what would be left of the country. The extraordinary point that I want to bring out is that in the small towns through which they passed these ambassadors of the treacherous Charles II were loudly cheered. Crowds raised frantic shouts of "Long live the King of England and the Prince of Orange!" and "Death to the States!" If William III had so wished, he might have sold the country. But he was not the man to play the part of a petty client to the Stuarts which his adherents were casting him for. He replied to the tempters that honor and duty bade him observe his engagements with the States. It was the greatest moment, perhaps, in the life of this great Orange, the moment in which he laid the foundation for all his later astonishing achievements.

De Witt's distrust, then, was put to shame. It is the tragic note in his life and in this period of Dutch history that, with what he had experienced so far, and knew, he had to act as he did. The tradition of the Orange party *had* for a generation been lacking in national purpose. How could De Witt have foreseen that the young William would have the strength of mind to break with that tradition? But it is worth noticing that William III chose his direction in close contact with other prominent representatives of that same Holland regent class that at that moment seemed, with De Witt, to have been brought low. Van Beuningen and Van Beverning, at one time intimately associated with De Witt, but who had been seeking *rapprochement* with the Orange court even before the crisis, were now William III's advisers. The young noblemen from the land provinces who surrounded him, like the infatuated Holland multitude, were all for accepting the English conditions and "hanging a dozen or so" of the States' members. William III was sufficiently realistic to understand that only with the States was a national policy possible.

The "ardent desire of the nation." It is a phrase that takes it for granted that the regent class was in a completely isolated position. One frequently comes across passages in our historical literature that seem to have been inspired by that thoroughly false assumption. The regent regime was an oligarchy, and it certainly was not without the vices that almost inevitably go with that system: nepotism, for instance; pride. But what were the alternatives? The experience of Frederick Henry's last years and of William II's short term of office had not given a high opinion of princely rule; and indeed under William III, too, great figure that he was, and sincerely living by an idea (an idea primarily concerned with international affairs), practices were used, all through the years from 1672 on, which were far from suited to elevate political life.

As for democracy, it was unthinkable. The people as a rule unquestioningly respected the authority of the gentlemen regents and saw in them their representatives. Only church questions and international crises were capable, occasionally, of rousing them against their lawful rulers, and if the idea of a change of regime was then raised, it meant in practice no more than that the Prince of Orange should be placed in the traditional position of eminence, to be a kind of popular dictator able to bridle the regents. The people might at times chafe at the existing order, but in constructive power they were completely deficient.

Take the year 1660, when the church-state question had once again led to shocking incidents. The town government, and also the provincial States, of Utrecht had exiled two ministers for having delivered offensive sermons; in order to bolster their capacity for maintaining order they had, before undertaking that risky measure, obtained the loan of troops from the States of Holland. After the two ministers had left Utrecht, the consistory of Medemblik (a Holland town) extended a call to one of them, but immediately the States of Holland issued an interdiction and once more dispatched troops to prevent disturbances—at Medemblik this time. "The citizenry of Medemblik," a burgomaster of the town wrote to De Witt, ironically, "regard the Reverend Van de Velde as a pattern of all Christian virtues." The irony becomes intelligible when one reads that "accursed and godless" were the qualifications applied by this man to the peace of Münster, then twelve years old. "The Lord God," he had assured his congregation, "has wept over this peace with a succession of rainy years; visitation after visitation have the provinces suffered since, and God has walked with us in contrariness."[13] De Witt, for his part, wrote that Van de Velde was "generally known for a man who seems to set his course to a madhouse rather than a pulpit." And here he indulged in a somewhat more general reflection:

I could have wished that the circumstances of the affair had permitted us, without risking disturbance of the country's quiet, to defer a little more to the inclination of the consistory and commonalty [of Medemblik]. But it has been judged the course of duty to look after the interests of Their Noble Great Mightinesses subjects [Their Noble Great Mightinesses refers to the States of Holland, which felt obliged to see to it that what was best for the people, the subjects, be effected], even against their wish or inclination; for they don't know themselves what will serve their peace and preservation; like the father of a family who, if he were to give way to the wish and preference of his children, would very likely do them the greatest harm.[14]

Such paternalism goes against the grain with us moderns. I hold, however, that the historian must see it in relation to the opinions and conditions of the time, and when I have tried to do so I can accept it as the perfectly sincere expression of the profound conviction of a ruler's duty. The States of Holland were a little too fond of mentioning their sovereignty and too eager to call the citizens their subjects. But with the best of the delegates the consciousness of being called to promote the interests of the community, and to do so after the dictates of conscience, without allowing themselves to be confused either by popular fury or by princely frowns, had the quality of an ideal. Human imperfections were not thereby ruled out, but the invigorating effect appears, as I see it, in a heightened style and bearing. The whole of De Witt's correspondence and state papers could be adduced in evidence; and De Witt, for all his individual greatness, was typical of an elite.

Many modern authors, Japikse for instance, will never use the current phrase to designate the system, the System of True Liberty, without an undertone of sarcasm. Up to a point this is understandable, for that liberty was found in the States of Holland's unrestrained fullness of power, unrestrained by a Stadholder, unrestrained by the commonalty. Nevertheless acceptance of the system was by no means limited to the regent class. There were first of all the non-Reformed, who generally looked to the regents to protect them against the intolerance of the ministers. The cultivated, even among the members of the Reformed Church, often were repelled by the fanaticism of the more extreme among the ministry and in consequence regarded the regent regime with the more sympathy. Vondel had glorified Oldenbarnevelt as the martyr of Liberty, afterward Oudaen and Paets did the same for De Witt. Vondel, of course, was, before he was converted to Catholicism, a Baptist. But it would be wrong to conceive of Reformed and Statist as necessarily making a contrast. Most of the regents of the True Liberty brand were as good Reformed as any, and many Reformed ministers accepted them with befitting respect and submission as their lawful governors.[15]

Not long ago a number of *Anti-revolutionaire staatkunde*[16] fell into my hands, in which was printed an article by Dr. De Pater, a well-known Dutch historian, entitled "The Policy of Johan De Witt," and directed against my *Oranje en Stuart*. The number dates from 1941, but at that time I was abroad,[17] and I had so far missed it. I found it most extraordinary reading and I will not conceal from you that it was this article that suggested to me my present reflections.

The writer takes exception to my remark that the System of Liberty found its firm basis in a healthy nationalism. That remark was the summing up of a lengthy exposition in which it was shown that the Orange party (in the years following upon the marriage of 1641) simply followed the line dictated by England (or by Stuart) and that this was one of the principal reasons why the States kept power so jealously to itself. But the policy of De Witt and *national*, this is for Dr. De Pater a contradiction in terms. Did not Bilderdijk write that the town government of Haarlem (one of the few generally Orangist towns in the States of Holland) proposed in the States assembly, at the time of the popular commotion of 1653, that "this entirely *national* desire should be satisfied and the young Prince be recommended to the States-General for the post of captain-general"? (The word *national*, by the way, was not used by Haarlem, but by Bilderdijk.) And does not Groen van Prinsterer, in his *Handboek* exclaim: "This form of government [of True Liberty] did not agree either with the people's rights and the constitutional make-up of the Commonwealth or with the spirit of the majority of the nation"?

It is true that Dr. De Pater does not suggest that the matter is settled by an appeal to the authority of those great names of Bilderdijk and Groen van Prinsterer. He goes on at length to argue the case by an examination of the facts. Nevertheless, both when he dissects my arguments (a large proportion of which indeed he ignores) and when he adduces arguments of his own, I cannot help feeling that he gives but another instance of the method of historical interpretation I have just observed with so much interest, and I must say amusement, in the "Wittian War" of 1757. Luzac, in his pamphlet, began by asserting that the stadholdership was an essential part of the form of government (in 1757). He first tries to prove the contention, with the aid of old "resolutions," but when Wagenaar and others pointed out that these were relevant only to the circumstances prevailing at the time they were taken, he tried to prove it by boldly advancing as a general truth: that a unifying authority is salutary and indispensable. This is to him so obvious that the people, when at the time of the foundation of the Republic they implicitly abandoned their rights, could not to his mind but have intended that there was at all times to be a stadholder. This argumentation really (as I put it in my essay) "describes a circular course," for "he uses the very thesis he had set out to prove as a chief argument." Luzac nevertheless concludes triumphantly that a statesman who wanted to abolish that stadholdership cannot therefore be called a faithful servant of the state, which dispenses him from the obligation to make an exact and unprejudiced study of the achievements and of the circumstances. He knew the conclusion before setting out on his investigation.

Now this is exactly how Dr. De Pater proceeds. He does not speak unkindly about my book, but, judging from what he has to say about it, it has simply not succeeded in piercing through the armor of tradition and convention with which he protects his conception of history. He takes hardly any notice of the facts and arguments with which the book is filled to overflowing.

But now let us analyze the pronouncements of those great antirevolutionary prophets, Bilderdijk and Groen, which De Pater accepts and attempts to substantiate. As regards Bilderdijk, I shall only refer to what I said at an earlier stage about the impossible and self-contradictory aim of the burgher movement of 1653. But Groen? With which rights of the people did the stadholderless regime disagree? Groen was probably thinking of the stadholders' participation in the appointment of councilors and magistrates. It is undeniable that as a result of the office being in abeyance the oligarchic system came to rest even more exclusively upon itself. But had the stadholder exercised this particular function with any regard for the interests or wishes of the people? No; mainly in order to get docile adherents into the corporations or magistratures. In 1672, William III, when the intimidated States of Holland had given him a free hand to change the personnel of the town governments, took no notice of a list of candidates submitted to him, at Amsterdam, by a group of citizens anxious to have the urban government regime democratized. At his death in 1702, in many towns there occurred outbursts of popular fury against the henchmen with whom, in his single-minded desire to obtain blind support for his anti-French policy, he had filled the councils. I have already discussed Groen's reference to "the spirit of the majority of the nation." It is surprising to find this leader of "antirevolutionary" thinking, who vehemently rejected the principle of popular sovereignty as a product of the Revolution, demanding, if only implicitly, that the legitimate authorities should alter the form of government after the pleasure of the multitude. But Groen would have contested, and so does De Pater, that *altering the form of government* is a fair description of what the enemies of True Liberty wanted. Restoring it, preserving it, is what they were out for. I quoted Groen to the effect that the stadholderless regime was itself a departure from "the constitutional make-up of the Commonwealth." And hear De Pater:

> The development in the direction of the centralized state, which had been arrested by the revolt against Spain, had been resumed by the Princes of Orange striving after unity and monarchical authority. But Johan de Witt, in his aversion to Orange, reversed this trend again. Once more particularism held up the advance toward unity and centralization, of which the Princes of Orange in their offices and persons had been the embodiment. Looked at from this angle, the form of government defended by De Witt and his party clashed with the historic and national principles of the constitutional law growing up in this country.

I pointed out already that this view, particularly as regards the role here assigned to the House of Orange, will be frequently found expressed in the historical writings of the liberal school. Fruin held it; so especially did Colenbrander.[18] I can only say that to me it seems to be a construction, a construction derived not from the facts as they present themselves to historical investigation, but from the authors' preoccupation with the outcome they know and value and which they impose upon the past as a postulate.

The Princes of Orange striving after unity? I believe that we should begin by recognizing that nobody in the Republic—among the Orangists any more than among the Statists—had any idea of transforming it into a truly unitary state. Nobody wanted to tamper with the independence of the provinces. The revolt, after all, had been directed against the centralizing tendencies of the monarchy, and the federation resulting from it could not but bear the stamp of that reaction. On a continent where absolutism and centralization went hand in hand, the Republic, down to 1795, stood apart as a medieval survival. At most, attempts were made, repeatedly, to introduce certain improvements in the machinery at the center, improvements intended to speed up decisions—decisions that even might make possible measures of coercion, however carefully qualified, in the case of a province being remiss in the actual payment of contributions to which it had consented. Already Oldenbarnevelt had mooted such projects—the States of Holland man par excellence. After the sensational victory of 1618, even though it had been won under the Generality cry, Maurice had neglected the opportunity (or do we only imagine that one offered itself?) to reform the constitution. Frederick Henry, it is true, attempted, fifteen years afterward, to get foreign policy entrusted to a Committee of the States-General (the *Secreet Besogne*), formed round his person, which might no doubt in the long run have meant a considerable progress in that sphere. By abusing the committee for his dynastic aim, unfortunately, he radically spoiled the atmosphere required for its harmonious working, and William II's reckless action in 1650, in the name of (as I put it) "a corrupt States-General," made matters worse.

But Orange was not the only rallying point for attempts of this nature. I recalled those of Oldenbarnevelt. As a matter of fact the preponderant importance of Holland supplied the potentiality of a cohesive factor and motive force on which a Union policy might be built. Under Frederick Henry and William II the States of Holland had been compelled, in self-defense, to fall back upon the impregnable stronghold of their provincial principles. During the stadholderless regime, however, De Witt, without losing touch with that safe backing, resumed the attempt to implement a somewhat more vigorous general policy, a policy of what he used to call "the general dear Fatherland."

I note that De Pater explains the provincialist reaction after 1650 simply by De Witt's "aversion to Orange." That the happenings under Frederick Henry and William II made that reaction inevitable, is a leading thesis of my book. De Pater does not even allude to this. In passing he draws his own picture—and what an idyllic one!—of William II's policy, but without making any reference to my argument. I do not of course claim that my argument, with conclusions and all, should be one hundred per cent accepted. I know that no account can put an end to the endless discussion that is history. But to overlook all the arguments adduced and just to repeat traditional phrases and generalities is not to make a contribution to the discussion—or to history.

After the revolution of 1672, William III like Maurice after 1618, neglected to recommend any constitutional reforms. His position, in which he had to work with irregular means of influence, no doubt had some effect for a little while. During the second stadholderless period, which followed, a grand assembly of all the provinces was held (in 1716) for the revision of the federal constitution. Here the most thoroughgoing proposals (although these, too, aimed at no more than a more expeditious organization at the center) were put forward by the Hollander Van Slingeland. Again the practical result was nil. The tradition of particular rights, the jealousy of each province, and within each province of each town or group, in guarding its own, the veneration of that impossible system as the only safeguard of liberty—these idiosyncrasies seemed to rule even more completely in the eighteenth century than before.

In 1747 William IV, married to George II's daughter, until then stadholder of Friesland only, was appointed stadholder of Holland and of each of the other provinces. Just as in the case of William III in 1672, a popular movement set going by a French invasion brought about that miracle. There being one and the same stadholder in each of the seven provinces did in itself contribute to the possibility of conducting a more vigorous Generality policy. Before 1747, in the war of the Austrian Succession, William IV had not scrupled to use his position in Friesland to obstruct the policy of Grand-Pensionary Van der Heim with all the traditional particularist methods;[19] this at least had now become unthinkable. But when he was in this unprecedented central position in The Hague, the idea of any drastic reforms occurred to William IV as little as it had to any of his predecessors. As for William V, he considered it to be his task to "preserve everyone by his rights" and loved to say that he was "no friend to novelties."

The incapacity for taking one step in the direction of centralization came to light most strikingly when in 1787 the Orange regime practically overthrown by the revolutionary Patriots' movement, had been restored by Prussian intervention. This last episode of the old Republic (1787-1795) shows Orange in alliance with all the forces of conservatism, not only with the Reformed Church, but (*mirable dictu*) with the regent class, which saw no salvation anywhere else in the face of the advancing burgher democracy. From the point of view of centralization these last years were completely sterile, however greatly Grand-Pensionary Van de Spiegel, an unexceptionable Orangist, of course, exerted himself. Yet how modest, how merely technical, how careful in leaving the seven provincial sovereignties intact, was Van de Spiegel's program. Only when the Revolution swept northward, in 1795, did the great transformation from sevenfold confederation to unitary state take place, through new men, backed by the dynamic power of revolutionary France. That is to say—and I said it already—the change came . . . in spite of Orange.

When one surveys this course of events, it becomes apparent how unhistorical it is to denounce De Witt's resistance to an excessive arbitrary power as if it were tantamount to blocking the development toward closer unity, of which only the House of Orange could be the agent. Let every epoch be viewed in its own setting. Do not let us require of the men of the third quarter of the seventeenth century that they should have guessed that at one time, in 1813, a unitary state under an Orange king was to be established. Let us rather try to understand that generation's particular problems, the memory of 1650, the shocking event of Buat's conspiracy in 1666, and so much more.

It is only fair to Dr. De Pater to assure you that his article, which, as I have noted, served as a starting point for these reflections, contains several shrewd remarks that give one food for thought. Nevertheless, the extremeness of the method is very marked, and I have fastened on that aspect in order to bring out the more clearly certain tendencies that are no doubt less prevalent in Dutch historiography than they once were, but that have by no means lost the significance of actuality.

Finally—I hope that you have not got the impression that I have wanted to sing a hymn of praise to the Holland regents. De Pater suggests that in my view the Dutch nation in Johan de Witt's time was constituted by the regents only.[20] Nothing can be further from my intention. And if I have observed the Orange party during a certain period to have been characterized by somewhat unattractive tendencies, I do not dream of wanting to extend my observation either to the entire party or to the entire period of its existence. All that I desire is that historians, in judging the men of the seventeenth century, should not use indiscriminately standards borrowed from our own time, as for instance, Democracy; or Free Church; or Unitary State.

(1954)

4

THE BATAVIAN REVOLUTION: 1795-1798

I propose here to offer an interpretation of the Batavian Revolution as it occurred during the years 1795 to 1798. Let me begin by recalling the main facts.

The Batavian Revolution had had a prologue, before the French Revolution broke out, in the Patriots' movement. In it at first the "regents"—that is, the governing patricians—especially of the province of Holland, co-operated with the middle class against the stadholders, but soon it developed into a middle-class democratic movement directed against the regent oligarchy. It was stopped in mid-course in 1787, when a Prussian army, backed by English diplomacy, invaded the country and re-established William V in The Hague. The regime overthrown in January 1795, when the French revolutionary army crossed the frozen rivers, was that of this restored Orangist party, blindly addicted to a policy of no-change and with no roots in broad middle-class opinion anxious for reforms. Thousands of Patriots had emigrated in 1787, most of them to France, where they soon witnessed a Revolution on lines at first simply parallel to those on which their own ideas had run, but before long reaching out to encompass extreme ambitions of which they had never dreamed.

When the French came, in January 1795, the Orangist regime collapsed. The Stadholder fled to England. The French left the revolution-making to the Patriots, who had a widespread secret organization and now set immediately to work. First in Amsterdam, then in one town after another, the oligarchic town governments were dismissed—all in an orderly and almost ceremonious manner—and, to the acclamations of the crowd, new men were installed: all this before the French troops were actually on the spot. Of these new men, a few were ex-regents of Patriotic principles; most were well-to-do burghers immediately below the regent class. There was, however, also a sprinkling of humbler men. A striking departure from the old ways was the appearance of Catholics and Protestant dissenters among the elected: the political monopoly of the Reformed Church was, after two centuries, broken. The revolutionized town councils in each of the seven provinces sent deputies to their respective provincial capitals, and thus the personnel of the provincial States assemblies was everywhere changed; the revolutionized States assemblies sent deputies to compose a new States-General in The Hague.

A new States-General, but still no more than an assembly of delegates of the provinces. The first task confronting the new men was to reorganize and strengthen the Union. It could be tackled only after relations with the French deliverers (or was it conquerors?) had been regularized. The treaty concluded in May 1795 was onerous and disappointing, but at least the Batavian Republic now had the recognition of the French Republic.

As for the establishment of a real union in the place of the old loose confederation, it was especially the province of Holland, crushed under the load of provincial debt, and radicals all over the provinces, who wanted the provinces to be merged into the Republic. Many of the old Patriots, however, anti-Orangist and enlightened as they might be, did not want to give up the provincial positions. Long disputes and negotiations were needed before, in the spring of 1796, a National Assembly could be elected by the Batavian people as a whole (including even the people of North Brabant, the Catholic region, which under the old Republic had been no more than "Generality Lands," not represented on the States-General, administered from The Hague), an assembly no longer dependent on the provincial States assemblies, but representing the nation.

Before consenting to this revolutionary innovation, however, the smaller provinces had stood out for restrictive conditions. The *Règlement*, in which these were embodied, greatly hampered the Assembly in its first task, that of devising a Batavian constitution —for even now the provinces were still completely self-governing, and the independence of the National Assembly with respect to them was more nominal than real. A first constitution was submitted to the primary assemblies (that is, to the electorate) in 1797 and was rejected by a combination of radicals and reactionaries. A second National Assembly was still hotly quarreling over a new constitution when the radical minority, supported by the French army still stationed in the Republic, carried out, in January 1798, a *coup d'état* after the French pattern. The Assembly was purged of moderates, and a unitary constitution carried through with a high hand. The radicals who thus came into power were driven out five months later, and the moderates now ruled the Batavian Republic, becoming more moderate at every successive crisis in the following years. Only, the unitary constitution introduced by the short-lived radical regime of 1798 was retained. The old system of provincial sovereignty was gone for good.

In 1810 the country was annexed by France. In November 1813 independence was proclaimed by Van Hogendorp and his friends at a moment when a French army was still in the country. The Kingdom of the Netherlands, under the House of Orange, was subsequently founded.

Neither the Patriots' movement of the middle eighties nor the Batavian episode beginning in January 1795 has had a good press with Dutch historians. It is small wonder, really, that the first generation after the restoration could not take an objective view of the passions and ideals of twenty years before. The intervening period had been a series of humiliations and disappointments, culminating in the complete loss of independence. Many ex-Batavians occupied leading positions under the new Orange king, but they were Batavians come to resipiscence; they preferred not to remember their giddy youth in any detail. "Forgive and forget," the official policy, suited them excellently. There was, too, a group of full-blooded counterrevolutionaries, not politically influential, but vocal, and indeed the inspirers of a revival of orthodox Calvinism; these men propagated a view of history in which the Batavians were no better than traitors to God, to their country, and to the divinely appointed House of Orange.

All this is as one might expect it to be. But long before the middle of the nineteenth century there was a vigorous liberal movement intent upon reforms that can be seen as aimed at the resumption and continuation of the work of the Batavians where it had got stuck or been undone by the conservative reaction that had set in soon after 1798. It is at first sight surprising that liberal historians should not have done more for the rehabilitation of the men of 1795. On the whole, these historians, too, were critical of Patriots and Batavians, although indeed they criticized them from a different point of view than did the counterrevolutionaries and the Catholics—for the Catholics, too, forgetting that they owed their emancipation to the men of 1795, were unsympathetic.

The liberal attitude of depreciation reached its zenith in the work of a modern professional historian who began writing just at the opening of the twentieth century, Colenbrander, later Professor of National History at Leyden. Every student of the period is in Colenbrander's debt, for he edited an impressive row of volumes (entitled *Gedenkstukken*) containing documents—not so much official, as correspondence from many sources both Dutch and foreign. (Among the documents there are many in French and in English: let nobody be frightened off by the title!)

But with all respect for the *editor* and his great knowledge and bold conception, the influence of the *historian*, in his introductions and in the monograph he published in 1907, was as unfortunate as it was profound. In examining the events and the men of 1795, Colenbrander could never rid his mind of the dogmatically held conviction that the spirit of the time, or the tide of history, was leading irrestibly to a change from the traditional society of privilege and particularism to the modern one of equal rights in State unity and centralization. But if the historian judges the men of the past by the standard of the actual outcome that environs him and allows *it* to determine and limit his awareness, if he requires of them that they should know it all beforehand as he knows it afterward, he will not be capable of a fair, of a truly historical, vision.

Now this was exactly Colenbrander's attitude toward the Batavians. And it was not only that he judged them by the outcome, he allowed his mind to be dominated by the grandiose spectacle (or so it seemed to him) of the French Revolution. He was not singular in this. Many Dutch writers took—unconsciously—the French Revolution as their model of how a revolution should be conducted, and poked fun at the Batavians, who prided themselves upon their *calmness*—a word frequently used with some complacency by the men of 1795. This revolution without bloodshed seemed but a poor specimen of the genus to later writers, although, and that is the funny part of it, they themselves were far from being in their own day such fierce revolutionaries—Colenbrander no more so than any of them.

And yet we find him writing that "the Batavians were ill fitted for the great work of renovation that awaited them. Only a small group among them was animated by a genuine revolutionary faith and had done with the past."

What an extraordinary saying, this, when one comes to think of it. How was it possible for a quiet, liberal, middle-class scholar of the early twentieth century so to identify himself with the Revolution? "To have done with the past" is indeed the customary illusion of all revolutionaries, but however sincere they may be, they will generally experience painfully enough, or at least the historian may afterward notice, that the past had not done with them.

Colenbrander, moreover, seems to think that all the Batavians had to do was to take their revolutionary wisdom ready-made from France. "The School of Revolution" is what he calls the exile in France of the refugees of 1787; and when the Batavian Revolution, after its hopeful start, appears to lose impetus and spirit so quickly, he blames it on the Patriots who had stayed at home and had missed that enlightening experience.

After getting to know the period a little more intimately than was possible from textbooks, I began to realize that the Batavian Revolution had its own character and necessarily tended to follow a course of its own. Tenderness toward the past, which one can indeed every now and again observe in many of its leaders, was a national feature distinguishing the Batavian from the French Revolution, and it sprang naturally from the circumstances and conditions in which the Batavian Revolution was set, circumstances and conditions differing markedly from those that made the French Revolution what *it* was.

There were two great problems, or sets of problems. Let me first take the problem of unity, of the merging of the provinces into a unitary state. I mentioned the confused bickerings in which three years were wasted, until the Gordian knot was cut by a *coup d'état* that was assisted by the French. Not a very inspiring story no doubt. But before one pours scorn on the small provinces and the conservatives generally, who resisted, and on Holland and the radicals, who proved unable to overcome that resistance more quickly or more independently—before, especially, one talks as if the French were gifted with more political insight or energy than these halfhearted, fumbling Batavians—it is well to remember one or two things.

The One and Indivisible French Republic, which emerged so

impressively from the Revolution—not without murderous party struggles however—had been for centuries prepared by the monarchy. Since Tocqueville's great work, *L'Ancien Régime et la Révolution*, which appeared in 1856, historians are familiar with that view. In France all local independence had been, if not destroyed, left an empty shell. The decisive figures in the administration had become the intendants, as against whom neither the provincial governors, drawn from the high nobility though they were, nor the provincial States assemblies, insofar as the provinces still had any, counted for anything, and these intendants were themselves but the executors of the orders of the central government. It was an easy matter for the Revolution to sweep away the remnants of a feudal past that had lost all reality and therefore all power of resistance. Whereupon the *Comité de salut public*, and soon Bonaparte, found in the monarchical tradition of centralization, firmly grounded in usage and habits of thought, the foundation—and more than that—for a rigid unitary system.

But was this system so salutary that we must blame that generation of Dutchmen when they jibbed at having it forced upon them? At any rate, nothing had prepared them for it. Under the old Republic, federalism[1] had very nearly preserved its medieval vigor. In his daily life the Zeelander knew no other than Zeeland authorities and laws, and the same was true for the Frisian, for the Hollander, etc. As for the building up of a system of officials who would meddle from The Hague in the internal affairs of the provinces, undermining, or even touching, the full authority of the provincial States assemblies—in the matter of finance, for instance, or of justice—such a thing had never even been thought of.

There can be no two opinions about the inconvenience of the existing system from the point of view of the Union. Defense and foreign policy, the only departments really with which the Union was supposed to meddle, had suffered only too badly from the need to make seven sovereign provinces agree before any decision could be taken. Yet the fact remains that no radical change had ever been so much as contemplated. *Corrections*, in order to strengthen the central government—even the Patriots had not gone any further than that.

Pieter Paulus, in his four-volume *Comment on the Union of Utrecht*, published in 1777, had written that, if only some small improvements were introduced, he could not imagine a better constitution for the Republic. This same Pieter Paulus in March 1796 became the first president of the National Assembly, an assembly that promptly went against the revered Union of Utrecht, and that was under the pressure of Paulus's province of Holland—and this with the full concurrence of Paulus personally

—to devise a new constitution that was to leave exactly nothing of it.

Paulus was not the only one to experience this sudden and drastic change of mind. Another Patriot wrote, a few years before 1795: "When I observe the pinnacle of enlightenment and understanding attained by Patriotism here [he means, in France, where he was living as a refugee], and I remember the ideas I used to entertain about Patriotism [before 1787, he means], I blush to think how narrow they were!"

Here we can see that exile in France did indeed serve as a "School of Revolution"—to some men, and especially, in some respects! The spectacle of the National Assembly at Versailles, soon at Paris, and later on, the fanatical detestation of *federalism* as tending to weaken the Revolution—these were the examples by which the French Revolution exercised its most direct influence on the Batavian. Unity! away with provincial independence!—this was indeed something novel. But just because it was, the idea proved hard to realize.

If the change could have been attempted in the first revolutionary onrush, it might have been feasible. But nothing came of the plan that the radicals had once entertained for a revolution carried out by a central revolutionary committee backed by French military power. It has been seen from the bare outline I have given how, on the contrary, the change of regime was carried out locally, in town after town, then in the provinces, and finally in The Hague by these provinces; the States-General was retained in 1795, only the men were changed. The Revolution, in other words, permeated the federal system, without overthrowing it. The States-General proclaimed all the new slogans, but it was still a conference of sovereign provinces; of the various provincial *peoples* or *nations*, in fact: could anything more augustly sovereign be imagined than the nation of Zeeland (150,000 souls), or the nation of Friesland (50,000)?

By the time the idea of a national assembly was seriously taken up, in May 1796, the Revolution was firmly settled in the old federal framework. Is it after all surprising, does it show the unfitness, or denseness, or feebleness, of the Batavians, that it proved so arduous an undertaking to break through that framework and to merge the many into one?

Principles or phrases could not alter the fact that round every provincial nucleus not only sentiments, habits, traditions, but *interests* had gathered which were bound to be put on the defensive. One has only to remember the present-day movement for European unity to realize that slogans and projects are not enough. To effect so fundamental a change by negotiation, by a reasonable exchange of thoughts, by common-sense give-and-take, is almost without precedent in history. What is needed, generally speaking, is violence, that is to say, war or revolution. In the Batavian Republic the idea was seriously mooted only when the revolutionary moment had passed. In the end the question was solved somehow, as I told you, by means of a *coup d'état;* if not by violence, by the threat of violence; and a miserable business it was, there is no denying it. But that does not alter the fact that the long-drawn-out debate between Unitarists and Federalists in the National Assembly, a debate within the orbit of the revolution, was an inevitable and natural product of the situation.

Colenbrander (to quote him once more, and for the last time) found the heavy tomes of the *Journal of the National Assembly* merely dull. To read these debates, he says, is exhausting work, to listen to them must have been awful. Indeed, there was a very great deal of talk, and that generation, not of Dutchmen only, was inclined to be long-winded in its eloquence. But to dismiss the speeches, and the whole of that contest between two opposing philosophies of politics and of the state, in so airy a fashion seems to me to be the sign of a curious lack of perception. I, too, have at times felt overcome by weariness while seeking my way through those many thousands of closely printed pages. But I was nevertheless fascinated.

The Federalists, champions of provincial rights and separateness, who are generally pictured as benighted reactionaries whose arguments are too contemptible to note, had a great deal to say for themselves and at times said it very well. They defended provincial independence as the palladium of true liberty, of liberty in the true Netherlands tradition. The radicals might talk as if the Revolution asked its adherents to speak all of a sudden of the Union of Utrecht with nothing but ignominy. "The Gothic monstrosity," "the misshapen constitutional abortion"—such were the terms the radicals seemed to look upon as obligatory when referring to it. But there were many who stood up manfully for the honor of the glorious ancestors. Thoroughly unrevolutionary utterances (utterances that Burke would not have disowned) were at times heard from supporters of the Revolution, and not only from citizens of the smaller provinces alarmed about their particular sovereign rights, but from Hollanders.

This is the question (I quote now from the pamphlet of a well-known publicist, Swildens):

> Where can the ultimate guarantee and mainstay of our civic freedom reside most safely, for every town, for every village, for every family, for you and for me, for each and for all? . . . In

a national assembly after the French example, that is, in the top of the tree swept by the winds? Or, in accordance with the nature of our provincial representative bodies, at the bottom, in the resisting fundamental roots?

And in the National Assembly itself similar sentiments were expressed. Long before 1798, when the stumbling block of the federalist *Règlement* was at last removed by the *coup d'état* of the radicals, there had been proposals to circumvent or get rid of it. Speaking on one such occasion in opposition to Vreede, the radical leader who later on, after the *coup d'état*, was to become one of the five Directors, De Mist, from Overijssel, warned against the tendency of domination inherent in all government, and against the despotism of an unfettered assembly. Bicker, an Amsterdam ex-patrician, did not scruple to give point to the allusion by reminding the Assembly of the French Convention under Robespierre three or four years before, which he had witnessed from near by, for he had spent the years after 1787 in exile. Apparently "the School of Revolution" had taught *him* to be on his guard. Bosveld, too, a Reformed minister at Dort, another Hollander, had nothing but contempt for the arguments of a radical speaker who had denounced, as bordering on sacrilege, all doubts of the wisdom of an assembly directly representing the people. To Bosveld, that was no more than a new fashion in flattery, similar to "the flattery that used to be showered on the great ones of this earth."

Must the resistance to a development that we all know has on the whole triumphed be dismissed with a shrug as the futile efforts of men who lagged behind their time? If one approaches these debates in that frame of mind, one will hardly *notice* utterances such as I have quoted, and all the protracted quarreling and shilly-shallying will appear senseless and indeed arouse no other feelings than those of boredom. But no, the opponents, too, can claim the attention of the historian, and as soon as he listens to them, he will understand that they, too, had a foothold in reality. The reality in this instance being that in the Netherlands—profoundly differing from France!—local autonomy was still untouched, and for all that it may have hampered and paralyzed the conduct of Union affairs, in its various particular domains it retained a full measure of self-confidence and of vitality. But indeed, if I spoke a moment ago of a development that has *on the whole* triumphed, this *on the whole* may well be particularly stressed. The moderates sounded a specifically Dutch note, and they did make their contribution to the future.

It should certainly not be overlooked that in France, too, a strong reaction was making itself felt against the dangers, which had been only too patent, inherent in one all-powerful assembly. This reaction had found shape in the constitution of the year III (1795) with its two-chamber system and five directors. In the debate about that constitution, Sieyès had roundly denounced the principle of absolute and monolithic public authority, and by implication the doctrine of Rousseau. But why was it, according to him, that the idea of popular sovereignty had taken on such overwhelming importance in the imagination of the French? Because (and I quote from the *Moniteur réimprimé*), their minds being still full of the superstition of royalty, the French had looked upon it as their duty to equip the sovereignty of the people with the entire heritage of imposing attributes and unlimited powers from which the usurped sovereignty (of the kings) had borrowed its splendor. This was the reason why (as Sièyes could not foresee in 1795) the new French constitution was soon to be displaced by one in which authority was again pushed to the farthest limits. Now this tradition was nonexistent in the Netherlands, and here we have one of the reasons why the radical-revolutionary solution could not really flourish there.

Moreover, in the Netherlands—and this has, of course, a great deal to do with the fact just mentioned—the social order left behind by the old regime still possessed a good deal of prestige. It had defects, no doubt. The blackest spot in the picture was the disarray of the country's economics caused by the falling off of the old carrying trade and resulting in permanent unemployment and a distressed proletariat, but the defects that had roused articulate political opinion were those that proceeded from the practical monopoly of political offices enjoyed by the burgher regent class and the nobility, and also from the predominant position of the Reformed Church. Most of these defects had been done away with by the Revolution in its first stage. And apart from this, there had never been those crying abuses of the unequal incidence of taxation, of the arbitrary methods of dispensing justice. There was not that deep-seated hatred between the various classes that had in France led to the dissolution of all social ties when once the Revolution began.

There, indeed, dissolution was far advanced even before the crisis. Tocqueville gives an impressive picture of a society broken up into a multitude of particles, all powerless, all separated one from the other by jealousies of rank or privilege; nowhere were a dozen men to be found who were used to working together independently for a public purpose. And indeed the Frenchmen reporting home on conditions in the country newly liberated (or conquered) remarked on the surprising number of men available in the Dutch provinces who were practiced in public business of some kind.

This brings me to the second problem, or set of problems. After the conflict between unitarism and federalism, the conflict between democracy and aristocracy, between—practically speaking—the lower middle-classes and the higher, close to, or connected with, the old ruling group of the regents. Here rises the question of "the people."

There was a good deal of unrest among the small middle-classes, focused in the agitation of the clubs, or popular societies. The clubs threw themselves into the forefront of the fight for unity, but what really moved the classes for which they spoke were social grievances and social aspirations. They demanded equality in real earnest. They fulminated against the men who, while professing to be supporters of the Revolution, wanted to preserve all that they could of the old order, who (as a speaker said in the National Assembly) "swore by Roman law and the Union of Utrecht."

Roman law, or indeed law, seemed to the radicals nothing but an obstacle in the path toward the rights of nature and toward enlightenment. A revolutionary regime had been set up late in 1795 in Friesland, with the connivance of the Holland moderates and of the French, both of which groups were working for more unity in the government and wanted to break the obstruction of the Friesland Federalists. Friesland now did indeed vote for the National Assembly, but the radical regime in the province pursued social aims that the Holland Unitarists (who were by no means radicals in the social sense) and the French government (which at this moment detested Jacobinism) were soon watching with grave concern. This Frisian government got involved in a violent quarrel with its own provincial Court of Justice, and in the course of it, it passed a decree expressly to abolish the ancient rule that in order to qualify for membership in the Court the degree of doctor of laws was required; after which it went on to compose a new court out of club agitators—a spirited publicist, a dissenting clergyman, and so on.

These were indeed ideas and actions inspired by the true revolutionary spirit. Advocacy of a total renovation, not only political but social; impatience with all restraints; and above all, a wholehearted conviction that the radicals' own views and policies were the only true ones, the ones needed for the well-being of *the people*. For—to complete the picture of revolutionary mentality and method—although so obviously representing only a minority and freely admitting the fact, the radicals nonetheless claimed the exclusive right to speak and act for *the people.*

Listen, for instance, to Vreede, who, even after the miserable failure of the radical dictatorship established by the *coup d'état* of January 1798, not in a single province, but in the Republic as a whole, remained firmly convinced of his having been in the right. After the five months of his directorship, he had gone into hiding and during this time wrote a memorandum to justify himself. What had been the purpose of the *coup d'état*?

> On January 22 it was decided that not all parties should participate in the conduct of the state, but that only one of them, the Republican party [he means the Radicals] should enjoy this privilege, in order that all the other parties, under its energetic lead, might passively enjoy the benefits resulting from the wise constitution *it* was to draw up.

The one-party state, the dictatorship of the proletariat, or at least, the minority dictatorship—offspring of Rousseau's conception of the *Volonté générale*, that is to say, not really the will of the majority, but the people's will toward its own well-being, of which the people, misled or divided, may not be conscious, but which must in that case be realized by an energetic minority—this thoroughly revolutionary program is here expressed with admirable lucidity.

Unfortunately, however, that short-lived radical regime of 1798 had, in spite of Vreede's self-assured tone, shown little else than its complete incapacity to govern. In the forefront of its propaganda there stood two points, and it was these that roused the clubs to the highest pitch of eloquence and fury, made the surest appeal to the wider circle of their sphere of influence, and indeed formed the issue of all the riots and commotions that occurred, not only in Friesland, but at various times all over the Republic, especially in Amsterdam and Rotterdam. These were the two points: the dismissal of all officials, down to the humblest, in towns and villages, to make room for good Patriots; and the confiscation of the property of all ex-regents, of all the numerous members of the local oligarchies overthrown in 1795, as a contribution toward the payment of the war tribute to France.

Jobs, and spoliation so as to obtain a relief from taxation. Not an impressive policy!

The small burghers, who had greeted the Revolution with high hopes, experienced in reality nothing but ever-more-depressing economic conditions due to the interruption of trade consequent upon the war with England to which the alliance with revolutionary France condemned the country. Envy of the security of office-holders and resentment at the easy circumstances of the ex-regents, who in their day of power (so the club orators kept on reminding them) had plunged the country into its distress by their wicked subservience to England—such feelings must have come naturally to these men.

So the radical regime of 1798 had become an orgy of the most reckless corruption and persecution. The popular societies now had it all their own way. The dismissal of the officials began at once. In a town like Amsterdam it led to chaos, for the club Patriots had more pretensions than experience or ability. Meanwhile, the voters' lists were revised in the most arbitrary manner by agents of the new directorate, and the names of thousands of citizens—not of Orangists, for these had never been admitted, but of Patriots of a more moderate way of thinking, who proudly regarded themselves as no less good Patriots than were the managers of the purge—were canceled. When the regime was swept away in June of the same year, 1798, the old officials were reinstated and the voters struck from the lists put on again.

What seems to me most noticeable in this course of affairs is the indignation to which opinion in the country had been roused by the spectacle of these wild doings. Notions of law, of decency, of respect for the social order, proved to be powerful, and not only among the Orangists, who had from 1795 on been standing aside, but among those who had taken an active part in the Revolution. Their own leading officials, their generals, Daendels, who had put them in power on January 22, turned against the Directors. The press, too, all Patriot of course, was openly critical. The spirit, the temper, of the Batavian Revolution, it becomes plainly apparent, was not truly revolutionary. Why so much less than was that of the French Revolution? When one remembers the derelict mass of the unemployed proletariat, one will hardly reply: because the society out of which it sprang was sound. Yet, such as it was, it disposed of powers of resistance that had been lacking in France. Viewed as a whole, the large middle-class, higher and lower, was still bound together by respect for law, for property, and by a willingness to co-operate in compromise.

Very characteristic is the tenacity, and the success, with which throughout those years the favorite scheme of the radicals, the confiscation of the goods of the ex-regents, was resisted.

The tone had been set at once when in January 1795 the new municipality of Amsterdam, put in office by popular acclamation, elected a well-known lawyer, Schimmelpenninck, to be its president. Schimmelpenninck promptly told the members of the Town

Council that if—perhaps soon—the cheering were to give way to discontent and grumbling, he would still expect them to follow the dictates of "fairness, justice, and generosity." And when as a matter of fact the cry for the spoliation of ex-regents was raised, he got the municipality to issue a proclamation—as early as February 1795—in which the demand was firmly declined.

> The order of law would be overturned if punishment were meted out for actions other than those that, throughout all times, apart from political considerations, are considered to be morally reprehensible.

It could not be stated more plainly that the Revolution must not lay hands on the "order of law." "Throughout all times": no new calendar was introduced in January 1795 (as had been done by the French in September 1792), and no new code of morals.

> If these principles are abandoned [the proclamation continued], all stability in human relationships will be undermined. . . . To counsel differently is in effect to preach the law of the strongest, the favorite law of tyrants.

The Amsterdam municipality, then, put its foot down. The radicals on their part never gave up their cherished idea. Now here, then there, the demand was put forward, often supported by violent popular demonstrations. And yet, never was the spoliation carried into effect anywhere. The radical regime set up in Friesland in December 1795 had at once attempted to do this. It had been stopped firmly by the National Assembly when it met in The Hague three months later. After January 22, 1798, the Friesland radicals, exulting at the triumph of their party, believed they would now be allowed to mulct the ex-regents of their province. But on the contrary, the National Assembly, although now purged of some fifty moderates, maintained the veto decreed before the *coup d'état*. Van Langen, one of the Directors, a Catholic, in a letter expresses his disgust at this proof of the hold that moderate counsels had on the minds even of his party.

Yet another principle besides that of respect for property or for the established rights of individuals was plainly stated in the Amsterdam proclamation of February 1795: the popular will was to have no absolute force. Quotations could be multiplied to make you realize the force and the clarity with which that fundamentally conservative view was maintained against the impetuous claims of the extremists. The presumption, too, of the popular societies in claiming to speak for the Batavian nation—for "the right-minded portion" they said at times, but at all events they claimed that *they* were entitled to lay down the course—that presumption was diagnosed as such and denounced.

It was a logical weakness in the position of the moderates that they had co-operated in enacting regulations intended to exclude Orangists. But the radicals reproached them for being far too ready to fraternize with Orangists at the first sign of a defeated adherent of the old order acquiescing in what had been done.

> It is proper to their principles [so Vreede wrote of the moderates in his memorandum of 1798] to unite with anybody willing to be reconciled, and in consequence they now count among their number men known to be moderate partisans of Orange, of aristocracy, and the rest.

Indeed, after the experience of the radical regime of 1798, the moderates did enter into an ever-closer coalition with the really conservative forces in Dutch life, even with the more pliable portion of the Orangists—as Vreede had foreseen. But it was Vreede's intransigence as well as his inability, while in office, to control his followers which had left the moderates no choice. One can regret this development. But it would be a very speculative and unprofitable regret. The radicals had been shown up in their insufficiency. The atmosphere of Dutch society apparently did not favor this kind of growth. The moderates were a truer expression of the national spirit. And they were far from being reactionaries. Even during the period of turning away from democracy after 1798, they did not break faith with the basic principles of the Revolution. The archmoderate Schimmelpenninck, who was placed in a semidictatorial position by Napoleon in 1805 (by 1806 he had to make way for Napoleon's brother Louis, who was to rule over the country as king until 1810) had among his ministers some of the ablest men of 1795 and enabled them to enact some important measures to carry these principles into effect—a system of national education, a system of national taxation. Even under Louis Napoleon useful work was done—and done by Dutchmen. But nothing came of the improvement of the lot of the masses, of which the radicals had talked. The radical movement fizzled out. and the masses had to wait.

But meanwhile, the co-operation between Batavian Patriots and Orangists had an important effect in securing the future of the reforms that *were* introduced, by "nationalizing the Revolution" —to use a favorite phrase of Schimmelpenninck's, who had worked deliberately to bring this about. It facilitated the change-over in 1813 and 1814, when the elevation of William I to the sovereignty was effected without any internal shocks. No opposition, no blind reaction: William I accepted the new position "only under the guarantee of a wise constitution," and the constitution drawn up by a commission of men of different shades of opinion in fact meant not so much a restoration as a consolidation of the main achievements of the Revolution, avoiding extremes, or what were then regarded as extremes. One can no doubt think that the result was but meager, and also, that the slowing down and stiffening of the public spirit that characterizes the period after 1798 was a high price to pay for it. In themselves, nevertheless, the achievements of the Revolution, such as the nineteenth-century Kingdom inherited them, were important enough. Provincial sovereignty, which had made the government of the old Republic practically unworkable, gotten rid of; North Brabant and Limburg incorporated in the nation; the Catholics, over one third of that nation, in possession of equal rights, at least legally; the oligarchic system overthrown; and the principle of popular election maintained, however restricted in practice: the basic conditions for a normal development in the modern west European sense were there.

And one has only to remember France, and the terrible scenes of the White Terror in the south of that country, indeed the permanent feud between supporters and opponents of the Revolution which remained behind and which was to trouble the life of the French nation for generations to come—and there will seem to be more virtue in moderation than Colenbrander was willing to admit.

"The virtues of moderation." It may have seemed that this has been the leading theme of my rehearsal of the Batavian Revolution. Let me assure you, however, that it has not been my intention to preach a political sermon—on that or on any other theme. It is only that the incorrigible (or shall I say indomitable?) moderation of this Batavian Revolution has struck me as its most remarkable feature and that I have therefore tried to bring it out, and at the same time, to explain it.

To be moderate is not possible for everybody in all circumstances. And we have all of us *that* within us which makes us feel that history would be the duller if moderation were to be universally practiced. And yet—is dullness the only alternative to high drama punctuated by shocks and violence? I must say that I have found the history of the Batavian Republic far from dull. I can only hope that I have succeeded in making that clear to you.

(1956)

IV

REFLECTIONS OF A EUROPEAN

1 THE IDEA OF LIBERTY IN HISTORY

The idea of liberty can assume widely different forms as it is applied to different domains of life. I shall confine myself to the domain of history, that is, of the aspirations, the fates, the struggles, of men living in community.

Just by way of contrast, not in order to embark upon theology, I begin by noting what liberty meant in the Bible, especially in the New Testament. Evangelists and apostles all use the word in the same sense. "The truth shall make you free" (John 8:32). "The Son shall make you free" (John 8:36). To be free means: "Free from the law of sin and death" (Rom. 8:2). "Where the Spirit of the Lord is, there is liberty" (II Cor. 3:17). "As free, and not using your liberty as a cloak for maliciousness, but as the servants of God" (I Pet. 2:16).

The liberty that is here meant is a moral, a spiritual conception;

it is a psychic state. In history, on the other hand, the idea of liberty refers primarily to man's relations with other human beings or to the community; it is a political conception.

The first Christians indeed honored authority and the State, but they did so as outsiders: political intentions did not enter their heads. Later, when the State became theirs, and, later still, when Christian states took shape, this mentality could not remain dominant. Yet it continued to exist, and, fundamentally unpolitical as it was, politics were sometimes measured by it, with unfortunate or paradoxical consequences.

I am thinking of St. Augustine and his doctrine of the *civitates*, one of the faithful, the other of those who live after the flesh. This, latter he seems to identify with the State, whose rulers, proud and divided by quarrels, strive after greater power by conquest, using God at best as a device to enjoy the world; while the faithful live in love and use the world to enjoy God. The *civitas terrena* will perish; the *civitas caelestis* will inherit eternity. Augustine's vision, marked as it may be with spiritual conceit, has grandeur. And as regards the political consequences to which I alluded, inherent in this doctrine is the danger that it will divert its followers' attention from politics, that they will look down upon earthly turmoil with self-satisfied contempt.

This consequence may be found unmistakably in Luther. More than a thousand years later, his *Liberty of a Christian Man*, that famous treatise of 1520, a powerful testimony of faith, seeks freedom in surrender to Christ and nowhere else. The Christian does not need the State. The State, on its part, must not meddle with men's souls. Apart from that, its power is unlimited; and again, apart from one reservation, the Christian, too, must submit to authority. The rulers are God's jailers and executioners. "God is a great lord, that is why he must have such noble, highborn, and wealthy executioners and executioners' servants, and it is his gracious pleasure that we shall call them gracious lords, throw ourselves at their feet, and be submissive to them in all humility."

The Christian's withdrawal into his spiritual life, quietly leaving the authorities to their task, which consists of nothing but the disciplining and chastisement of the wicked, represents an attitude of mind by which Lutheranism has certainly inhibited, not promoted, the cause of secular, or political, liberty.

But the European world took its traditions not only from the Bible, and Christianity itself could not stay within the narrow confines of this conception of the State. Side by side with the line that I have indicated, there is one that has its origin in the pre-Christian civilization of Greece, one, moreover, to which the Church had adapted its theory of the State long before Luther's time. I am not thinking of Plato, whose system, it is true, centered on an idealized state on earth, conceived, however, in no less arrogantly absolutist a sense than was Augustine's kingdom of the elect, and claiming liberty as its own monopolist prerogative. I am thinking of Aristotle's *Politics*, in which he proceeds from the simple observation that man is a social being. This view was adopted by Thomas Aquinas, the great thirteenth-century philosopher of the Roman Catholic Church. And it was enough to prevent the self-righteous isolation of the faithful and their indifference toward the State from becoming a current proposition in general Christian ethics.

The implications were of immeasurable importance. As soon as the State was accepted as an institution naturally appertaining to man, interest in its organization was bound to be aroused. Thomas follows Aristotle also where the ancient philosopher distinguishes three forms of political constitution: monarchy, aristocracy, and democracy. Discussing the merits of each, he concludes in favor of monarchy. Monarchy become despotism is, he admits, the worst polity imaginable; but the advantage of one-man rule, if the king sincerely tries to promote the common weal, is that it engenders harmony and through harmony that order, or quiet, which is the State's highest aim. A much more positive definition, this, than was Luther's chastisement of the wicked!

The word "liberty" is not used with any emphasis by Thomas. It *was* by Aristotle. Liberty, so he wrote, appears to flourish particularly in democracies. Too often, however, it is the liberty to act as you please. And it is an error to think that to live in accordance with one of the other possible constitutions is to be considered slavery. Order, whatever the polity, means the security of the individual.

A contrast is making its appearance: liberty, order. Indeed, much controversy had raged about this contrast in ancient history, and in the later Middle Ages, too, it dominated the political struggles of the Western world. Thomas, so much is plain, has chosen order. The same can be said of Erasmus, in whom I see the line of Aristotle and Thomas continued. There is no trace in Erasmus of that Augustinian contempt for the world and its potentates. Far from indulging in the cynicism of Luther, who in his personal assurance of grace took pleasure in seeing rulers play the executioners to the wicked and honored them for it as the performers of God's awful judgment, Erasmus lovingly sketches the portrait of the Christian ruler. He must be like a benevolent father; he must not only punish, but admonish and teach. He must not act arbitrarily, but be the embodiment of the law. More, Erasmus would like to see monarchy softened with a certain admixture of aristocracy and of democracy; *sic volo sic jubeo* he abhors.

The word "liberty" does not occupy a central place with Erasmus either. He was a monarchy man, as indeed were, then and for generations to come, most intellectuals. They distrusted the unreasoning multitude and feared that popular liberty would interfere with theirs. But a liberty of a different kind than that of pure democracy had been inherited from the political arrangements of the Middle Ages, and by and large it was this that the monarchy in its striving after expansion of power found in its path—I mean the liberty of privilege, the particular liberty, the liberties (for here one should really use the plural) of groups, of corporations, of towns and provinces. When from the theories expounded by Luther and Erasmus, mutually so widely differing, one comes to the reality of their day, it must be noted that it was *this* conception of liberty that was the issue of much contest. Traces of it are indeed to be found in Erasmus's treatise, where we saw him attempt to make the monarchy come to terms with it. The combination, or mingling, of the two which he recommended still actually existed, although not always leading to harmony.

In the centuries after the great migrations, serfdom had formed the sharpest contrast to personal freedom in the areas of Germanic settlement. The serfs had for the most part won their freedom, but the free had forfeited a good deal of their liberty. The feudal system as it came to cover the entire empire over which Charlemagne had reigned may be likened to a pyramid of subordinations. Personal loyalty in exchange for protection was its leading principle. But it did not for long retain the simplicity suggested by my parallel. Great ones made themselves practically independent. Other relations of dependence crossed the original ones. And gradually, exceptions, or exemptions, were conceded. The towns, the monasteries, broke loose from feudal cohesion and obtained their own charters, their privileges, their "liberties"; privileges became the prized possessions of many groups.

To these exceptional positions, to these particular distinctions, the conception of liberty became almost exclusively attached. For the state, or states, that had originally continued the tradition of the Roman Empire this process of feudalization, subsequently complicated by the privileges, meant little less than dissolution. But in the late Middle Ages a movement in the opposite direction set in. Rulers, influential over wide areas, like France, or over parts of a wide area, like the German Empire, were trying to restore princely power and began building up the centralized and bureaucratic states from which the modern states were to spring.

And this led to that struggle between liberty and order which I mentioned before.

The liberty of privileged groups, corporations, or districts, should not be disposed of as mere egoism, disorder, a caricature of liberty. It meant something real. A striking token of this is the vigorous life springing up under these auspices in the towns. Yet the falling apart into separate areas, and within these areas, into more or less independent parts, the inequality of groups, each with its particular status and rights, constituted a hindrance for the development of Western society. In the struggle between liberty, as represented by feudalism or privilege, and order, as represented by the rulers, a struggle that was carried on for many generations and with varying success in the whole of western Europe, the modern observer will not find our conception of liberty a ready criterion by which to determine his preference. Each side made its contribution to the future as we know it.

Take Netherlands history. The Act of Abjuration, by which in 1581 Philip II was deposed as sovereign of the Netherlands provinces, is still so largely ruled by the idea of the privileges that it appeals less immediately to us than does the American Declaration of Independence two centuries later, in which liberty is proclaimed in more general terms. Yet in the older document, too, the love of liberty in general speaks with unmistakable accents. This document has its honorable place in the European history of liberty.

The subjects [so it was said in the famous preamble] were not created by God for the sake of the Prince, to be subject to him in all that he may ordain, whether it be godly or ungodly, right or wrong, and to serve him like slaves; but the Prince [was created] for the subjects' sake, to rule over them after right and reason and to protect them, like a father does his children and a shepherd his sheep.

And if he does not do so, but instead of protecting his subjects tries to oppress and overcharge them, to rob them of their old liberty [mark the singular], privileges, and inherited customs, and to treat them like slaves, in that case he must be considered, not as a Prince but as a tyrant and may, particularly by the country's States assembly, be deposed and replaced by another.

Their "old liberty"—but immediately after that—their "privileges, and inherited customs." The Netherlands revolution of the sixteenth century was not, indeed, one inspired by a general or abstract ideal (I leave aside the religious motive, which in the early stage of the crisis was of secondary importance); it was not intended to found a State in which liberty was to be carried through to its logical conclusion. It was intended to safeguard what was prized as an old possession.

The Act of Abjuration has been explained as proceeding from Calvin's constitutional doctrine set forth in his *Institutes*. And indeed, although expressly rejecting a change on the ground of theoretical preference or purely rational argument, Calvin approves of resistance under the conduct of inferior historic magistrates when existing rights are being violated. But the drafters of the Act were not so Calvinistic. I should rather say that both they and he proceeded from the same medieval tradition of liberty, one that was firmly rooted in the Netherlands, both North and South. It was even the fourteenth-century Charter of Brabant, the Joyous Entry, that supplied a particular inspiration for the Act of Abjuration (both Flanders and Brabant were still represented in the States-General that passed the impressive decree).

At the same time it is worth noting that Calvin, in marked contrast to Luther, did accept the State as a domain belonging to God's positive order and in which the Christian therefore had a task to fulfill. This alone is enough to explain how the Calvinists, so much more than the Lutherans, have been able at times to do something for the cause of liberty.

The Netherlands revolt, at any rate, was not one that in principle aimed at a renovation; it was a defensive revolution. Consequently, the Republic to which it gave birth north of the rivers can, considered purely in its constitutional appearance, be called a medieval survival. Provinces and towns, each equipped with its particular liberty; the rights of the citizens guaranteed by old privileges and supposed to be protected by authorities themselves deriving their power from old privileges and in whose election the townsfolk had no say: our conception of liberty is not satisfied by this oligarchic constitution of the old Republic. And yet it must not be overlooked that in the struggle against Philip II's despotism the general idea of liberty had obtained a strong sway over Netherlands political thought.

But whose liberty? Liberty to do what? These are the questions that must always be asked, and the replies could not always be edifying. The cynical but sharp-witted mid-seventeenth-century chronicler Aitzema taunted the Frisians, whose province was always backward in contributing to federal expenditure, with their habit not only of exclaiming indignantly at every attempt to make them pay more, but of accompanying their resistance with grandiloquent boasts of their famed liberty: "Libertas, et speciosa nomina," he comments (Liberty, and more such specious terms).

In France Louis XIV gave expression to similar sentiments with regard to the current conception of liberty. In his *Mémoires*, written for the benefit of the Dauphin, he explained that to promote the well-being of the people at large, to protect the little man's interests against the nobility or the urban magistrates and their egoistic use of privileges, one single authority is needed, raised above all and shared with no one, inviolable; only thus can the absolute king carry out his noble task. Many intellectuals were inclined to agree, some on the same high idealistic grounds, the majority, however, rather because they feared a democratic liberty that seemed to them tantamount to the worst possible tyranny.

We are now in the presence of a widespread state of mind. I hinted at this when discussing Erasmus. Shakespeare thought likewise. Even an early seventeenth-century Dutch patrician like Pieter Corneliszoon Hooft, the great poet and historian, looked with some regret upon the beneficent monarchy in France. And much later still, Voltaire expected everything from that monarchy, on condition, of course, that it would be "enlightened," and he kept hoping against hope that it would prove so. Those to whom culture was the highest good expected the absolute monarch to protect them against the mob, the populace, which might break loose and destroy everything. It was in particular the susceptibility of the masses to religious fanaticism which roused the intellectuals' feelings of contempt as well as of fear.

The classical example is the English philosopher Hobbes, who, shocked by the spectacle of the civil war in the 1640's, developed a theory of the state which was to exercise an immense influence.

What was the object, Hobbes asks himself, for which men in the condition of nature concluded the State contract? (For he makes use, like most of the seventeenth- and eighteenth-century theoreticians, of the fiction that the State was created by a deliberate agreement.) What was their object? To escape into security from the misery of "the war of all against all" (the condition of nature was, according to him, nothing better). Given man's unruly nature, power is required for that purpose, and in order to be effective that power must be unassailable, raised above all discussion. By that (imaginary) treaty, therefore, men completely and irrevocably transmitted their rights to the State. To the State they have since owed their security, their life, their society, their civilization, their law. Good and evil, unknown in the condition of nature, exist only thanks to the State. The State decides what is good and what is evil, what true and what untrue. Errors containing the germs of revolt must be suppressed; the State will see to it that the universities teach only the true doctrine.

Even for this horrifying system Hobbes enlists the help of the patient word, "liberty." It is a mistake, he says, to think that liberty should consist of lawlessness or should require that authority be unable to issue laws out of the fullness of its power. And in any case: "The measure of liberty must be calculated after the well-being of the citizens and of the State." A good deal of harmless liberty, harmless to the State, will, so he reflects, remain, and he does not grudge the citizens that boon. It will even flourish the better when, thanks to the State's all-powerful character, penalties have been fixed for good and all, and arbitrary measures have become unnecessary.

But is not it likely that this all-powerful State should consider, occasionally, or even frequently, an arbitrary measure to be good? In that case, nothing would be left to the citizens, and to Hobbes himself, according to his theory, but to acquiesce, or rather, to agree. *Leviathan* is the title he gave to his book. The State that swallows all, indeed. Totalitarianism, the denial of liberty.

I spoke of the immense influence exercised by Hobbes's theory. One sees the traces of it even in a country where the tradition of the liberty of liberties was strongly embedded, as it was in the Dutch Republic. Take Spinoza.

Spinoza's philosophical conception of liberty could not but make his mind susceptible to the attraction of Hobbes, although at the same time it caused him to preserve a certain independence. "Free is, not he who acts upon his individual pleasure, but he who can wholeheartedly live in accordance with the precepts of reason." If Spinoza regarded the all-powerful State as indispensable for liberty, he therefore at the same time postulated that it should behave rationally. But to say that he *postulated* this is saying too much: he *hoped* for it. And when he, who was personally not only rational but humane, attempts to smooth out the rough edges of Hobbe's system, his treatise takes on the nature of a plea rather than a doctrinal exposition. He describes all dictation on matters of inner conviction as "violence"; he judges a government to act unjustly toward its subjects if it lays down what should be accepted as truth or be rejected as untruth. That the government is entitled to do this, however, he does not question. "We are not now speaking of its right, but of the wisdom of its actions." He seeks comfort in the thought that no government is likely to be rash enough to offend its subjects, knowing, as it must, that its right only lasts as long as does its power (this, too, is pure Hobbesian theory). And Spinoza is happy in being able to point to the example of tolerance given by the wise rulers of Amsterdam.

He did not, like Hooft, indulge in an aberration into monarchism. He reposed confidence in the actual rulers under whom he lived, the patricians (the "regents"). To them he applied this high theory of the absolute nature of authority. Nor was he the only one to do so. Even more rigidly absolute was the sovereignty claimed for the States of Holland by the lawyer Graswinckel. The brothers Jan and Pieter de la Court, in their remarkable pamphlets, went no less far, although they permitted themselves inconsistencies, casting glances in the direction of democracy, using the *word*, at least.

It is a striking fact that all these men were faithful followers of De Witt, and that the great Grand-Pensionary and his friends in these same years called their regime the regime of "True Liberty." This elicited a good many sarcasms at the time, and also from later historians. The phrase does indeed appear paradoxical when it is remembered that among the citizens there was widespread displeasure at their complete exclusion from all political control. This "True Liberty" was the liberty of the new sovereign, the States assembly. "Their Noble Great Mightinesses" wanted to be free from the supervision of a stadholder, which might easily have become princely absolutism; free, also, from the interference of the commonalty, of the stupid, shortsighted masses, which allowed themselves to be incited by the ministers of the Reformed Church.

Now, every time the people raised their own democratic demands against this oligarchic liberty—and the history of the Dutch Republic is thickly sown with disturbances of that very tendency—they recalled the theory of the Act of Abjuration. The prince for the people's sake, not the people for the prince's sake, was its great tenet, and this was now directed against the new oligarchic sovereignty claim. The patricians were reminded that they wielded power for the people, not for their own interests. And for this course, too, liberty was invoked.

All through the two centuries of the Republic, "liberty" remained a great word. It was a word to which the Dutchman liked to lay claim for himself and for his nation, and it made him look down with a feeling of superiority on the slavery of the French, the Germans, the Italians, of all peoples living under despotism. In spite of the theories put forward at the time of De Witt, people and patricians were generally one in this. The Hobbesian doctrine had no more than a passing influence. The patricians might often be presumptuous, but they did not generally forget that their rule bore a representative character. This had in fact been expressly stated, in the early phase of independence, by the States of Holland in its famous Deduction of 1587. Representative, although not elected: to us this may seem surprising, but in the Middle Ages, and in the early modern period, "representative" and "elected" were not felt to be necessarily connected.

Until at last, late in the eighteenth century, the tradition of the Act of Abjuration and the Deduction was merged, quite naturally, with the new formulas of the people being free only if it is consulted or elects its rulers to carry out its wishes. In the American Declaration of Independence these new ideas, of course, occupy a central place; but yet, even it can be read as a late-eighteenth-century version of the Act of Abjuration, a modern confirmation of the old tradition of liberty originally wedded to privilege and to history.

The influence of Hobbes, however, was not wiped out by this development. It even appears most strikingly in Rousseau's *Contrat social*, of 1762. But before I come to that, I shall consider in its wider European aspects the countercurrent that I have just been noting in the Dutch Republic.

Two great names present themselves: Locke and Montesquieu.

Locke wrote in order to justify the Glorious Revolution of 1688. A king dethroned because he was violating the constitution. According to Locke, and this is the essential point, the subjects on entering upon the State contract had *not* transmitted all their rights. Men had had rights in the condition of nature already, and it was to safeguard these so much the better that they had formed a State equipped with no more power than was needed for that purpose. Life, liberties, and property, these were what mattered, and if the government laid hands on these, it laid hands on the State contract to which it owed its existence and no longer *was* a government. Resistance consequently became lawful.

Observe that this is precisely the argument on which the Netherlands Act of Abjuration was based. Locke stands indeed squarely in the tradition of medieval liberty, but by virtue of his generalizing way of thinking and arguing, and no less because the transaction of 1688 gave rise to the durable English constitutional monarchy, he also points into the future. The modern term "liberalism" can be applied to him without seeming overly anachronistic.

This is even more true for Montesquieu. Montesquieu wrote under the impression of the derailment of absolute monarchy as he had witnessed it in Louis XIV's last years. Those fine-sounding phrases in the young King's *Mémoires* about a task for the benefit of the people, how little did the practice of the reign agree with them! Power policy had become all, and endless wars had exhausted the country and hindered all useful reforms. Versailles, where the court was established in 1682, had isolated the monarchy from the nation. In the view of independent-minded Frenchmen, it no longer was the ordering, and when necessary, reforming, power—although Voltaire, for one, in spite of all disappointments, clung to this view almost to the last—but was instead a despotism, enamored with its own greatness, stifling all independence, becoming more and more arbitrary.

The theory of the State, then, as Montesquieu developed it, was inspired by the wish to safeguard the nation from this despotism. Putting it positively, what he wanted was liberty, liberty for the individual—actually, he was primarily thinking of the well-to-do bourgeoisie—liberty resting on a feeling of security. The laws, and the State, should keep their hands off certain fundamental rights, freedom of thinking and speaking, freedom to do everything that is not harmful to fellow citizens or to the community. But how to obtain that the State should stay within those limits? By dividing authority and at the same time strengthening organs that might resist it.

Not for Montesquieu, then, the one, indivisible, absolute authority advocated by Hobbes and so many others. On the contrary, Montesquieu wanted to have the executive, legislative, and judicial functions established as three separate, mutually independent parts of government; the *trias politica*. The exaltation of sovereignty, in which rulers and writers were on all sides indulging, was an abomination to him. Authority was not to be simply derived from the pretended right of sovereignty. It could not will after its pleasure. The highest resort to him, was reason, crystallized in law.

But moreover there were the historic bodies of inferior rank, to which he assigned in the life of the nation and of the State a role of essential importance. First of all the *parlements*, the courts of justice, manned by the *noblesse de robe*, to which Montesquieu himself belonged. He even went so far as to defend the vicious system under which the councillors' seats were purchased or inherited, because this engendered in the *parlements* an independent *esprit de corps*. Besides, there were the provincial States assemblies, urban magistratures, guilds, clergy—all these *corps intermédiaires* (to use Montesquieu's own expression) were useful in that they might resist all-too-importunate intrusions of central authority.

It was a broadly devised system. Reason, as we saw, is the ultimate, the decisive criterion, but to Montesquieu reason is not necessarily opposed to history. On the contrary, he likes to call history to its support. Consequently his system is, like Locke's, related in spirit to the Netherlands Act of Abjuration. But, again like Locke, Montesquieu nevertheless spoke for the future. His theories for the moment lent support to his class, the members of the *parlements*, in its opposition to the arbitrary actions of the monarchy under Louis XV, an opposition that a generation later was to create the situation from which the great Revolution sprang; but when I affirmed Montesquieu's significance for the future, it was not of this that I was thinking. Rather does his advocacy of the *parlements* reveal a reactionary trait in his thought. The *parlements*, which did so much to create the revolutionary situation, never for one moment dominated the Revolution, which was immediately directed against the privileged, that is to say, against *them*, at least as much as against the monarchy; and in fact all of those *corps intermédiaires*, to which Montesquieu attached such importance, were brushed aside by the Revolution.

In the American Revolution, Montesquieu's influence made itself more directly felt or rather, in its sequel, the fashioning of a constitution to take the place of the Articles of Confederation. The separation of the powers, which actually came to be a feature of that constitution, was advocated by Madison with arguments borrowed from "the celebrated Montesquieu."

But the French Revolution very soon turned away from Montesquieu and let itself be inspired by the unhistorical, absolutist spirit of Rousseau. Montesquieu's time, however, was to come when the Bourbon restoration seemed to have written off the radical interpretation of the Revolution as a failure. It was partly to Montesquieu that nineteenth-century liberalism owed the strength of a certain tendency characteristic of it, a tendency that had been presented with great force by Burke, in his famous *Reflections* (1790) when the Revolution had only just begun. Liberty? Yes, but liberty as an inheritance from our ancestors, liberty in historic forms; no nicely thought-out system, no abstract (or as Burke himself put it, metaphysical) argumentation taking no account of fact or circumstances. Because of his passionate detestation of the Revolution, all this has a strongly conservative bias, as presented by Burke. That he is, nevertheless, fundamentally a liberal, becomes clear at once when one places him beside a counterrevolutionary thinker like Joseph de Maistre, who, writing in the early years of the Restoration, openly mocks at liberty; or like the great Dutch eccentric Bilderdijk, who wrote, as early as 1793:

> The cheering subjects of a king,
> That is where liberty flourishes.

Montesquieu and Burke stand at the beginning of a line that was to be continued by Mme de Staël, Tocqueville, John Stuart Mill, Lord Acton. Of a liberalism, in other words, that was concerned about the danger threatening liberty and civilization from the leveling effect of a new despotism, that of the masses. Not that they, as in *their* time Erasmus or Voltaire, looked for protection to an enlightened monarchy, but they attempted to impregnate democracy, which they accepted, with respect for law and reasonable moderation.

But was not Rousseau the greatest preacher of liberty of them all? With what vehemence, in the very opening paragraphs of his *Contrat social*, does he take Grotius and Hobbes to task for having assumed men capable, by the founding contract of their State, of transmitting their liberty to a monarch or to a small number of rulers! No! exclaims Rousseau—for even in this succinct, almost pedantically positive, little book the new personal and emotional tone with which in his earlier works he had made so deep an impression breaks through every now and again—no! "To renounce one's liberty means to renounce one's quality as a human being, the rights of humanity, one's duty itself."

What could be more promising! But note that Rousseau goes on cold-bloodedly to assert that only one social contract is in agreement with nature, namely the contract by which each and every partner surrenders himself totally, with all his rights, to the community. From that moment on, this community is the sovereign. Upon the sovereign no fundamental law can be imposed. Nor is this necessary, for since *this* sovereign is composed of all the individuals having made the contract, it has not, and cannot have, any interest opposed to theirs. The General Will (*la volonté générale*), by which the State under this contract is governed, is always right and pure. "Whoever refuses to obey the General Will, shall be compelled to do so by the whole body; and this means only that he will be *compelled to be free*."

This, then, is the liberty that Rousseau at the outset so strikingly proclaimed to be the distinguishing mark of human dignity! He is back with Hobbes, of whose influence he, while denouncing him, carries the indelible imprint. The General Will in the place of the monarch, but equally absolute!

And now let us try to understand what Rousseau means by this General Will. It is not necessarily the will of the majority. The majority can have been misled. Separate groupings, parties, churches, those *corps intermédiaires* that in Montesquieu's eye rendered such useful services in helping to protect liberty—according to Rousseau all they can do is divide and confuse the community. The General Will, however, is the will toward the general weal; this will, Rousseau assures us, is present in all men whether they know it or not, and it can therefore be safely assumed never to err. It remains in all circumstances the sovereign expression of the community's true will; it *is* the community's true will.

This, too, points into the future. Toward the immediate future of the Revolution at its most violent, when Robespierre, with his small group of Jacobins, was unshakably convinced that he was the embodiment of the General Will ("inaltérable et pure") and that he was by it entrusted with the task of exterminating all who seemed to endanger the realization of the ideal State. But it also points into a much later future: toward all the minority dictatorships that we have seen, and are still seeing, in action.

Not long ago a French Socialist had a conversation with a member of the Central Committee at Moscow. "You tell me," so the Russian countered his arguments, "that only where the individual has a right to give utterance to opinions opposed to those of the government can liberty be said to reign. This may hold good for a middle-class state, where people and government are contesting forces. But how is it possible with us for an individual to hold opinions different from those of the government? All that we have is at the disposal of everybody. We are the government of the people; we *are* the people."

This is completely in agreement with Rousseau's doctrine. The State is a community into which the individuals have been completely merged. That State can never wish for anything that would go against the interests of its members. It represents the General Will, and the General Will is always right. If an indidividual wills differently, he must, for the sake of his liberty, be coerced.

It seems a far cry from Rousseau to the Soviets. I am not suggesting that this Moscow Committee member had read the *Contrat social*. But Rousseau's spirit, Rousseau's *trick*, this horrifying adulteration of the word "liberty," this argument leading to the conclusion that the citizen must find his liberty in the submission of his will to the State—to the democratic State, it is true, the State founded by the surrender of each to all—this Rousseauan doctrine has become the property of quite a school of thought, and it has come to the Russians via intermediaries. I am thinking in the first place of Hegel.

Hegel, too, saw the individual merged in the community, in the State, able to realize himself only through the State, and only thus finding his liberty. In his imposing system history is a development of the Absolute, thinking itself toward liberty—the ultimate goal. The way this happens is through a struggle of States, now this one then that being the elect of the Absolute and bearer of the Idea of History. Germany, Prussia, had been designated by the Reformation to attain the goal, as it was understood in his, Hegel's, mind.

The vision of St. Augustine's work, I said above, was one of grandeur. How are we reminded of Augustine here! Hegel's *Absolute* is Augustine's *God*, and the predestined goal of liberty toward which Hegel's Absolute is thinking itself is St. Augustine's predestined Day of Judgment, when he and the like-minded faithful will inherit the Kingdom of Heaven.

Hegel's "liberty" is, like that of Rousseau, a mere philosophical, or rather, romantic liberty; a liberty in the prophet's imagination. In reality the term is made to palliate a veritable enslavement to the State; and in Hegel's case, to war. For to him it is war that necessarily marks the stages of development.

Many men have since operated with this "liberty" paradox, and to suit very different purposes! There was Treitschke, who saw the triumph of liberty in Germany's victory over France in 1870, a victory willed by history. And there was Marx, who announced that triumph for the day when the proletariat should have wrung supremacy from the bourgeoisie and have founded the classless society.

"A community," so we read in the Communist Manifesto of 1848, "on which the free development of every individual will be a condition for the free development of all." The whole of previous history had been, in Marx's view, a struggle, not, as for Hegel, between peoples or States, but between classes. The bourgeois rule, under which men were still living at that moment, was in all ways objectionable and rotten, it must and it would be forcibly overthrown, to make room for the predestined final state of affairs.

The belief in one solution, the only and final one, to be forced through irresistibly, be it by Providence, by Reason, or by History, after which there will be no more strife and practically no more history: this absolutist trait all these ways of thinking (St. Augustine's, Rousseau's, Hegel's, Marx's, and that of the Moscow Committee man) have in common. And it is this very characteristic—absolutistic, simplistic, fatalistic, and, I add, unhistorical, however much its presentation is accompanied by rummages in the storage rooms of the past—it is this that lends these systems their power to impose and to fanaticize, and at the same time, charges them with deadly danger to liberty.

"There are two schools of democratic thinking," Professor Talmon of Jerusalem wrote not long ago, and he distinguishes them as the Liberal and the Totalitarian. One regards politics as a matter of trial and error and leaves a large domain of life outside its sphere; the other assumes a sole and exclusive truth in politics, and its messianism pretends to embrace the whole of life. "Both schools affirm the supreme value of liberty. But while one finds the essence of liberty in spontaneity and the absence of coercion, the other believes it to be realized only in the pursuit and attainment of an absolute, collective purpose."

I need hardly say that I belong to the Liberal school—liberal of course not in any party sense. Not only does the other attitude seem illusionary to me, but I see in it the negation of liberty. And yet I must add that by this other road, too—at the cost of heavy shocks and of a deplorable waste of energy, no doubt—mankind has sometimes made headway. Moreover, whenever it took this dangerous turning (for that at the very least it must be called), it was practically always the blind obstinacy of conservatives, or perhaps the shortcomings or hesitations of fellow democrats of the other school, that had tempted it to do so.

The liberty of the privileged under the *ancien régime*, and later on, that of the propertied bourgeois class continuing their tradition, was before everything *their* liberty. Nineteenth-century liberals too often shut their eyes to the fact that the propertyless masses, left to the free working of economic laws, were bound to be anything but free. These are undeniable truths. And this implies that Marx's criticism was up to a point justified and had its relative usefulness. The social struggles of the nineteenth century have made a contribution of irreplaceable significance to liberty. But that the cause of liberty would be lost without resistance by counterforces grounded in civilization and history—I for one am firmly convinced of it. Tocqueville's conservatism is at times somewhat obtrusive; in Mill's thought the neglect of the State and community factor constitutes a weakness; yet the emphasizing of the value of an elite by the one, and the other's insistence on the need for individual diversity and for totally unfettered discussion, count in the history of liberty.

I shall not dream of attempting to draw up, by way of conclusion, a definition of my own of the idea of liberty, or of "True Liberty." There have been too many such attempts already. Of the results some appear to me to be no more than impudent sophisms. Others do strike a chord. But to sum up in a formula the conception of its numerous aspects and implications—personal liberty and liberty in relation to the community, political liberty and liberty in social and economic terms—one formula, one definition, one recipe? I feel unequal to the task, and what is more, I believe that it is impossible.

Liberty in the full sense of the word cannot, in the imperfect society in which we imperfect beings live, exist. All that we can do is to strive after conditions in which as much liberty as is practicable will be attained. To strive—not by abolishing history and making an entirely new start. "Liberty": this word, full of wisdom, was spoken by Lord Acton, the Englishman who devoted a long life to collecting materials for a *History of Liberty*—which he never wrote: "Liberty is the delicate fruit of a ripe civilization." To strive, in the path opened for us by preceding generations, making use of their achievements, learning by their mistakes. To strive, and if need be, to fight. For unless they had the courage to stand up for it, liberty has never remained the lot of men; and that to fight, or to be prepared to fight, may still prove the only way to retain of it as much as we have, the years in which we live have made abundantly plain.

(1956)

2

"HITLER'S EUROPE"

The first volume of *Hitler's Europe* (edited by Arnold and Veronica M. Toynbee; issued under the auspices of the Royal Institute of International Affairs, London, 1954) is a co-operative work of seven hundred large and closely printed pages; I count nine contributors, apart from the two editors, of whom Professor Toynbee opens the volume with ten pages of introduction. In six parts we get accounts of the fateful six or seven years—in Germany, politically and economically, in Italy, in France, in the smaller countries of western, and in those of eastern Europe. An additional volume, of over three hundred pages, contains documents.

I cannot, of course, dream of trying to criticize in detail each of those parts and their several chapters. There are aspects with which I am insufficiently familiar, but besides, I am sure that you would soon get bored if I attempted to deal with the book in that fashion.

Speaking quite generally, I have found most of the chapters both informative and absorbingly interesting, and the book as a whole stimulates a number of reflections. But before I can try to lay some of these before you, I feel I must relieve my mind about the chapters on Holland and Belgium. I confess to being astonished that the Royal Institute of International Affairs should have entrusted these chapters to a writer who does not appear to know the language of Holland, which is also the language of the majority of the Belgian people. It is to this deficiency that I put down the errors and general superficialness of Viscount Chilston's account of what the Hitlerian occupation amounted to in those two countries.

A very great deal of serious, scholarly work is being done in Holland on the history of the occupation. The State Institute for Documentation, in Amsterdam, which exists solely for this purpose, has brought together an immense collection of documents pertinent to the subject of the occupation; monographs have been published, and are still being prepared, under the Institute's auspices. How is it possible that Chatham House has not consulted the able experts in charge of that great work?

Confining himself to German sources and the few Dutch sources available in German or English, the author has been unable to establish any real contact with the problems. All that he has to say on the evolution of public opinion under the occupation, on the part played by the Queen while in exile in England, on the resistance movement, gives but a blurred, and at times, seriously distorted, picture.

As regards Belgium, because a large portion of the national sources is in French, he has been able to give a more consistent and more penetrating account. Only, his inability to take any notice of what has been written by the Flemings has resulted in a deplorable one-sidedness. What, for instance, is one to think of the following statement?

> In view of the undeniably closer kinship of the Flemings with the Germans in the matter of race and language it was not unnatural that the Nazi movement should have deeper roots in Flanders than in Wallonia.

If "kinship . . . in the matter of race and language" really was the decisive factor, how does Lord Chilston explain that the *Dutch*

National Socialists remained so completely out of touch with the realities of Dutch national life? The fact is, of course, that among the Flemings there had for a long time existed a sense of grievance with respect to the Belgian state, French-administered, and favoring French as it did, a sense of grievance that could be worked upon in a moment of crisis. It is true that the most glaring injustices had been remedied, but nationalist resentment often survives its immediate cause (need I remind you of South Africa and of Ireland?), and in any case it leads quite easily to dabbling with National Socialist theories and to adventures in association with the self-styled avengers of the wrongs inflicted by the alleged imperialist nations. This side of the story is not even mentioned by Lord Chilston. Nor does he state with sufficient emphasis that, even so, the large majority of the Flemish people proved obstinately refractory to National Socialist teaching, and while he gives the names of a few French-written Belgian underground papers, he does not mention a single Flemish one. Let me assure him and his leaders that the Flemings did have an underground press of their own.

But I must come to the more general reflections to which the work as a whole gives rise.

What *was* Hitler's Europe? It was in fact no more than a part of Europe conquered and held in a stifling grip while the conqueror went on fighting for more, and finally for bare life. There was much talk in the early stages, of a New Order that victorious National Socialist Germany was going to found, a United Europe, united not only for Germany's but for its own good. Mr. Clifton Child brings out very clearly—it is one of the interesting points of his excellent chapters on Germany—that Hitler himself never believed in this fine talk. What he was after was the expansion of German power and the establishment of German supremacy over as many subject peoples as he could manage. For international consumption he could at times speak the high-flown language of the New Order as well as anybody, but in the circle of his intimates he once said in a burst of confidence: "Why proclaim German aims to the world? As far as our might extends we can do what we like; and what lies beyond our power we cannot do in any case."

We have here perhaps the fundamental reason why the Germans could not during the four or five years of their supremacy make any lasting impression upon the occupied countries of Europe. Suppose that they had taken seriously the conception of a European unity which the propagandists loved to proclaim. One can imagine that on those lines something might have been wrought with which, for better or for worse, the liberators and the liberated of 1944 and 1945 would have had to reckon. As it was, no planning, no large-scale political or social reconstruction was possible, nothing that might be termed a *policy* for the occupied territories. Nothing but subjugation, oppression, exploitation. And as soon as the occupied nations gave signs of having discovered that the occupation meant indeed no more than the advancement of the interests of the occupying power, all they got was worse subjugation, worse oppression, and worse exploitation.

The parallel with Napoleon's conquests readily presents itself, and Professor Toynbee, whose mind runs so naturally on parallels, does, in his introduction, mention it. He is, in my opinion, inclined to take Napoleon's European unity too much at its surface valuation. I am not forgetting that the Napoleonic occupation did have a policy, and that it did leave lasting results behind. But that Napoleon was in many ways Hitler's prototype becomes, I should think, clear when one remembers that he, too, might be described as the conqueror for conquest's sake, the conqueror who would not state his aims because he never knew if he could not go beyond them, the despiser of ideology too, ever ready to use phrases that might result in procuring him useful dupes—such as the unfortunate Poles.

But where Toynbee seems to me to go more definitely wrong is when he identifies the purely personal policy of the disastrous maniac Hitler with the Prussian tradition. To talk of "a Prussian tradition of finding no pleasure in the acquisition of power without savouring this by tasting blood," or of "Hitler indulging in the Prussian pleasure of offensively asserting his domination over satellite states and conquered peoples," is mere rhetoric, replete with prejudice. I have no call to defend the Prussian tradition wholesale, but I cannot help remembering how Prussia, when she acquired, at the peace of Vienna, the western German territories of the Rhineland and Westphalia, managed to weld these into her system; and the same happened after 1866. Mere denunciation of Prussia, in view of such facts, appears woefully inadequate. Indeed, Professor Toynbee here seems to depart from the argument of his own contributor, for Mr. Child insists, as I hinted before, on the purely personal nature of Hitler's naked power policy. Far from representing it as the resultant of a deeply rooted historical tradition, he opposes to it "the proposals for the re-organization of the European continent along the more liberal lines occasionally suggested by the German publicists."

It is at all events one of the central problems of Hitler's Europe, this conflict between the attraction exercised by certain tendencies of the New Order and the growing disillusionment attendant upon the practice of the conquest. There had been, in the late thirties, in most countries a weariness of the weaknesses of democracy and of the confusions and calamities resulting from the political and economic anarchy in which Europe seemed so hopelessly stuck.

That the opportunities offered by this state of mind of the victims were missed, is not to be explained by Hitler's individual opinions or peculiarities alone. His was not the only influence accounting for the completely amoral, immoderate, destructive tendencies of the National Socialist movement, for its *nihilism*, to use Rauschning's description of it. There were many, in all the conquered countries, who never for one moment were under any misapprehension as to the evil nature of the New Order suddenly imposed upon them by brute force and making ready to shape their lives. Yet in the first weeks, or months, of complete discomfiture due to resounding, and as it then seemed irretrievable, defeat, people experienced a kind of relief to find themselves still alive and the German soldiers not the fiends they had seemed while the battle was raging; the public at large was to a certain extent malleable, the New Order did in some ways appeal to it. It took the peoples, in all the occupied countries, some time to wake up to the hard truth that there was no possibility of compromise with the conquerors or with their system.

It would be interesting to draw a comparison between developments in the various countries. In a book in which these are treated separately by various authors one cannot expect this comparison to be fully worked out. But in reading the chapters of *Hitler's Europe* I was struck by similarities and differences; every now and again I felt myself faced by the problem: Why was it that things took this turn here? Why did they assume so different a shape there?

I indicated one particular factor that made itself felt in Belgium: the peculiar position of the Flemings and their feelings, or the feelings of a radical group among them, with regard to the Belgian state. There was another factor there: the most unusual position of the King, who personally acted as commander in chief. When he thought the hour had come for a capitulation, he elected to stay with his army, and rather than retiring to England and heading a refugee government there, as at that moment the Queen of Holland was already doing, he became a prisoner of war. There is no doubt that King Leopold's unfortunate decision was immensely popular, just as there is no doubt that the flight of Queen Wilhelmina and her government had been viewed by most Dutchmen with feelings of dismay and indignation.

I can well remember how men who had always professed (and professed in all sincerity) love and reverence for the House of Orange talked bitterly of desertion and betrayal. It was left to a minority to reason with them—to men who had not, perhaps, been very zealous royalists, but who had studied the international situation and cherished no illusions about Hitler and his crew. We had to explain what after a while became so obvious that it needed no explanation any more: that the Queen and the government would have been powerless, under the occupation, to prevent anything; that the Germans would have tried to use them as tools; that it was only in England, last remaining free spot in Europe, that they could preserve the continuity of Dutch sovereignty and prepare for a better future.

Yet it was not, as Lord Chilston thinks, the example set by the Queen which revived the feelings of self-reliance and of fortitude among the people of Holland. There was a hard core in the traditions of Dutch society and of Dutch civilization which needed no outside incitement. It was nevertheless a great and inestimable service that the Queen and the government rendered the nation by their going away and by their determination to stay away until Holland had been freed. And here the Queen played her personal part—I can think of no better word than: manfully.

One automatic effect of there still being a Dutch government was that it prevented the setting up in the country of a lawful government under German supervision, round which all the forces of defeatism, of compromise and collaboration, might otherwise have gathered.

As happened in France. The story of Vichy, as told by Professor Cobban, is an instructive, although a depressing one. The old Marshal, enjoying his triumph in the midst of defeat, partly through vanity, partly out of an honest but stupid hatred of democracy, presents a far from pretty spectacle. Yet that of the intriguers by whom he was surrounded is worse. Then there were the colonial governors sheltering behind legality and taking pride in carrying out the orders that were the price Vichy had to pay the Germans for its semblance of independence. But what makes it all so particlarly humiliating an episode is the fervor with which the majority of Frenchmen indulged in a veritable cult of Pétain as the savior of their country, because in the turmoil raging all around them he seemed to be securing them the comfort of peace.

The Dutchman cannot help congratulating himself that the history of those years in his country did not present the exact match of all this. But he should not therefore imagine himself to be immune from the weaknesses shown so glaringly in France. We were saved from the most insidious temptations thanks to the timely departure of the Queen and her government. And even so, the problem of collaboration remained, and people's attitudes toward it were often enough similar to those that can be observed in France. Indeed, everywhere, the reactions of the public will be found to have been similar; it was the different circumstances—different in France from what they were in Holland, different again in Belgium or in Denmark—that turned them into different channels.

But everywhere, there was this fundamental fact: people in responsible positions could not altogether refrain from co-operation with the invader. Their individual desires to withhold from him all services that could even remotely be construed as assisting him in his nefarious practices had sometimes to give way to considerations of the immediate welfare of the population. Exactly at what point co-operation became collaboration was a question that could not be answered offhand. It was apt to involve serious-minded and patriotic men in the most painful conflicts of conscience.

Resistance and nothing but resistance, resistance caring nought for all these nice distinctions and considerations, was a great moral asset. In France, too, it helped to save the soul of the nation. But it must always and everywhere be the affair of a minority.

I have broached a question here which can still arouse the passions of people in all the occupied countries. It is a great question, a question touching deep-seated chords of feeling. I can say no more about it now, but I am sure that later historians, too, will consider it to be one of the most fascinating as well as most trying problems of Hitler's Europe.

(1954)

3

OPENING LECTURE (OCTOBER 1, 1945)

When, on October 1, 1945, I lectured to my students for the first time since my transportation to Germany as a hostage five years earlier, I felt that the occasion required some introductory remarks of a general nature. I had no thought then of publishing the little piece I prepared, and I had even completely forgotten it when I happened to come across it some eight years later. I then included it in a volume of essays published in 1954 under the title *Historicus in de Tijd*.

If I have now thought it worth translating, it is not because I believe it will add much that is new to the views on history which I have already expressed on several occasions. But the circumstances in which it is set and to which it is a response do perhaps impart to this confession of faith a peculiar quality of immediacy.

(1960)

It is five years ago since I last lectured in this building. On October 7, 1940, I was arrested by the Sicherheitspolizei, and when I was released, on February 14, 1944—nearly three and a half years later—I had in the meantime been dismissed from my chair by the Reichskommissar.

So it is like a new beginning for me to be able to address you once more.

I have asked myself whether, under the impression of what we have been through, I shall speak to you differently from how I used to, whether the spirit of my teaching, of the information and the guidance I shall try to impart to you, will prove to have undergone a change. I believe not. Oh, certainly, events have not passed by without leaving their imprint upon me. You will occasionally, in what I shall from now on have to tell you, hear the echoes of the fight that we have all of us fought. But a different attitude toward life, a different attitude toward history, that is not what you must expect from me. The air resounds with admonitions: everything must now be changed, so we are told from many sides; the older generation and its wisdom have had their day. It is at moments as if people regard the catastrophies by which we have been struck as the doing, not of Hitler and his armies, but of our own shortcomings; as if civilization and society in this country before May 1940 were rotten through and through; as if salvation can come only through a new generation prepared to try new ways.

Now this is of course no more than hollow talk, and I haven't the slightest fear that you, as you are seated here before me, representatives of a young generation, are looking at me suspiciously or arrogantly, thinking in your own minds: Now what can this old fogy still have to tell us? Let me at any rate give you plain notice what I can give you is the same that I tried to give before the war. I have not been renewed or made over, I am still what I was—at least I hope so. I am not ashamed of my past; I am not appearing before you in a penitential mood. The best service I believe I can do you, and I hope with all my heart that I may to some extent achieve it, is, through my teaching, to put you in touch with the old civilization that the fury of National Socialism assailed and threatened, but God be thanked, did not extinguish. Through my approach to historical problems, through the whole of my mental attitude toward history, I hope to do my bit toward restoring and reviving old cultural possessions that in five years of oppression have shown their soundness and resilience.

Perhaps you attended, a week ago, in the Aula, the meeting called to found the "Civitas Academica," and very likely you supported the declaration of principle to the effect that the University must not stand apart from public life, that scholarship and science have a social task to perform. I am myself cordially of that opinion, but really I did not discover it only in the course of the last five years. The study of history in particular has in my eyes always had a social, a national, function. I have always been profoundly conscious of this, and I believe that before the war my teaching was already animated by that thought.

But let us take care. The community, the nation, have claims upon us; but we cannot give to the community and the nation the best that is in us if we don't cultivate our individuality. Science, and also the study of history, has a social, a national, function, granted; but it can only fulfill it if it scrupulously maintains its independence and proceeds undeviatingly in accordance with its own laws. Those precious acquisitions of our civilization which I said a moment ago I hoped to help you in restoring to their previous freshness from the ignominy and the neglect of the years behind us, are precisely those laws and the respect for them; it is the true historic spirit as it has been evolved in generations of European civilization. I have no doubt but that we, you and I, not in the least troubled by our belonging to different generations, shall be able to find each other in that service and shall be able to co-operate in concord toward the mental recovery that is needed after the malicious attempts at confusion and subversion that we have experienced.

I don't want to confine myself to generalities. What do I mean by the laws of the study of history, by those invaluable cultural possessions in the guard of our profession, which during the occupation were exposed to disregard and to distortion and to which we must be true if we want to be good Dutchmen and good west-Europeans?

I mean the sense of criticism, the courage to apply criticism, the fearless use of our rational capacity, daring to go where it leads us, even though in effect this may at times seem to put a distance between us and those verities that we can every day hear being proclaimed as eminently and obligatorily Dutch, or it may be, west-European. You know how National Socialism tried to enslave scholarship, and particularly history, to its pet ideas, to its myth. National Socialism had nothing but scorn for the independence of scholarship. History had to prove the cohesion and the worth of the People, the greatness and the power of the *Reich*, or of the Germanic Race—or rather, those great truths were to be taken as starting points, they were sacred, not to be tampered with, but to be glorified. The historian bold enough to criticize was denounced as a heartless individualist, a traitor to his nation. We take our stand against National Socialism, we prove our faith to our national traditions of culture, when we dare to think for ourselves, when we apply criticism, when we serve scholarship in accordance with its own laws, regardless of persons, regardless of people or nation.

'That is the first duty of historical scholarship, criticism, again criticism, and criticism once more. A hard duty at times, for it may bring us into seeming collision with other duties and loyalties. But in reality by being true in this respect, we are true to the highest values of our civilization, that is to say, to our noblest traditions, to what we owe before everything to our own people and our nationality.

Without allowing ourselves to be misled by current views we should search fearlessly for the reality behind conventional terms, behind nationalistic or party phrases. "L'histoire est une fable convenue"—there you have a cynic's statement, but insofar as it contains truth we must not acquiesce in it, we must attempt to dig more deeply, and our first task in doing so will be to apply criticism, to look at the facts dispassionately and unafraid, to use common sense. To train us in this exercise is one of the great gains that the study of history holds out for us, and I do not mean for the individual historian only, but for the community to which he belongs. It is salutary that there should be a group of men schooled in that discipline by which the dangerous clouds of fine-sounding words and of thoughtless repetition, of romanticism and of mental laziness, can be dispelled. This is one of the great social functions of—in a sense of all study, but I believe that the study of history is particularly important from this point of view.

I lay so much stress on this aspect because some of the effects of the deceitful and crafty propaganda carried on by National Socialism against the true scholarly spirit, against criticism, against the intellect, are still with us. *Intellectuals* is a word that still has to many ears a somewhat suspicious sound. *Rationalism* evokes the idea of *cold; criticism*, of *destructive*. But let us try to look at what has happened to the world collectively, as if from a distance, and we shall see that the most cold-blooded despotism and terrorism that have ever reigned, and the most terrible danger of destruction that has ever threatened European civilization, were made possible by a systematic extolling of instinct and passion above reason, by detestation and contempt of criticism. Reason and criticism are among the bulwarks of Western civilization.

But this is not all. A sense for criticism is necessary. But no less needful is a sense for tradition, love for what has grown, love for what is distinctively ours, or to put it more briefly, love and respect. Is there an insoluble contradiction between the first requisite and the second? Certainly not, although undoubtedly there is a tension. In any case, as it seems to me, this sense for continuity, the capacity for discerning it and the zest for bringing it out, constitutes an equally indispensable feature of the historic attitude. And it, too, is a precious feature of the civilization that has helped to shape us, to which we belong, and which after the brutal outrages of revolution and fanaticism we must patiently try to nurse and to develop.

Reason and criticism are factors we cannot do without, but they are not enough. Even he who stands up for the rights of reason and criticism, and, more, maintains that they belong to our most valuable cultural possessions, will know nowadays that the great creative forces of life, of society and civilization, lie elsewhere. Rationalists such as flourished in the eighteenth and nineteenth centuries are an extinct species. Nobody will nowadays regard the world as a mechanism driven by reason alone and to be controlled by reason. How shall we name those great creative forces? How shall we approach them? I am not lecturing on philosophy, and this is a question I don't feel called upon to deal with. Ask various individuals or groups of our national community, and the solution will assume sharply differing shapes. Here come into play deep springs of personal conviction. Our Dutch civilization, the whole of west-European civilization, is long past the phase of one interpretation of life common to all.

But this I think I may say, that the study of history can strengthen in men of divergent religious or philosophic sentiments a feeling of—how shall I put it? I have already used the words *love* and *respect*, and indeed I think that they render better than any the historian's attitude of mind. Without indulging in romanticism or mysticism, unbefogged, after having given to criticism its full due, we can by the spectacle of history feel fortified in our love for life, in our respect for life. The true historian may detest deception and violence with all his might, yet, placed before the great currents and upheavals of history, he will not scoff, he will not rage, he will feel awed; before everything, he will attempt to understand. In the manifestations of communal life, in that ceaseless alternation of the noblest intentions and the direst lapses, he will see more than did the eighteenth-century English thinker who described history as "the dreary record of the crimes, the follies, and the miseries of mankind." It is not as if I should want the historian to see everything in a rosy hue, to lay aside his intellectual or moral standards when contemplating the men of an earlier age; far from it. But the historian will learn to see those men in their human surroundings, and he will understand that the imperfections of both are the concomitants of that human imperfection of which he and his time still have their share.

History does not only fashion that understanding and participating attitude of mind in the most general way with respect to life and humanity; it calls forth feelings of kinship with the group to which the spectator belongs, it strengthens the sense of community. With understanding grows love for what one is part of, and a more profound and firmer love as it is free from illusions. A feeling of kinship, moreover, that can do without the incentive of hatred. Hatred for another people is not a historic state of mind. Hatred for oppression and cruelty, certainly; hatred for crime and deception. But the historian who seeks the support of reason and of criticism knows how to make distinctions, and the rejection of an entire people, or of that people's civilization, which is in so many ways intertwined with European civilization as a whole, cannot pass muster with a true historic appreciation.

In resuming my lectures after the liberation, I had to unburden myself of these general reflections. We stand at the opening of a new era in the history of our country, in the history of Europe and the world. If that is taken to mean that *tabula rasa* has been made and that we are starting afresh, history would be a subject that could have little contact with reality and with our actual problems. But that is a view I resolutely reject. In this new era the past will be seen to be continuing. Every revolution has imagined that history, so to speak, began with it, but when the dust clouds of upheaval and destruction settled, the uncommitted spectator was able to observe how many of the old trends were going on under the new surface, how much of the old framework of society and of civilization had resisted the impetuous passion for renovation. So it will be now, and more so even than was the case, for instance, after the French Revolution, because, although the material shocks have this time been more violent, Europe was not, as was the case in the eighteenth century, enamored of the new ideas even before the crisis, and when Hitler triumphed, these ideas, instead of being sucked in and assimilated by the conquered people, were on the contrary resisted and rejected.

History, then, will carry us to the sources of what still is our civilization, the civilization of our time. And it is a work of restoration, it is a work of reconstruction, to devote attention to our past, to study history. It is not an escape from the present, it is strengthening ourselves for the struggle that is calling us.

I tell you so, and I hope that you will feel it yourselves, or will learn to feel it. But this does not mean that I want to impress upon you that in your study you should be continually animated by present-day preoccupations. Not a bit of it. On the contrary. Plunge into the subject, work hard, stick to the laws and the rules of the subject, exercise your powers of criticism and of discrimination, treat the problems as technical problems. The other thing will come, if it can come, of its own accord.

Bringing the University closer to life—about which we heard so much at the meeting of the Civitas Academica—does not mean that we, in studying history, must all the time be on the lookout for the actual, the practical, the national, or whatever it may be in the sphere of interest of the community. If you have followed my argument that the historic attitude itself—the critical faculty, the sense for discrimination as well as for connection and continuity—that this true historic state of mind is in itself a precious asset for the national as well as for the wider European community, you will understand that I can urge you to give yourselves to the subject, to the study, simply, without distracting commitments, with wholehearted devotion. That, once more, will be reconstruction; that will be making your contribution to the restoration of our civilization.

4 THE VITALITY OF WESTERN CIVILIZATION

The great problem of our day is that of the salvation of Western civilization.

Let me tell you at once that you will not hear me speak in an alarmist fashion. Prophecies of downfall, laments about the decline of Western civilization—these are moves in the undermining tactics of its assailants. My theme will be, on the contrary: the vitality of Western civilization. But we must not hide from ourselves the fact that our life and our work lie under the shadow of a total menace, a menace from the outside, from Russia and her Communist or semi-Communist accomplices in our midst.

It is our duty, in the face of this menace, to maintain our position. A task that is perhaps all the harder because we must not expect the sudden and rousing challenge of a war: the atom bomb is the paradoxical safeguard of world peace. What is needed is an alert spirit of resistance to the insidious encroachments of a system that, in spite of all we now know of its practical effects, still casts a spell over backward or badly apportioned groups, over absolutistically inclined minds, and that turns to its advantage all our weaknesses, economic and social, but more especially, intellectual and psychological.

That is why it is worthwhile to examine a little more closely the campaign of pessimism and self-criticism which has the effect, whether intended or not, of weakening our morale. A variety of tricks are employed in that campaign. Pessimism even at times takes on the appearance of optimism and adopts a tone of cheerfulness and hope. Not that this is required on all occasions. There is in human nature a trend that responds to visions of ruin and decay. Against them the divine promise of eternal bliss can shine with greater radiance. Take Augustine, take Bilderdijk, the great early nineteenth-century Dutch counterrevolutionary poet. But even Spengler's unadulterated pessimism found a receptive public.

The course of the world's affairs has not so far followed the prophecies of doom. The generation that accepted Spengler as a prophet did, it is true, live through a severe trial of the West, but instead of this trial leading to dissolution, Western civilization came through it triumphantly. One has only to cast one's mind back to those anxious years before the war when the outlook seemed so gloomy: that powerful Germany, led by a lunatic—its ambitions aimed at the very pride and value of our life. The most oppressive phenomenon in those days was the fumbling, the disunity, the willful blindness, among the peoples of the West. The economic depression, which had done so much to bring Hitler into power, the paralyzing unemployment—there were moments when all this seemed irremediable.

But see: the war roused the spirit of resistance. Our civilization turned out to be possessed of profound reserves of strength. England's example proved fruitful because in the rest of western Europe too, the traditions of freedom and of human dignity were still alive. And the greatest miracle of all, the most hopeful happening, was when, after the collapse, the German people too came to their senses. After the destruction of their cities and the exhausting and upsetting experience of an inhuman regime and its savagery, German society was seen to have preserved the life germs of its better past. The German people were able, after that evil dream, again to unite with the West. History triumphed over the nihilistic revolution.

Yet our problem had not been solved. The Soviet Union had

moved into central Europe, and it seemed to be western Europe's turn next. In fact, history hardly knows solutions. As a Dutch poet puts it:

> Drama without a denouement; every decision
> glides over into a resumption of the plot.[1]

In any case, the plot of National Socialism had had an ending that we may count as a striking proof of the West's powers of resistance and of recovery. And this especially because there was more than a mere having survived a threat, more also than the reviving of the historic German people. I mentioned the economic distress and unemployment in the thirties. Today the Western peoples have succeeded, in spite of that destructive war, in raising the general well-being of their masses and at the same time in guaranteeing to the common man a security such as he has never known before. The welfare state is not, of course, a sudden post-war product. It had been prepared in a long period of social strife. It is now, at any rate, a striking testimony to the inventiveness, the creative power, and the humanity of our civilization. In the new contest that we face, the economic base of our civilization constitutes, moreover, a considerable element of strength.

I think I may already conclude that prophecies of doom supply no objective indications about the vitality of the periods in which they are pronounced. They must be explained by the subjective state of mind of their authors, or by the reaction of those authors to social phenomena that signified less than they imagined.

One might well ask whether the phrase "decline of a civilization" has any sense. A civilization is an extraordinarily composite phenomenon. Moreover, it is subject to incessant shifts and changes. Here old branches will wither away; there, at the same time, new foliage will be sprouting. We cannot expect contemporaries, not even the most learned sociologists, to be able to comprehend the whole in a balanced view and to speak of *flourishing* or *decaying* stages in a way that has absolute and universal validity. To pronounce the prognosis "hopeless" will always be a risk, and even with a "hopeless unless" (*unless* whatever the observer happens to have thought of as a remedy) one is presuming upon the sovereignty of the inexhaustibly inventive future.

Why then, these recurring fits of discouragement or dissatisfaction? Our civilization draws on the resources of a rich past, but it keeps on changing. Without change no life, and this is a sign of health. Nevertheless every change, however salutary for the community, or however salutary in the long run, will disturb individuals or groups and will indeed actually cause them hurt or damage. Here is a plentiful source of those complaints against the age which were indeed heard in previous ages just as they are in our own.

In the middle of the nineteenth century an optimistic belief in progress was prevalent. The triumphs of human reason were celebrated; science, technology, opened glorious prospects. Yet even then one can perceive a constant voice taking the counterpart and uttering the most dismal warnings. This very belief in man's independent power to determine his fate was regarded by some as proof of impending disaster. I might quote De Maistre or Carlyle or the Dutch Calvinist thinker Groen van Prinsterer. But instead I shall let you hear that voice as it is raised today.

The religious-minded man today is shocked by the ever-advancing de-Christianization. Over against this, the triumphs of science, and the multiplication of material goods, count for nothing in his estimation. Sometimes he even regards them as a snare and discerns tragic evidence of man's sinfulness in allowing himself to be deluded by the semblance of power over "all the realms of the world and their delight." I quote a contemporary Dutch Catholic writer: "Wealth has spread over a large part of the earth." When he adds "the wealth against which the Gospel warns us," he explains that the *attachment to wealth* is meant, the *striving after wealth*. "This desire, which has mastered mankind more than ever before, constitutes the veritable desert of God's Absence."

Now has desire for material well-being really mastered mankind more than before, and is it causing us to neglect the spiritual? If every prophet of doom, denouncing his age from whichever system of thought it may be, is inclined to invoke the comparison with the past, it is because the past lets itself be fashioned or simplified in the way that suits him. Past reality may get lost in the process, but the contrast needed for the effect will be obtained. The *historian* knows—or should know—that in the ages of the supremacy of the church, or of the churches, man was at least equally tied to the material; that his childlike or dogmatic faith did not guard him against passion or avarice; that the social arrangements with respect to property, public authority, and the dispensation of justice were accompanied by an oppression and a cruelty from which one might at least as readily conclude God's Absence. It would be an unwarranted, in the deepest sense unhistorical, conclusion. But this is true also for the present. Forms have become different. Dogma and organization have lost much of their power over the spiritual. But that is not the whole story.

The service of knowledge and of social justice and its rationalization can satisfy the need for the spiritual in a way that I imagine is in harmony with God's plan no less than was, in the ages of faith, the Council of Trent or the Synod of Dort.

But another motif governs the protests against the spirit of the age. Progressive optimism in the previous century dominated especially the minds of those who believed in and continued the rationalistic and humanistic tendencies of Western civilization. Among those very men a reaction manifested itself from before the middle of the century on. Tocqueville and J. S. Mill were concerned. Burckhardt, Renan, Flaubert, Taine, expressed bitter aversion to the development they witnessed. The year 1848 gave the first rude shock to bourgeois liberals. The Paris Commune of 1871, coming on the heels of the crushing defeat administered to France by Germany, made an even more profound impression, and not on the French only. While Nietzsche launched his imprecations, Jakob Burckhardt withdrew in stoical resignation. Fruin, too, the great nineteenth-century Dutch historian, who at first was all satisfaction and confidence, in the later decades of the century gave way to gloomy forebodings.

Numerous are those who nowadays would be inclined to think that these fears have come true. A friend wrote to me, not long ago: "Our century is a calamitous century." I replied: "Certainly, the twentieth century cannot exactly be called an idyll. But that is a description which, when you look at the history of mankind, no century has ever deserved. And true calamitousness does not reside in the measure of human sorrow, in the numbers killed in battle or murdered. It should appear in the irremediable dissolution of human society. Well, as far as I am concerned, I am struck rather by the astonishing power of resistance and resiliency that has been displayed—in the West; but is not that our world?"

In fact, there is more than power of resistance. The social reforms alone show undiminished creativity. But these very reforms explain the disgruntlement of so many intellectuals, then and now. The nineteenth-century men I mentioned were frightened and embittered by the rise of the masses. They feared the consequences it might have for international relations, but more especially for conditions at home.

Civilization seemed to them to be safe only with a social *élite*. It seemed to them the property of the aristocratic or well-to-do bourgeois group to which they themselves belonged, and they could not help thinking that its fate was bound up indissolubly with their own. And as for *their* position, it was indeed menaced. Swiss democracy did not win so quickly as Burckhardt, as early as 1846, was afraid it would. The Commune, which threw Renan,

Flaubert, Taine, into paroxysms of fright and fury, never came anywhere near success. Yet in the whole of the succeeding period, and until today, the well-to-do bourgeoisie felt uncomfortably threatened in their pre-eminent position in society.

Now the same fact can be stated in the reverse: we can observe that the masses were being gradually raised out of the pitiable and dehumanizing conditions in which, during the heyday of aristocratic and bourgeois civilization, they found themselves. And did civilization suffer a corresponding loss? Were humanism and education ruined, as prophesied by Treitschke and Renan? Did our society become a *waste land*, and we ourselves *stuffed men* or *hollow men*? to use the words of T. S. Eliot—in whose case one can wonder whether it is his Christian faith or rather his aristocratic feeling of life which makes him seek comfort in such wholesale condemnation. Ought the present state of our civilization to be characterized as *quantitative* in contradistinction to the *qualitative* civilization of the past?

It seems to me that there was something lacking in this nineteenth-century civilization that overlooked so lightheartedly, or condoned with such fervor, the misery around it. The utterances of aversion to the people, the arguments that civilization needs a substructure of poor and docile wage-earners, which were heard on all sides, were really sadly devoid of that humanism these prosperous bourgeois imagined was their monopoly. Their qualitative civilization was without at least one quality, a quality by which, at least by the potentiality of which, Western civilization has always been distinguished. I mean a sense of responsibility for the whole of the community. Here is an organ of our civilization which a development, accelerated in our reputedly calamitous century, has strengthened, resulting in a heightened sensitivity and a finer perceptivity.

Of course I know the usual complaints. Technology exposing mankind to self-destruction; the progress of science leading to narrow specialism; films and television estranging the rising generation from serious reading; art broken away from tradition, desiring nothing but immediate reflexes. There even are plenty of talented young men who take delight in systematically extolling anxiety and absurdity as the hallmarks of true artistic feeling. This mentality truly denies some of the most precious tendencies of our civilization. But let ever so many critics be eager to praise that wild talk as the purest profundity, I see in it no more than the ephemeral aftereffects of the shocks of war and revolution, and I am quite sure that it will not affect the main current of development.

Perhaps every one of those complaints contains a grain of

truth. I am not singing a song of praise of our times the burden of which would be "All is as it should be, sleep well." I want, on the contrary, to rouse and to warn. I mention weaknesses, and no doubt there are more. But I know no greater weakness than when the constant changes to which our thinking and our ways of life have to adapt themselves, or which they have to overcome, are met only with a sigh of fatigue or a revulsion of fear. True, every change is apt to disturb us in our customary train of life and to confront us with problems. But we should not expect civilization to be served up to us like the sweet fruit to the inhabitants of the Land of Cockaigne. Civilization means struggle. And struggle we do.

To me the present spectacle of that struggle seems downright impressive. In the command of matter, in the knowledge of human life, social as well as individual, Western man is making progress as never before, and every discovery, every new theory, every shift in conditions causes tensions that necessitate provision. I say, "Western man," for it is he who continues to lead in these respects, and if Russia at times seems to be in front in the technological sphere, the regime of compulsion which prevails there calls into being tensions that are concealed rather than solved. The contrast between the semblance of unity there and the continual controversy here does not denote strength as against weakness. Our liberty, with all its drawbacks, is sure proof that Western civilization is very much alive.

But no doubt the process of democratization and removal of inequalities, which is far from having come to an end, will continue to offend groups that are still in a better position than many to make themselves heard. Here we still have, together with the uneasiness of organized believers, a source of alarmist opinions about the voyage on which History is taking us and of fears that Western civilization will not come through unharmed.

But now I come to a third factor, which serves more than anything else to create, in some, feelings of frustration, of lost greatness. I mean the demolition of the overseas position of the western European countries, the rise of Asia and Africa, and coupled with this, the weakening of Europe's power in world politics. The time when world history seemed to revolve around Europe is gone. Beside the United States and against Russia the voice of western Europe does not count for much any more in the neutral world of countries recently come to independence. This is a development that is being used by people of radically different outlooks for radically different arguments, all tending to prove that Europe has no future.

There are, first of all, the convinced colonialists, who keep on declaiming about the halfheartedness and feebleness with which in the critical years from 1945 to 1949 our democratic regime abandoned the bastion, and about the betrayal of the West committed by the United States. Suez was to these men a new proof of the degeneration of the West, while France's obstinate fight in North Africa seems to them a last chance, in which, however, they can hardly believe any more. In short, a "calamitous century."

I cannot, of course, go into any detail about these questions. It seems to me, leaving on one side the blindness displayed by American political leadership and all possibilities of compromise or gradualness that may thereby have been neglected, that we were faced here by an ineluctable development. The colonial peoples had been shaken out of the immobility of their social conditions by their Western rulers; intellectually, too, they had been touched, set in motion by ideas and slogans with which we ourselves made them acquainted. Add the suicidal wars in which the European countries involved themselves, and the position of mastery, even of leadership, became untenable.

But does this course of events, and does this issue, imply a death sentence on Western civilization?

This civilization may have been stimulated by its colonial expansion and its position of world power; it has thereby been led into errors and illusions as well, and at any rate, it never owed its essential values to that development. And similarly, even our economic prosperity—the miraculous revival after 1945, or rather, after 1948—has taught us that we can do without that artificial support. Looking at the Netherlands alone: the rebuilding of the devastated cities, the bold Delta scheme for mastering the estuaries and securing the low-lying land, the almost revolutionary industrialization, the search for new markets; and no less, the control of the social and cultural consequences of those material changes—it all gives plenty of scope to our energies. We can resign ourselves to putting the colonial episode behind us.

And as regards world power—we Dutchmen lost our modest share of that some centuries ago. It is helpful to observe that our national civilization was not thereby doomed. Shall we not conclude from that experience that Europe, too, can lose her world supremacy without necessarily losing the vitality of her civilization?

Provided, once more, that the Atlantic peoples—we western Europeans and Americans—remain conscious of having in common the task of self-preservation against the system entrenched so powerfully in the Soviet Union and which would prove inconsistent with the fundamental principles of our civilization. For democracies, co-operation is always difficult, and there is only too much disagreement in the Western world.

This is partly due, no doubt, to the gloomy speculations I am tracing and which have unsettled too many minds.

Take, for instance, Professor Barraclough, a year or two ago appointed to Toynbee's London professorship of international history, previously known as a sound medievalist. In his book *History in a Changing World*, of 1954, Barraclough warns us that the history we have learned and practiced has lost all sense. He himself was converted to the realization of having wasted his life, as suddenly as was Saint Paul on the road to Damascus, by the spectacle, in 1943, of the Germans being compelled to raise the siege of Stalingrad. Russia was thereby revealed to him as the great power of the future. He regretted the time he had spent in studying the papal chancellery or the emperors in the thirteenth and fourteenth centuries: owing to that, he now knew nothing of the Piasts, the Przemyslids, the Ruriks, or of Casimir the Great of Poland. "Farewell to Europe," is the title of one of his lectures, and he contemptuously dismisses Louis XIV, Napoleon, and Bismarck as "neolithic figures," completely irrelevant for any purpose today. *The European Inheritance*, the title of a collective work recently published in England, is to him a senseless phrase: "The old Europe has given up the ghost."

Now this kind of writing simply revolts me. As a historian I protest against the denial of a truth to which history owes its irreplaceable value: the indissoluble concatenation of the ages. As a European I detest the defeatism. And then the implied proclamation of success as the supreme standard of values! Must we see the whole of history culminate in the Kremlin because the Russians won at Stalingrad? It was a near thing if Hitler did not bring off his *coup*, and in that case I suppose Barraclough would have told us our first duty was to search the past for the signs of the Third Reich.

I do not close my eyes to the change we see materializing. It amounts to a revolution. I know, too, that contemporary events of this magnitude do not leave our view of the past unaffected. We now see in Louis XIV, Napoleon, and Bismarck, in addition to all that they were besides, the unconscious contrivers of the present-day collapse of European power. But one thing I hold firmly: that we are still Europeans and that our past, including those great national power fanatics, contributes toward shaping our present; that in us there lives the tradition of a great civilization, great and beneficent in spite of all the shortcomings and errors which are inseparable from human nature; and that it is our task to go on working toward the prospects and within the confines set to us by that tradition.

All this is nowadays obscured in theorizings propounded from many parts. *Eurocentric history writing* has become a term of reproach. We are told to practice *universalism*. But because Europe does not now hold the central place in world events, must we therefore forget that for a long time it did? And does not that period still in many ways affect the present? But indeed, as a basis of history writing, universalism seems to me impracticable. The stage is too wide, the action on it too confusingly varied. If one wants to depict it all in an intelligible connection, one will have to survey it from a point of view, and how can anyone in doing so detach himself from his country and civilization?

That would be a superhuman effort, and what is more, one that would go against human nature. I am quite ready to admit the right of Indians or Chinese to write the world history that suits them; but equally firmly I stick to the conviction that we Europeans are entitled to, and need, the world history that will help us to discern more clearly our place in the well-nigh incomprehensible whole. This does not in the least mean that everything must be seen in subordination to the European interest, or that admiration must be reserved for what was done by Europeans. Nor does it mean that European or Western civilization should, or can, be interpreted as a rounded-off entity on which no outside influences have made, or are making, themselves felt. But how can a human being—and the historian must not, above all, try to pass himself off as anything but a human being—allow his mind, shaped in his own cultural environment and by its centuries of sustained action, to be dissolved in an unorganic and anarchic *world* without losing hold of his most fertile life-principle? We must approach world history through the smaller formations in which we grow up. To each of us his national history, to all of us the history of our Western cultural community, must provide a point of departure and always a point of orientation.

But now read a man like Professor Locher of Leiden University, who does his best, unmistakably, to remain critical and matter-of-fact. Even he proposes that we should prescribe extra-European history as a subsidiary subject to (mark well!) our best students; and he wants time to be found in the secondary schools—at the expense, inevitably, of the study of the Greek and Roman world out of which our own civilization has partly sprung (and let me remind you that Greek and Latin still are compulsory subjects in the secondary classical schools in Holland)—to familiarize our next generation of intellectuals with . . . with what? with

China? with India? with the Arab countries? with Russia? That there are specialists studying those civilizations does not satisfy him. I remark in passing that I regard such studies as an enrichment of the intellectual life of our community, and no civilization has, and has had for a long time, so wide a curiosity as ours. But to extend this to the school programs, as Locher imagines should be done, could, I fear, lead only to a disintegration of that intellectual life and to hotchpotch in the pupils' heads.

However, this is nothing compared to the naïve illusionism to which the true universalists abandon themselves. They form a numerous host, and their influence is felt in an even wider circle. I shall have to say something about Toynbee and the Amsterdam professor Romein—a Marxist, and at the same time, curiously enough, a fervent admirer of Toynbee. But first of all a few words about the Moral Rearmament enthusiasts. The caricature presented by them in such deadly earnest will sharpen our eyes for the unhistorical features in the views of those historians.

I suppose that many of you will have seen those delightful periodicals. We got one in Dutch as well recently. How charming are those pictures! The happy, beaming faces of all those Filipinos, Negroes, Chinese, Burmese—they call up before our inner eye a better world than the one we know. And indeed, I read: "Will Asia lead the way?" Nothing is expected any longer from poor Europe. Nothing but *repentance* for former *pride* and *self-sufficiency;* and now *humility*. "We have plunged mankind into two world wars. We have exported materialism. . . . Humbly we ask you, Asia and Africa, to forgive us."

I grant that pride and self-sufficiency, and also the wars, are evidence of the wickedness of human nature which even Western civilization has never been able, and never will be able, completely to check. But that human nature in Asia and Africa contains nothing but this irresistible kindliness so ably pictured by Mr. Buchman's photographers—I can't believe it. I shall not enumerate the sanguinary despotisms in the Oriental world of former days; nor the murderous outbursts of religious fanaticism or the terrible social abuses still to be noticed today. If I recall them, it is not in order to argue that these peoples are incapable of anything better. But those better potentialities will not be realized at one stroke by congresses where world citizens in picturesque attire utter, and cheer, amiable platitudes. Only by strenuous labor, by generation after generation struggling with stubborn traditions and prejudices, will progress be made—as has been the case with us.

This fundamental error, this lighthearted overlooking of history and decreeing that everything will be different from now on, I also find in Toynbee and in Romein, his Marxist admirer in Holland. And these two men similarly belittle the part that western Europe can still play. The present commotion in the until recently colonial world proceeds—both Toynbee and Romein admit it—from the impact of Western civilization on the forms of social life prevalent there. But what did we bring them? What have we still to offer? According to Toynbee only the Russians have a faith to impart, that is their advantage over us: a faith derived, however much distorted, from Western civilization. All that *we* have is technology: "a stone instead of bread." It is exactly what we heard the Moral Rearmament man say: "Nothing but materialism."

Isn't it astonishing that Toynbee keeps silent about the sense for social justice which has led to those profound reforms in the West during the last few generations and which did undeniably inspire the civil servants of England, of France, and of Holland in the East to attempts at alleviating the oppressive feudal arrangements there? But even more astonishing is it that in another passage, concerning Turkey, Toynbee himself observes that what the revolution in that country has borrowed from the West is "the sense of fair play and moderation in politics which, we Westerners believe, is one of the good gifts that the West is able to give to the world." Astonishing, because he forgets this later when he speaks so bitterly of "a stone instead of bread."

What is the key to this contradiction? It is that Toynbee in his heart nourishes an urge to ostentatious depreciation of his own side, an urge to disparage and impeach. Worse, on one occasion he went so far as to write that we must not expect another escape as was the last war; mankind's patently increasing submissiveness makes it certain that a future would-be world conqueror will find us an easy prey. A heart taking pleasure in a pernicious defeatism. And with Toynbee this heart scores off the mind every time.

The same can be said of Romein. He has in the last seven or eight years given much of his attention to the relationship between Europe and Asia. In his case, too, the resulting picture testifies to an unresolved conflict between his knowing and his wishing. His wish is to make us believe that we, that the whole of our aggressive Western society, have misbehaved toward the gentle East, which has never committed aggression against Europe; and that for us it is now time to come to resipiscence. It would be enough, in his view, if we remained neutral between an America playing with thoughts of war and a peace-loving Russia. That is what history demands of us, but he is afraid that we shall not have the strength even for that modest role. Need I point out that western European neutrality would indeed be *enough* . . . for Russia and Communism to triumph?

But the astonishing thing, in Romein's case, too, is that elsewhere he does give a realistic sketch of the monstrous feudal conditions in Asia at the time the Europeans came to know it, and that he even admits that the invaders contributed something to their improvement. But yet again, when speaking for an audience at Gadjah Mada University, at Jokjakarta in Java, he lets himself be carried away to exclaim: "Asia has in its history known higher triumphs that can be bestowed by martial glory, triumphs in the works of peace!" Europe, apparently, has not . . .

And yet the cultural influence exercised by the West upon the East is a leading theme of Romein's argument. He has summarized his vision of world history in one of those attractively brief formulas with which he loves to operate—and he is particularly proud of this one—formulas that may seem, at first sight, striking, but to which the rich variety of historic life will always refuse to adapt itself. He starts from the assumption that the communal life of all peoples in its early stages bore the same features everywhere. This is the Common Human Pattern. From it *the European peoples* gradually deviated. So here we have the fundamental secret of Western civilization, that it is a Deviation from the Common Human Pattern (I hope you hear the capitals). Now, however, the Awakening of Asia, brought about unintentionally by those aggressive and interfering Deviators, has set in motion a process of assimilation. The world is being Westernized, soon the Deviation will be a deviation no longer. In principle, and lately more particularly under the influence of Soviet Russia and of the United States, it has already been accepted by the whole world. In principle the world is one already.[2]

In 1955 I heard, in London, Toynbee deliver the speech on "World Unity and World History" which soon afterward he repeated at The Hague with Romein acting as chairman. I said to Toynbee when he had concluded. "You spoke of mankind being one large family. It doesn't look much like it." To which he retorted like a flash: "No, it looks more like a slaughterhouse." He meant, of course: We must. It is our only alternative to annihilation. And this is also the idea of Romein. To me it seems a depressing idea: our only alternative—a phantasm!

For this Westernizing of the world, this removal of that extraordinary Deviation—can it take place so readily? Civilization is no currency, which will retain its value when passed on to somebody else. It is a commodity shaped in the course of centuries and tied indissolubly to its possessor, to his history, to the qualities and capacities that are proper to him and that also owe their existence to his experiences and those of his forefathers, to their exertions and tribulations. The civilization of a people is but the aggregate of those qualities and capacities, of those memories. It is a product of history and powerless without living contact with history.

How lightheartedly did the Americans believe, after the war—and numbers of Europeans likewise—that colonialism only needed to be demolished and the West might count on the Asian and African peoples as sympathizers and allies. Actual developments brought a good deal of painful disappointment. A passionate nationalism, quick to take offense, was among the first fruits of Westernization—a strange introduction to the one-world paradise that in the imaginations of Toynbee and Romein seems as good as realized.

But now the explanation has been thought of that the cause of the trouble is in the poverty and "underdevelopment" of the ex-colonial world. Let us remedy that, and everything will be all right. I have all sympathy with the policy of assisting the underdeveloped countries, but it is already beginning to dawn on the supporters that even here, in that apparently technical and material sphere, matters are not so simple. The assistance does not yield much result if the technical abilities of a population fall short (and in most cases they do, inevitably) and if, moreover, the class contrasts within the underdeveloped area (and most of them suffer from that evil) direct the assistance into wrong channels. (This was pointed out in the inaugural oration recently given by the new professor of non-Western economics at Leiden University, Dr. Brand, who speaks from the experience of his work with the United Nations Department of Social Affairs. A book on the subject from his hand is soon to appear in English.)[3]

Here again history will not be ignored. Impatient idealism is doomed to sterility. Hollow optimism is as dangerous as is the most destructive pessimism.

The optimistic and the pessimistic speculations I have discussed agree in this: all of them tend to disparage the vitality of Western civilization. A state of mind is encouraged in which whenever a cultural phenomenon is discussed without reference to Asia or Africa, the word *hubris* is thrown at the speaker; and the more bitterly so, of course, when he has dared to mention the backwardnesses or imperfections of Oriental societies. And one who professes love for the grandiose tradition of Western thought, or of Western poetry, will be called a *Western chauvinist*.

There is something thoroughly unhealthy in that habit of

depreciating our own spiritual heritage. The West has no faith any more, it is asserted, and the accusers vie in offering, one this, the other that, which might serve. As if an ideology could be plucked from the air! No faith? Well, I believe in ourselves, in our own tradition, which with its tireless experimenting and trying out changes, gives evidence that it still has something to offer to the world.

But in any case, even if, either because overpowered by an alien force or owing to our own shortcomings, it might have to pass through another time of trial, to us it will still remain an indispensable source of strength. All those other faiths are no more than wishful thinking, and they divert attention from the devoted labor and the incessant struggle which are needed.

Strife is the law of life. I am far from suggesting that we should underestimate the deadly character of a third world war. We must avert that catastrophe with all our capacity. But by breaking faith with Europe and her past, by cringing before Russia, by hollow confessions of guilt with respect to the peoples of Asia, we shall not show that capacity or avert threatening misfortunes.

A calamitous century? It is a century that makes demands on us. And in spite of the lamenters and the dreamers, I see around me heartening signs of the will to respond.

(1958)

5

THE HISTORICAL BACKGROUND OF THE IDEA OF EUROPEAN UNITY

1.

European unity. We hear the cry on all sides. Everyone agrees that the times demand its realization and implementation. This can be argued on political or political-strategic, as well as on economic grounds. The organization that is being planned, and is already partially effectuated, is related to those orders of ideas and in the practical discussion of its realization considerations derived therefrom prevail. Yet at the base of it all there lies the fact of a spiritual affinity which, across distinctness and discordance, reaches far into history.

With this cultural cohesion there were in former days connected certain political, or ecclesiastical-political, institutions, which although seemingly imposing, were actually decaying and increasingly impotent. And although there was no lack of attempts to renovate them or to found others in their stead, the history of attempts at European unity can never give much encouragement to the strivings of the present day. It presents a series of failures, and one will even detect in it a tendency of "going from bad to worse." But we must not turn to history for encouragement only. It is equally salutary to allow history to show us the limits set to our ambitions. Not that we need be satisfied with an admonition to be cautious. The demonstration of "from bad to worse" may make us conclude that "if we don't show sense, the worst will be upon us." Therefore: "We must." I don't believe for a moment that the future will simply bow down to our imperative, but that does not mean that we should abdicate. This mood of "it never came off, but this time we shall see that it does come off" may inspire fresh attempts that will perhaps help to fashion the future. There will be less chance of disappointment to the extent that we have a clearer perception of the limits of our capacity.

It has sense, then, for the present in which we live, for the problems with which we struggle from year to year, to consult history—primarily in order to refresh and strengthen our awareness of that cultural cohesion on which in the last resort we must rely. History is a vital need of culture.

Let me begin by stating that our European civilization springs from two historic roots: the Graeco-Roman tradition and Christianity. There is nothing novel about this statement. One hears it repeated to satiety. But that does not make it less true or less important. Yet, when one tries to elaborate it in detail, one has to work one's way through a maze of complications and contradictions, by a twilight very often in which the outlines seem to be blurred. This observation will not cast doubt upon the simple thesis that I stated, but the centuries-long process through which the synthesis of the Graeco-Roman and the Christian came into being is far from characterized by simplicity. Every account of it will differ from every other and be marked by the particular preferences and opinions of the observer. And when developments unfold the diversity by which the cultural cohesion is manifested in cultural forms of its own (I am of course thinking of national forms), when the all-embracing Christian unity is torn asunder and faith itself weakened in consequence, the multiplicity of possible presentations and interpretations is certainly not diminished.

I shall first of all indicate—very briefly, and with an almost shameless neglect of shadings and distinctions—what was the heritage of Greek culture.

In the Homeric world already one is struck by the appearance of clearly marked personalities and by the keen attention given to the individual. The Greeks themselves were conscious—in a somewhat later stage at least—of the contrast they presented in that respect with the Asiatic Orient, the world of power states, of despotisms, of arbitrariness and subjection. What they defended against the Persians was, in their own estimation, liberty. The victories of Thermopylae and of Salamis created a respite of some generations, during which the Greek spirit could work on. Its most distinguishing quality—the Oriental civilizations had a brilliance of their own and often displayed a striking technical inventiveness, but in this they were lacking—was the mathematical exactitude of its thinking, its aptitude to appreciate the fact and to subject it to criticism. Plato and Aeschylus still make a glorious appearance, but the modern mind feels a more direct affinity with Thucydides and Aristotle.

In the Roman Empire, in which the independence of the Greek cities and small states was dissolved, the Greek mind—to quote the well-known phrase—conquered its conqueror. The riches of Greek civilization were given shelter in the Empire, and its influence could then spread over a much wider sphere than previously. The Romans, too, had in their republican period valued political liberty, but it was an aristocratic liberty, and by the time of the emperors, little more than its memory was left. Yet the Roman Empire had its contribution to make. Even when it had fallen apart, the organization of power itself, the administration, still proved in its aftereffects a fertilizing influence. Especially significant for the future was Roman law, and indeed it was closely bound up with the other factor. After the interruption of the Dark Ages it was dug up and put to practical use, and its firm theoretical foundations and clear definitions, its formulas and modes of argument, formed ties between the Western peoples almost as firm as those of their common Christianity.

Now as regards Christianity. This, too, was able at first to spread within the confines of the Roman Empire. It might be thought that with its renunciation of the world, and directed as it was toward eternity and the hereafter, it offered the sharpest contrast imaginable with the mundane and human traits that seem to be so characteristic of both Greek and Roman civilization. Not, in fact, the sharpest imaginable. The Christian religion has been described as the most Western of the many Oriental religions or mystery cults that in the latter days of the Roman Empire wooed for the soul of a population menaced by decline and ruin. If it took hold, it was because of the unique importance it assigned to the human personality, while the equality of all before God which it preached was to prove a positive and dynamic strengthening of tendencies already present in the Greek city and in the frigid, matter-of-fact law of Rome. It was, in any case, one of the great facts in the development of Western civilization that in the later Middle Ages not only was Roman law "received," but that also the Church, in a way, "received" ancient thinking.

"After a long contest and in a process taking some generations" —I quote from the Dutch Cardinal De Jong's *Manual of Ecclesiastical History*—"and which was completed by Thomas of Aquino, the Aristotelian philosophy, purged from errors, was placed in the service of theology." All this was a truly European achievement. The language used by the theologians, the lawyers, and generally speaking, the scholars, continued to be Latin. This facilitated exchange from country to country. And who does not know that it was the monks who, industriously copying old Latin texts of all kinds, contributed to the salvation of the treasures of ancient culture until succeeding generations reached the stage where they could put them to advantage—there were indeed several stages, the great Renaissance of the fifteenth century being long preceded by similar movements.

I have boldly traced a line from Homer to the fifteenth century. Taking into account all the shocks and revolutions, and moreover all the new departures and goings astray, one can observe continuity. Not until the last phase did this civilization assume forms that we immediately recognize as being our own, but we may say that it is the early history of our European culture that I have been talking about.

Let me point out, however, one aspect that from this point of view constitutes at first sight a difficulty. The geographical delimitation of the process of development I have sketched has been subject to very considerable shifts. (I apologize for the word "sketched," which has to my own ears far too pretentious a sound. I shall indeed, after dealing with these geographical changes, have to say a little more about the political and ecclesiastical history of that early period. But first the shifts in the geographical compass.)

The world of the Greeks had exceeded Greece, but remained bound to the Mediterranean. The Roman Empire, in which Greek civilization found a refuge and in which it so profoundly affected the original human element, still had the Mediterranean for its axis. Asia Minor in the East, and on the other side of the water, North Africa, belonged to it. To the north it stretched toward the Alps and the Rhine, even toward the Danube and the lands of the Black Sea. This, then, was the territory where Christianity was to strike roots, soon recognized, even fostered, by the emperors' authority. But the imperial power falls into dissolution. From their still "barbaric" central European home, the Germanic peoples, crossing the rivers, invade the Empire. The invaders are assimilated, but political unity is broken up. Only in the East, with Byzantium as its center, does the Empire maintain itself.

In the West, in Gaul, the kingdom of the Franks has been formed; Rome is now only the see of a bishop, who, however, manages to become acknowledged as the head of Western Christendom. The split is confirmed when Charlemagne, in 800, has himself crowned emperor. It is a split, but at the same time an attempt to continue the tradition of unity. And in so far Charlemagne is indeed the true representative of the civilization built up in the Roman Empire, that in expanding his reign across the Rhine he also expands Christianity to these Germanic regions, which had never known imperial sway. After his death, when his ostensibly old, but in fact new, empire is divided, it is even there that the imperial dignity, with its claim to representing unity, is transplanted. A hollow claim, at least in terms of politics. And as political unity kept decaying, the cohesiveness of the European world was more and more embodied in the Church and its supreme pastor in Rome. I say "of the European world," for it was to Europe, west and central, that the civilization whose vicissitudes I am trying to trace was now practically confined.

Russia, which was Christianized from Byzantium—let us say in the tenth century and mention the dukedom of Kiev in order to give our thoughts a momentary hold—went through an entirely different political and social development from that of Latin-Christian Europe (to which belonged, let me remind you, Poland and Bohemia, that is, Czechoslovakia). Yet Russia cannot on that account be considered Asiatic and excluded from Europe. Christianity made its influence felt there in different forms—it showed for one thing much less resistance to state despotism—but it did make its influence felt; and ancient civilization penetrated as well, although less profoundly no doubt, through the medium of Byzantium. Let us say then that Russia was a variant of general European civilization, which—to cast a glance into the future—was able in the eighteenth and nineteenth centuries to approach the West, only to take up in our time an attitude of bitter and dogmatic aloofness.

North Africa and Asia Minor, on the contrary, were completely alienated. From the seventh century on, the dynamic Mohammedan movement managed to detach those regions from Western civilization and Christianity. Europe herself was menaced and directly attacked. The rise of an aggressive power on Europe's southeastern border heightened the feeling of solidarity between what had already become independent European powers. The Crusades were a striking sign of this.

The Church, in the early Middle Ages the strongest factor for unity in all spheres of life, could play a particularly active part in this development. It not only dominated thought, without, as I pointed out, barring pre-Christian forms, but it disposed of the only effective organization on the European scene. The Pope exercised his spiritual authority over all rulers; and in spite of the bitter contest over competence between the papacy and the imperial power (which was now in fact confined to central Europe), this had real significance. The Holy See had not yet become so exclusively an Italian institution as it was to be later on. And in any case there were the monastic orders, whose unifying influence made itself felt perhaps even more directly.

The oft-quoted phrase *respublica christiana* must not, however, be taken in too literal a sense. It denoted a vague, and mainly spiritual, conception. Politically it served at most an aspiration which was never realized. There was never anything like a regular, permanent organization embodying the European feeling of kinship. The period resounded with endless quarrels and fights between Christians, on a local scale mostly, because effective action in a larger context was beyond the capacity of the loosely constructed communities. The later Middle Ages indeed, saw the rise, very gradually, of somewhat more strongly organized separate states.

This was a development that spelled danger to European unity, but it is idle to complain. It was an indispensable stage. The medieval world lacked the resources needed for the establishment of an authority over the whole of the Europe. For the time being nothing more could be expected than the formation of states of some size, within whose domain local particularism or chaos could be superseded and order guaranteed. No doubt new tensions were thus created, which were to prove increasingly violent and destructive, down to the times in which we live. Disputes and wars between these ambitious new formations were inevitable, and from them the unity of Europe was to suffer worse shocks than from the small-scale scuffles of the preceding period. Yet even now the awareness of a common bond between otherwise hostile nations was not extinguished.

And this although simultaneously the influence of the all-embracing Church was growing weaker. The Renaissance was not anti-Christian. Yet within the Church wholehearted dedication was sapped by abuses, while in the world outside, thinking was not ruled by its initiatives as exclusively as before. Thought was to some extent secularized, although it is worth noticing that in those terms, too, the idea of European cohesion and homogeneity was expressed. Machiavelli, for instance, in *The Prince*, contrasts Europe and Asia. In ancient times already, he saw Asia personified in Darius, the despot, all the rest being no more than slaves; while in Europe *many* shared the work of government. In Machiavelli's own day he personified the same contrast in the Great Turk, the unreservedly despotic Sultan, and in the King of France, who could not rule without the aid of his barons. Machiavelli no longer mentions the *respublica christiana*, nor does he seem to hanker after unity: the numerous states in Europe, each with many men sharing responsibility, create a courage and talents such as are not to be found in Asia. To all appearances, he does not consider their fratricidal warfare too high a price for that advantage.

But the Renaissance was not to be all. Soon the Reformation burst over Europe, and the Church, of old the guardian, even the creator, of unity, was torn asunder.

Thomas More, who refused to take an oath to Henry VIII's supremacy over the English Church and who was therefore brought to the block, was a martyr not only to the cause of papal supremacy, but also to England's historic partnership in a Christian Europe. (This is how an English historian, not himself a Catholic, puts it.)

The Reformation did indeed stimulate and intensify the process, which had long been gathering strength, of the formation of absolute and sovereign states. The religious wars of the late sixteenth and early seventeenth centuries contributed to this development and moreover created other than purely religious ambitions and contrasts. Their violence and destructive effect was such that even Machiavelli, had he lived to see them, could hardly have taken them so lightly. Even before those wars, Erasmus had sounded a very different note: Peace, peace! had been his deep-felt wish. Grotius's *De jure belli et pacis* was inspired by the same sentiment. Erasmus, however, had not gone beyond philanthropic, pacifist preaching. Grotius, basing himself (curiously enough) on the work of Spanish Jesuits particularly, constructed a complete system of international law which was to be valid for princes and republics alike and which was to make it possible to identify the unjust war and to brand it as a crime. The questions of *who* was to do this, and *who* was to intervene—to prevent or to punish—he left unanswered; indeed he hardly posed them. The author's ideal aim, the establishment of an international community ruled by law, was not brought any nearer to practical realization by his famous book. Yet the mere thought of a generally acknowledged international law, which was its message, served to strengthen the common bond.

The division of Europe into Protestant and Catholic did not apparently make an absolute separation any longer: that is what we may conclude from Grotius's building upon foundations laid by Spanish Jesuits, and indeed from the respectful attention given to his book all over Europe. There are many signs of the European idea still living in men's minds. Toward the close of 1646 Charles I, in his turn head of Henry VIII's national church, was a prisoner of his own people. And now he addressed himself to the other Christian rulers, who were at that moment negotiating peace at the Münster Congress, reminding them that his cause was theirs also and exhorting them to come to his aid when peace had been restored. It was indeed an appeal to a shadowy solidarity, and it found no response.

Nor can it be denied that after, no less than before, the peace of Münster, in the actuality of international politics, the cause of unity fared worse and worse. In the cultural sphere, too, there was more than only the schism in the Church, which had, when it was the one and only Church, tended to impart a single general direction to the underlying variety. The dominance of Latin had long been weakened, and the prestige of literature in the popular languages was increasing all the time. This was only one aspect of a development that sprang, as it were, automatically from the operation of states embracing much larger entities and affecting people's lives much more profoundly, a development of national consciousness within each particular state. In the episode of Joan of Arc one sees an early sign of this. How strongly and articulately does it speak in Shakespeare! And in Holland, a generation later, in Vondel!

But it is in the *politics* of the seventeenth century that the movement away from universality can be observed most strikingly. It was the century of Richelieu, and in its second half, of Louis XIV: the sovereign state that was a law unto itself, that strived systematically after more power, more prestige, more territory—the great minister, and after him, the Sun King, "le grand roi," as his admiring subjects called him, were its most conspicuous personifications, and they regarded the glory and the advantage of the wearer of the crown as the glory and the advantage of the entire nation. *National* glory and *national* advantage were the stakes for which the century's indefatigable power-policy, and its wars, were carried on. And no room was left for any thought of the interest of Europe. Europe was no more than the field of contest where every contestant was intent upon nothing but his *own* preservation, his *own* gain. At most, Europe could figure as a unity in the overstrained ambition to shine with a luster superior to all other rulers, to establish a *universal monarchy*. This was the mood that was also prevalent at the Emperor's court, and one can observe it, if not, naturally, with the same wide-straying tendency, in princes like the dukes of Savoy, the electors of Brandenburg, and many others.

France furnishes the most striking example because it was the most powerful among the states that had emerged from the medieval confusion, and because in the course of time the others began to feel menaced by Louis XIV's insatiable land hunger. And so the very excesses of that unbridled ambition, that policy inspired by the most exclusive national and dynastic interests, tirelessly intriguing, thinking out combinations, and interfering, if not directly resorting to arms, did in the end evoke a manifestation of European solidarity.

I am thinking of the coalitions that William III spent his life in trying to build up in order to restrain France. That generation was still inclined to see the real danger arising from the Catholic versus Protestant contrast. To the Dutch, Louis was the persecutor of the Huguenots; what mattered now was to defend the Protestant religion, at home and in the whole of Europe, against his aggression. In 1688 William III set out for England as the champion of that country's *liberty and its Protestant religion*. The Catholic Hapsburg ruler at Vienna, however, was the great rival of Louis, and the coalitions were mixed Protestant and Catholic. When Protestant-Catholic co-operation was aimed at, the fear that statesmen could openly advance was only that Louis was out for *universal monarchy*. In 1707 the English Parliament declared—and nothing could be more in harmony with William III's way of thinking—that it meant to stand up to Louis for the sake of *the liberties of Europe*. The European solidarity to which the English Parliament thus appealed was, after the Glorious Revolution and after Locke, of a different conception from that which had occurred to the mind of Charles I in his hour of need. This word *liberties*, however, was far from denoting a universally admitted principle. The principles of dynastic prerogative and of popular coresponsibility would still have to wage a bitter contest, in which indeed the latter principle was to gain the upper hand. However, now, at any rate, solidarity could consist in nothing but resistance to the one most powerful, in the instinct of self-preservation of the numerous independent weaker ones. Peace and security were sought in a balance-of-power system.

It was exhausting work to have to lead those coalitions. Was I justified in describing them as a manifestation of European solidarity? William III at one moment grumbled about his Englishmen, who cared so little about what happened on the Continent and seemed to imagine that they were alone in the world; then again about his Dutchmen, who preferred to make themselves small in their little corner, hoping that the storm would spare them; and all the time he was plagued with the particular demands of the Emperor and of the petty German and Italian princes on the anti-French side and with their mutual rivalries. These coalitions themselves bring out the weakness of the sentiment of European community of interest in the existing disruption into sovereign states.

The danger of French domination was averted—for the time being. But the eighteenth century still had no better system for the organization of Europe than one of combinations keeping each other more or less in check. What did the balance of power mean? In the instruction of a French ambassador the answer was given as it were with a shrug: "C'est une chose de pure opinion" (all interpret it in accordance with their own views or interests). And the great French historian Albert Sorel (late nineteenth century) concludes: "There was no Europe, there were but nations and states." And to be sure, one war succeeded another. Prussia now is the most dynamic player in that game, but the situation was not a little complicated by the conflict between the colonial ambitions of England and France in Asia and America. Principles of law were much invoked in international relations, and theoricians, following the example of Grotius, filled many books on the subject. But the moral norm that Grotius had placed in the center was lost sight of, and Vattel raised state sovereignty into an absolute. The Polish partitions, for which Prussia, Austria, and Russia conspired in time of peace, were an insolent negation of that order of law which was still given the homage of words and in which the small states sought their security. The first partition, in 1772, created considerable alarm among them.

As a matter of fact, there were thoughtful men everywhere who understood that something was wrong. It was a time when there was a good deal of thinking done, critical thinking. The Enlightenment undertook to apply the standard of reason to all phenomena, national and international. If the spectacle of practical politics must make one sigh "There was no Europe," an examination of intellectual life will on the contrary evoke a clear picture of true European homogeneousness.

This new spirit is seen at work everywhere—in fact it was in many respects no more than the acceleration or intensification of older tendencies. Society had long been undergoing shifts and changes as a result of which inherited institutions and customs were often felt to irk. Everywhere an ambitious middle-class had grown up. With veritable passion the existing state of affairs was criticized and the desire for reforms rationalized. From the late Middle Ages on, the rulers, with the wholehearted co-operation of their lawyers and ministers, had already dared, within certain limits, to lay hands on traditions and to carry through reforms. The period was now marked by the Enlightened Despots, who carried on this work with a new zeal and in spheres hitherto left alone. Even Russia, where that broad middle-class was lacking, had been by Peter the Great, and was now by Catherine, opened up for this Western influence. Everywhere the Enlightened Despots were applauded by the philosophers (as the leaders of the Enlightenment were called in France).

Intellectually, or propagandistically, France played a leading role from the middle of the eighteenth century on. This was partly due to the position the French language had acquired among the aristocrats and the intellectuals of all countries, so much so that it had almost become a European *lingua franca*, a substitute for Latin, which was more and more losing that position. The conceptions and the methods, however, were no specifically French possession. They resulted from the centuries-long process to which all peoples had made a contribution of their own —of late, and very particularly, the English. The Germans, the Italians, the Dutchmen, who proved receptive to that great movement and went enthusiastically along with it, cannot be dispatched as mere disciples of either the English or the French. Among them, too, this spirit worked from the inside. There was a concordance of views and aspirations arising naturally from each nation's particular as well as from the universal-European development.

The intellectuals of the period were aware of this. Each might feel warmly for his own country and at moments of international tension side with it unhesitatingly, yet each knew that Europe constituted a cultural unity. Burke, who, of course, cannot without qualification be called a spokesman of the Enlightenment, said that in manners and education, in the modes of intercourse and in the entire conduct of life, there was from country to country so much similarity that no citizen of Europe could be wholly an exile in any part of it. Montesquieu went even a little too far when he described Europe as one state composed of several provinces. Another remark of his is, on the contrary, very true: "What all countries of Europe have in common is a spirit of liberty, which has always made it difficult to subject them to an alien power." And Voltaire says it most strikingly of all: "Europe is a kind of large commonwealth, divided into several states, all of which support the same principles of public law and politics, unknown in the rest of the world."

In France the spirit of the Enlightenment developed in a more vehement sense and acquired more radical tendencies than elsewhere; soon the Revolution set to work to carry through reforms more thoroughgoing and less respectful of old traditions than those of the Enlightened Despots in Prussia, in Austria, in Belgium, in Russia. Why precisely in France? No single answer will fit that question, but let me concentrate on one of the many factors that any full explanation will have to consider: in France the monarchy was not enlightened and had allowed the reforming task that it, too, had somewhat fitfully attempted, to get completely stuck. In fact, the Enlightened Despots elsewhere had not been so enterprising or so consistent but that in their countries, too, the French example was bound to make an impression. The French Revolution, moreover, presented the dramatic aspect of a struggle for the ideal of liberty, a struggle against despotism as such. This could not but evoke a response among the peoples that were governed despotically, in however enlightened a sense.

What I want to bring out is that in the period opening in 1789 the unity of Europe, its unity in the sphere of civilization and society, was strikingly demonstrated; more, was strengthened and deepened. Especially if it is realized that the period was not exclusively dominated by the Revolution. The Revolution has largely shaped the future, but the resistance, too, has left profound traces. And this resistance was equally firmly rooted in European traditions. It is the contest between rationalistic reforming zeal, whipping itself up to excesses, and traditionalist conservatism, tainted with class interest and selfishness no doubt, but nevertheless representing an indispensable form of life—it is this contest, to which the Restoration did not put an end, in which divided Europe once again attested its essential unity. Action and reaction were both European, and both fruitful. If one tries to think that thought through, one is presented with the conclusion that Europe realized herself even in the wars to which the Revolution gave rise. Paradoxical as it may sound, I can accept that conclusion.

2.

I shall now look a little more closely at the significance of the French Revolution for our problem—the problem of European unity. Before everything, I want to underline the fact that the Revolution in its first phase presented itself in the conceptions and the terminology of the Enlightenment, the thinking of which was so markedly universalist. Reason, common to all men, undertook to lay down what was good for all men. The preamble to the famous "Declaration of the Rights of Man and of the Citizen" of August 1789 spoke, not for the French citizen, but for mankind. It meant indeed to brush aside what had grown up historically in favor of what, from before the formation of states and governments, before their abuses and misdeeds, had always been, and would always remain, the rights of man. Not long before, England's rebellious North American colonies had introduced in similar terms the declaration by which they announced their independence to the world. There has been a good deal of dispute as to how far the French was an imitation of the American declaration. I believe that we must explain the similarity by the fact that all peoples of Western culture (and the Americans who were in revolt against England can safely be regarded as Englishmen) shared the cult of reason and natural rights typical of the Enlightenment. This makes it at the same time understandable that both these declarations, and particularly, of course, the French one, made so profound an impression upon the European peoples.

I said a moment ago *universalist*, and I have now switched over to *European*. The Enlightenment may have progressively become more antireligious; it built on the foundations inherited from Christianity. In its absolutist attitude of mind this becomes manifest. It demanded the entire person and the entire world. Thus it was that the French in their initial ecstasy did not reckon with frontiers, and thought, not beyond France only, but beyond Europe. *Mankind*, that is how the enthusiasts felt it, was reborn in 1789. In practice, however—and is it not natural? for in practice history does not allow itself to be disposed of so easily (we experience this truth today at every turn, as our predecessors have experienced it in their time!)—in practice the influence of the enthusiasts remained limited—for the time being, if you like, but certainly for a long, long period—to the countries where men's minds were prepared for it, where they had already been touched by the Enlightenment, that is to say, it was limited to Europe. Anacharsis Cloots, *l'orateur du genre humain*, remains a figure of fun.

But as far as Europe is concerned, then, did the spirit of 1789 lead to a strengthening of the sentiment of unity? For that is where my argument seems to tend. Everybody knows that the contrary is often maintained, namely, it is maintained that it was the French Revolution that created nationalism—nationalism that was to prove the greatest threat to European unity. Well, I admit an element of truth in that thesis too—although I do not agree that the Revolution *created* nationalism; let us say, stimulated, stirred to a particular virulence. We are faced, then, with two opposing tendencies both of which can be attributed to the Revolution.

It is a fascinating spectacle to see how in the thinking and the acting of the men of the French Revolution the two tendencies appear in close conjunction: how nationalism was fed by universalism, until the latter ideology, sucked empty, was thrown away. What facilitated the transition from universalism to nationalism was messianism. In their early enthusiasm the French wanted the entire world to share their happiness, but they could not think otherwise than that *they* should bring that boon to the others. They were carried away by an exalted feeling of having a mission to fulfill. They promised support to all peoples seeking liberty—but it must be *their* kind of liberty. When it comes to war—war with the monarchs as it was termed—the old and all-too-human ambitions of the French monarchical policy spring to life in the hearts of the revolutionaries: the cry of *the natural frontiers* drowns out that of humanity. The passion of the Revolution allies itself automatically with the passions that always accompany war, and the struggle with hostile Europe, a Europe, blind, backward, slavishly attached to its evil traditions and its princes (that is how French enthusiasm sees it), becomes a popular cause such as wars under the old regime had seldom been. Some of the conquered peoples—the Belgians, for instance—would not understand what blessings the conquerors showered on them. It is small wonder that the horrors staged during the Terror turned the original sympathy for the self-styled liberators into feelings of suspicion and aversion. But such peoples were with a heavy hand "forced to be free"—to use a horrifying phrase of Rousseau's.

When Napoleon enters the stage of history and curbs the Revolution, nothing is left of liberty at all. But did he not attempt to unite Europe? Purely and simply as a conqueror. Even so, there were those in Europe who were ready to accept him and his enforced and despotic unity. In Holland, for instance, the orthodox Protestant Bilderdijk, in the days of the Republic a fervent supporter of the House of Orange, prophesied in 1806, in his *Ode to Napoleon*, that the upshot of all the suffering would be salutary. Dirk van Hogendorp, too, the brother of G. K. van Hogendorp, who was to play so courageous and statesmanlike a part in the insurrection of 1813 and the restoration of Dutch independence, in 1808 applauded Napoleon as the hero who would give the world peace. Germans and Italians joined in that chorus.

The large majority of the French themselves for a long time venerated Napoleon as the man who not only had established order in their country and won it glory, but who spread the beneficial principles of the Revolution over Europe. Pitt, who at the Lord Mayor's banquet of November 1803 spoke those famous words, "England has saved herself by her exertions and will, as

I trust, save Europe by her example," was in *their* view the leader of the English aristocracy and of the powers of darkness everywhere. English liberty in those days was certainly far from perfect, yet the consciousness of fighting for liberty was by no means alive among the aristocracy only.

In the end, Napoleon's coercive rule proved unable to found a firm system of European unity. It goaded the peoples, the Germans, the Spaniards, in 1812 even the Russians, into open resistance, or at least, it fostered feelings of resentment and aversion; it made the peoples aware of their own particular natures, interests, aspirations; in short, against French nationalism it called into being multiple nationalisms.

The first thought of the victors at the Congress of Vienna was, naturally enough, to organize Europe in order to prevent a new period of war. But after the downfall of Napoleon Europe was the prey of an indescribable confusion and fermentation of minds. The nationalist movements had been directed against a France that still pretended to be the bearer of the principles of the Revolution, and they had thus sought strength in historical, religious, legitimist, conceptions. But Napoleon had at the same time been the military despot, and so the revolutionary ideology had done service together with or against the other. How easily it could now be mobilized against rulers who bluntly interpreted the Restoration as meaning a return to the untenable conditions of the past, against rulers who, as in the Hapsburg monarchy and in Italy, were alien to the populations!

The Holy Alliance, concluded, at the initiative of Czar Alexander, between himself, the Austrian Emperor, and the King of Prussia, was intended to be the nucleus of the desired organization of Europe. Quoting Holy Writ, the partners testified to the most complete community of interests, in which their peoples were to share: they were to form *one christian nation.* The true aim was, however, to restrain whatever might still stir of the diabolical tendencies of the Revolution. In spite of all the fine phrases, Metternich turned the Alliance into an instrument of espionage and suppression, using it in the provinces of the Hapsburg monarchy, and outside it, in the German Confederation and in Italy, against all democratic or nationalist movements. England, little more liberal under Castlereagh, acceded by a separate treaty. As early as 1818 France, now under Bourbon rule, was admitted as a fifth partner. Congresses were held regularly to maintain strict supervision over the affairs of all countries, to prevent, in other words, the Revolution from raising its head anywhere.

It was, as it were, a last attempt on the part of that dynastic Europe to which Charles I in 1646 had made his vain appeal.

At that time it had hardly had shape, and now that it did constitute itself it proved unable to master the spirit of the time. After Castlereagh's death, England, under Canning, freed itself from Castlereagh's reactionary tendencies. The English government openly disapproved of the expedition undertaken by France —where reaction still had the better of revolutionary stirrings— at the instigation of "Europe," to suppress a rising against the King of Spain. With regard to the revolt in Greece and to the collapse of Spanish rule in South America, too, Canning followed a line of his own. The solidarity of the great powers had thus fallen apart even before, in 1830, the Bourbons were chased from France. The reign of Louis Philippe, the Citizen King, did not in the long run satisfy the radical elements, and in the forties a powerful revival of revolutionary sentiment manifested itself, and raised echoes all over Europe.

A moment ago I spoke of "the spirit of the time." But I must not be understood to mean that there was no ideological countercurrent. I recall Ranke, to whom the states—not the peoples— were "ideas of God"; in the state alone the individual can realize himself, even without any democratic share in the responsibility; power is the primary quality of the state. Yet from our point of view there was a positive element in the mind of the historian whose work was to do so much to shape political thinking: he believed in Europe. He saw the power game of the great European states controlled by an eternal equipoise and European civilization benefiting from their variety and their struggles. An optimism that was to be sadly put to shame by what later generations had to suffer.

As a matter of fact, this kind of European idealism stood outside what was coming to be the reality: the development of popular nationalisms. The existing state formations in Central Europe— in Italy, in Austria and Hungary, in Ranke's own Germany— became the butt of the aspirations once stirred up by Napoleon: the clamor now was for a state based on each particular nationality, covering the whole of a linguistic area. *The people* and *a share in the government*, those were the slogans. Everywhere, national movements allied themselves with liberal or radical sentiment, sentiment tracing its origin to the Revolution. And here, too, the universalist thinking of the Enlightenment and of the Revolution was in evidence, although practically speaking, once more, *universalist* meant *European*. The synthesis of nationalism and Europeanism was embodied in Mazzini. The passionate Italian nationalist and republican looked beyond Italy. He maintained close contacts—mostly in common exile—with the radicals of other oppressed and dissatisfied nations, and with them he dreamed of: away with kings; Europe a federation of free republics!

The Communist Manifesto of 1847—"Proletarians of all countries, unite!"—belongs organically to the same state of mind. To Marx, however, nationality was but a category of capitalism and fated to be superseded with it. In his view it was only the fight against the bourgeoisie that counted.

In February 1848 revolution broke out in Paris. The memories of 1789 and 1792, revived in the preceding years in a flood of historical writings, by Buchez, by Lamartine, by Louis Blanc, by Michelet, now demonstrated their dynamic power in actual fact. Messianism was always an important factor; in practice it meant: French conceit; French chauvinism. "When Providence desires an idea to inflame the world, it kindles it in the soul of a Frenchman." So says Lamartine. And Michelet: "France believes that she cannot render a greater service to the world than by presenting it with her ideas, her ways of living, her fashions." And it should not be thought that he disapproves or writes ironically. He *glories* in this "assimilation des intelligences," this "conquête des volontés"; according to him this is something quite different from the mere egoism of Rome's, or England's, imperialism.

We see again how Europeanism might slip over into a dangerous kind of nationalism. Meanwhile, in Poland, in Italy, in the German Confederation, the cry of national liberty, national unity, rises to a higher pitch: the growths of history are to be drastically corrected. And the French revolutionaries acclaim what they consider to be the effect of their example. All European nations will be liberated, all united in fraternity.

Failure was followed by disillusionment. The middle class, which had after all the tempestuous courses of the Revolution of 1789 in the end pocketed the gains, maintained itself now too and presented a bold front to the future. But when we think of European unity, the striking fact is that the historic power consolidated in the states so dear to Ranke's heart did indeed hold the field. It is true that in Italy and in Germany the movements for national unity bided their time and were in the end to prove irresistible. But here, too, the lead was no longer with the idealists, deriving their thought from the Revolution and striving after a synthesis with Europe. It had fallen to men devoted to that same historic power, men who only *used* nationalist enthusiasm and who did not regard Europe with any feelings or aspirations of fraternity, men to whom Europe was (as it had been to Richelieu and Louis XIV) a field of contest, where combinations could be devised to create constellations enabling them to bring off their *coups*.

What was at hand was the time of Cavour, and above all, of course, of Bismarck.

Bismarck had in 1848 resolutely opposed all those revolutionary doings of the German nationalists who had wanted to dissolve Prussia into a liberalized, or even radicalized, Germany. All he wanted was to serve the state and the King of Prussia. He was as little satisfied with the German Confederation as were the enthusiasts for German unity, for in it Prussia played second fiddle to Austria. In any case, he never believed that solutions could be obtained as a result of popular excitement and eloquence: "blood and iron" was the only way. The power policy he had carried out in the sixties, as the King of Prussia's minister, he continued after 1870 for the Emperor he had helped to make. First its aim had been conquest, now it was consolidation, but as regards the fundamental principle—that his royal, now imperial, master's interest must come before all other considerations—there was no change. The sensational successes of his policy, even before 1870, dazzled the German liberals and made them forget *their* principles. The historians moved away from Ranke's European view and began to take the interest of Prussia, as the predestined creator of German unity, for the standard by which to judge all things. Treitschke, who had started as a liberal, later proclaimed the tenet: "To cultivate its power is the state's highest moral duty." Unconditional submission to the purpose of power, this now came to be an article of faith in Germany, and one result was—especially after Bismarck's gigantic personality had gone—that the army, or the officer's caste, acquired a dominant position in the direction of the state.

For the European idea this development meant a regression. And at the same time, in France the loss of Alsace-Lorraine left an unappeasable sense of grievance. The feud between the two leading powers of the Continent poisoned the entire European atmosphere. In France, too, there grew up a nationalism of a much more virulent kind than Louis XIV's primarily dynastic policy or than the nationalism of the Revolution which, chauvinistic as it became, still retained an element of idealism. This new nationalism indeed set itself squarely against the ideology of the Revolution. The messianism of those heroic years, so it was now argued, had contributed toward bringing about France's weakness. It was time to stop this madly generous, this ruinous, devotion to the salvation of *the world;* France must think of herself.

In Charles Maurras's *Action française* this new attitude found its most uncompromising expression. "La France seule" was one of his slogans, and it could not be put more briefly and more pointedly. In the Dreyfus affair Maurras had considered the question of guilty or not guilty of less importance than the safety of France, which was guaranteed only by the army: no doubt must be cast on the honor of the devoted officers' corps for the sake of a Jewish intruder. The *Action française* glorified *le grand siècle* of Louis XIV as a source of inspiration for the present; the movement advocated a return to the Monarchy: the Republic, according to its teaching, was a revolutionary and impotent abortion. This, while the Republic was preening itself on having concluded an alliance with Czarist Russia, which exposed Germany to the danger of a war on two fronts.

The *Action française* never succeeded in cutting a figure in practical politics. It exercised, nevertheless, a powerful influence over the public mind. Intellectual circles took Maurras very seriously indeed. The sham logic he presented with bitter passion somehow touched deep springs of the French soul.

The French-German feud was at the basis of the intolerable tension prevailing in Europe, but there were several hearths of unrest, especially in the southern-Slav world, where rising national sentiment began to clash with existing arrangements. Austria-Hungary felt itself menaced and looked upon Russia as a possible enemy. The great powers were allied in two groups, and although peace was for a long time preserved, a mad armament-competition kept nerves on edge. In 1899 a peace conference assembled in The Hague. The initiative had been taken by the young Czar Nicholas II, and what he had had in mind originally was to bring about a coming together of all the states that were willing to make world peace secure. "Stupid blunder of a young dreamer," was Kaiser Wilhelm's private comment; "grist on the mills of socialists and antimilitarists." But for decency's sake the conference could not be declined. It became a hollow show. The German representative declared, bluntly, but at least frankly, that his country did not feel oppressed by the cost of armament and that the German people discharged their military service with feelings of pride and satisfaction. The conference was to have met again, but the Boer War, which broke out in that same year, 1899, caused the plan to be shelved.

The acutely nationalistic mood was not confined to Germany and France, not to the Continent. In England men like Gladstone and Cobden, much as they differed in mental structure, had had this in common: the conception of Europe meant something to them. With Joseph Chamberlain, nationalist conceit and self-righteousness came to prevail in a particularly offensive manner. It is true that a revival of the liberal outlook soon followed, and in France, too, attempts were made to temper the international contrasts. But the catastrophe, prepared by a generation of power politics and nationalist narrowness could no longer be averted.

The war of 1914 to 1918, with its mass armies deadlocked in the murderous trenches, with Russia thrown into revolution and Austria-Hungary in dissolution, shook Europe more violently than even the Napoleonic wars had done. At the Congress of Versailles, as at Vienna a century before, the victors felt that an attempt must be made to prevent a repetition. The League of Nations, planned by the peace treaty, was in a way a counterpart of the Holy Alliance. If the Holy Alliance had failed, it was largely because it was so blunt a negation of the principles of the Revolution, which, related as they were to some of the oldest and most distinctive features of European civilization, had proved too powerful for a merely conservative "restoration." The war itself had been waged by the western European powers under the slogan of protection of democracy against autocracy and militarism, even before the idea found its prophet in the president of the great extra-European power that came in the last stage to intervene in European affairs, for the first time—and decisively.

Wilson came to Versailles with definite conceptions about the principles that ought to govern the drafting of the peace treaty; he had formulated them in advance in the Fourteen Points. He also had a project for the League of Nations ready: it was in his idea to clinch the arrangements to be laid down by the peace treaty and to insure permanency. The exhausted European victors could not but listen with due respect to the man who seemed to command the unimpaired strength and wealth of America. Why did it all once more end in disappointment?

The Fourteen Points had been dictated by a well-meaning care for the interests of a peaceful world community. But it proved not so easy to translate them into practice. Historic insight was too completely lacking in Wilson's mentality for him to foresee that old prejudices and blind sentiments would put up strenuous resistance and that the truths he preached would be interpreted variously in various countries. The Italians and the southern Slavs, for instance, each claimed that the right of self-determination supported their cause. The French and the English could not at once get the better of the hatred and suspicion of the Germans into which they had worked themselves up during the war years. The French were inclined to look for their security, as of old, in a weakening of the redoubtable neighbor country even though it might now disguise itself as a republic. They wanted the Rhineland, at least the Saar district. The English public joined in the chorus claiming crushing war-indemnities. Wilson, with his generalizing and moralistic preoccupations, was helpless in the face of such unregenerate manifestations.

He spoke of "American principles" that he advocated. According to him they were "the principles of mankind" and they *must* prevail. The tone of messianism is unmistakable. It was not the French, this time, who knew, but the Americans, and so they were *called*. But the sequel shows once again how easily this spirit can turn into the most selfish nationalism.

Coming home with the result of the Congress, in which little was left of the Fourteen Points, and with the League of Nations project, which must still put everything right, the President was abandoned by his own people. The mood of the American public was no less self-righteous than was his own, but its conclusion was to wash its hands of this incorrigible Europe, quarrelsome and divided by nationalisms. The Senate voted down the League of Nations, and the United States withdrew for many years into a sterile isolationism.

Not only the United States, Russia too stood aside. For a long time the Western powers regarded the Russian Revolution as an irregularity that was bound to be straightened out sooner or later. On its part, the authoritarian minority rule that had become established in that country interpreted the slogan "Proletarians of all countries, unite!" in so dogmatically one-sided a manner that an absolute separation from the rest of Europe came about.

By themselves the western European powers were unable to make a success of the League of Nations. Such paper arrangements cannot in one blow change the course of history. Zealous Europeans said at the time—and they still say—that the League of Nations could not do it because it had not been fitted out with supranational authority. But that nostrum won't cure everything either. The forces that make history come from the bottom, and in Europe they were indissolubly tied (and still are, of course) to the nations and states that, with their several interests and traditions, composed the European community. In order to understand the failure of the League of Nations the observation of its organizational weaknesses will not help much: the political conditions and feelings actually prevailing in Europe will have to be examined. It will then be noticed that, certainly, the cultural cohesion maintained itself, also that many in all countries realized the danger threatening all of us and urged the necessity of international co-operation, but that nevertheless there was still, as a legacy from the preceding period, in each country a large public opinion passionately cheering on its government's unrestrained selfishness.

The most pernicious phenomenon was the ever-rankling Franco-German feud. Instead of giving a fair chance to the German Republic (of Weimar), seriously trying as it was to master the evil tendencies of the Wilhelminian period, the French kept making things difficult for it; especially the French, but the English, too, often behaved unwisely in this respect. Practically, western policy encouraged the German nationalists of various descriptions in their reckless opposition to what they denounced as the weaknesses of their own German government. This German opposition inveighed against the humiliations that the treaty of Versailles was still inflicting upon Germany; the economic crisis by which the country was being overwhelmed, too, they explained as an effect of the treaty. An impassioned nationalism burst forth.

We now see the fateful figure of Hitler rising up. I pay a tribute in passing to Stresemann and Briand, who still did what they could to avert the disaster; I mention Locarno. But National Socialism did come into power. And glorifying race as it did, clamoring for a strong state that, inexorably one, was to make the German will prevail at whatever cost, it was the denial of all European order, of Europe itself.

I quoted Maurras's saying, "la France seule." In 1932, shortly before the *Machtübernahme*, I attended a students' congress in Germany and got acquainted at first hand with the National Socialist madness. Among my most vivid memories is the abhorrence with which I heard Count Reventlow's contumelious rejection of the entire conception of Europe. There was no sense in it, there was no such thing, there was only Germany: Europe was a phantasm invented to paralyze the courage and the energy of a great nation.

Well, we have seen to what all this led the Germans and the world. Europe was renounced not only politically, but culturally and morally. Triumphant National Socialism amounted to a veritable revolt against Western civilization, to its negation.

In the end, however, Europe did have a place in the National Socialist imagination and in the National Socialist propaganda, but only as an object of conquest and of domination. And it is to be noted that many people outside Germany hoped—you will remember my pointing to the corresponding phenomenon in the days of Napoleon—that the longed-for unity of Europe might in this fashion be realized. So spoke our Dutch N.S.B.-ers (members of the Dutch "National Socialist" movement), and there are a few left who still do. But there were men of an entirely different outlook who were impressed by this slogan of European unity. They deluded themselves into believing that the excesses did not belong organically to National Socialism: they would not last. No doubt, authoritarianism was the very essence of the German dynamism that seemed to be changing the world. But they were prepared to sacrifice democratic liberty to this idolized unity. A strong impetus was given to this way of thinking in 1941, when Hitler made war on Russia. "Europe united against Bolshevism," was the cry then raised. In that enchanting vision the national particularisms of Europe could appear insignificant. England? Did England *belong* to Europe? Had not England at all times been the enemy of European unity? Had not England thwarted the great work time and again—as it was trying to do now?

Actually England was then making a stand, as it had done against Louis XIV and Napoleon, for the salvation of European liberty. William III, Pitt, Churchill—they form a sequence. And what is Europe without liberty? I have stressed how from the beginning liberty has been the guarantee and the hallmark of Western civilization. One of the most fertile forms in which the resulting diversity appears, is the national. No unity can be allowed to stifle or to blur it—or disturbing reactions will result. Diversity, that is how the great Swiss historical thinker Burckhardt put it in 1869 (without expressly mentioning the national, but it is implied in the passage): diversity, the struggle between individual forces, and the harmony arising out of those various sounds of tendencies, groups, and individuals, this is the essence of European civilization.

> It is menaced by only one danger that might prove fatal: that of an oppressive mechanical power, whether on the part of a conquering barbaric people or of the aggregate means of power within its own confines mobilized in the service of one tendency.

This is how the large majority of the Dutch people felt it under the occupation, and more intensely as the visitation lasted longer. In France, which went through an unprecedented moral collapse and where Pétain had concluded his unholy pact with the victor, men's minds were divided much more profoundly. There, moreover, a factor rooted in history was at work: the old distrust of England, mixed with envy. To range Churchill in one sequence with William III and Pitt would probably be regarded by a Frenchman with very different feelings than I meant to evoke.

Nevertheless, in the last instance the mood was determined everywhere by the aversion and hatred the occupying power roused against itself with its increasingly brutal methods. In the end we owed our liberation to the stubborn perseverance of the English people and the overwhelming power of the United States.

But what about the problem of European unity after the downfall of Hitler and his system? Was the story of the years after 1918 to be repeated and the German people, while trying amid the ruins to recover its senses, to be confused and goaded into fresh outbreaks of fury by the nationalist ambitions of the others? Even in Holland there was wild talk of annexations at the expense of Germany. For a few years France persisted in its eastward expansionist ambitions—I am thinking of the Saar region. But the acute menace presented by Stalinist Russia, whose power now stretched westward down to and across the river Elbe, made the aid of what remained of Germany indispensable. The antagonism between Russia and the West (that is to say, Europe, insofar as it was still free, and the United States) soon paralyzed the organization of the United Nations, which had been meant to be an amended League of Nations. From the point of view of my theme the United Nations hardly comes into sight. The League of Nations, too, had been projected for a world organization, but the European powers and their mutual relations had held the stage at Geneva. In the United Nations, Europe was submerged in the mass of extra-European countries animated by a new consciousness of their importance. But in fact the Russian vetoes undermined the effectiveness of that grandiose enterprise. At any rate, it could not play a part in the organization of Europe. Only America made its influence powerfully felt once more.

In these circumstances a deliberate endeavor to reintegrate Germany into the West soon won through, and it is one of the most auspicious phenomena of recent years that this process has followed so smooth a course. The most beneficial aspect has been the settlement of the Franco-German feud that had for generations dominated the European scene. An atmosphere has been created in which it is possible once more to work with some hope for the unity of Europe (of a Europe, it is true, suffering from an amputation on its eastern side).

After all periods of war this idea emerges: after 1815, after 1918. The lesson has been more severe this time; the ardor is more intense; the chances are more favorable. The fact that there is, compared with earlier periods, a larger measure of consensus on democracy—due to the experience with National Socialism as well as to the new menace of communism—is, in particular, an inestimable gain. Something has been achieved already. I am thinking of the Council of Europe and the European Parliament at Strasbourg; of the Organization for European Economic Cooperation; of the North Atlantic Treaty Organization, too, even though the leading part in it is played by the United States. It is more, and it seems more solid, than anything that was built up on earlier occasions.

And the Europe of "the Six"?

I have repeatedly given expression to my doubts about the

wisdom as well as the practicability of that undertaking. I think that for the smaller partners (the Benelux countries) it contains downright dangerous possibilities. This does not belong to my subject. But I want to indicate very briefly how my view of the history of Europe, as I have unfolded it very sketchily here, leads me to these doubts.

The first thing that fills me with astonishment is that the creators of the association of "the Six" have presumed to claim for it the name "Europe," and that the Europe enthusiasts exultingly applaud an arrangement that may well turn out to have prepared a cleavage in Europe. This small Continental Europe has never been on the order of the day in history except under circumstances unacceptable for the true European. If we seek the unity of Europe in liberty, it is absurd to leave England outside, England, which has on three occasions stood in the breach for the liberty of Europe —and the last time the most glorious.

Speaking generally, throughout the unceasing changes to which conditions and ways of thinking are subject in the course of the centuries—and our generation has lived through some dizzying changes—I am struck by the persistence, the stubborn durability, of fundamental characteristics. The belief of the idealistic or revolutionary mentality that we can at a given moment begin, so to speak, on a clean slate, is a dangerous illusion. Such, for instance, is the idea that the French and the Germans are from now on nothing but Europeans. They are still, respectively, Frenchmen and Germans, and so are we Dutch still Dutchmen, and it is right that we should, and we must, be. But can we make our influence felt with regard to the powerful nations to which we have tied ourselves by the treaty of Rome? Does not our enthusiasm for the idea of supranationalism impede us in our freedom to watch over our interests?—more than it does them? Do the articles of the treaty leave us room, for instance, to promote the extension of the association that our government assures us it desires, but that seems to hitch every time on the unwillingness especially of the French? I shall no more than mention the directly elected parliament that is in course of preparation and that to me seems to be a most questionable experiment. Not only because it is likely to prove an unsurpassable obstacle to the English, but in itself: how is it possible to expect reliable guidance from so heterogenous a body, one whose members will be drawn largely from nations that have not made a conspicuous success of parliamentary government at home?

Enough of questions. The historian is no prophet. The future is to him an impenetrable mystery as it is to all of us mortals. But for all that, history sharpens the eye for possibilities and impossibilities, and I shall be satisfied if I have made you feel for a moment that the past—*not*, holds us enslaved—thank heaven, no!—*but*, that it participates.

(1959)

POSTSCRIPT

From 1953 on I had watched with misgivings the establishment of a closer relationship between "the Six." Not because I am opposed to European federation, but because a partial federation from which England and the Scandinavian countries (to mention only those) are excluded seems to me not to advance that ideal, but on the contrary, to place a very serious obstacle in its way.

I know as well as anybody that England bears a large share of the blame for the development that we are now witnessing. But I have felt all along that our statesmen, for their part, were shutting their eyes to the dangers of the course in which they engaged; and the enthusiasm for the treaty signed in Rome displayed by the fervent supporters of the European idea in our midst seemed to me incomprehensible. To listen to them, indeed, the association of "the Six" was only a beginning, made necessary by England's hanging back, and in the end it would be seen to have promoted a more truly European solution.

These explanations and excuses could never convince me. I was, and still am, afraid that, on the contrary, the block that has been formed will evolve a particularist sentiment, supported by vested interests growing stronger with every year that passes. I am afraid that, under cover of a devout use of the name "Europe," a dangerous division of Europe is being prepared.

This is not what the Dutch statesmen wanted, or want. But in this association with states of so much greater strength, their wishes can already be seen to count for little.

I have repeatedly expressed my "unorthodox" views on this matter.[1] In 1959 I devoted the address I was invited to give at Harvard on Commencement Day to the subject.[2] For years mine was a somewhat lonely voice in my own country, and if many of my compatriots now seem to be waking up to the unfortunate consequences of the Common Market, it is becoming increasingly clear that there is now very little we can do to avert them.

One can still hope that England will realize that the Continental block her policy of abstention has allowed to be constituted may in the long run weaken her own position, not only economically, but (and I am inclined to think, especially) politically. There are at this moment signs of a change in English public opinion. Have those who used to say that the association of "the Six" would act as an incentive and would prove to have been only "a beginning" been in the right after all? If England does join, I shall be only too happy to apologize to them. But I am still afraid that this will not happen unless "the Six" will adopt a somewhat more forthcoming attitude, and I am also afraid that not all the partners will be as ready for concessions as will be Holland.

(1960)

V

ON SOME CONTEMPORARY HISTORIANS (MAINLY CRITICAL)

1

JAN ROMEIN, OR BOWING TO THE SPIRIT OF THE AGE

There is something both uncommon and attractive about the personality of Jan Romein (born 1894; Professor of History at the University of Amsterdam from 1939)[1] as it is revealed to us in his latest volume of essays, *Commissioned by the Age*. He moves by preference among great problems, and his intellectual intercourse—as a reader, I mean—is by preference with great minds. This cannot be said of all historians, and indeed a historian does not need that particular quality to make an outstanding contribution to the historical discussion. But Romein here obviously obeys a deeply felt want, and it is enough to give him something distinctive. What makes him attractive—and this, too, sets him apart from the every day type of our profession—is the intensity of his struggles with those great ideas and the sincerity with which he reports on them. For that is characteristic of his work. He does not build a proud and imposing system in accordance with a project preconceived in the cold transparency of an intellectual universe. He is a seeker. His heart impels him as much as does his mind. His examination of history, his conception of what it can give and of how it may best be approached, his discoveries and his doubts—it all means something to him in his life, and in his essays there transpires something now of his hope, then of his disappointment or of his uneasiness. They have something to tell us on a different plane from that of mere curiosity about the past.

A seeker—after steady truth. In fact, he imagines that the remedy against his tormenting vision of dizzying chaos is to be found in Marx. He often testifies to this belief, but he belongs to those whom the revelation of truth does not once and for always satisfy; he must labor to experience it every day, he must put it to the test. And this is what he does in these essays, in a charming fashion, confidential, disarmingly frank, obviously yearning after what is noble and good. He does it in a thoroughly human style, at times sensitive in a way bordering on the coquettish, but also shot through with flashes of humor.

This testing of a truth postulated by the heart makes a spectacle both fascinating and instructive. Convincing, however, if that is to mean that the result will every time seem to the reader as conclusive as it does to the author—convincing it can be only to those to whom the same revelation has already been vouchsafed, to his companions in the faith. Terms as here used flow automatically from the pen when this work is discussed. By its nature it is related to writings giving an account of the experiences of religion.

The first essay is from this point of view the most important. In it the central problem of "certainty and uncertainty in the science of history" is treated. One can readily go along with the author as long as he describes the uncertainty that is so obviously inherent in history and the inadequacy of the various methods with which it has been thought this could be overcome. "We cannot, however, forever linger at the inn called Zero and must proceed. How?" A statement, and a question. But should we not, with respect to what is denied and affirmed so unhesitatingly, first of all like to know *Why*? and *Why not*? Why can we not stay on in uncertainty? and who has told Romein that we must—or can—proceed? The answer, in fact, is not far to seek: because Romein finds uncertainty unbearable, and because he hears his soul cry out that the certainty without which it feels itself lost *must* exist. So he goes out to seek, and (so indeed it is written) he finds.

And what is the certainty he offers us as the result of his reflections? He begins with a twofold, or rather threefold, unprovable assumption. The past has an objective reality, which, moreover, has sense; which sense we can know only through and by way of our mind. Especially the last point, which he seems practically to take for granted, would seem to stand in need of some serious argumentation. *Can* we know this sense? know it in a way that amounts to certainty? For Romein apparently it is enough that he wants to, that he must; therefore he can.

But how?—Here Croce's dictum points the way for him: "All true history is history of the present." This is how Romein himself formulates it: "Objective is, and certainty gives, *that* history-writing which is in agreement with the spirit of the age." (Let there be no mistake—he means: with the historian's age.)

Romein admits that he does not write down those words without "some trembling," and he expects "a cry of protest." I must say that, for my part, it is especially the way in which he overcomes that trembling and tries to silence that protest which makes me stare.

Romein knows, and he says, that the present spirit of the age will be succeeded by a different spirit of the age, and that the devotee's certainty will thereby be superseded. Does he then acknowledge the relativity of his certainty (of "the certainty as I understand it")? His entire argument is intended to turn that relativity into an absolute.

For that purpose the conception of "the spirit of the age" must be simplified and fixed. For Romein there is at every time but one spirit of the age—or rather, there are two, the true one and the false. Only *he*, at any rate, can claim objectivity or certainty who, as our author puts it, "has made the right choice." But how is one to know that one is not in error? At first sight it might be thought—thus Romein lets us share in his cogitations—that only the future will decide this point.

I cannot see on what grounds we should have to let the future judge on true or false. Moreover, the future? The future is a most variable entity. Romein here clearly gets himself involved in difficulties. To which future, how far distant, must we defer the judgment? He adduces the striking instance of the German historians who saw the past in the terms of Bismarck's "Little-German" solution of the unity problem, and in their lifetime this did indeed command the future. Must we therefore call them objective? By Romein's own standard we know better now. The ever-continuing shifts in the development of the ever-moving times have indeed opened our eyes to a thing or two. And has the development come to a stop even now? Besides, the historians who read the past by the light of a policy that was indeed to triumph did not have the field of history all to themselves. Must we conclude that the true spirit of that age was after all represented by their critics because a more distant future seems to be putting them in the right, or at least, showing the fallacies in the outlook of the others? and must we therefore accept these critics as the better, or even greater, historians? Klein-Hattingen greater or more famous than Treitschke? For fame with posterity, too, supplies Romein with a criterion by which to judge the historian's true significance in his own time. He may be right in thinking that the historian becomes "truly famous" only after his death and that only then can his greatness appear. But neither his fame nor his true greatness is determined, and no more is the view we take of his objectivity or of any timebound certainty that he may offer, by his being representative of the true spirit of his age. Many other factors, differing among themselves, will count in the final reckoning.

But indeed, the comfort that the future may give is not enough for Romein. He wants to know *now* that he is on the right track.

> After the choice between the true and the false spirit of the age has been made, it appears possible to check it in another way than with the help of the future alone. The choice can be checked by the *inner* certainty of the historian who made it, on condition, however, that the choice was the right one. For—and this is most noteworthy—this inner certainty, this, so to speak, higher peace of mind of the historian who made the right choice creates (and *because* he made it) the psychological condition that will help him when writing history to overcome his other, personal and group, subjectivity. . . . [And a little later he avows:]
>
> As for me, I have made that choice. I see the true spirit of our own age in the emancipation struggle waged by laborers and peasants, and as long as it lasts the critical method of knowledge that goes with it is the dialectical-materialist. It is that method, therefore, that in my opinion guarantees, for us, the largest possible measure of knowledge about the past.

Romein, in other words, not only has the conviction of his social-political conceptions, but he knows that, taking his stand upon them, he possesses the only true view of history that our time affords. He is certain. Certain with an inner certainty that can never be the part of other-minded men. So while *he* can overcome personal or group subjectivity, those others, who—perhaps against their better judgment, against their better nature—follow the false spirit of the age, live in a constant unrest caused by self-reproach; and blinded by egoism or hatred, doomed to indulge their passions of partiality, they will never find that radiant inner certainty.

It is worth noting that Romein appeals to Groen van Prinsterer, the mid-nineteenth-century Calvinist and antiliberal, who wrote: "It may sound paradoxical, but it is true: only he who chooses a side can be impartial." And indeed, Groen too was a man possessed of an inner certainty that the truth concerning his own time and concerning the past had been revealed to him. Whether it was the truth that was to be confirmed by the future I leave to Romein to judge; the question must worry him more than it does me; I suggest to him that he reread *Unbelief and Revolution.*[2] In any case, Groen was a famous, and if not a great, an important historian. But not a historian, really, who impresses us as having been remarkably objective. He began by representing the Prince of Orange as a hero of the faith, then he revised that interpretation, without being able essentially to alter it, under the influence of the criticism advanced by writers who, if *he* had a monopoly of the true spirit of the age, must have been sadly devoid of it. To how untenable a picture of the Earl of Leicester his partiality made him cling down to the end of his life, can be seen in *Maurice et Barnevelt.*[3]

"The certainty *as I understand it,*" so Romein wrote—and we can now see how badly needed was the qualification—"does not exclude, but on the contrary includes, doubt. This is in accordance with the experience of psychology telling us that the strongest believers are the strongest doubters."

There is no trace of this inclination to doubt in Romein's title, in which the writer gives us to understand that the age commissioned him to compose his book. But what strikes me above all in the passage just quoted is the comparison, which is in effect an identification. Romein's conception of history is a faith. His conviction that he has the true view of the past, and others, dominated by the false spirit of the age, the false view, is not a thesis that can be proved, it is not even liable to discussion: it is a faith.

Finding this faith formulated as we saw it done by him—he insists that the true spirit of the present age consists in the emancipation struggle of laborers and peasants—one is inclined to add that it is a hopelessly short-range faith. I am quite ready to agree that this emancipation struggle is a phenomenon characteristic of our age; I trust that it will prove fruitful. But the abundance of life does not let itself be imprisoned in so narrow a definition. There are contrasts of endless variety on all sides—exceeding or crossing this only one that Romein is willing to observe.

We are confronted here, and not for the first time, with a peculiarity of the author that is connected with his deepest being. In another essay in this same volume he quotes a "thesis" appended to his doctoral dissertation (of 1924): "The science of history must accept historiography as its final aim, and historiography must concentrate on the historical account, or story."

Striking words indeed, and Romein says he still agrees with them. But why, then, do we now receive from him so little "historical account, or story"? Why has he given his heart to what he calls "theoretical history"? I regret this, for although a historical account impelled by so emotional, and at the same time, so narrow a faith would not be likely to excel in objectivity and could hardly embody more than a fragment of the spirit of our own age, its inspiration might lend it pace and fire, and even those other-minded men whom Romein abandons to the contempt of posterity might be grateful for the light thrown if only on an aspect of the truth about the past. But no, Romein the historian seems to be succumbing to the danger of allowing his mind to be so engrossed by general conceptions that the historical sense for the concrete, for the particular, for the multiform and the refractory to system, is escaping him.

"The conception of the spirit of the age is so vague." This, so he says, is the objection that will be raised against the considerations he propounds. He continues:

To this I must reply that the historian always works with vague notions. Race, people, nation, state. Nobility, bourgeoisie, small middle-class, proletariat. Republic, monarchy, dictatorship, democracy. Feudalism, capitalism, socialism, fascism. Renaissance, baroque, romanticism, liberalism. Where is the historian whose hand will not hesitate when venturing to define any of these conceptions? But where, also, is the historian who will refrain from using them as being too vague? The historian must work with vague notions because his object does not admit of exact ones.

The problem, however, presents itself in a totally different fashion from that suggested by Romein. The historian does not work with notions or conceptions primarily, but with representations, or delineations. What vagueness there is in conceptions must become exact in his concretization. The notion *monarchy* is vague. But in a history of Louis XIV we must get a clear picture of what monarchy was under him. The true historian will feel some diffidence in the, indeed unavoidable, employment of vague generalizations. He will at once be ready with questions, with criticism; he will desire greater precision and do what he can to supply it.

And so I conclude that the reckless employment of the term *the spirit of the age*, the simplistic distinction made between *the true* and *the false spirit of the age*, the presumption of measuring every writer of history by his being an adept of either the one or the other—I conclude that all this making play with a conception of indeed so vague an import must be called thoroughly unhistorical. If Romein did not content himself with a general presentment of his idea, but tried to apply it in particular cases, the results would probably provide an ironic comment on his all-saving theory of certainty. The rightness of a historical representation, and the greatness of a historian, depend on many factors, among which are prominent those of personal qualities and personal ways of thinking not simply to be derived from the historian's intellectual position with regard to his own age.

How dangerous is this doctrine according to which objectivity is not a capacity to be acquired, or approached, by dint of labor and discipline, but a state of grace obtained once and for all by adhering to the doctrine itself! How must it, and in what treacherous ways, strengthen the temptation, to which we are all of us exposed, to let our cherished fancies and our constructions have the better of the facts!

(1947)

2
OTHMAR F. ANDERLE, OR UNREASON AS A DOCTRINE

I will frankly confess that I read reviews of my books with a good deal of interest. In the course of a lengthening life, in which hardly a year has passed without some publication or other, I have had innumerable reviews in half a dozen countries. There were some that annoyed and some that infuriated me; others pleased or even delighted me; a good many, laudatory as they might be, moved me to no more than a shrug.

But I have seldom experienced the mixed feelings of astonishment and indignation giving way to sheer amusement that were roused in me on reading a review of my *Debates with Historians* in the solemn pages of the leading historical journal of Germany, the *Historische Zeitschrift*.

The writer, Othmar F. Anderle, is a fervent admirer of Toynbee, and his article is concerned mostly with those essays in my volume in which *A Study of History* is criticized. But indeed so full of Toynbee is the writer's mind that even when I write about Ranke, Macaulay, Carlyle, and Michelet, about the American Civil War and Talleyrand, he imagines that I am indirectly tilting at the prophet.

Now, none of this very greatly disturbed me, but what I thought extraordinary is that Toynbee's apologist should admit the correctness of practically the whole of my criticism. When I point out the errors in the factual foundations of Toynbee's superstructure of theory and generalization, he thinks I am in the right. Even when I assert that the whole method is faulty and that Toynbee's repeated insistence on proceeding empirically and arriving at conclusions by a concatenation of proved facts is no more than make-believe, he agrees. In fact, he considers my opposition to be the most careful and well-founded statement of the many that international scholarship has made against Toynbee.

But now Herr Anderle brushes aside all the defects in the great work as irrelevant, and because I seem to consider them important and indeed conclusive, rates me down for an antiquated representative of out-of-date "classical" scholarship. I reveal myself as being a mere stickler for the correct statement of facts, a despiser of theory and generalization, a man blind to the greatness of this startling new panoramic vision. Toynbee, according to Anderle, is helping to bring about a revolution in historical scholarship, and only if we will do homage to the principle, *Credo quia ineptum, quia absurdum*—I believe because it is preposterous, because it is absurd—shall we be allowed to enter the brave new world this revolution is opening up for the elect.

The argument reveals a state of mind with which it is impossible to argue. Was I right in saying that the ultimate feeling the article aroused in me was one of sheer amusement? At any rate, when the next issue of the *Historische Zeitschrift* brought an article in which Herr Anderle gave his views on Toynbee's work at greater length, and when the issue after that presented us with a third article, in which he set forth his own theory of history (in both I came in for renewed denunciation), I began to think, not only that the joke was growing rather wearisome, but that, after all, the matter should perhaps be taken seriously.

My protracted dispute with Toynbee has from the first exceeded the limits of strict historical scholarship. I have championed against him not only, as Anderle will have it, the canons of the profession but—that, at least, is how I have felt about it myself—the vital traditions of Western civilization.

Nothing is more absurd than to suggest that I, or historians in general, believe in nothing but facts, that we despise theories of generalizations as such. History must reveal to us a meaning in life, or we are not worth our salt. History, as I have expressed it on another occasion, is a key to life, as is art or literature.[1] But history has its own methods and obligations, and although it will not get far without imagination or intuition, it must always accept the control of reason.

There is in the whole of the Western world, as there has been before, a movement of revolt against the claims of reason. Toynbee's great work, and the popular acclaim that greeted it, were signs of this, and I have done what I could to point out that behind the pretense of scientific empiricism there was the reality of emotional and defeatist fantasy. I was not, truth to tell, alarmed overmuch, because I believe that our civilization, which has no more distinctive feature than its rationality, disposes of abundant powers of resistance to master (again, as it has done before) these stirrings of impatience and petulance within its own fold. But Herr Anderle goes one better than Toynbee. He dispenses with the pretense and boldly invokes the principle of Tertullian, which has undeniable greatness in its own sphere, but which, when applied to history, cuts at the foundations of scholarship and clear thinking.

When a great European historical review, not once but three times running, allows this doctrine of unreason to be proclaimed in its pages, one has an uneasy feeling that among the custodians of our heritage some are not fully aware of the dangers that beset us. The powers of resistance of our civilization are, I said, abundant. The rational approach is among its most effective weapons of defense. We must be careful of it.

(1958)

3
HERBERT BUTTERFIELD, OR THINKING AT TWO LEVELS

The leading idea of Herbert Butterfield's *Man on his Past* (1955) is that of the importance of the history of historiography. Four lectures included in it were delivered under the auspices of the new Wiles Trust at the University of Belfast. In these we are first shown the history of historiography in historical perspective. The origin of the notion in a more significant form than that of a mere listing of books and authors is traced back to the Göttingen School of History in the decades before and after 1800. Quotations from Gatterer (1760), Schlözer (1785 and later), and Rühs (1811), bear out the conclusion that these men were the spiritual forebears of Ranke and Acton.

The importance of Germany's contribution to the emergence of the view of history that we have come to consider as characteristic of modern civilization is beyond dispute; the recognition that historiography is itself governed by the process of development is a natural concomitant of that view. So it is not surprising that the second essay deals with "The Rise of the German Historical School." The third, on "Lord Acton and the Nineteenth-Century Historical Movement," is again largely concerned with German ideas, which it was Acton's ambition to introduce into England, although at the same time he set his face against the consequences of relativism and acquiescence to which "historicism" so easily led, and insisted on the need for upholding the independent and unchangeable standards of morality.

The fourth lecture, "Ranke and the Conception of 'General History,' " deals with general history as much as with Ranke. We are given disquisitions of the author's own on the problem of the importance of foreign policy, the idea of Providence, the Renaissance, and the division into periods.

Finally there are two essays, published earlier, one on "Lord Acton and the Massacre of St. Bartholomew" and the other on "The Reconstruction of an Historical Episode: The History of the Enquiry into the Origins of the Seven Years' War." In these the author gives samples of his own of the history of historiography in connection with concrete questions.

The first thing that must be said of this work is that it is the product of profound and meticulous research and testifies to a remarkable erudition. The accounts of the origins of the notion of a history of historiography and of the rise of the German historical school are particularly useful since they show—once again—that what one is accustomed to look upon as a revolution and to associate with a few great names, had in fact been long prepared, and prepared by "little men," or men, at least, whose names have been forgotten.

One aspect of the general history of historiography which has Professor Butterfield's special interest is the treatment of individual historians. "Since the Second World War," he writes, "three men in particular have been repeatedly examined, both in Europe and in America," Ranke, Burckhardt, and Acton.

Personally I believe that the attention lavished upon Acton in England sometimes surprises Continental historians. That extraordinary devourer of books and scribbler of notes, whose *magnum opus* never got written, produced only essays in a style that has been described as "crabbed, tortuous, contorted, elliptic and allusive."[1] In his voluminous private notes, no doubt, he often found for his unceasing and profound reflections phrases of an unforgettable quality, and Professor Butterfield deserves our thanks for having culled so many more from those mysterious black boxes in the Cambridge University Library. How could the idea inspiring the history of historiography be stated more pregnantly and more simply than when he says: "Teach to look behind historians, especially famous historians." And how can the opposition to historicism, which he welcomed with such fervor, be better expressed than in a note unearthed by another recent student of his work: "Resist your time—take a foothold outside it."[2]

The treatment of Ranke is admirable. To approach him from the angle of "general history" proves really fruitful, and in a few pages not only the special qualities of the great historian, but the various aspects of the concept "general history" (European and world history, western European history, the relations between political and cultural history, nationality, power and the moral factor) are illumined.

On one point I think Professor Butterfield goes too far along with Ranke. He confesses to having felt shocked at first when he found Ranke arguing that "in spite of Goethe, German culture and German cultural influence gained their great momentum with the rise of German power and confidence in the nineteenth century," and then: "Yet when I reflect on the cultural leadership which the United States and Russia have come to enjoy since the Second World War . . . I am staggered to see how such matters are affected by a mere redistribution of power." I am not at all sure that it is right to speak of "cultural leadership" of the U.S., however highly I esteem the American contribution to our common Western civilization. But I am quite sure that it is wrong to speak of a "cultural leadership" of Russia. I write under the fresh impression of the wilfully one-sided and propagandist Russian contributions to the proceedings of the International Congress of History recently held in Rome.

But perhaps the author will brush this evidence aside as irrelevant, for he, who devotes so much attention to Ranke and Acton, does not seem to rate history very high as a cultural force. In trying to establish the usefulness of the history of historiography he takes a somewhat narrow ground. He speaks as the teacher of history, he considers the equipment of the research student, he hopes for the unraveling of the bewildering entanglement of researches in certain fields. For the two practical examples of his own application of the method, too, he has (in the two essays alluded to above, the fifth and sixth in his book) chosen problems of a concrete and factual nature.

Stress might have been laid on matters of wider significance. As for instance, that every personal view of a historical episode or figure being to a certain extent one-sided or biased, more of the fundamental truth may be revealed when we watch the ever-changing interpretations offered by successive generations of historians,—no mere kaleidoscopic sequence, but one in which every next picture will be seen to have incorporated elements of the preceding ones, a gradual conquest of reality over myth. Also, how much do historians unconsciously reveal of the spirit of their own times! The ideal history of historiography would be a contribution to the intellectual, social, and political history of the times in which the works were written. Moreover, the historian as the exponent of contemporary tendencies has often exercised a direct influence on the development of ideas, conditions, and events.

This, of course, Professor Butterfield knows as well as anybody, but he regards this influence with suspicion. He dwells on the case of the post-Rankean school in Germany which, as he puts it, misled the German people. And he concludes that particular story with a reflection of even wider import: "It would seem that the decline of religion gives undue power to history in the shaping of men's minds—undue power to historical over-simplifications, and multitudes of young students have even come to the study of technical history in the expectation that it would help them to shape their fundamental views about life. It is an expectation that is often disappointed." (Curiously enough, according to Acton, as recorded by Professor Butterfield himself: "history lay at the basis of European religion," and if what Professor Butterfield means is not really "history" but "historical over-simplifications," the question might well be asked whether many of these were not inspired by religion.)

"Technical history"—what our author means by this becomes clearer in another passage. "Technical history," the kind of history that we can teach and that, when we write it, will pass the tests of scholarship, "is a limited and mundane realm of description and explanation, in which local and concrete things are achieved by a disciplined use of tangible evidence." Professor Butterfield is here concerned to place the concept of Providence beyond the reach of the "technical historian." "Thinking at different levels" is what he advises.[3]

In his *Christianity and History*, when apparently he was thinking at the other level, he explained the defeat and destruction of Germany in the second world war as the divine punishment for the sins of the German people. The explanation required the concept of "vicarious punishment," for is it not obvious that many Germans were not guilty? The fact that other countries, I mention only the Baltic countries, which had not sinned (insofar as sinlessness is humanly possible), had to suffer as grievously and are still suffering, remained without explanation.

At any rate the technical historian, according to *Man on His Past*, "is arguing in a circle if he thinks that his researches have in fact eliminated from life the things which for technical reasons he had eliminated in advance from his consideration." But do historians have to eliminate things in advance? Professor Butterfield now even switches over from religion to literature and maintains that "the poet, the prophet, the novelist and the playwright command sublimer realms than those of technical history because they reconstitute life in its wholeness. The history of historiography may help us to keep the technical historian in his place."

This is a view of history which I for one can never accept. History must claim the whole of life for its province. It is hampered by a deficiency of data, admitted; the human mind is incapable of embracing even those which it can gather and of bringing them into a stable equilibrium, of that too I am fully aware. I do not claim that history will solve the riddle of our existence. But the true historian, whose mind has been touched by the great revolution in historic thinking which Professor Butterfield so well describes, does not come to his material as a technician, or not *only* as a technician, but as a human being. He will eliminate nothing in advance. He will never expect to reach the absolute, but he will strive, despite his handicaps, with all his soul and mind, like the poet. He will in his way be a servant of truth, like the preacher or the prophet. He will not mind being put in his place, but he will not belittle history, nor will he be discouraged.

I know that this is just stating view against view. I am, however, grateful to Professor Butterfield, not only for his excellent specimens of technical history, but also for the shock he has made me experience by his philosophy, a shock which is to me confirmation of my own belief that history cuts down to the deepest issues of life.

(1956)

4

GEOFFREY BARRACLOUGH, OR THE SCRAPPING OF HISTORY

It so happened that I read Barraclough's *History in a Changing World* immediately after another volume of essays, *Six Historians*, by Ferdinand Schevill, which was published posthumously. I shall write here only of the first-named work, but it is impossible not to remark upon the contrast presented by the two.

Professor Barraclough, who for a number of years occupied the chair of Medieval History at the University of Liverpool, recently succeeded Arnold Toynbee as Research Professor of International History at the University of London. His essays, fifteen of them, for the most part quite short, give evidence, no less than do those of Schevill, of a vast range of learning. But instead of a firm rooting in the Western cultural tradition, and the balance and mellow understanding characteristic of the older man, we find here a restless dissatisfaction with the old ways of historical scholarship, carping—wildly, as it seems to me—at prejudice, convention, antiquated methods, and calling on us to cast all our textbooks onto the dustheap and learn the world's history anew.

For Barraclough, "historicism" is the enemy. Historicism, which sees history as a process of continuity, to which one period is as important as another, by which everything is judged according to time, place, context, and environment, etc.; I abridge the eloquent passage.

No doubt such tendencies have at times been promoted by historicism, but it seems to me absurd to write as though they constituted the prevailing attitude among historians of the last generation. Historicism is not for me a term of reproach, for I regard these demoralizing and deadening kinds of relativism as excrescences. I find its true significance in the fact that it enables us to feel ourselves, not enslaved by the past, but in touch with it—a touch that is invigorating as well as restraining.

But here comes Professor Barraclough to bid us study the periods of crisis, of change and revolution, for continuity is a delusion and we are ourselves in just such a period of crisis, which makes all our inherited notions of the past "irrelevant." What exactly does the new prophet mean? In his introduction he lays much stress on the immorality of historicism, but his own philosophy, as he develops it in a variety of contexts, is not preoccupied with morality or the free choice of the individual, but with power.

Western Europe has lost its dominant position: America, Russia, Asia, now make world history. Let us not shrink from the conclusion, then, that we have been wrong all along in picturing to ourselves a world history centering on Europe. So runs Barraclough's argument.

The loss of the dominant position is indisputable, though to suggest that "in the late twentieth or in the twenty-first century Europe is destined to enjoy (if that is the right word) something not unlike the colonial status which in the eighteenth and nineteenth centuries it imposed on Africa, much of Asia and the New World," seems to me just shock tactics unworthy of a serious historical argument. But admitting that the dominant position is gone and irretrievable, does it follow that in our view of the past, when the dominant position was undeniable, Europe must no longer be seen as the central force in world affairs?

To me it seems obvious that the peoples of America, Asia, and Africa, all of whom have been deeply and permanently affected by the enterprises and traditions of western Europe, will for a long time need to study the history of that region in its period of greatness if they want to understand themselves. But it does not seem obvious to Barraclough:

The traditional Europe—the Europe of our history books, the Europe of Louis XIV and Napoleon and Bismarck—is dead and beyond resurrection, and we may disabuse our minds of the illusion that there is any special relevance, from the point of view of contemporary affairs, in studying these neolithic figures.

It was in 1943, when Stalingrad was relieved by the Russians, that Professor Barraclough suddenly awoke to the fact that he had misspent his life. Why, he asked himself, had he and all Westerners been so blind to the actual distribution of power? It was because he, who knew a great deal about the machinery of the papal chancery in the thirteenth and fourteenth centuries, knew nothing of the Piasts, the Przemyslids and the Ruriks; because, in short, he knew nothing of eastern European history. This strikes me as an extraordinarily naïve remark. In the first place, why wait until 1943? And although the victory at Stalingrad may have been an unanswerable power pronouncement, was it the natural culmination of a process beginning with the Przemyslids and the Ruriks? One has only to read the story of the 1941 campaign to realize how uncertain were the chances of war and how near Stalin came to ruin. Would we then have had to accept Germany as the true center of world history and rewrite everything accordingly?

It is not only the decline of western Europe's world position, it is the rise of Russia and of Communism which often makes our "universalists" give way to what I regard as a detestable defeatism with respect to the vitality and prospects of Western society. They are so obsessed with the idea of change that they no longer care to preserve our heritage. Their outlook is akin to that truly revolutionary mentality that Croce, twenty-five years ago, described under the name of "anti-historicism":

That feeling that true history is only about to begin, and that we are at last escaping from the bonds of false history and struggling into freedom and space.

I used the term "our heritage." *The European Inheritance* is the title of a three-volume collective work that appeared in England two or three years ago. Barraclough devotes a largely sarcastic article to it, the title especially moving him to scorn. Though some of his remarks are to the point, his bias appears in the use he makes of Geoffrey Bruun's gloomy description of the state of affairs, especially in France, after the miscarriage of the Revolution of 1848 and of the 1871 Commune: "A runaway technology; the implicit contradiction at the heart of liberal philosophy: the unresolved contradiction between political equality in theory and economic inequality in fact; the confident premises were no more." All this is quoted from Bruun, Barraclough seeming to forget that it is related to one particular period. Indeed the final sentence of his paragraph, "When the end came, old Europe's last breath was a sign of relief, as it concluded the unequal struggle, cast aside its burden, and gave up the ghost," is *not* based on Bruun, though the reader must think so.

Has old Europe indeed given up the ghost? One might maintain with greater justice that the twentieth century, which has seen the ruin of Europe's power, has also seen a new proof of the vitality and resourcefulness of its society and civilization—seen it in the welfare state, which has largely resolved the distressing contrasts of the preceding century. But the welfare state comes in for nothing but sneers from Barraclough:

> In Russian eyes today [he said in a lecture] Western society is a weary, decadent society, the relict of a dying bourgeoisie, which has lost faith in itself and is incapable of renewal from within. To you, luxuriating in the manifold delights of the "welfare state," this may seem a curious and perverse judgment.

He does not actually say that he considers the judgment sound, but this is the impression one gathers from his many pronouncements. And indeed he tells us in so many words that our civilization has nothing to look forward to but gradually being superseded by "the coming civilization," of which he can already see "the dim shape." Elsewhere he bids us take comfort from the thought that "European values, though they may be modified and re-assessed, will not perish, because they are embedded in both American and Russian civilization."

Yet he warns us not to think of America as an integral part of western European civilization. He is at pains, on the contrary, to argue that Russia is more truly of Europe than most of us are inclined to believe. He does not, in fact, seem to find much to choose between America and Russia:

> Already the Soviet Union and the United States have their European satellites; already eastern Europe can only defend itself with Russian help against American domination [!], and western Europe can only defend itself with American aid against Russia.

Power, I said, is the dominant factor in Barraclough's view of the world. Nowhere in his book is there a clear indication of the true nature of the Soviet system in which we are to be glad that "our Western values" are being "embedded." The tendency of this latest prophecy of a historian (in a book, let me add, abounding in acute and stimulating remarks) seems to me pernicious.

(1957)

5

SOVIET HISTORIANS MAKE THEIR BOW

For a full week in September 1955 the Tenth International Congress of History was assembled in Rome. Two thousand historians of all nationalities discussed, in I don't know how many sections, innumerable subjects. Before leaving home they had received six heavy volumes containing elaborate reports, and at Rome there waited for them a seventh, with brief summaries of the communications to be delivered orally. It would be an impossible task to survey the activities of the Congress as a whole. But one fact was of so unusual, and at the same time, of so arresting a nature that it still dominates my memory of that crowded week: there were Russians there, flanked by Poles, Hungarians, Czechs, Rumanians, and they were anxious to give an account of themselves.

Into the babel of voices they certainly introduced one that was distinctively different. Unfortunately, it is impossible to affirm that they added to the possibilities of a real exchange of thought. On the contrary, the most remarkable feature of their contribution was that the Russians did not really take part, and obviously were unable to take part, in that argument without end which is to us of the West the study of history. No doubt this is what one would have expected, but to have one's untested expectation so abundantly confirmed is a significant experience. They had come just to *tell* us—for they were certain that they had a monopoly of true historical method and true historical insight, revealed for all time by Marx and Engels. They were unshakably certain that the materialistic conception of history is the indispensable condition for history being raised to the status of a *Science*; with the aid of it alone can work be produced that will be both *progressive* and *objective*. These latter terms, which at first sight do not seem to go together too well, they would reel off confidently in one breath—for it is part of their doctrine, not only that history is governed by the development of the means of production and is essentially the history of the class war, but also that its direction is *determined* toward a future of pure democracy, of a classless society.

When I speak of *them* in the aggregate, I only echo their constantly referring to *us*: "We Soviet historians"; "the school of historical materialism to which I belong"; and so on. In the West, however, all of these axioms are still problems: one historian may accept more of them; another, less; a third will reject them altogether. Most of us will count spiritual or instinctive factors in history in addition to purely materialistic ones. There will be fairly general agreement that these various categories are somehow interdependent, but there is nothing like a *communis opinio* as to the order in which the connection makes itself felt. The different factors will be differently apportioned. As regards the course of history, Western historians may hope or fear, accept or doubt; few will affirm that they *know*. They are far, then, from constituting a unanimous chorus, and here we have the first and principal characteristic of the performance and the testimony of the Russians at Rome.

Or rather—a unanimous chorus?

A close phalanx is what they appeared to be. Their leader was A. L. Sidorov. His contribution to the activities of the Congress was a survey of Soviet Russian historical problematics and achievements.

"Soviet Russian historiography," so he tells us without mincing matters, "continues the materialistic tradition, which has found its most consistent and fullest expression in Marxism." Led by it, Lenin in his writings "has explained in a new way all major events of Russian and modern world history." Nothing less. Also: "It may be said with certainty that the materialistic conception of history has completely triumphed in our country and is universally recognized by historians of both the younger and older generations."[1] As for this last positive assurance, I do not for a moment doubt it. But it does not seem to strike the Russians that what we are confronted with here is an extraordinary phenomenon, which cries out for historical explanation.

Truth to tell, their own recipe for historical explanation is easily applied, and one guesses that for them Sidorov's first sentence says everything: "Soviet historiography came into existence, after the great revolution of October 1917, in the conditions of the new socialist society." But *is* there no more to be said? The spectacle of this intellectual discipline, of this well-drilled array of historians all trotting obediently through the same curious processes of thought, all pretending to master the refractory material of mankind's historical vicissitudes by the same formulas—it not only rouses the disgust of anyone who has not had his thinking molded by Soviet dictatorship, it makes the outsider ask questions to which no satisfactory answers will ever be forthcoming from those well-schooled adepts of historical materialism and its special kind of dialectics.

How much compulsion has been needed to achieve this state of affairs? Is there any Soviet historian left who, in the privacy of his study (if he has any), thinks differently? Are there any younger men trying to widen their outlook by surreptitiously scanning the writings of unorthodox ("reactionary," "bourgeois") Western historians? Do not doubts stir in the brain of one or another of these speakers who, after having arrived in Rome with passport and all in order, is now proclaiming with brazen forehead the Marxian truths, doubts that perhaps he hardly dares to admit to himself?

And as regards the future, of which these lights of Soviet historical scholarship dispose so masterfully—does it really belong to them? Is their "history" really destined to become *History*? Have they discovered the means by which to shackle once and for all the human mind, which, as Burckhardt said (a reactionary bourgeois if you like, but somewhat more besides!), is "a worrier" (*ein Wühler*)? I cannot believe it, and what strengthens my disbelief is that very disgust with which the achievements they so confidently offered us have filled me.

I have heard them. But I have, more especially, read them. In Volume VII of the Congress publications there is to be found, for instance, another brief theoretical treatise, by Madame Pankratova, agreeing completely in both thought and terminology with Sidorov's survey. "We start from a materialistic view of history [so she tells us] in which history is conceived as an objective process, at the base of which lies the development of the means of production of material goods." Proceeding in that way one will learn "rightly to understand the laws of history and how these are to be applied in order to solve the problem of the present." Western historians get lost on unscientific paths, as did Spengler, who drew a gloomy picture of the past, and Croce, Beard, Collingwood—all submerged into subjectivism or pessimism. And what can be worse than the opinion, suggested in the American *Report on Theory and Practice in Historical Study* of 1946, that history is unknowable!

A worse case of mixing up representative and unrepresentative names (Spengler!) and of neglecting shades and subtleties of opinion, it would be difficult to imagine!

Sidorov has an explanation of this reluctance of Western historians to deduce laws from their observation of history and to speak dogmatically about the true meaning of history: it is because they are afraid of the future; it is their way of trying to halt history in its march and to delay social progress. Indeed, according to Madame Pankratova, "the study of history shows that socialism is the normal result of the entire preceding development of society, the result of the struggle of the mass of workers for their liberation." If, by looking at realities and refusing to shut up one's mind in the schematic, one realizes what is meant here by "socialism" and the "liberation" of the workers (another author will give me occasion to come back to this point), there is indeed plenty of reason to be afraid. Fortunately, the equation of Soviet society with the future requires a violent mental somersault, which there is no need for us to imitate.

But what about the practical achievement, the works of history *in concreto*? Sidorov follows up his theoretical introduction with an enumeration of what is being done in Russia in the field of historical study. Judged by the numbers of research workers and the variety of their subjects, an impressive show of arms. The proclaiming of generalities is not all; historical sources are being ransacked, and no doubt much of that technical work will be useful. Nevertheless it does remain subordinated to the preoccupations, to the *idées fixes*, of the system—that this is so, Sidorov affirms with pride at every turn. But, as a matter of fact, we were put in a position to form our own judgment at leisure. One morning it was announced that in Room Thirteen Soviet Russian historical literature was obtainable, and I managed to get hold of some eight booklets, in Russian, with translations into one of the Western languages (Sidorov's paper was among the lot, with translations into all three). Of the rest I only mention Khvostov on the Franco-Russian alliance of 1891, Nikonov on the origins of the second world war,

Stepanowa and Lewiowa on the struggle for a united Germany in 1848 and 1849, Volgin on humanism and socialism.

Here, then, Soviet historiography shows the West what it can do, and it is a pitiable exhibition. How frightful is the superficiality, and at times, downright falsification resulting from that dogmatism, that willful one-sidedness, that parrotlike repetition of the same formulas all over again!

Take for example Nikonov. He begins (as they all do) with a grandiloquent proclamation of theory. The origins of wars can only be ascertained correctly and scientifically (how fond they all are of the word "scientific"!) by a veracious analysis of concrete historical facts. Fine! Who would not applaud so virtuous a statement! But wait a moment. The field on which "science" is to operate is at once drastically restricted. To begin with, the attempt to explain wars by man's biological or psychological make-up is not allowed to pass for "scientific." It amounts to "calumniating mankind." To represent kings or rulers as responsible for the outbreak of wars, too, is to indulge in a fable from the unscientific phase of historiography. Chance is ruled out: to admit it into the picture would amount to rejecting history as a science. In order to be scientific one has to believe in the goodness of human nature, in mass movements as the true motive forces of history, in the obedience of those movements and consequently of history to laws, and in a few more axioms. Accept them, and you will *know*. In a tone of triumph Nikonov assures us:

> Modern historiography investigates all historical phenomena, wars included, in their organic connection with the concrete socio-economic conditions of the development of society, [and thus] determines and discloses the objective laws of the historical process. History has become a systematized science. . . . Modern progressive historical science, and Soviet historiography particularly, proceeds from the fact that every war is the result of preceding economic and political development, the result of the home and foreign policy of the respective classes and states.[2]

And he goes on once more to reject specifically every explanation based on fortuitous circumstances of a phenomenon so patently "law-governed" as war.

In the whole of this passage one detects a polemical undertone against Western historians, not mentioned by name, but in the aggregate untouched by grace and unenlightened. The implied criticisms are, to begin with, unfair. There are few of us who will try to explain everything by man's corrupted nature, or by the ambition and lust for conquest of rulers, or by chance; there are few also who will not include in their argument "the concrete socio-economic conditions of the development of society." The only thing is that Western historians—or had not I better say "good historians"?—will not take the all-too-easy way of confining their attention to one order of factors. They will as a rule offer pluricausal explanations. Factors of a spiritual nature will not be left out of account, and although ideas at times seem to us to be a reflection of social or economic conditions, we shall recognize in them a vital principle of their own, one capable of overcoming such conditions. To strike a balance between factors belonging to different orders is indeed our insuperable difficulty. And so, we are often led, not, as Pankratova blames the writers of the American report of 1946 for being led, to the verdict that history is *unknowable*, but indeed to the admission that in the final, all-embracing judgment there will necessarily remain a quantum of arbitrariness. This modesty might more justly be called scientific, while Nikonov's crude one-sidedness and his boast that he and his party have mastered the laws of that immense happening of mankind's life on earth strike me as in the deepest sense unscientific and unhistoric.

But indeed, Nikonov's essay, following upon his pompous introduction, has no other purpose than to lay the responsibility for the second world war on the shoulders of "the reactionary politicians" of the West. Everybody knows—and disagreeable truths of this description can be safely uttered on this side of the Iron Curtain—that Neville Chamberlain, supported by considerable conservative groups in England and France, carried on a very questionable policy, at the back of which fear and distrust of Soviet Russia were undeniably present. To suggest that the ruling circles in England, France, and the United States, driven by their capitalistic interests, "were unwilling to halt the impending world war" is nonetheless a monstrous distortion of what actually happened. How recklessly Nikonov can let his preconceived notions prevail over "concrete facts" appears when he writes that the Munich agreement was greeted with indignation "in the democratic circles of the various countries." Take England. Who was more indignant than Winston Churchill, Leo Amery, Duff Cooper?—to each of whom, in Nikonov's terminology, the description "reactionary politician" would apply. "The peoples," so he goes on, undaunted, "realized that the deal with the aggressors at the expense of Czechoslovakia was fraught with the gravest consequences to peace." "The peoples" indeed! the masses, that deified figure in the theory of Communism (*only* in its theory, however)—what was more striking in those tragic days of 1938 than the naïve enthusiasm with which the peoples everywhere acclaimed Chamberlain as the savior of peace!

But the reactionaries, the capitalists, *must* be the guilty ones, and to the exclusion of the rest. Granted that fear and distrust of Russia had an unfortunate effect in the critical days of the summer of 1939. But in every "scientific," or more simply, honest discussion of the crisis the fact will have to be recalled that there were only-too-real grounds for that fear and that distrust. Those feelings were alive particularly in Russia's unhappy neighboring countries, which have since been conquered and assimilated; and this constituted for the leaders of the West an objective obstacle (apart from personal sentiments or prejudices) to a consistent and straight-lined course of policy.

But to admit this extenuating circumstance on behalf of the West would amount to allotting to Russia at least a share in the responsibility. Now this can never be allowed. Over against the guilty West, Russia must appear in pure nobility. The Nazi-Soviet nonagression pact of August 1939 is therefore represented as an act of self-defense which was forced upon Russia. In order to stifle all objections to that interpretation (which is at best a half-truth), Nikonov has been careful to avoid all recognition of the altogether exceptional, the lawless and inhuman, character of the Hitler regime. To him it is merely a variant of the capitalist system. He never notices the essential difference between National Socialism and the political and social conditions prevailing in west European countries.

Only a man caught in a system that turns a blind eye on the pluriform reality of peoples and of individuals can write like this. But there is more. This system compels its adherents to defend through thick and thin the rulers who profess it, or make use of it. "Science" has nothing to do with this. What goes to shape the picture is really not even the system; it is, clothed in Marxist formulas, an intention that is purely tactical. It is the determination always to appear to be, and always to have been, right; and to supply to the Kremlin—whether smiling or frowning—what it needs in its struggle with the West.

The tactical intention is transparent, and it becomes even more so when in another one of these Soviet historical booklets we find the Franco-Russian alliance of 1891 discussed in a surprisingly different tone. Czarism and the French Republic of those days were of course capitalistic powers of the deepest dye. In spite of this, Khvostov sees in their alliance the illustration of a constant historic truth, namely, that "the peoples" of France and of Russia need each other against the menace of German militarism; both are aware of this, and each cherishes for the other "ineffaceable sentiments of sympathy."

It is no accident that the language into which Khvostov's essay was translated is French. The author conceived it with an eye to the anti-German feelings and the fears still present in French opinion, feelings and fears to which, when it suits them, the French Communists also appeal. A Marxist confession of faith is not lacking—practically all these writers on special topics feel bound to begin with one. "The school of historians to which I belong," says Khvostov, "the Marxist, takes for a starting point the fact that in the transition from the nineteenth to the twentieth century, capitalism was entering upon its last stage, that of imperialism." And again: "The Marxist historian starts from the fact that under capitalism the various countries go through unequal stages of development." This latter thesis, which is taken straight from Marx (as is the earlier one), has to do service in the whole of this literature to smooth out such obstacles as the system may encounter. But in Khvostov's argument the categories of Marxism—the production process as the determinant of events, the class struggle, the inevitable self-destruction of the capitalist system—seem to have receded to the background altogether. The essay is a piece of national propaganda and nothing else.

These tactical maneuvers[3] are faciliated by the confusion of thought which Marxist determinism has engendered in Russian heads. Determinism will not work in human relationships,[4] and so its adherents are forced to use subterfuges in order to maintain it in theory while evading it in practice.

When, for instance, the ladies Stepanowa and Lewiowa deal with the German revolution of 1848, they indulge in vehement exclamations against "the treason" of the liberal middle-class and against "the cowardice and indecision" of the lower-middle-class democrats, who refused to be dragged along by the socialist revolutionaries. It is very questionable, so it seems to me, whether at that juncture the social revolution ever stood a chance against the conservative forces entrenched in the old dynastic states. I am quite ready to admit that the dissensions breaking out between the three oppositional groups hastened its failure. But do not the Marxists themselves hold that these dissensions were determined? Why then these words, heavily laden with moral reproach? It is not even necessary to think in the strict terms of materialistic determination to realize that the liberal middle-class and the smaller bourgeoisie acted in accordance with class convictions. If the story of 1848 and 1849 is told so as to make it appear that "the people," in the Marxist sense, would have been able to dominate the German revolution and that on the other groups rested the moral obligation to admit this and to follow in the people's track, clearly something from the historian's own philosophy is forcibly imposed upon a period to which it is in fact alien. This is a completely unhistorical way of proceeding—always to approach the past with that one query and to overlook the problems as they presented themselves to the contemporary generation in their own rich setting of ideas and strivings.

But the Soviet historians are on the watch all the time—they say so themselves every now and again, and several of these publications deal with nothing else—for popular movements, popular revolts, revolutions, these in their eyes constitute the real, the beneficent motive power in history. Every expression of doubt as to the people's capacity to govern is to the Soviet historians an attack on what they consider to be an eternal truth. Sidorov says this in so many words when Mignet writes in this way about the years of the French Revolution. Similarly, according to Stepanowa and Lewiowa, in 1848, only Marx and Engels saw matters in their true light—and this not only for the future, but for the actual historical moment itself. How much more natural, however, is the traditional view that, given the entire course of events, these two men badly misjudged the situation and that, moreover, if 1848 made anything clear, it was the prematureness of an attempt to let "the people" govern.

But even as regards the future! We heard Madame Pankratova exult in the liberation of the masses. Volgin quotes, with a reverence hardly less than would be due to Lenin, a dictum of that other great doctor, Stalin: "What is the essential feature and the effect of the fundamental economic law of socialism? It is to assure the maximum satisfaction of the ever-growing material needs of society, by continually increasing and perfecting socialistic production on the basis of a superior technique." And Volgin adds, proudly, that in this formula no mere utopian society is sketched any longer. "The realization of the elevated humanitarian aims posed by it as assured by the fundamental principles of the Constitution of an actually existing socialist state, the U.S.S.R."[5]

What beautiful reading is made by the passages that Volgin goes on to quote—and what a gap between them and the reality of life as lived by Soviet man! In no case does the gap yawn more widely than where clause 123 seems to suggest that it is "the people" that governs. Regarded "objectively" and "scientifically," developments in Russia since 1917 would almost seem to confirm the opinion of that "backward," if not "reactionary," Mignet, who wrote over a century ago that "the people" is not capable of governing. For is it not the fact that the masses in

Russia *are* governed, and with a heavy hand, by a group, or a clique, asserting that they are called to carry out what will redound to the masses' well-being and what they *ought to* want—what indeed has been hammered into their heads as their salvation and their dearest wish for so long now that perhaps they hardly know any better?

And are Soviet cultural needs really being satisfied? One shudders when one reads Sidorov triumphantly citing the printings of historical textbooks. There are those that run to 15,500,000, to 18,600,000, copies. All, we may assume, composed on patterns designed by these masters. Brainwashing on a gigantic scale! One can hardly expect the masses to be able to resist so well-organized a "satisfaction of their cultural needs." But may we not hope that among Russian intellectuals, the intellectuals of a nation that not longer than a few generations ago produced so rich a literature, so humane, so open to all problems—that among them doubts will occasionally stir? One really does not need to have been schooled in historical method to be struck by the crooked logic, the contradictions, and the dull, lifeless coloring, the poor quality, of this kind of history writing.

A few opinionated intellectuals will not bring about a revolution, I know. But I believe that they can keep a spark aglow, from which, under a favoring constellation, and after a development the "laws" of which I shall not presume to guess at—let alone to lay down—a beneficent fire might be kindled.

I believe it. Indeed, I, too, have a faith. Not a faith in Marx or any other prophet; not a faith, either, in historic materialism or any other system. But a faith in life, a faith in the human spirit.

(1955)

POSTSCRIPT

At the Twentieth Party Congress, held in Moscow in March 1956, Mr. Khrushchev delivered his famous speech revealing the tyrannical character of Stalin and his regime. One would expect that this must have given Soviet historians furiously to think. Had they not been taught to regare Stalin as a doctrinal guide no less authoritative and reliable than Lenin? But indeed, at the same Congress, Mr. Mikoyan said in so many words that the history of the October Revolution and of the Communist party had been misrepresented, not by "reactionary," "bourgeois" historians of the West, but, under the influence of Stalin, by Soviet historians themselves.

These same men whom I had heard lecturing us on our "unscientific" methods, and telling us with inimitable self-assurance how we should go about things, were thus, on coming home, reproved by a politican who may not be a historian but whose authority to decide what is orthodox and what heretical history they will not for a moment dare to dispute. They were reproved, and at the same time instructed to present the party and the government with more acceptable history. One can imagine them writing away laboriously in a feverish attempt to obey orders.

A very unsettling experience, one would think, and it must have added to the trials of these unfortunate men that the mood of the Kremlin has kept going through dizzying changes since. Is it possible that they remain unshaken in the belief that Communism knows the answers to all the riddles of history? I am afraid that they will go on docilely convincing themselves that every new version is, no less than was the previous one, in strict conformity with the precepts of historic materialism, that is, of *Science*.

(1959)

VI

LOOKING BACK

When I was asked to talk to you tonight I said that if the committee would not object, I meant to talk about myself. A man who has just completed his seventieth year may be allowed this luxury. I am in a reminiscent mood. And I have a good many memories to draw upon.

If I may say so by way of introduction, I have a feeling that my life has been a happy one, in spite of all the sorrowful moments and all the difficult circumstances that I have known; and much of my happiness I have found in what I always used to describe as "my own work," as distinct from the functions more directly attached to my professorship, which has indeed also given me a good deal of satisfaction. But "my own work," my writing, my creative work—that is where I shall inevitably place the emphasis when I survey my life. And my creative work shall always be indissolubly connected with the part I have, from time to time, taken in politics, in the exchange of thought or the controversy about great questions in the public life of my own day.

I was aware of a desire to express myself at a very early age. The same observation has been frequently given a different twist—sometimes in a friendly manner, sometimes with caustic undertones—by suggesting that I have from boyhood on been animated by burning ambition. But are the two motives mutually exclusive? I think not, and however critically I look at myself I cannot doubt that in my case the first one was perfectly genuine.

It was not history to which I immediately turned as my natural form of expression. At first I wished to be a poet—in my *gymnasium* years at The Hague. Next, a novelist—in my first years at Leyden. I had chosen "Dutch language and literature" as my main subject, and while history was not in those days admitted to that discipline, it was an obligatory subsidiary to "Dutch." How little I knew of history—although I had been really interested, at the *gymnasium*, by Van Aalst's history lessons—appears from an incident that has stuck in my memory. It happened in my first year at Leyden. An older student showed me his books. One he took from the shelf: *there*, he said, lay his true interest. It was Fruin's *Tien jaren*,[1] and the name, not only of the book, but of Fruin, was completely new to me.

History soon gripped me. Yet I continued for a few years to ride two horses at once, and it was not until Verwey[2] to whom I had sent the manuscript, dismissed a novel of mine with a shrug that I decided: I must choose. Afterward the thought would rise occasionally: Verwey! But was he the man to judge a novel?

Nevertheless history had won. Writing poetry—it had been sonnets, mostly—I had given up long ago; my faith in that work had gradually withered away. History, then, as a second—or third! —best? Failed as a poet and as a novelist, and now a historian for want of something better? No—here too, I am inclined to reject the all-too-simple contrast; and this much is certain, I never rued the choice, and, then and all through my life, I had a strong feeling of having found my calling.

Not that early aspirations were therefore completely stifled. The contrary became clear during my internment at Buchenwald.[3] Suddenly interrupted in my habitual work and torn from my routine, there sprang from me, to my own surprise and delight, a series of sonnets, and also a novel. You may smile when I mention those sonnets. I belong to a different generation from the men who now dominate the scene of poetry and of poetic criticism, and since my poems are strictly and regularly constructed and have a clear and sometimes incisive meaning, these younger men are inclined to regard them as not really poetry. I can only say that I take my sonnets very seriously myself and that I reject the new fashion in poetry as wholeheartedly as they do a tradition that I am sure it is not in their power to kill, however successful they may be in confusing the minds of their docile readers.

But you will *certainly* smile at my mentioning my detective novel. I remember very well how, when I came home from my internment early in 1944, and the rumor of that peculiar indiscretion was spread about, more than one colleague asked me, with concern even more than with astonishment: "Are you going to publish this under your own name?" Yes, indeed I did, and I am still glad to have, with my historical work, a volume of sonnets and that "lighthearted" tale laid in the river country that I love, standing to my name.

History, nevertheless, became and has remained the ruling interest of my life. History such as I have always understood it: not an inventory of dead people and dead things, but a key to life—as literature, too, is a key to life. Not long ago I found in a review of one of my latest publications a passage quoted from the preface to my first, that is, to my doctoral thesis of 1913. I was much struck—for I had completely forgotten the passage—to find this idea already forcefully stated then. It has continued to inspire me.

Life in its fullness, life in all its shadings and aspects. This is one reason why I have never shrunk from contact with politics, why, on the contrary, I believe that history can benefit thereby. Not that history should *serve* politics. The position of bondage is not for her. History has her own laws, and only by remaining true to those can she match herself with life. *Distance* is her contribution to life, but without *contact* it can never be a contribution of much value.

Fate smiled on me when I was appointed, in 1913, correspondent of the *Nieuwe Rotterdamsche Courant* in London. I had not disliked schoolmastering, at the small *gymnasium* of Schiedam (summer 1912 to December 1913), but what wider prospects did this correspondentship open up for me! The work first of all. I owe a great deal to this journalistic episode for my formation. The introduction to men and to conditions in another country—and a great country—the need to write quickly and intelligibly, was a basic training. Especially so in those blessed times when a foreign correspondent—at least at the *N.R.C.*—had latitude both as to space and as to expression of opinions. I could let myself go, I could write as much as I pleased and on anything that struck my fancy. Politics was, of course, an obligatory topic, but then, politics interested me very particularly.

And also, entrance into the Anglo-Saxon world was in itself an event in my life. I had not dreamed of this a year or two before, when I had been granted a traveling scholarship and had spent six or seven months in Italy, in Venice more especially (first half of 1912), where in the Frari archives I had collected the material for my thesis. I had had visions then of a future devoted to Italian history, literature, art. But now I was drawn westward.

I was to spend twenty-two years of my life in London. After the 1914 war, which I "did" for my paper (what an experience!), I became the first incumbent of the newly founded chair of Dutch Studies at the University of London. History could now come into its own. Not that the first years were not very difficult. A young and untried man, with an out-of-the-way subject, having to find his way in that enormous, self-sufficient, and indifferent organization! But after a while the position began to give me very real satisfaction. I came to feel at home in the English academic world; I made friends there; every year a few students placed themselves under my particular guidance. Yet how much, as the years went by, did I begin to hanker after a return home.

I taught Netherlands history; I wrote Netherlands history; and just about the time of my entering upon that first professorship I began to follow, with passionate interest, the development of affairs in Flanders and of the relationship between Holland and Flanders. I had grown fond of London; I was happy in my position and circle there; but my heart was across the water.

My first contact with the Flemish problem dated, in fact, from 1911, my last year at Leyden, when I had attended a Flemish students' congress at Ghent. The profound impression the experience made on me[4] is evident in a long essay I got accepted by the serious-minded, conservative, professorial monthly *Onze Eeuw*. That impression was never effaced; yet my residence in England, and then, especially, the war, had for a while cut me off from what went on in Flanders. But now I got immersed in the counsels of the newborn Flemish Nationalist movement as intimately as if I had been a Fleming.

This too—but the reflection I am going to make came to me only after the event, for at the time I took it all with too wholehearted a devotion—was training for a historian. "The captain of the Hampshire grenadiers," says Gibbon in his autobiography, after having described his activities in that capacity, "has not been useless to the historian of the Roman Empire." So from my association with a nationalist movement, from the internal quarrels and intrigues, from the enthusiasm that was liable to deteriorate into fanaticism, from the moderation that might become flabbiness, from the derailments and disappointments, and from the permanent achievements, I learned a good deal that has somehow helped to fashion my writing about the past.

It has for many years dominated my life, this Flemish question. From London I crossed over to Holland several times a year. I could manage to do this because the Batavier Line had, as its contribution to the Dutch chair, granted a permanent free pass to the professor. In Holland the Great-Netherlands Students' Union,[5] a small but active group promoting closer relations with Flanders, provided me with a platform. And no less frequently I lectured to Flemish students or academic and other organizations in Flanders. My relations were with the Flemish Nationalists, the radical wing of Flemish movement, the group of my generation.[6] At first my closest connection was with Dr. Antoon Jacob, whose acquaintance I had made at the students' congress in 1911. I now visited him several times in the prison at Antwerp where he was kept from 1919 to 1924 for his "activist" misdeeds during the war. I still possess a large batch of his prison letters. An impressive personality! He was my junior by a year or two, but from the cell he acted as my teacher of Flemish Nationalism. Even before he was set free, however, I began to detect in his mind a rectilinear quality that roused me to opposition. Soon Herman Vos became my most intimate ally. Next to him Rik Borginon. These two were successively to lead the Flemish Nationalist "fraction" in the Belgian Chamber. Both were intellectuals of a high caliber; both were, like Jacob, of my age or a little younger.

In the twenties and thirties Flemish Nationalists were somewhat undesirable connections in the eyes of the Belgian authorities, and also of Dutch public opinion at large, as well as of the academic and the official world. In Holland all Flemish Nationalists and Great-Netherlanders were lumped together in the same reproval: revolutionary elements, a threat to the very existence of the Belgian state. That my closest associates were not extremists was not noticed, nor that I myself was throughout those years carrying on a fight on two fronts. On the one hand I found ranged against me the indifference and the misapprehensions governing the minds of my fellow Dutchmen, and on the other hand the recklessness of the extremist groups among the Flemish Nationalists and of the hotheads in the North who took their cue from them. I used to remind audiences of the Great-Netherlands Students' movement of the "European order," and I warned them against indulging in irredentism. And all the while I polemicized indefatigably against the preachers of total unadulterated nationalism, against the weekly paper *Vlaanderen*, and against the group gathered around that typical scholar-fanatic De Decker, a Flemish exile (now teaching Latin at an Amsterdam *gymnasium*).

In *Vlaanderen* De Decker and his associates tried with bitter persistence to make the movement as a whole toe the line of their "integral" Great-Netherlands program. "Death to Belgium! A Great-Netherlands state!"[7] As I saw it, the activities of these men hampered or paralyzed the attempts of the Flemish Nationalists in the Belgian parliament, who of necessity worked within the reality of Belgium, and who were indeed achieving something there, if only—and to me it seemed much—by putting "Belgicist" Flamingants, like Van Cauwelaert the Catholic and Huysmans the Socialist, on their mettle. It has indeed been the most tangible result of the Nationalist clamor for a federal system that it helped the "Belgicist" flamingants to obtain from the Chamber, about 1930, a number of "language laws." Divisions within the ranks of the Nationalists, so it seemed to me, must slacken the pace of actual reform, and I was more intent on attacking these doctrinaire troublemakers of the *Vlaanderen* weekly and their partisans in Flanders than were the parliamentary Nationalists themselves, than was Vos particularly, who was inclined to laugh at these adversaries and shrug off their "nonsense." His feeling of superiority and his contempt were intellectually understandable enough. But politically his attitude had fatal consequences, for those men did undeniably undermine his prestige with the rank and file in the country, with the young men particularly. His disdainful silence was apt to be interpreted as embarrassment or weakness.

But however strongly I opposed the false logical consistency of the doctrinaires, neither in Brussels nor in The Hague was there much inclination to draw a distinction between moderate and radical in the Great-Netherlands movement. In 1929 I was made to feel it as far as Brussels was concerned.

I had been invited to give a lecture in three Flemish towns. I had received warnings from more than one side (there had even been statements to that effect in Belgian newspapers) that the Belgian government had decided that I should not be allowed to speak. In London, at the Belgian exhibition of ancient painting, I had happened to meet Vermeylen, the well-known writer, at that time a Socialist Senator, and he told me that the warning was meant. I gave him to understand that he ought not to acquiesce in such a thing, and he did do his best in Brussels, but (as he wrote to me) without result. I went all the same. In Antwerp and in Ghent I was not interfered with. But when I came to Louvain, with the same speech, of my usual historical kind—and it had not, on the two earlier occasions, caused the Belgian state to shake on its foundations—here, in the hall of the hotel where I was to have dinner with my friends before the meeting, a little old gentleman came up to me. "Have I the honor," so he began, in Dutch, "to address Professor Geyl from London?"

The question flashed through my mind: Is this an admirer, or is it the police? It was the police. Orders from Brussels: he showed me the paper. "In French," I said: "Against the law." But of course that did not alter the situation. I was allowed to dine with my friends and was then, with unfailing politeness throughout, conducted to the train out of Belgium to Holland. (A few years later I met with a similar contretemps. On that occasion I was expelled together with a member of the Dutch Chamber, Moller, and the well-known novelist Antoon Coolen. That excellent Coolen, a child in politics, simply could not understand what was happening to him!)

But in Holland, too, the distinction between moderate and radical was not generally made, although I must say that I had no reason to complain of the press reactions to my expulsion in 1929.

This could not leave me indifferent. The affair might have had very unpleasant consequences for me. In London I combined with my professorship the position of an unofficial press-attaché. There would be a great deal to tell about my experiences in that function too: how I wrote articles, for instance, to explain the Dutch case in the long-drawn-out Scheldt dispute with Belgium in the decade following the war, articles under my name, under a pseudonym, at times under somebody else's name; how I tried to influence editors. I received for that work a salary from the Dutch Foreign Office—and I needed that supplement to my somewhat scanty professorial stipend. Our Foreign Office—if I may say so—really valued my work in England, but my activities in Flanders were always regarded with suspicion. The Plein[8] was always completely lacking in understanding of the value to our own country of the potentiality for Dutch civilization in Flanders. When the question of my lectures in Belgium cropped up in 1929, the Foreign Office had explicitly warned me not to give occasion for an incident. And now I had risked it, and the fat was in the fire.

The train that was to take me from Louvain to Holland stopped in Antwerp, and there I got out to devise with Vos the way in which we were to give publicity to the affair. When I arrived in The Hague, the Dutch press was in possession of a leading article written by him in his paper *De Schelde*, in which the offensive, incomprehensible action of the Belgian authorities was denounced in his most dignified and tactful manner. I myself made straight for the Plein. Attack is the best way of defense. I had a talk with my friend Van Kleffens, who was at that time chief of the Political Section, and I demanded that an explanation should be exacted for the ignominious treatment meted out to a reputable Dutch citizen and scholar. Van Kleffens explained that this would hardly be possible since the Dutch government itself set too much store by its right to expel undesirable aliens without stating grounds. But the conversation took place in an atmosphere of good humor.

In my own mind I made the observation that apparently, without having in the least departed from the line that I felt was dictated to me by principle, I enjoyed a reputation for moderation. A little to my surprise. Not that I want to decline that praise—if praise it is, and on the whole I think so—but in certain circles I knew I was regarded as a difficult customer, too readily spoiling for a fight. In certain circles, and especially among my fellow historians.

A few years afterward, when political conditions had already profoundly altered, the old confusion of thought concerning my association with the Flemish Nationalist and Great-Netherlands movement still appeared to prevail—in the University of Utrecht, in the Faculty of Letters.[9] Here a vacancy was created by the retirement of G. W. Kernkamp, Professor of Modern History. A vacancy on which I had had my eye for years. Here was my chance!

The Faculty has to make the first recommendation. In this company, consisting at that time of not quite twenty men, several, for no other reason than that I was associated with a nationalist movement, regarded me as little better than a National-Socialist. In consequence of my long residence abroad, they hardly knew me personally. They judged by a reputation that had very little to do with reality. My historical work? Hardly any attention was given to what I had written on other subjects, but my polemical essays directed against the Little-Netherlands interpretation of our history and against the complementary Belgicist interpretation—and also my *History of the Netherlands People*,[10] of which by then two volumes had appeared (1930, 1934), covering the period down to 1688—had given me in the profession, not of course without exceptions (and they were notable exceptions) the reputation of a man abusing history for political purposes. A disturbing element.

In the early twenties I had already questioned the authority of Fruin, next that of the leading men among the living, of the generation that was now in control, that preceding my own: my masters Blok and Kalff; then Colenbrander, Japikse, Huizinga, Brugmans; and in Belgium the great Pirenne. Pirenne was admired quite uncritically in Holland, and I never gave more offense than I did in 1927 by my review—I must admit cutting, but in substance incontrovertible—of the sixth volume of his *Histoire de Belgique*, dealing with the late decades of the eighteenth and the early decades of the nineteenth century. Then, in 1933, there had occurred the sensational affair of the plagiarism committed by a well-known professor of history,[11] an affair about which I shall say no more now. The impression created was that I was likely to prove a troublesome colleague.

The easiest way to dispose of my work on the North-South relationship was to dub it "politics." No doubt it was my profound feeling for Flanders that had inspired me to my novel interpretation of the sixteenth-century split and its causes and of the entire North-South relationship. Indeed I had always affirmed the connection of historical views and contemporary conditions, nor had I ever tried to disguise or disavow my wish to contribute by means of my historical work to the breaking down of the narrow conceptions in which the Dutch public, including the intellectuals, allowed itself to be imprisoned, conceptions concerning the foundations of Dutch nationality, concerning the Belgian state, concerning the Dutch-Flemish relationship.

But was it right on that account to attach the label "politics" to *my* views more particularly?

It is a well-known dodge to use that word to discredit the historian who goes against established opinion. It was tried on me in yet another historical field about which I made myself heard throughout those same years. I refer to my views on the conflict between the princes of Orange and the "regents," of Holland especially, in the history of the Republic. For although I said a moment ago that the Flemish question dominated my life, I did not therefore neglect the opportunity to do research work in the Public Record Office and the British Museum, and I delved deeply in seventeenth- and eighteenth-century North Netherlandish history. The connection of the House of Orange with the Stuarts, and in the next century with the House of Hanover, and the way in which this influenced the party struggle in the Republic and its foreign policy—this was the theme that I dealt with in my *Orange en Stuart* (which did not appear in book form until 1939, but of which the chapters constituting the first half had already been published in various reviews[12] in the twenties) and also in *Willem IV* (of Orange) *en Engeland* (1734-1748), of 1924. A theme that again took me into the heart of highly controversial matter.

I had been struck, when I came to be familiar with the particulars, by the astonishing partiality toward the stadholders prevailing in our historiography. Groen's religious philosophy[13] would lead one to expect this of him, but I found the same attitude rampant even among the liberals. Later, after the second war, I have shown the effects of this bias somewhat haphazardly in the work of Fruin, and more systematically in that of Colenbrander. But it was in the early twenties that my opinions on this point took form. All the well-known assertions that Orange or the Orange party was identical with *national*, and States of Holland or regents party with *egoistical*, *class*, or *provincial* interests; that the princes of Orange had prepared the way for unity while Holland did nothing but block it with her commercialism; that Orange was the people's protector, while the regents were no more than a group out for their own profit, a group outside the nation—all these assertions I learned to see as belonging to an Orange-myth at variance with past reality.

It is the historian's task to demolish myth—"in spite of those who do not like it." In this particular case too, most certainly, there were those who did not like it. The myth is, by its nature, intimately bound up with sentiment, and unyielding to reason. When my *Willem IV en Engeland* appeared, it was described in the *Times Literary Supplement* as a kind of anti-English pamphlet. But it is unfortunately a fact that the way in which the English government, cheered on by English opinion, treated the Dutch during the War of the Austrian Succession did not come very graciously from an ally, was indeed, frankly, rather shabby. I laid that bare in all its ugly detail—the first modern historian to do so, I believe. Does that prove me to be "anti-English"? On his part, Professor Krämer, a predecessor of mine in the Utrecht chair of modern history, at that time House-Archivist to Her Majesty the Queen, pictured me in a review in *Museum* as a bitter enemy to Orange. But could I help it if William IV was so feeble a character, unable to follow a consistent line of policy, now indulging in rabid Frisian provincialism (until 1747 he was stadholder of Friesland and Groningen only), then prepared to swallow whatever England, his father-in-law's country, dictated, and all the time more accessible to personal ambition than capable of taking a large view of the national interest? To observe these things, does that show me to be anti-Orange? There is a great deal of difference between one prince of Orange and the next. Unless, at least, you look at the lot through orange spectacles. Such spectacles were still much the fashion in those days, but I have never consented to wear them.

I am not taking these old controversies too tragically. The instinctive opposition soon proved to be really powerless. The reception of my book in the professional journals, both English and Dutch, was quite satisfactory on the whole.

The fate of my Great-Netherlands arguments and interpretations was not essentially different, but the opposition was more vehement, and there was quite a lengthy and to me painful intermezzo when it seemed as if it would triumph and my return to Holland be prevented. "Nothing but politics! Unscholarly!" was what the adversaries said. In fact all I had done was to take issue with a prejudice, demonstrating that it was historically untenable. As for politics, I had maintained all along that, on the contrary, this unreasoning sentiment was, with the current historical view, the product of political events, and that what my opponents used that false history for—unconsciously perhaps, but in that case so much the worse for historians—was to justify existing political arrangements and abuses (like the partial Gallicization of Flanders).

Anyhow, in 1935, when my name could not be suppressed altogether in connection with the pending appointment at Utrecht, some, or many, wanted to bar me as a rabid nationalist, a recruit, most likely, for the N.S.B.[14]

The men who talked (or muttered) like this not only knew nothing of the attitude that I had consistently taken in the Great-Netherlands movement, but even my historical work, which they industriously played off against me, they had read very carelessly. They suspected me of leanings toward National Socialism. Yet in the preface to the second volume of my *History of the Netherlands People* I had, in 1934, in dedicating the book to my particular friends the Great-Netherlands students, admonished them to remember that, according to the Netherlands tradition in both North and South, "variety, and respect for private rights" were among our most precious goods—as clear a warning against slipping down in an eastward direction as one could wish. And I quote only one utterance out of many. Had no attention been given to this evidence of my true feeling?

In the end I was appointed—against the recommendation of the Faculty,[15] and after a behind-the-scenes struggle shifting from Utrecht to The Hague and lasting many months. Once I was there in person, however, the misunderstandings melted away like snow before the sun. My inaugural oration, in February 1936—you will understand that after all that had transpired during the long-drawn-out tussle over my appointment, it was attended and listened to in an atmosphere of unusual tension—cleared the air. Yet I said in it no less on the delicate subject than I had done on so many earlier occasions. I well remember the warm congratulations I received, when I had concluded, from Bolkestein, the ancient history man, who had been among my antagonists. In the Faculty, where as a matter of fact I had been generally received in an unexceptionable manner, I came to be on particularly friendly terms with Bolkestein.

And since I have recalled that I was suspected of National Socialist inclinations, it is amusing to remember that not much more than a year afterward, Bolkestein and I both figured as speakers at a meeting in Utrecht of E.D.D. I am afraid that the younger generation will need to have those initials explained: they meant "Unity Through Democracy," and they represented a movement, to which men of all the democratic parties were welcome, intended to rally the Dutch people to close ranks (for the time being with a view to the general election to be held in the summer of 1937) against the dangers threatening from the N.S.B. Politics again. Bolkestein was uneasily aware of this. When we were mounting the platform together he whispered to me: "An academic scandal," pointing out that we seemed to be the only professors present in the overcrowded hall of Tivoli.

Were professors of that generation really so shy of politics? Perhaps only of taking so public a part. There were quite a few, nevertheless, whom the rise of National Socialism shocked out of their ivory towers. I myself spoke two more times the following year, in the huge R.A.I. Building in Amsterdam, before crowds compared with which that Tivoli audience seemed to shrink into insignificance. A popular orator! Never had I dreamed of such a thing!

An amusing aside to the story of my appointment at Utrecht is that the support I had received, in all the successive stages through which a professorial appointment has to pass, came from conservative elements. If the others were relieved when they at long last saw me in their midst, *they* were soon disagreeably surprised at the quick evolution through which I passed in the Dutch air, an evolution that nevertheless amounted to going on in the direction of my earlier thinking and writing; and really, I had never tried to mislead anyone as to my political convictions. The climax came, I believe before the year 1936 was out, when I told an archconservative colleague of another Faculty, who had so recently employed all his influence on my behalf, that now that I was back in the country I did not in the circumstances prevailing in the world want to remain an isolated intellectual but was planning to join a party, and the party for me was the Socialist party. If I had said "N.S.B.," he could not have been more shocked. I did not take the step, after all; not yet, because after exchanges of thought with leading personalities in that quarter I came to the conclusion that the process through which the S.D.A.P. (the Socialist party) was going at that moment, the process of freeing itself from doctrinaire antimilitarism and cosmopolitanism, had not gone far enough. I did join the S.D.A.P. immediately after the war, just before it changed its name to Labor party in order to mark the definite break with Marxist doctrinairism. Let me just add that the explanation that I used to give to my friends, in all sincerity, was that I looked upon the Socialist party as the last refuge for a liberal. For of course what I really am is a liberal. But our present-day Liberal party, which professes to continue the tradition of Thorbecke, strikes me as a typically conservative Party.

The danger that threatened in the late thirties did not arise after all from the N.S.B. (which suffered large losses in the election of 1937), but from Germany. Even when, in September 1939, war broke out in Europe, many people still attempted to obscure *that* stark truth with vague talk about neutrality being our bounden duty and about the need of being on our guard with respect to England and France just as much as with respect to Germany. I wrote a pamphlet pointing out the hollowness of that view. I also went on speaking at E.D.D. gatherings. In May 1940 the catastrophe broke over our heads. I happened to be a member of the Senatus Contractus and at our daily conference with the Rector I could observe how even then the situation was too much for the political acumen of many of my colleagues. There were moments in that little group when tension ran high.

The real difficulties for the University did not begin until toward the end of that year. I was spared the painful struggle with them because I had already been seized as a hostage, in the early days of October 1940. When I came home, in February 1944, I still had nothing to do with them, for in December 1942, while still in internment, I had been dismissed by the Reichskommissar from my post at the University. The ground given was: "seeing that his general mentality does not hold out any guarantee for loyal cooperation. . . ." In May 1945 I looked upon myself, and so, naturally, did my colleagues, as reinstated. But it was not until September that the royal decree was issued in which my reinstatement was actually confirmed. Here, too, grounds were indicated; to wit, that "nothing had transpired of disloyalty toward Her Majesty the Queen or the Kingdom of the Netherlands." I could not help feeling that this was not the happiest way of putting it.

But I have strayed with my memories into a different world. Let me look back again and offer some general reflections on those years between the two wars and on my activity in connection with the Flemish and Great-Netherlands questions.

The memory of that struggle (it always was a struggle) over the Great-Netherlands versus the Little-Netherlands vision of our history and—within the Great-Netherlands and Flemish Nationalist movement—over moderation or extremism, realism or doctrinarism—that memory is very dear to me, although a certain melancholy goes with it.

No movement ever leads directly to the aim that its adherents have set for it. *This* movement was derailed in the thirties under the impact of the demoniac and powerful Nazi aberration. Even before I came to Utrecht, this development had estranged me from many whom I used to regard as engaged in the same cause. That cause was as close to my heart as ever, but in practice I was aware of a growing isolation. When, at Brussels in 1939, as speaker at a lunch of Flemish Catholic university graduates, I made a challenging appeal to the democratic principle, I was cheered by other Flemings than those with whom I had been most closely allied.

My most intimate friend in the Nationalist camp, Herman Vos, a consistent democrat, had left the party as early as 1934 and had rejoined the Belgian Socialist party. I could not but understand his decision. But I had continued my friendly relations with Rik Borginon, who now led the Flemish Nationalist group in the Chamber. Only, my letters to him (which I still have) are one uninterrupted series of warnings and admonitions. Not that he personally had any leanings toward National Socialism, but I wanted him to take a stronger line with the untrustworthy members of the "fraction," and particularly I wanted him to state publicly the views he professed to me in private. The semblance of National Socialist influence inevitably weakened the recruiting capacity of the conception of Flemish Nationalism among Flemings at large and at the same time alienated Dutch opinion.

Borginon, unfortunately, did not succeed in keeping his wild men in check. He never gave in to German blandishments himself, and the sentence of twenty years' imprisonment which was pronounced against him after the liberation of Belgium was a striking instance of the way in which the triumphant Fransquillons used the repression to eliminate as many potential leaders of Flamingantism as possible. In fact, although he was set free quite soon afterward, an active political career is no longer open to him. He is still numbered, however, among my friends. Jacob, too, went back to prison in 1944, but indeed *he* had lost his head completely under the influence of the German lunacy; he died in prison in 1948. With him I had had no contact for many years.

Vos, on the contrary, came to look me up very shortly after the liberation of Holland. A fortnight before the liberation my house had been raided, and we were now camping, my wife and I, in the one room that it had been possible, more or less, to furnish.[16] Vos came quite unexpectedly: we still had hardly any means of communication with the outside world. I was quite startled to see him get out of a splendid Belgian government car driven by a uniformed chauffeur. I had heard a rumor—although it seemed hard to believe—that he was now a Cabinet minister. But there he was, both he and his chauffeur, loaded with good things that to us, in the famine from which Holland was as yet but slowly emerging, seemed simply marvelous. We embraced, French fashion—it is the only time in my life that I took part in that emotional ceremony—and tears (it must have been an extraordinary spectacle) trickled into both our beards.

My friendship with Vos was resumed on as cordial terms as ever, and yet there was no longer room for the kind of co-operation that had attended it in earlier days. Vos was now a member of the Belgian government! He was as true a Fleming as ever he had been, and I built high hopes on his new position and how he could make it serve our old ideals. In practice, not much came of this, and if I had pestered Borginon with "warnings and admonitions" in the thirties, it was now Vos's turn to receive reproaches and exhortations, which he laughed off—or tried to—as he had done the carpings and slanders of *Vlaanderen* twenty years earlier. In spite of my impatience, I felt his early death in 1952 as an irreparable loss to me, not only from the point of view of friendship, but also because with him there went my firmest *point d'appui* in postwar Belgium.

Not that I have no contacts there any more. The new climate would even seem particularly favorable to relations such as I have always dreamed of. The ideals that have meant so much to me and to which I have remained faithful, have partially been realized. Only—in other ways, in other forms, and I can no longer feel as intimately connected with their development as before. No doubt I have been able to do some work, but on an entirely different basis.

From 1946 on I have been a member of the then formed Mixed (that is to say, Dutch-Belgian) Commission, appointed by the two governments, for the execution of the cultural agreement between them. The promotion of cultural co-operation and exchange with the French-speaking part of Belgium belongs to the program, and I can of course wholeheartedly accept it. My zeal for Dutch in Flanders has never meant that I want to exclude French or French culture. Such has never been my type of nationalism. It is true that I can work for relations with the Walloons only on condition that the special and natural connection existing between Holland and Flanders be admitted. In the new circumstances, after the enormous change that Belgium has gone through as a result of the linguistic laws passed about 1930, it has indeed been possible to have that principle unquestioningly observed by the Commission. The Belgian members are all Flemings, with the occasional exception of a Walloon with a perfect command of Dutch. The discussions are never carried on in French. I have always been able to take part in the work with conviction, although, frankly speaking, commissions are apt to make me impatient.

Two years ago the Commission celebrated its tenth anniversary.

One precious moment stands out from that occasion—a moment full of irony. The celebration took place at The Hague. The Belgian Ambassador had invited us to lunch at the Embassy. And there, before we sat down, he started a little speech and began to distribute a few decorations. Suddenly I found myself a Commander in the Order of the Crown of Belgium. The irony was not lost upon the Flemish friends who came up to congratulate me. "Who would have thought so twenty-five or thirty years ago!" they grinned. To which I could only reply: "Yes, Belgium *has* changed!" The thought that I, too, had changed did cross my mind and caused me a little embarrassment.

Belgium changed—in itself the fact is not open to doubt. The most crying linguistic grievances have been remedied by the legislation of 1930 and the immediately following years. A generation of Flemish intellectuals schooled and educated in Dutch is beginning to take its place in Belgian life—a phenomenon that had been unknown for well over a century. And yet how many weaknesses can still be observed in the cultural and social position of the Flemish population! Just because the most crying grievances have been removed, it seems as if the reaction against remaining maladjustments—I mention only the progress of the Gallicization of the Brussels population and the formidable influence exercised by Brussels on the entire life of the Flemish-speaking region—has become less spontaneous and less strong. I sometimes regret the absence of a *movement* such as I knew it—for there is now hardly anything left that might be called a Flemish movement. And I still see dangers for the future.[17]

I sometimes ask myself, with self-reproach, what do I do to support the Flemings who are still struggling? Ought not I, also, to denounce, much more insistently than I do, the optimism of my Hollanders, who are only too much inclined to cherish the comfortable belief that Flemish grievances have now been remedied. On the whole I, too, acquiesce far too readily in a state of affairs that, in spite of the remarkable improvement I have witnessed in my lifetime, is not really satisfactory.

But life has disposed of me otherwise.

It is not only the state of affairs in Belgium, which makes a difference between then and now; it is not only the difficulty of finding points of contact for action there, as I found them in the past. Before the second world war the rise of National Socialism had already upset my view of the world. I thought and felt (and I think and feel) about Flanders, and about the significance to us of Flanders as a potential territory for the flowering of Netherlands culture, as I had thought from my youth onward; in that view I continue to find inspiration for historical work. But civilization's life-and-death struggle of the last twenty-five years is set on a wider stage. From the first moment I had thrown myself into that struggle, and that too was in my mind automatically transposed into historical forms. Thus something within me, too, has changed; the change, however, when all is well considered, is not one that ought to cause me "embarrassment." I have shifted the focus of my interest, or rather, I have enlarged its field. Hence, even during the occupation, *Napoleon For and Against*;[18] hence polemical essays against Romein and Toynbee, against Butterfield and Barraclough; hence studies about great foreign historians, about Bilderdijk and Groen, and Ter Braak, about *Use and Abuse of History*.[19] Hence, also, the twenty years that have elapsed between the publication of the last original volume of the *Geschiedenis van de Nederlandse Stam* and the completion of a new volume, which I was able some time ago to entrust to my publisher.

I touch here upon a painful point in my career as a writer of history. I am deeply aware that I have put my publisher's patience to a test more severe than was permissible. That his patience has held out is more than I deserve. And there was not only the publisher: often enough readers gave utterance to impatience or annoyance—utterances that warmed my heart as evidence the work meant something to them, but that at the same time I could not read without experiencing pangs of conscience. Among my colleagues I believe that there was a fairly widespread opinion: "Geyl will never do it now; obviously he has lost the inspiration for his work."

But in reality I had never abandoned my intention to go on with the task so lightheartedly undertaken in 1927. In the midst of my other activities I sometimes worked on the *Nederlandse Stam* for months at a stretch as hard as ever. And I can say in all sincerity: with as much conviction, with as great a zest as ever. Only, every now and again, I found myself in the grip of a polemic, or an essay seemed the only way to free my mind from the fascination of a problem. How many times have I said (and promised my wife): "This has been my last escapade, my last essay." And before I knew what I was doing, I found myself in the midst of one again.

The worst of it is that, warmly as I feel for my great work and deeply concerned as I am about its slow progress, I cannot declare that I regret those other activities. The reason is not in the first place that they have, to my own surprise, evoked such a response in England and the United States. But these explorations in fields into which I had never dreamed that I should venture—Shakespeare and Napoleon and the American Civil War and Russian historiography and Romein and Toynbee and what not—I have learned a great deal from all these adventures, and I have enjoyed them, too, just as much as I have the *Nederlandse Stam*.

"Give it up, that *Nederlandse Stam*!" so friends have at times advised me. "If you take another twenty years for the volume after this one, you will be ninety, and how many volumes will be still to come? And, after all, you have already made good the main thesis. Why go on driving a point that you have already made? Write essays! You have found your line. And no doubt you have more to say about historiography and the theory of history."

Certainly! much more! enough to fill another life. Yet, advice like this always rouses me to opposition. I don't in the least intend to take another twenty years for the next volume. I want to go on. I must go on. And it is not true—this at least I can swear to in any court you choose—that I have no heart for the *Nederlandse Stam* any more. I want to go on, not only because I feel obliged to, but because I am longing to give form to my conception of William I's United Kingdom and of the Belgian Revolution of 1830, and after that of the rise of the Flemish movement and . . . . But I stop. I can only bear witness to my feeling and to my will. I am not master of the future. This I can say, that writing history is still the joy of my life, and that I shall enter my retirement, not without feelings of regret certainly, but mainly with cheerfulness at the thought that I shall have so much the more time to give to "my own work." Concentration I dare not promise, but I am not without tenacity.

History "a key to life . . . in its fullness and all its aspects," that is how I put it at the beginning of these remarks. It is a phrase apt to counsel modesty when I survey what I have written so far. But I also hear in it an exhortation to persevere and ever again to delve and to search for treasure. To master life is not what history will permit us, but under history's colors to struggle with life will be our fulfillment and our prize.

(1958)

NOTES

Shakespeare as a Historian: A Fragment

1. I follow here E. M. W. Tillyard, *Shakespeare's History Plays* (1944). The spiritual background of the English plays in particular is excellently evoked.
2. It was in France that its dominance was most complete. Voltaire, who prided himself on having discovered Shakespeare for his compatriots, did not understand him in the least. When later on other French writers had the impudence to admire Shakespeare in their own way he flew into a rage, which he wreaked upon his one time protégé. His outburst against "le sauvage ivre" has remained famous. An American writer, Thomas R. Lounsbury, has described Voltaire's eventful relationship to Shakespeare in a book that is amusing as well as instructive: *Shakespeare and Voltaire* (1902). Even Taine's sketch of Shakespeare, in his *Littérature anglaise* (1869), is little better than a caricature.

Not all Frenchmen, naturally, were to that extent the prisoners of the classicist tradition. Mézières, *Shakespeare, ses oeuvres et ses critiques* (1860), has great merits, and the very able book of Stapfer, *Shakespeare et l'antiquité* (1879-80), not to mention any later authorities, excels in understanding.

3. See especially P. Alexander, *Shakespeare's Henry VI and Richard III* (1929). For Homer, see J. A. Scott, *The Unity of Homer* (1921). The effect of Alexander's study reminds one of that created by the child's ingenuous remark in Andersen's tale, "The Clothes of the Emperor of China."
4. This has been pointed out particularly by A. C. Bradley in his great book, *Shakespearean Tragedy* (1904).
5. Tous ces crimes d'Etat qu'on fait pour la couronne,
Le ciel nous en absout alors qu'il nous la donne,
Et dans le sacré rang où sa faveur l'a mis,
Le passé devient juste, et l'avenir permis.
Qui peut y parvenir ne peut être coupable;
Quoi qu'il ait fait ou fasse, il est inviolable.
6. J. A. R. Marriott, *English History in Shakespeare* (1918), p. 69, considers it improbable, in accordance, as he says, with most critics, that the play about Richard II performed on the eve of Essex's rebellion was Shakespeare's *King Richard II*. E. K. Chambers, *William Shakespeare: A Study of Facts and Problems* (1930), Vol. I, p. 354, and John Dover Wilson, *Essential Shakespeare* (1932), p. 102, although differing on many points, both very positively assume that it was.
7. This is also the view taken by the modern historian; see J. H. Ramsay, *Lancaster and York, 1399-1485* (1892).
8. Bradley, in his *Oxford Lectures on Poetry* (1909), says that in Falstaff we admire "the bliss of freedom gained in humour." As a matter of fact, the effect of the character probably rests upon that illusion of amoral freedom, but cool reflection will lead to the conclusion that it *is* an illusion. The attitude postulated reminds one of that of Lamb toward Congreve, Wycherley, and company. Lamb argued that one need not be offended by their immorality since their world is but a theatrical world and has nothing in common with the true world, where standards of good and evil hold sway. Macaulay disposed of that argument in a well-known essay occasioned by Leigh Hunt's edition of Restoration dramatists.
9. The commentators are often all too anxious to whitewash Henry V both in his princely and his royal phase. Mr. Losey (who edited *King Henry IV* for one of the modern editions of Shakespeare's works), for example, finds something to admire in the Prince of Wales's seeking "low company": it is the young man brimming over with life who prefers intercourse with "the people" because it can teach him more than would the chilly sphere of the court. As if Falstaff and his crew were "the people"! They were highwaymen and gamblers.

The same Mr. Losey sees in the King's fatherly remonstrances to his son (the true King's this time: *King Henry IV, First Part*, Act III, Scene II) cold-blooded calculation and in that relationship finds the superiority on the Prince's side. To my mind the genuine and vigorous personality of Henry IV comes out convincingly in that scene; striking, in particular, are the reminiscences to which, in the softened mood of the moment, he abandons himself. But to a certain type of Englishman Henry V must be in all circumstances the ideal figure.

10. *Shakespeare's Roman Plays and Their Background.*
11. *Twelfth Night*, Act II, Scene III.
12. Edward Dowden, *Shakespeare, His Mind and Art* (1875).
13. Cf. notes by Ralli, *A History of Shakespearean Criticism* (1932), Vol. II, p. 391.
14. Cf. above, p. 14.
15. Pieter Corneliszoon Hooft (1581-1647), son of an Amsterdam burgomaster, wrote lyrical poetry of a very high quality and devoted the last half of his life (when he was bailiff for the town of Amsterdam, in the rural district of Gooiland, and resided in the castle at Muiden) to his large-scale history of the revolt of the Netherlands. That work, a masterpiece of Dutch prose, would occupy a very considerable place in European historiography if Dutch were more widely read. The dramas discussed in the text are not Hooft's greatest achievement.
16. A Dutch writer of the late thirteenth and early fourteenth centuries. His *Rijmkroniek* ("Rhymed Chronicle") is particularly important for the events of his own lifetime, covering the reign of Count Florent V of Holland, murdered in 1296, and his immediate successors.
17. N. W. MacCallum, *Shakespeare's Roman Plays and Their Background* (1910), p. 76.
18. Stapfer, whose ideas will be more fully discussed below.
19. Vit on jamais une âme en un jour plus atteinte
De joie et de douleur, d'espérance et de crainte.
20. Non qu'Albe par son choix m'ait fait haïr vos frères.
Tous trois me sont encor des personnes bien chères;
Mais enfin l'amitié n'est pas du même rang,
Et n'a point les effets de l'amour et du sang;
Je ne sens point pour eux la douleur qui tourmente
Sabine comme soeur, Camille comme aimante.
21. See above, p. 16.
22. De pareils serviteurs sont les forces des rois
Et de pareils aussi sont au-dessus des lois.
23. Similar remarks were made by Fontenelle.
24. Mais on doit ce respect au pouvoir absolu,
De n'examiner rien quand un roi l'a voulu. . . .
Quoi qu'on fasse d'illustre et de considérable,
Jamais à son sujet un roi n'est redevable.
25. Les princes ont cela de leur haute naissance:

Leur âme dans leur sang prend des impressions
Qui dessous leur vertu rangent leurs passions.
Leur générosité soumet tout à leur gloire.

26. I agree, generally speaking, with Lytton Strachey's dictum, in his famous essay on Racine: "If, instead of asking what a writer is without, we try to discover simply what he is, will not our results be more worthy of our trouble?" But I am not writing on Racine; I am writing on Shakespeare; and if I have to apologize to the shade of the great Frenchman, it is only for using him as a foil to bring out more effectively the distinguishing qualities of Shakespeare.
27. Even Taine. His *Histoire de la littérature anglaise* is uncommonly brilliant (as is all that he wrote), but as a picture of the English mentality, it is no less uncommonly one-sided and *outré*. And in any case, Taine committed the error of proclaiming all that he observed in his own day (and he observed only what fitted in with his preconceived opinion) as permanently and unalterably fixed in the English character, civilization, and society. Cf. F. C. Roe, *Taine et l'Angleterre* (1923), p. 144.
28. A very fine example of this approach is Bradley's characterization of *Macbeth*. See *Shakespearean Tragedy*, pp. 264 ff. The atmosphere of the play, he summarizes, is that of "blackness," but "not that of unrelieved blackness. On the contrary, as compared with *King Lear* and its cold dim gloom, *Macbeth* leaves a decided impression of colour."
29. This is not, of course, the only instance. Even in the quarreling scene with which the play opens, typically English and un-Italian traits can be observed. I mention only Sampson's comical anxiety, while challenging the rival party, to keep "the law" on his side. One should not look for exact archaeological faithfulness in Shakespeare.
30. The most striking example of how the compulsion of the unities hampered Vondel in his presentation of history is afforded by his *Maria Stuart*. What a subject! The conflicts with Knox, the murder of Darnley, the murder of Riccio, the flight to England, the imprisonment, the conspiracies against Elizabeth! But Vondel stages for us only the last day of the martyred Queen's life. The Catholic propagandist conception of the drama ruled out, in any case, the possibility of its imparting any truly historical impression.
31. I recall here Racine's *Athalie*, which also owes its old Testament setting to an atmosphere definitely distinct from that prevailing in the poet's other plays.
32. The contrast between *Batavian Brothers* and Rembrandt's "Conspiracy of Claudius Civilis" was indicated by Schmidt Degener, *De Gids*, 1919 (reprinted in *Phoenix*, 1942, pp. 142 ff.). As for the reasons underlying the rejection of the picture, stress is usually laid on the offense given by its baroque style to the still dominant classicist tradition. The whole question remains debatable. See Seymour Slive, *Rembrandt and His Critics* (The Hague,

1953), p. 78, where, however, the point made by me, and before me by Degener, of the departure from the legendary representation of Claudius Civilis the Liberator, is not even mentioned.

French Historians for and against the Revolution

1. For instance, Benjamin Constant in 1797; see Stanley Mellon, *The Political Uses of History: A Study of Historians in the French Restoration* (1958), p. 27. The book was reviewed by me in *The Annals of the American Academy of Political and Social Science.*
2. Quoted by Mellon, op. cit., p. 23.
3. Liable to be subjected at pleasure to forced labor, to taxation, to death; now only to imprisonment.
4. It is this controversy that forms the subject of the book by Stanley Mellon cited above.
5. That is to say, to break up the unity of the state for the benefit of provincial self-government.
6. One of the first writers to make use of it was Carlyle, in whose *French Revolution* (1837) one will find frequent references to it.
7. I have dealt with Michelet at greater length in an essay included in *Debates with Historians* (1955).
8. Carl Becker's phrase: *The Heavenly City of Eighteenth-Century Philosophers* (1932).
9. Michelet and Louis Blanc, it should be remembered, had been no less industrious in this way than Tocqueville.
10. See, for example, *Correspondance entre Alexis de Tocqueville et Arthur de Gobineau* (Schemann, 1858), pp. 311-12, 333.
11. "De la manière d'écrire l'histoire en France et en Allemagne," in *Questions historiques* (1893—published posthumously; Fustel de Coulanges died in 1889).
12. See my *Napoleon For and Against*, pp. 86-105.
13. De la Gorce, *Histoire du Second Empire*, V.
14. "La Monarchie constitutionnelle en France"; reprinted in his book *La Réforme intellectuelle et morale* (1871).
15. Published together with the one of 1869, and several others, in the volume cited in note 14, above.
16. There is indeed a striking resemblance between the views quoted from Renan and those that Treitschke developed about the same time on more than one occasion. See, for instance, A. Dorpalen, *Heinrich von Treitschke* (1957), pp. 199-200.
17. Compare to this the opening paragraph of De Gaulle's *Mémoires de guerre*, I.
18. George Sand's reply to these outbursts is very moving. See *Correspondance entre George Sand et Gustave Flaubert;* Flaubert's letters of March 31, of early May, and of September 8; George Sand's of September 14, 1871.
19. Treitschke, indeed (see note 16, above), was equally virulent. He, too, of course, had started as a liberal.
20. "Vice and virtue are products, like vitriol and sugar."

21. *Correspondance*, IV, 30; letter of 1877.
22. This is a passage that Mathiez has missed in his penetrating article "Taine historien," in *Revue d'histoire moderne et contemporaine*, VIII (1906-7), an article to which I owe something for the following paragraph.
23. *L'Ancien Régime*, p. 35.
24. See, for instance, Daniel Mornet, *Les Origines intellectuelles de la Révolution française* (1938), p. 474. Georges Lefebvre, *Peuples et civilisations* (1938), XIII, 50, summarizes the story of the Assembly as follows: Infléchir les principes ou les contredire, tantôt pour combattre l'aristocratie, tantôt pour contenir le peuple, tantôt pour se le concilier, ce n'est point faire oeuvre abstraite, mais réaliste." The name of Taine is not mentioned, but the polemical *pointe* is unmistakably directed against him.
25. *Correspondance*, IV; letter to Monod, July 6, 1881.
26. "The Revolution is a block, from which no parts can be detached."
27. "France? . . . Yes, but a great France, a strong Republic, the France of the Revolution, and the Republic that represents in the world Right and Justice."
28. "France, but . . . France, if . . . France, on condition that . . . No! Frenchmen before everything and unconditionally."
29. Bussemaker and Colenbrander.
30. *Annales révolutionnaires*, 1908 (first year), pp. 340-57.
31. A few years later, in 1916, Cochin was killed in the first world war—undoubtedly a loss to scholarship.
32. Crane Brinton, in the "Bibliographical Essay" with which he concludes his brilliant volume *A Decade of Revolution: 1789-1799* (the "Rise of Modern Europe" series, New York, 1934), p. 298, has not, I think satisfactorily unraveled Cochin's somewhat involved argument. In stating that Cochin adhered to *le thèse du complot* he is certainly mistaken.
33. Lefebvre (who died in 1959), though born in the same year as Mathiez (1874), survived him by nearly thirty.
34. A stenciled volume in *Les Cours de Sorbonne*. The date of publication is not given. I believe it was 1953, although there is internal evidence that the lectures were composed before the second world war.
35. Op. cit., p. 250 (edition of 1938).
36. "Side by side with, and independent from, the 'scientific' labor." Cf. my little essay on Professor Butterfield, pp. 331-35, below.
37. Langlois thought (or said) that history serves only to satisfy curiosity; Seignobos, to form democratic citizens. Against them De Marans quotes a passage from Fustel de Coulanges. I gave part of this passage above (p. 117); the following is also, I think, worth reproducing: "L'histoire imparfaitement observeé nous divise, c'est par l'histoire mieux connue que l'oeuvre de conciliation doit commencer." And elsewhere: "La connaissance du moyen âge, mais la connaissance exacte, sincère et sans parti pris, est pour notre société un intérêt de premier ordre. . . .

Pour remettre le calme dans le présent, il n'est pas inutile de détruire d'abord les préjugés et les erreurs sur le passé." Comte and the positivists attributed to history a leading task in the work of ordering and controlling society. One can see a connection between Fustel de Coulanges's insistence on history's beneficent influence and the positivist dogmatism and arrogance in his view.

38. I mentioned that Madelin's book on the Revolution was awarded a prize by the *Académie*. On the strength of his Napoleon book he was later elected a member.
39. See my *Napoleon For and Against*, pp. 390-402.
40. A situation full of irony resulted in 1957 when the committee of party chairmen in the Chamber in an unguarded moment decided to request the government to organize a national commemoration of the bicentenary of Robespierre's birth. On second thoughts, when Pinay and Bidault had issued resounding protests, several of the gentlemen were seen to waver. *L'Humanité*, the Communist newspaper, poured scorn especially on the Socialists who were trying to explain away the great man's inhumanities. As if any apologies were needed for the Incorruptible! These lackeys of the bourgeoisie were only trying to decorate their miserable cause with the name of a man of whom they would be mortally afraid if he were not safely dead! . . .

    Insofar as the memory of the Revolution still does have an immediate impact on French politics, the Communists have found it a useful asset.
41. That was in 1956—before the coming into power of De Gaulle. And what seems finally to confuse the picture is the fact that General Massu, the instigator of the military *coup* in Algeria by which the Fourth Republic was, in May 1958, overthrown, organized his adherents in a *Comité de salut Public*!
42. Clemenceau's phrase, see p. 130. This "block" theory was expressly refuted many times, very strikingly by Vandal, quoted with approval by Madelin.

Orange and Stuart: 1641-1650

1. *Brieven van N. van Reigersberch aan Hugo de Groot* (Utrecht: Hist. Gen., 1901), p. 51.
2. Vreede, *Geschiedenis der Nederl. Diplomatie*, I, 58.
3. In August 1634, for instance, the Groningen member of the Secret Committee, on being told that he must not give any information about the negotiations then proceeding to the States of his province, replied that he would abstain from taking any part in further proceedings except insofar as directed by that States (L. Aitzema, *Saken van staet on oorlogh*, III, 267). Opposition of Groningen did not need to be taken too seriously, but we shall see that this was the very point on which Holland, in 1643, was to aim a deadly blow to the Secret Committee. Under

William III the Secret Committee was revived (*Recueil des instructions données aux ambassadeurs de France, Hollande*, II, 168) and again this point at times caused friction; see Sylvius, *Historiën onzes tijds* (1684), p. 41. The history of the Secret Committee would repay systematic examination. Brief and vague remarks are all that is to be found in Vreede, op. cit., Van Riemsdijk, *Griffie van H. H. M.*, p. 21, Fruin-Colenbrander, *Staatsinstellingen*, p. 187.

4. Arend, *Algemeene Geschiedenis* (1868), III, v, 261.
5. Vreede, op. cit., I, 212, n. 2.
6. See the evidence from the *Archives de la maison d'Orange-Nassau* and Van der Capellen cited by Ising in *Bijdragen*, New Series, IV, 255. Fruin has shown, by a reference to the *Clarendon State Papers*, that the suspicion was unfounded. In May Sir William Boswell was already reporting similar rumors from Holland (*State Papers, For., Holland*, CLV).
7. Ranke, *Französische Geschichte*, II, 506 ff.; Lavisse, *Histoire de France*, VI, ii, 350.
8. I do not think that Marie de Médicis can have been quite honestly in favor of the idea. Sommelsdijk declares that in January she as well as her daughter were enthusiastic about the Spanish marriage (*Archives*, II, iii, 161).
9. Arend, op. cit., III, v, 248; cf. Aitzema, op. cit., IV, b, 75. The instructions, December 6, 1639, are given as an appendix in T. J. Geest, *Amalia van Solms en de Nederl. politiek van 1625 tot 1648* (1909).
10. February 6, 1640 (*Archives*, II, iii, 197).
11. All that we know about this incident is to be gathered from a letter from Sommelsdijk to Frederick Henry of February 2 (ibid., p. 198). Brill, in Arend's *Algemeene Geschiedenis*, III, v, 259, n., drew attention to this. The emphatic tone of Sommelsdijk's words leads one to suspect that he thought the Prince needed persuasion.
12. *Venetian Calendar* (1640-42), p. 110.
13. Cf. *Archives*, II, iii, 161, 206.
14. The inequality of the marriage may be illustrated by contrasting the forms used by Frederick Henry in his letters to Charles II with those of the King's letters to him. The Prince of Orange writes: "Sire, la gracieuse lettre dont il a plu à V. M. m'onorer. . . . Je lui témoigneray tousjours par mes devoirs et très-humbles services que je suis avec passion, Sire, de V. M. très-humble et très-obéissant serviteur. . . ." The King writes: "Mon cousin, Vous verrez . . . Je suis, mon cousin, votre très-affectionné cousin. . . ."
15. *Archives*, II, iii, 161.
16. Geest, op. cit., p. 91.
17. *Archives*, II, iii, 217.
18. Ibid., p. 220.
19. With Mademoiselle, known later as "la grande Mademoiselle" (ibid., p. 218).

20. See *Venetian Calendar*, p. 124.
21. L. Aitzema, *Saken van staet en oorlogh*, V, 336 (I quote from the quarto edition), in relating the visit of the Queen to Holland, remarks in his caustic way that she "seemed to have been informed of the Prince's great authority and power" and that "he did as he willed with his state." Indeed, that is how the position was regarded at the English court: early in 1939 Secretary Coke had written in a letter to Boswell, the resident at The Hague: "The building of the fort at Breda, as it secureth that place, so it showeth what great power the Prince of Aurenge hath among them." (*State Papers, For., Holland*, CLV). See below, n. 171.
22. *Venetian Calendar*, p. 119.
23. It stipulated, among other things, that the bride should remain in England until she had reached her twelfth year; that the marriage portion should be £40,000, payable in four half-yearly sums of £10,000.
24. *Archives*, II, iii, 430.
25. The suspicions of the Parliament had so increased by March that the King's commissioners insisted at the last moment that the envoys of the Prince of Orange should be content with an informal and secret ratification of the contract (ibid., p. 400; see also p. 460). This is what Baillie, the Scottish Covenanter, must have had in his mind when on May 7, 1641, O.S. (May 17, N.S.) he wrote from London: "The precipitation of this marriage is feared by manie." (*Letters and Journals*, I, 351; cf, also *Venetian Calendar*, p. 115.)
26. "De bruid niet in de schuit." (*Brieven*, p. 649).
27. Ibid., p. 674: "Die praem wat langer zullen willen gebruycken."
28. May, *Life of Duke of Gloucester and Princess Mary* (1661); quoted in Green, *Lives of the Princesses of England*, VI, 128.
29. Agnes Strickland, *Lives of the Last Four Princesses of the Royal House of Stuart*, p. 28. Miss Strickland's historical appreciations are if possible even more amusing than Miss Green's, but she, too, has done some archival research. Cf. also Clarendon, *Rebellion*, p. 819, and P. C. Hooft, *Brieven*, IV, 344.
30. By an act of February 10/20, 1641/2, *Rawlinson Letters* (Bodleian Library), A, cxv. This volume contains letters written by the Orange family and the Stuarts to Heenvliet and his wife, together with a few official documents of personal interest to them both.
31. Reigersberch, *Brieven*, p. 605.
32. Ibid., p. 719.
33. ". . . Hen die van Godt tot Godheid zijn gewijt Ten dienst van 't algemeen."
34. *Venetian Calendar*, p. 158.
35. For 1642 alone Knuttel, *Catalogus*, mentions some seventy pamphlets connected with the differences between the King of England and Parliament, mostly translations of declarations, proclamations, and justifications of the two parties.

36. "We have met at length sometimes with Dr. Rivett: he is one fullie in our minds and against the Bishops." (Baillie, *Letters and Journals*, I, 181.)
37. Although Baillie later on encouraged him to do so (ibid., pp. 169, 181).
38. William Spang, cousin of Robert Baillie and one of his most regular correspondents (see Baillie, op. cit., II, 75, 115, 180). From the last passage it appears that Spang was sometimes responsible for the printing of the writings that the other man inspired. Apparently the reference is here to the pamphlet numbered 4990 in Knuttel, *Catalogus*.
39. Knuttel, *Acta der . . . Synoden van Zuid-Holland*, II, 505.
40. Ibid., pp. 466-504.
41. *Ernstig gesprek . . . tusschen drie personen* (1652 [Knuttel, *Catalogus*, no. 7256]), p. 35. In *De Nederlandsche Nijptang* (1652 [ibid, no. 7251]), p. 13, the same accusation occurs.
42. It is true that they were often offended at the worldliness of Frederick Henry and his protégée the refugee Queen of Bohemia (another Stuart!)—I find for example in *State Papers*, *For.*, *Holland*, CLV, a letter from Samson Johnson, "from Her My's Court at The Hague" (i.e., from the court of the Queen of Bohemia), to Archbishop Laud, dated December 5, 1639, in which he says: "The consistorye in this towne have done all they could for suppressing of the French players licenced by the magistrate and protected by the P[rince] of Orange as his servants, but their invectives for condemning of all stage-players or the like shewes have bin soe intemperate in theyr pulpitts, that they ar gone backward rather than forward; all the preachers were with the P[rince] of Orange to represent the unlawfullness, but it seemes used noe argument that could worke on him, his counsell was that they should preach better and the playes would be less frequented. They came also to her Matye and desired shee would forbeare going; her Matye told them that shee conceaved 'twas a pastime that might be lawfully used and shee would use her discretion; and wondred at their incivilitye. I had nothing to doe in the business, they came not to me but formerly they desired me to preach against barenecks, by reason her Matie uses to goe toe, which I refusing as being not sent to tell her Matie, how to dress herself, they let me pass in this business. Beside there has been a proposition made to the consistorye here by the persons of best qualitye that they might have organs for to play with the psalms as in some townes of these countryes, but they plainly denyed it." The festivals in honor of Henrietta Maria gave offense in the same way (see Knuttel, *Catalogus*, no. 4869). Down to the time of his deepest humiliation Charles never ceased to demand that the stipulations of the marriage contract, guaranteeing the observance of the Episcopalian form of worship at his daughter's court, should be adhered to. On 6, August 1647, O.S. (August 16,

N.S.) in connection with the report that there were differences of opinion at the court itself on this point, he wrote to Heenvliet from Stoke with strict injunctions to the same effect (*Rawlinson Letters*, A, cxv).

43. Knuttel, *Catalogus*, no. 4870; *Lettres inédites de Henriette-Marie*, ed. Baillon, p. 66.
44. According to Reigersberch, op. cit., p. 707, the ambassadors in England "had been generous in promising as much as 50,000 guilders a year, but this without the knowledge or authority of those who would have to pay. . . . The States of Holland, seeing many provinces anxious to play the generous at their expense, resolved to give what they wished to give apart and of themselves, leaving the others to carry out their own liberality." See also Aitzema, op. cit., V, 343; *Venetian Calendar* (1642-3), pp. 21, 28.
45. Aitzema, op. cit., V, 335.
46. "Many are only just seeing the results of this alliance "writes Reigersberch, March 24, 1642 (op. cit., p. 708), and he adds "and all do not see it yet."
47. Green, op. cit., VI, 129. The statement of source is not satisfactory: "Letter of La Fin, page of the Prince of Orange, to his brother, 10th March, 1641." The date is obviously March 20, 1642, O.S. Some of the details, too, are obviously apocryphal. For instance, mention is made of a tribunal of the States-General at The Hague. The letter is to be found in *Somers Tracts*, IV.
48. Aitzema, op. cit., V, 467; *Archives*, II, iv, 166.
49. Reigersberch writes (op. cit., p. 740) on November 1643 to Grotius that "the present vigor of many has its origin more in umbrage on account of English affairs and religious ideas than in steadfast principles of state policy and freedom." Reigersberch, a Remonstrant republican, objects to the English policy of the Stadholder but he regrets that the new vigor against the Prince's supremacy had no more steadfast principle as a basis. By "religious ideas" he means, of course, the Calvinist sympathies with the Presbyterian Parliament.
50. See the dispatch of the States-General to Joachimi, July 26, 1642, in Muller, *Mare Clausum*, p. 318, n. 3.
51. "Il ne faut pas que le Prince laisse périr le Roy"; this is what Henrietta Maria said to Heenvliet in January 1642 (*Archives*).
52. Joachimi (corresp. in 19th cent. copies at Br. Mus.) constantly reported bitter complaints. He could in reply only point to the resolution laying down a policy of neutrality. That gave no satisfaction because at that time the States-General still held that allowing the export of arms was consistent with neutrality.
53. See the letters of his treasurer, Volbergen, in Worp, *Briefwisseling van Constantijn Huygens* (Rijks Geschiedkundige Publicatiën), III, *passim.* Volbergen had a great deal of trouble in raising the 300,000 guilders in Amsterdam. They had to submit to an interest of 7 per cent.

54. How entirely dependent on his favor everyone was in such cases appears very clearly in my article "Troepenlichten en schepenhuren in de dagen van Frederik Hendrik," in *Bijdragen*, 1918.
55. Eva Scott, *Rupert, Prince Palatine*, p. 59, gives "Coulster" as the name of the captain of the ship placed at their disposal by the Prince. Reigersberch (op. cit., p. 728) writes on June 30, 1642 that Rupert and Maurice, "with a following of some hundred officers," left for England "yesterday." That must have been the first unsuccessful attempt to cross, which Miss Scott, however, places in August.
56. *Archives*, II, iv, 40.
57. Ibid., p. 42.
58. Ibid., p. 39.
59. Reigersberch (op. cit., p. 701) wrote immediately: "The state will profit to this extent: the bride being brought home, they will not have to court England's favor so much [*men minder schoon op sal hebben te dienen*]." The Queen herself wrote to the King (March 17, 1642): "Je travaille avec le Prince d'Orange et espère en avoir contentement, quoyque ce soit une personne malaysée à engager; mais les intérests ont de grands pouvoirs" (*Lettres inédites de Henriette-Marie*, p. 25).
60. "Dearest Daugther, I desyre you to assist me to procure from your Father in Law the loane of a good ship to be sent higher to attend my commands. It is that I may safely send and receave Expresses to and from your Mother" (Charles to Mary, Newcastle, September 16, 1646, O.S. [September 26, N.S.], *Rawlinson Letters*, A, cxv). The date 1646 is obviously wrong; it must be 1642.
61. See, for instance, *Archives*, II, iv, 43.
62. Ibid., p. 49.
63. In April 1645 Charles I gave him a barony with the title of Baron de Kerckhove. Whereupon Jermyn wrote to Digby that this was not enough, in view of the fact that the Queen in Holland "upon the important services she received from Heenvliet" promised a title for his son by Lady Stanhope. On June 7, 1649 Charles II fulfilled this promise by creating the son himself Baron Wotton of Marley (*Rawlinson Letters*, A, cxv).
64. *Archives*, II, iv, 43.
65. *Lettres inédites de Henriette-Marie*, p. 402.
66. Arend, op. cit, III, v, 383.
67. *Archives*, II, iv, 71. The Hollanders were particularly moved by the report that there were "canons d'état" on board these ships. They found none, but this does not mean that the report had no foundation in fact.
68. Ibid., p. 69.
69. Letter to Heenvliet, ibid., p. 75.
70. Reigersberch, op. cit., p. 727, writes: "Actually the alliance is made with the King, so that it cannot rightly be proved that arms may be denied to him." He says also that Amsterdam and

Rotterdam in the States of Holland were against a prohibition of export (in June 1642), "under the pretext that trade must be free."

71. A year later Boswell still writes about this resolution with the greatest indignation, in a letter to his government which happens to have been preserved because it was intercepted by the parliamentary party (*State Papers, For., Holland*, CLVII).
72. *Archives*, II, iv, 73. "Notorious" for his corruption.
73. On November 11, 1642, Strickland writes to Pym that he has given information about a munitions ship to the States-General, "but there is so much form in their resolutions as to make the work fruitless. When I sought to hasten it the Greffier, who is to despatch the order, told me that he cared not whether she were gone or not. I find him harsh in all that concerns the Parliament" (*Hist. MSS. Comm., Xth Report*, vi, 91). See also *Archives*, II, iv, 43. The Council of State allowed itself to be used by Frederick Henry, and up to a certain point, as it appears, the Admiralty College of Amsterdam. Concerning Musch, as late as April 16, 1645, Dr. Goffe writes to Jermyn (*Digby's Cabinet* [see below, n. 100]): "He is a very serious servant of her Majesties, and ought to be gratified whatsoever becomes of other businesse." And, as a matter of fact, at the end of May 1645 he received a gift of 3,000 guilders (ibid., p. 39).
74. *Hist. MSS. Comm., Xth Report*, vi, 93. Renswoude, like Musch, was one of the confidants of the Prince of Orange (*Archives*, II, iv, 97).
75. Reigersberch, op. cit., pp. 730 ff.
76. *Lettres inédites de Henriette-Marie.*
77. *Archives*, II, iv, 9.
78. Ibid., p. 17.
79. Ibid., p. 18.
80. Reigersberch, op. cit., p. 707.
81. Arend, op. cit., II, iv, 371.
82. Willem Boreel (Elias, *Vroedschap van Amsterdam*, I, 540), a member of a well-known Zeeland family, had settled in Amsterdam and had become pensionary of the town in 1627. He was nonetheless an Orangist. Heenvliet took him into his confidence over the question of the crown jewels (*Archives*, II, iv, 43). One of Heenvliet's sons became a gentleman at the court of Frederick Henry and Boreel took a warm interest in the career of this young man (see Worp, op. cit., V, 55). He himself owed his appointment as ambassador at Paris to William II. According to a note, the source of which I cannot trace, he received in that capacity 1,000 livres a year from the Prince over and above his salary.

    Renswoude, the well-known Orangist deputy for Utrecht in the States-General, was a brother of Reede van Nederhorst, who belonged to His Highness's council (Waddington, *La République des Provinces Unies*, II, 257, 260). In December 1642 Strickland wrote, with great annoyance, concerning Renswoude as a strong antiparliamentarian (*Hist. MSS. Comm., Xth Report*, v, 93). Henrietta Maria received a visit from one of the two which very much pleased her (*Lettres*, p. 31).

83. *Archives*, II, iv, 39. See also Reigersberch, op. cit., p. 726.
84. The French ambassador, Harcourt, too, writes in the same spirit (*Archives*, II, iv, 97).
85. *State Papers, For., Holland*, CLVII.
86. Reigersberch, op. cit., p. 699.
87. Observations on the wrecking of the Secret Committee by means of this new instruction are to be found in Van der Capellen's *Gedenkschriften*, II, 173; Waddington, *La République des Provinces-Unies*, II, 35 (d'Estrades to Mazarin); and in a French memorandum of 1647 published in *Bijdragen en Mededelingen* (Hist. Gen.), XV, 134. The instruction: Aitzema, op. cit., V, 552 ff.
88. Aitzema, op. cit., V, 619.
89. Ibid., p. 563. See also Duanne Lon in *Venetian Calendar* (1642-3), p. 220: "The Prince knows how much his authority has suffered since the alliance of his son with the Princess Mary of England, because of what he has had to do in the interests of that Crown." (December 31, 1642).
90. Reigersberch, op. cit., p. 734.
91. Baillie, op. cit., II, 113.
92. See his letters to Huygens, the Prince's secretary, in Worp, op. cit., IV, *passim*; Worp calls Renswoude by his family name, Reede. In these letters Renswoude makes no secret of his anti-parliamentary leanings, e.g., "the government of the Parliament means ruin to our state" (November 4, 1644, p. 95) and, "I understand that Joachimi is working secretly in Holland that he may come with us, which will be to the disadvantage of His Highness and the King; must therefore be prevented" (March 10, 1645, p. 131).
93. Baillie, op. cit., II, 143. Shortly after this, he says simply that they were "sent by the Prince of Orange to serve the King's ends."
94. Arend gives a detailed résumé of the report handed to the States-General by the ambassadors on their return.
95. Baillie, op. cit., II, 155, 167.
96. Arend, op. cit., II, v, 501.
97. See Huygens to Joachimi, February 6, 1645 (*Archives*, II, iv, 128): "Il a esté procuré que nos ambassadeurs n'auront à bouger d'Angleterre pour quelque temps, vers où donc, si la France se résoult d'en envoyer de son costé durant leur séjour par delà, ils pourront entrer dans les communications que vous sçavez et veoir à quelle sorte de concert les affaires se pourront conduire entre leurs mains."
98. More particularly of the Independents.
99. Arend, op. cit., II, v, 518. See also the bellicose tone of a letter from Renswoude to Huygens of August 14, 1645 (Worp, op. cit., IV, 192).
100. On March 6, 1646, O.S. (March 16, N.S.), the House of Com-

mons issued an order for the publication of the papers of Digby, which had fallen into its hands in the previous year in a battle at Sherburn in Yorkshire. They were published under the title *The Lord George Digby's Cabinet. . . .* A Dutch translation of the parts of most interest to Dutch readers appeared under the title, *Eenighe extracten uyt verscheyde missiven, gevonden in de Lord Digby's Cabinet. . . .* Tot Londen, ghedruct by Robert Wood; Knuttel, *Catalogus*, no. 5252; "Holl. druk" according to Knuttel.

101. *Digby's Cabinet*, Goffe to Jermyn, April 17, 1645, O.S. (April 27, N.S.), "When the ambassadors are returned, all endeavours shaal be used to induce the States to a League defensive and offensive."
102. Ibid., Goffe to Jermyn, 8/18 May 1645.
103. Ibid., Goffe to Jermyn, 15/25 May 1645.
104. Ibid., Goffe to Jermyn, 1/11 May 1645.
105. Ibid., Goffe to Jermyn, 29 May/8 June 1645.
106. Aitzema, op. cit., VI, 75.
107. Gelderland and Friesland voted with Holland for the reception of Strickland. The Frisian delegates, it is true, conformed at the express bidding of their Stadholder, although their States had made the opposite decision (Aitzema, op. cit., VI, 77).
108. See Kernkamp, *De Sleutels van de Sond*, p. 44.
109. The suspicion that it probably was not that, but "also on account of the marriage alliance between himself, the King of England, and Denmark," is expressed in Van der Capellen, *Gedenkschriften*, II, 98, and Van der Capellen was by no means inimical to the Prince.
110. Ibid., p. 98: "om deze coorde niet te stijf te trecken, opdat daeruyt niet erger kome te ontstaan." The candid man's name is not given.
111. By the revelations contained in *Lord Digby's Cabinet*; see below, p. 178.
112. *Archives*, II, iv, 97.
113. Worp, op. cit., IV, 473.
114. See Gardiner, *History of the Civil War*, I, 328.
115. *Archives*, II, iv, 98.
116. Arend, op. cit., II, v, 493.
117. *Archives*, II, v, 103.
118. Ibid., II, iv, 97.
119. The attitude of France toward the English differences was no more honest than that of the Orangist majority in the States-General, but it was certainly more cautious. In the British Museum there is a bulky volume comprising "Négociations de M. de Sabran en Angleterre en 1644" (Add. MS. 5460). The Instructions, dated April 19, 1644, say that the attempts of Grécy to mediate between King and Parliament were not acceptable to the Parliament because he showed himself too much an adherent of the King. Sabran is now to "appuyer les justes prétentions du Roy et le favoriser en tout et par tout," but "avec tant d'adresse qu'on ne puysse luy imputer qu'il soit son

partisan." "La raison d'état" requires this, because he is to appear as a mediator and also because "la raison d'état exige qu'en une chose incertaine on ne se déclare pas si ouvertement que, s'il arrivoit un changement qu'on n'eust peu prévoir, l'on ne se trouve pas hors termes de s'accorder avec celluy qui sera resté le Maistre."

120. *Archives*, II, iv, 134.
121. *Digby's Cabinet*, Goffe to Jermyn, 29 May/8 June 1645.
122. See Gardiner, op. cit., II, 258.
123. In February 1645 Huygens had frankly put the case to Lord Jermyn: there were two tendencies to be distinguished there, the one dependent on the will of His Highness, the other on the States; as for the first, there would never be cause for complaint; as for the second, His Highness could only do his best (*Archives*, II, iv, 128).
124. Arend, op. cit., III, v, 560; *Archives*, II, iv, 128; *Digby's Cabinet*, *passim*, particularly pp. 37 ff. These ships were used for the export of tin from the west of England, the only source of income for the Queen; also to keep up communication between the royalists on the Continent and the King. Captain Colster, or Coulster, who is mentioned in nearly all these reports, took Prince Rupert and his company over to England on the instructions of the Prince of Orange. See n. 55, above.
125. Charles IV of Lorraine, who, after having been driven out of his country by France, as a leader of irregular bands generally fought with the Spaniards.
126. *Archives*, II, iv, 142, 144; Worp, op. cit., IV, 226. Negotiations had been entered into with Dorp, Huygens's brother-in-law, to act as admiral.
127. Le Clerc, *Négociations secrètes touchant la paix de Münster et d'Osnabrug* (1724), III, 52, 107, 112.
128. Ibid., pp. 56, 57.
129. I have described this incident more fully in "De Oranjes en Antwerpen, 1646-50," *Tijdschrift voor Geschiedenis*, 1925; reprinted in *Kernproblemen van onze Geschiedenis*, 1936.
130. *Archives*, II, iv, 152.
131. Ibid., p. 151.
132. Ibid., p. 166.
133. Ibid., p. 152.
134. Ibid., p. 162.
135. *Archives*, II, iv, 180.
136. The treaty, as noted above, provided that neither of the contracting parties was to conclude a separate peace.
137. *Archives*, II, iv, 235, August 5, 1647.
138. Ibid., p. 262.
139. *Hamilton Papers* (Gardiner, 1880), p. 228, letter of Sir W. Bellenden from Amsterdam, July 9, 1648 (presumably O.S.): "At all time of my acces to the P. of Orange I did moue him what was to be doin be ws for the conjunction with the Staits,

but the trewth is that he is not so ripe and painfull in and for business as his condition doeth requier."

140. Memorandum from William II to the Prince of Wales, September (?), 1648, *Archives*, II, iv, 267.
141. This matter is known from the letters of De Wilhem to Huygens in *Archives*, II, iv, 263 ff.; published more fully by Worp, op. cit., IV, 491 ff. Further, a letter of Sir Edward Hyde in *Clarendon State Papers*, II, 455 ff. He gives the number of men as 900; De Wilhem 500.
142. De Wilhem received a receipt from Bellenden for these munitions.
143. At a later date the Prince of Wales expressed this gratitude most emphatically (letter from St. Johnston, January 21, 1651, *Rawlinson Letters*). From the moment that they had first met in Helvoetsluis, says the King (as he then was), Heenvliet's services had been inestimable.
144. "Pleust à Dieu que nostre maistre ne s'engageast plus avant avec ces gens sine luce, sine cruce, sine deo; jamais de ma vie je vis un tel désordre et confusion"; September 18; this is to be found only in Worp, op. cit.
145. According to Eva Scott (*The King in Exile*, p. 51) it was again the generosity of the Prince of Orange which enabled this fleet to set sail; he had equipped it with three months' provisions. The writer, however, gives no source.
146. The Prince of Wales was received at The Hague in accordance with his rank, and entertained for the customary ten days at the expense of the States-General; the States of Holland refused to allow this term to be prolonged at the pleasure of the Prince of Orange (De Wilhem to Huygens). The young Duke of York, too, was still living at the expense of his brother-in-law. In order to relieve him, the Duke of York went to France in December, while the Prince of Wales's court was curtailed as much as possible (Aitzema, op. cit., VI, p. 575). According to Aitzema (op. cit., VI, 782), William II gave pensions to the lords of Charles II's court in 1649 of 2,000 guilders each. Cf. also Carte's *Ormonde Papers*, I, 199, 209.
147. William was at the time of these decisions in Groningen. Thence, on September 15, he wrote to Heenvliet that he had sent a letter to the Princess Royal for the Admiralty of Rotterdam in case the Prince of Wales might like to have a ship to go to Scotland. On September 20—apparently Heenvliet had in the meantime enlightened him as to Preston—he wrote the following characteristic words: "J'ay receu vos lettres. Je voy que les affaires sont bien incertaines et qu'ils ne savent de quel bois faire flèce. Me semble qu'il vaut toujours mieux un Royaume [understand: *one* kingdom—Scotland] que rien, mais le temps perdu est beaucoup" (*Rawlinson Letters*).
148. For at that time most people were still loyal parliamentarians, says Aitzema.

149. Aitzema, op. cit., VI, 682.
150. Eva Scott, op. cit., p. 73.
151. Aitzema, op. cit., VI, p. 694.
152. See above, note 119.
153. Aitzema, op. cit., VI, 685.
154. The Latin dissertations, both translated into Dutch, were followed by two more pamphlets. See Knuttel, *Catalogus*, nos. 6377-83. The name of the Utrecht writer is not known to me.
155. Graswinckel, *Korte onderrechtinge raeckende de fundamentale Regeeringhe van Engelandt* (Knuttel *Catalogus* no. 6375). *Beduncken op de onderrechtinghe*, etc. (Knuttel no. 6376). Of this latter pamphlet no mention is made of either printer or author.
156. Aitzema, op. cit., VI, p. 688.
157. See above, note 38.
158. Baillie, op. cit., IV, 73 ff. Spang wanted to speak English or Latin, but William II preferred Dutch. Lord Byron, the envoy or Ormonde, says: "He understands English very well, though he speak it not, so that your Exc. shall not need trouble to write in French" (Carte, *Ormonde Papers*, I, 269).
159. Spang is, as one might imagine, very well disposed toward William II: "Ye will find our young Prince of Orange one of the hopefullest youths that ever Europe brought forth, and willing to doe all good offices for the cause" (Carte, op. cit., I, 83).
160. Ibid., pp. 88, 90.
161. Ibid., 239.
162. Sophia of Bohemia wrote this to her brother Rupert on April 13, 1649 (*Cal. St. P. Dom.* [1649-50], p. 85). Baillie, himself one of the Scottish envoys, wrote home to the same effect.
163. The Queen of Bohemia hoped to win Charles for Sophia. The Bohemian family was Calvinist, but most of its members were far from faultless in doctrine. The accusation against Sophia was that she accompanied Charles to common prayer. Cf. Sophia's *Mémoires*.
164. Carte, op. cit., I, 264.
165. Byron, for instance, after giving the conditions of the Scottish envoys, writes: "But the King being now unfortunately in a Presbyterian country cannot resent these indignities so as otherwise he would" (Ibid., p. 268).
166. *Thurloe State Papers*, I, 115; September 19, 1649.
167. *Clarendon State Papers*, II, 482.
168. *Archives*, II, iv, 309. The assertion in the *Nicholas Papers*, I, 127, that the moneys were procured for the King by William II, "underhand provided by the States," is most improbable. A similar account is found in 1650 (Gardiner, *Letters and Papers Illustrating the Relations Between Charles II and Scotland in 1650* [1894], p. 77). Strickland wrote in September 1649: "Pray, sir, doe but gratifie the States of Holland, and my life for it. P.C., who hopes only to retrieve his game from hence, shall doe noth-

ing, notwithstanding the greatness of the greatest heere" (*Thurloe State Papers*, I, 119).

169. Aitzema.
170. *Archives*, II, iv, 315; October 19, 1649.
171. Gardiner, op. cit. The Princes of Orange had a special connection with Breda and owned a place of residence there.
172. Ibid., p. 60.
173. His reports appeared in *A Briefe Relation*, the organ of the English Council of State, and are reprinted in Gardiner's book.
174. Ibid., p. 30.
175. Ibid., p. 51. About Voetius, see above, p. 183.
176. Gardiner, op. cit., p. 76, *et passim.*
177. About this time the Prince managed to borrow two million from the town of Amsterdam. See below, n. 184.
178. Wynne, *Geschillen over de afdanking van het krijgsvolk*, p. 93. Reprinted in Gardiner. Unfortunately these documents are not dated.
179. Gardiner, op. cit., pp. 81, 85.
180. Not far from Delft. He had spent another month in Breda after the conclusion of the treaty, according to the English spy, because he did not want to face the displeasure of the States of Holland at The Hague (Gardiner, op. cit., p. 119). In the *Rawlinson Letters* there is a letter from the Princess Royal to Heenvliet, from Breda, undated but apparently of May 1650. She asks him to show this letter to her husband, and continues: "afin que nous puissions vennir à La Haye. Le Roy est en grande impassiance et ne fait que demander quand vous viendrés icy."
181. Even William II wrote (June 13) from Schoonhoven to Heenvliet: "Je croy qu'il sera bien périllieux après avoir attendu cy longtemps de s'embarquer, et il vaudroit mieux remettre l'affaire à une autre fois" (*Rawlinson Letters*). The King was then already on board.
182. Gardiner, op. cit., p. 90.
183. Cf. below, p. 192; also note 184.
184. Cf. *Br. Rel.*, Sept. 9, 1650 (Br. Mus.; not in Gardiner, op. cit.; published by me in *Bijdr. en Meded.*, 1924): "They [the Hollanders] wish verie well to your affaires in Scotland." I don't quite know what is to be made of the fact that in April 1650 Amsterdam advanced two millions to William II on the security of estates—a capital sum that the Prince certainly did not need merely to wipe out old debts, but that at the same time enabled him to come once more to the assistance of Charles II, who just at that time was preparing to go to Scotland (Wagenaar, *Amsterdam*, I, 550). It looks like a sort of reassurance, an attempt, just when Schaep had been sent to England, to pave the way for friendly relations in the other camp as well. However, in the absence of any certain data as to how the Prince spent the money, it is impossible to decide the exact significance of this fact. This much of course is certain that he, who two or

three months later carried out his attack on Amsterdam, did not allow his gratitude for this loan to exercise any influence on his line of policy.

185. *Thurloe State Papers*, I, 113 ff.
186. Ibid., p. 118.
187. Aitzema, op. cit., VI, 831.
188. One instance of the way in which William II used to get a hold over the deputies. In 1649 he gave a lieutenancy to the six-year-old son of Jonkheer Boldewijn Jacob Mulert, deputy in the States-General for Overijssel. The towns of that province (each province was responsible for the pay of particular regiments of the Union army assigned to it) were so indignant that they decided to refuse payment (Bussemaker, *Geschiedenis van Overijsel, 1650-72*, I, 25). This same Mulert was after William II's death criticized in the States of Overijssel for having voted, unauthorized, in the States-General for the resolution of June 5, 1650, on which the Prince had based himself in undertaking his *coup d'état* (*Brieven aan De Witt*, *W.H.G.*, I, 33).
189. *Archives*, II, iv, 317.
190. Aitzema, op. cit., VII, 23.
191. Article X, of the Union merely prohibited the members from entering into separate "alliances or treaties" with other states.
192. *Archives*, II, iv, 317.
193. August 16, 1659: P. L. Muller, "Spanje en de partijen in Nederland in 1650," in *Nijhoff's Bijdragen* (Nieuwe Reeks), VII (1899), 149. In my opinion Muller is quite wrong in calling this "a certainly somewhat curious utterance." His incredulity merely proves how completely neglected have been the aspects of the foreign policy of Frederick Henry and William II which I am putting forward in this study.
194. As it is expressed in the very bitter pamphlet, *Openhertig Discours . . . rakende de subite dood van Z.H.* (Knuttel, *Catalogus*, no. 1651), William II would have liked to subdue all the provinces; he wanted to dismiss the independent magistrates everywhere and replace them with "servile" officers, "and then we should have been plunged into two wars at the same time; to wit, against the Parliament of England in order to help the King of Scotland, and against Spain to please the frivolous French, in whom he placed all his faith."
195. *Archives*, II, iv, 298. The document is not dated. Groen puts it down to the end of February 1649.
196. See *Archives*, II, iv, 318. Brasset promises William that France will not insist on French troops being sent back, while Holland would like to see the foreign regiments removed.
197. *Archives*, II, iv, 317.
198. *Gedenkschriften*, II, 281.
199. See, e.g., a pamphlet of 1652, *Ernstig gesprek tusschen drie personen* (Knuttel, *Catalogus*, no. 7256). The author is a States party man. Of the three characters he lets the one he has cast for the part of victim of Orangist propaganda say: "Our country has before

been sold to the English, when our last Prince of Orange [William II, who died in November 1650] was still living. He, knowing this, for that reason went to lay siege before Amsterdam in order to stop them delivering it." In *State Papers*, *For.*, *Holland*, CLIX, there is a letter of August 11, 1650, from Utrecht, signed Cha. Ledison (one of the pseudonyms of Sir E. Nicholas), about the attack on Amsterdam; in it credence is given to these stories: "Its reported that in order to render themselves sover-aigns and to curbe the rest of the provinces a factious party in that city hath by their Agent Monsr Scape now in England, and other underhand instruments, treated with the Rebells there to send them to Amsterdam by the Tassell [Jexel] 10,000 men, whereof 5000 were to have come very speedily being (some say) alreddy levyed and reddy to be shipped under pretence of being sent for Irland, and the other 5000 were to be sent a monthe or 6 weeks after. By their complices in England its easy to make a judgment of their designe and intentions; but I be-lieve untill the English rebells see the success of their forces now marched into the Northe, they will be wary how they send many men into any foreigne partes." But Nicholas uttered more rad-ical doubts very soon afterward. On August 15 he wrote: "Methinkes those who are of the Prince of Orange's counsell should use all possible industry to get proofe of the truth of what is printed concerning the agreement between Scape and the Rebells of England, which is a business of very great im-portance for these States to knowe."

200. See above, n. 184.
201. See Wicquefort, I, 522, and "Briefe Relation" in Gardiner, *Charles II and Scotland in 1650.*
202. Who had left the court of Charles II and had betaken himself to Leyden (Gardiner, op. cit., p. 115).
203. Ibid., p. 114.
204. "Be pliant, friend, whoe'er thou be, A virtue 'tis will profit thee." From "The Reed and the Oaktree." Cats is remembered as a poet more than as a statesman. His didactic and rather trite poetry enjoyed immense popularity in his own day and much later.
205. Pelnits to Nanning Keyser; *Bijdragen en Mededeelingen Historisch Genootschap*, XVIII, 356.
206. Aitzema, op. cit., VII, 53; *Briefe Relation*, September 9, 1650.
207. The quotations are to be found in a pamphlet of 1668, *Zeeuwsche vreugde . . .* , (Knuttel, *Catalogus*, no. 9675). It was against this dedication that Vondel wrote his impassioned little poem; "On the Rebelliousness of the Godless Zeelander Max. Teellinck."
208. Aitzema, op. cit., VII, 11.
209. See, e.g., Fabio Chigi to the Cardinal-Secretary of State, *Bijdra-gen en Mededeelingen Historisch Genootschap*, XXXV, 121.
210. *Gedenkschriften*, II, 281.
211. Elias, *Vroedschap van Amsterdam*, p. scix.
212. The strength of these appears from a letter to the Van der

Capellen of the *Gedenkschriften* from his son, published in Wicquefort, op. cit., I, 448. Here the dissatisfaction of the "common man" is spoken of, and it is said that "most people thought His Highness was in the wrong."

213. Aitzeman, op. cit., VII, 155.
214. *Briefe Relation*, September 9, 1650.
215. Wynne, op. cit., p. 156 (Duyst van Voorhout), 166 (Nanning Keyser); Ruyl's performance was even worse.
216. Ibid., p. 179.
217. Fruin, *Verspreide Geschriften*, IV, 166 ff.
218. Brun writes (August 28, Muller, op. cit., p. 166): "My confidants in the province of Holland say . . . that despite all this their province is not overthrown, as people think, but that she is still as powerful as before and watches her interests and safety more closely than she formerly used to do." It is true he did not place much faith in these professions.
219. *Briefe Relation*, September 9, 1650.
220. A republican correspondent in London wrote on November 18, 1650, to the Netherlands: "La mort de Son Altesse d'Orange fauche les espérances de nos ennemis et nous fera sans doute voir quelque grand changement aux affaires d'Escosse." *Bidragen en Mededeelingen Historisch Genootschap*, IV (1880), p. 239).
221. Aitzema, op. cit., VII, 155.
222. "The party in these parts increases every day in faction against the Prince of Orange" (*Nicholas Papers*, I, 198).

Historical Appreciations of the Holland Regent Regime

1. "Regents" refers to the numerous class of men who in the Dutch Republic held office—generally for life—in the corporations of "voting towns" or were members of the provincial nobilities. Together the towns and the nobility constituted the States of a province, the assembly that represented the province's sovereignty. I mention the nobility with the town gentlemen, although commonly the word "regent" will suggest only the latter.
2. The title of advocate was later replaced by that of grand-pensionary.
3. "Het Stadhouderschap in de Partij-literatuur onder de Witt" (1947); "Democratische tendenties in 1672" (1950); "De Witten-oorlog, een Pennestrijd in 1757" (1953). (All three in *Mededelingen* d. Kon. Akad. van Wetenschappen for the years indicated.) Essentially I have studied the same problem as presented in the sermons, pamphlets, and poems with which the fiftieth anniversary of the Kingdom was celebrated in 1863, in an essay, "1813 herdacht in 1863," *De Gids*, July 1954, pp. 14-51.
4. The so-called private schools, which, under the legislation of 1921, are fully subsidized by the state. Together, the private

Protestant and the private Catholic schools accommodate a considerably larger number of pupils than do the neutral public schools.

5. *Gereformeerd* is the bastard Latin form of the Dutch word *Hervormd.* The old State Church, which in the seventeenth century called itself *Gereformeerd*, now goes by the name of *Hervormd*, while the secessionists have revived the word *Gereformeerd* and laid hold of it for themselves. In English the distinction cannot be rendered.
6. Maurice was seventeen years old when his father was assassinated in 1584. Maurice was appointed stadholder of Holland in that year. The office was not hereditary.
7. The Twelve Years' Truce, 1609-1621, interrupting the Eighty Years' War with Spain, 1568-1648.
8. *Verspreide Geschriften*, IV, 16.
9. Fruin does not entirely overlook this, although his statement to that effect seems to me somewhat perfunctory. A striking instance is the following remark made by J. C. Naber (no more a Calvinist than was Fruin) in his well-known book *Calvinist of Libertijnsch* (Utrecht, 1884), p. 57: "There are not many instances in history where a government that counted supremacy over the church among its prerogatives extended its authority so far as did the States of Holland on this occasion." To which one can only reply: the history of the Reformation, both in Germany and in England, is full of such instances.
10. See the preceding essay.
11. The statement occurs in *Oranje en Stuart, 1641-1672* (Utrecht, 1939), p. 76, which is in the chapter that follows the two printed in this volume. In the second of these will be found the remark on the corrupt character of the States-General that drew Dr. Japikse's ire. See below, p. 199.
12. *Verspreide Geschriften*, VIII, 76.
13. L. Aitzema, *Saken van Staet en Oorlogh*, IX (1664), 1054.
14. *Brieven van De Witt* (Utrecht: Hist. Gen., 1906-13), II, 311, 313.
15. M. Th. Uit den Bogaard, *De Gereformeerden en Oranje* (Utrecht: *Historische Studies*, 1954).
16. The Antirevolutionary party, that is, the party opposed to the principles of the French Revolution, is the party of which Groen may be considered to be the spiritual father. Its voting strength is drawn largely from the members of the *Gereformeerde Kerk.* The other orthodox Protestant party, which also claims Groen as its patron, is called the Christian Historical party; it is supported mainly by orthodox members of the *Hervormde Kerk.* Together the two parties muster some 20 per cent of the seats in the Chamber, as against the Catholics over 30 per cent.
17. Abroad: at Buchenwald.
18. As regards the latter, I pointed this out in detail in an essay of 1950, reprinted in *Studies en Strijdschriften* (Groningen, 1958).
19. See my *Willem IV en England tot 1748* (The Hague, 1924); reviewed by Sir R. Lodge in *English Historical Review*, October 1925, pp. 616-21).

20. It is possible that he misread one sentence in *Oranje en Stuart.* This at any rate is what Dr. Japikse did in *Bijdr. Vad. Gesch.* (1940), and also G. N. Clark in *English Historical Review* (January 1942, pp. 139-43) in reviewing the book. On p. 389 I referred to "groups of the population politically so little schooled or so much isolated from national life as the commonalty with their ministers and the court nobility." Both my reviewers understood this to mean that I regarded as well "the commonalty and their ministers" as "the court nobility" as groups outside national life. I may have committed a stylistic error, but at any rate, this much is certain: what I meant was that "politically so little schooled" should be connected with "the commonalty and their ministers," and "isolated from national life" with "the court nobility."

The Batavian Revolution: 1795-1798

1. Let me warn the reader that I use the word "federalism" in a sense exactly opposite to that which was current in the early days of American independence. In the Batavian Republic the Federalist party wanted to preserve as much as possible of provincial sovereignty. The party out for strong government was called the Unitarist party.
2. Since I wrote this lecture, the new volume of my *Nederlandsee Stam* has appeared; in it I deal with the episode in considerable detail.

The Vitality of Western Civilization

1. The Dutch poet quoted is myself. The lines are taken from one of the sonnets I wrote during my internment, see below, "Looking Back," pp. 356-7.
2. An essay by Romein on the Common Human Pattern (in English) was published in the issue of *Delta* that followed that in which the present lecture was first published.
3. This book has since appeared, under the title *The Struggle for a Higher Standard of Living: The Problem of the Underdeveloped Countries* (The Hague: Van Hoeve; Glencoe, Illinois: Free Press, 1958).

The Historical Background of the Idea of European Unity

1. "Onorthodoxe bedenkingen over Klein-Europa" was the title of an article I published in *Het Parool* in January 1954, when E.D.C. was on the tapis. I had it included in *Studies en Strijdschriften* (1958).

2. See the *Harvard Alumni Bulletin,* July 4, 1959, and *The New Leader*, August 31, 1959.

Jan Romein, or Bowing to the Spirit of the Age

1. To 1959.
2. *Ongeloof en Revolutie* was based on lectures given in 1845 and 1846. In it the author derived the Revolution, which he saw still continuing its nefarious work, from the rejection of Christianity springing from the philosophy of the Enlightenment.
3. This book of Groen's old age—it appeared in 1875—attacked the interpretation of the church and state crisis of 1617 to 1619 given by Motley in his *Life and Death of John of Barneveld.* To Groen, Maurice was the hero who had preserved the life principle of the Dutch Republic, orthodox Calvinism, which the old "advocate," Oldenbarnevelt, had jeopardized by the protection meted out to Arminianism. Moreover, he traced the issue, which to him was at all times the one of essential importance, throughout the history of the Republic and recalled the polemics in which he himself had been engaged in his lifetime to vindicate its true significance. See in my *Reacties* (1952), the essay "Groen contra Motley."

Othmar F. Anderle, or Unreason as a Doctrine

1. See below, in "Looking Back," pp. 357, 372.

Herbert Butterfield, or Thinking at Two Levels

1. Lionel Kochan, *Acton on History* (1954), p. 36.
2. Op. cit., p. 97.
3. Compare the remarks made by De Marans, quoted above, p. 138.

Soviet Historians Make Their Bow

1. I follow the English translation of the pamphlet distributed at the Congress. The version in Volume VI of the official Congress publications is in German.
2. I quote from the official English version.
3. Signalized by Dr. R. van 't Reve in his little book *Sovjet-Annexatie der klassieken.* His observation of these maneuvers in the field of literary criticism is a help toward understanding what goes on in historiography.
4. As Isaiah Berlin remarks in his little book *Historical Inevitability.*
5. This is according to precept. To utter doubt with respect to the

actual existence of the socialist society would be an unforgivable heresy. On October 9, 1955, after this article had been written, I read in the newspapers that Molotov had made a bad *faux pas* by stating in a speech that "in the Soviet Union the *foundations* of a socialist society are already in existence." In a letter to the periodical *The Communist* Molotov has since confessed to having committed "a theoretical error": the nineteenth Party Congress had found that the party had already succeeded in building up a socialist society; that all that remained to be done was "to build up a communist society by way of a gradual transition from socialism to communism."

Looking Back

1. *Ten Years of the Eighty Years' War* (1588-98). This book, which appeared in 1857, when Fruin was thirty-four years old, is still regarded as a classic.
2. Albert Verwey, 1864-1937, a leading poet and critic.
3. October 7, 1940 to November 1941, when the group of hostages to which I belonged was transferred to Holland; I was released from internment only on February 12, 1944.
4. Compare what is said on this point in *Debates with Historians*, pp. 219-20.
5. The organization was called Dietse Studenten Bond. The word *Diets*, an archaic word for Netherlandish, was revived in those years by the adherents of the Great-Netherlands idea. It has since fallen into disrepute owing to its similarity to *Duits*, that is, *German*, a similarity that seemed ominous when later on a number of "Dietsers" gravitated toward National Socialism and in the end collaborated with the Germans. It is hardly necessary to say that no such proclivities were intended or even thought of, by the original "Dietse Studenten" in the twenties.
6. Flemish Nationalism had come into action during World War I in two distinct forms. One was the "activism" of those Flamingants who used the presence of a complaisant German occupying authority to carry through reforms that were indeed long overdue. Secondly there was the clandestine, but at one time powerful, organization of Flemish soldiers at the front who resented being commanded by officers ignorant of their language. After 1918 the Activists were prosecuted; many fled the country, settling in Holland (some in Germany). In the practice of Belgian politics there soon took place a merging of the forces of Activism and of Frontism. The common appellation now became Flemish Nationalism. See A. Willemsen, *Het Vlaams Nationalisme, 1914-40* (Utrecht, 1958).
7. This is what was meant by the cry "Politiek Groot-Nederland!"
8. The square in The Hague on which the Ministry of Foreign Affairs is situated.
9. Dutch universities embrace seven or eight "faculties," each

faculty being concerned with a particular field of study: theology, science, law, medicine, etc. The faculty of letters is perhaps the most heterogeneous one of all, embracing not only languages and literatures, Dutch and foreign, ancient and modern, Oriental and Western, but history, geography, psychology, philosophy.

10. *Geschiedenis van de Nederlandse Stam* (Vol. I, 1930; Vol. II, 1934; Vol. III, 1937), reprinted in two large volumes (1947-8); a new volume dealing with the period appeared in 1959. The portion on 1555 to 1609 appeared in English under the title *The Revolt of the Netherlands* (1932; third impression 1958); 1609 to 1648 under the title *The Netherlands Divided* (1936); a new edition of this latter work and a further installment covering the period from 1648 to 1702 are in preparation (the title to be: *The Netherlands in the Seventeenth Century*, I and II).
11. In January 1933 the leading monthly *De Gids* came out with a long article in commemoration of the fourth centenary of the birth of William the Silent. It was written by the Managing Editor, Professor of National History at the University of Leyden. In a letter published in the press, signed jointly by my friend Van Eyck (my successor as London correspondent of the *N.R.C.*, a well-known poet and critic, in 1935 appointed Professor of the History of Dutch Literature at Leyden) and myself, it was pointed out that the article was plagiarized from Pirenne's *Histoire de Belgique*.

    The affair created an enormous sensation. Leyden students publicly protested against "an attack on Leyden." Meanwhile a committee of three professors of history of the other public universities were invited by the Curators and the Rector of Leyden to examine the charge; after a long delay they reported that they had found it to be justified. Their report went on, however, to blame Van Eyck and myself for having rushed into publicity. To this we retorted (all these statements were published *in extenso* by the daily press) that "apparently many people in this country have a greater aversion to publicity than to deceit." The Curators publicly endorsed the report, and subsequently stated, at our request, that this naturally meant: "insofar as the report related to the Leyden Professor of History."

    Let me add that the retiring Utrecht Professor of Modern History, whose place I was eventually to take, had been, two years earlier, one of the committee of three.
12. Chapters I and II in the *English Historical Review* (1923) and *Scottish Historical Review* (1923) respectively. Cf. above, pp. 152-81.
13. See a long review by Sir Richard Lodge in the *English Historical Review*, 1925.
14. Nationaal-Socialistische Beweging—the National Socialist organization in Holland, led by Mussert.
15. The procedure is as follows: The Faculty makes its recommendation to the Committee of Curators. This is a body of five, now-

adays seven, men of standing and independence. In the last resort they represent the authority of the Minister of Education, by whom they are appointed and by whose decisions they have to abide. They will generally advocate the University's views in The Hague and will often do so with tenacity, but in the exchanges preceding the Minister's decision, they can also, and frequently do, take their own line. In the matter of professorial appointments it is they who make a recommendation to the Minister. In the large majority of cases they will make the Faculty's recommendation their own, although they are by no means bound to do so. The Minister, for his part, will generally follow the recommendation of Curators, although he, too, can depart from it.

My case was an unusual one from beginning to end. The Faculty placed me third on its list of three candidates. The Curators recommended me; this decision was reached in July 1935, when months had already been spent in confabulations. But it was September before the Minister expressed a wish that I should call on him. I came over from London the next day. He then told me that he felt inclined to follow the recommendation of the Curators, but that, as I was sure to understand, there were difficulties. I told him that I did not understand at all. After which he said, in an impressive tone of voice: "Belgium, of course!" He even said, incredible as it may appear, that the Great-Netherlands movement might lead to WAR!! with Belgium. I asked him whether he knew anything of my particular position within that movement and promised to let him have a memo I had drawn up earlier for our Ministry of Foreign Affairs (for I had had misgivings that there might be opposition from that quarter). He told me that he had brought the matter up in the Cabinet and that no voice had been raised against the appointment, although his suggestion that he would have a serious talk with me before coming to a decision had been welcomed. He assured me he would be glad to see the memo.

This memo did not contain any apology for past action or any promise of different conduct in the future. It consisted of a string of quotations from speeches and articles of mine over a period of twelve years or more. Its effect on the Minister was to make him write me a letter in which he told me that he was laying my name before Her Majesty the Queen. My friends in the Department congratulated me, advised me to go to Utrecht to present myself to the Secretary of Curators and to look for a house before returning to London. Next Thursday the Queen was to sign royal decrees.

In the evening of that day I was rung up by the head of the Universities Section, who told me, much embarrassed, that the Queen had not signed.

But I had the Minister's letter, and if I was not appointed I could let the world know (and meant to) how the original decision had come to be revised. The affair caused quite a commotion in political circles, without, however, being ventilated in the press. I received a good many expressions of sympathy and promises of support, from the then Prime Minister among others, but I had to wait for another painful three months before the decree was duly signed.

I entered upon my duties on January 1, 1936.

16. The house was raided because it had transpired that we were hiding in the cellar arms and munitions of the Dutch underground forces. Also, a secret telephone had been installed in a top room overlooking the main road east, and young people were regularly attending it. We had been warned in time and had gone into hiding ("dived under" was the technical term), which meant that we went to stay with friends in another part of the town. In our absence the Sten guns and hand grenades were discovered and the German military police carried off all our belongings. When we came back, a fortnight later, the house was completely empty and the dining room had been wrecked with one of "my own" hand grenades, the only use to which any of the lot was ever put.
17. I am glad to be able to add now, in 1961, that a remarkable revival has taken place.
18. English translation 1949 (London: Jonathan Cape New Haven: Yale University Press).
19. The Terry Lectures for 1954, published in 1955 (New Haven: Yale University Press).

NOTE OF ACKNOWLEDGMENT

Of the seventeen essays included in this volume, three are here published for the first time:

FRENCH HISTORIANS FOR AND AGAINST THE REVOLUTION, originally two lectures delivered at Oxford in 1956;

THE IDEA OF LIBERTY IN HISTORY, originally a lecture given in "Studium Generale" at the University of Utrecht, 1956;

"HITLER'S EUROPE," a talk delivered over the B.B.C., London, 1954.

Six are here published for the first time in English:

SHAKESPEARE AS A HISTORIAN: A FRAGMENT, published in the periodical *Nieuw Vlaams Tijdschrift*, Antwerp, 1947, and reprinted in the author's *Tochten en Toernooien*, 1950;

THE BATAVIAN REVOLUTION: 1795-1798, originally a lecture given at a conference of the Dutch Students' Association held at Woudschoten, published in the periodical *Bijdragen voor de Geschiedenis der Nederlanden*, 's Gravenhage, 1956, and reprinted in the author's *Studies en*

Strijdschriften, Groningen, 1958; English version used for a public lecture at the University of London, 1956;

OPENING LECTURE (OCTOBER 1, 1945), published in the author's *Historicus in de Tijd*, Utrecht, 1954;

THE HISTORICAL BACKGROUND OF THE IDEA OF EUROPEAN UNITY, originally two lectures given in the Aula of the University of Leyden in October 1959, published in *Viermaal Europa*, together with three other papers by experts in European federation;

JAN ROMEIN, OR BOWING TO THE SPIRIT OF THE AGE, published in the periodical *De Gids*, Amsterdam, 1947, and reprinted in *Tochten en Toernooien*, 1950 (the concluding portion of this essay, containing criticisms of detail, has not been included here);

LOOKING BACK, a talk given to the Utrecht Historical Students' Circle in March 1958, published in *Studies en Strijdschriften*, 1958.

MOTLEY AND HIS "RISE OF THE DUTCH REPUBLIC," a talk delivered over the B.B.C., London, was published in *The Listener*, London, 1956.

The first and second parts of ORANGE AND STUART: 1641-1650 were published respectively in *The English Historical Review*, London, 1923, and *Scottish Historical Review*, Edinburgh 1923, and later became the first two chapters of the author's *Oranje en Stuart 1641-1672*, Utrecht 1939.

HISTORICAL APPRECIATIONS OF THE HOLLAND REGENT REGIME, originally a paper read for the Royal Flemish Academy, Brussels, 1954, was published in the Academy's *Mededelingen*, Brussels, and reprinted in *Studies en Strijdschriften*, 1958; the English version, which is included in *Essays in Diplomatic and Constitutional History*, 1961, a volume presented to the historian Dr. George Peabody Gooch, is reprinted by permission of Longmans, Green & Co., Ltd., London.

THE VITALITY OF WESTERN CIVILIZATION, a valedictory oration delivered in the Aula of the University of Utrecht on the occasion of the author's retirement from the chair of Modern History, May 31, 1958, was published separately and was reprinted in *Geschiedenis als Medespeler*, 1959; the English version appeared in *Delta, a Review of Arts, Life, and Thought in the Netherlands*, Amsterdam, Spring 1959.

OTHMAR F. ANDERLE, OR UNREASON AS A DOCTRINE was published in Meridian Books' newspaper, *The Meridian*, New York Fall 1958.

HERBERT BUTTERFIELD, OR THINKING AT TWO LEVELS first appeared in the *Historical Journal*, Cambridge 1956.

GEOFFREY BARRACLOUGH, OR THE SCRAPPING OF HISTORY was published in *The Nation*, New York, April 13, 1957.

SOVIET HISTORIANS MAKE THEIR BOW was published in the periodical *De Gids*, Amsterdam, December 1955; an abridged English version appeared in *The Nation*, New York, April 14, 1956.

In reprinting some of the essays, translating or retranslating others, the author has availed himself of the opportunity to make a few minor corrections and to add several explanatory notes; short prefaces have been added to the SHAKESPEARE essay and OPENING LECTURE; short postscripts to THE HISTORICAL BACKGROUND OF THE IDEA OF EUROPEAN UNITY and SOVIET HISTORIANS MAKE THEIR BOW.

MERIDIAN BOOKS

published by The World Publishing Company
2231 West 110 Street, Cleveland 2, Ohio

M1 ABINGER HARVEST *by E. M. Forster*
M3 ROUSSEAU AND ROMANTICISM *by Irving Babbitt*
M4 IMPERIALISM AND SOCIAL CLASSES *by Joseph Schumpeter*
M5 WAYWARD YOUTH *by August Aichhorn*
M6 THE PLAYWRIGHT AS THINKER *by Eric Bentley*
M7 THE PHILOSOPHY OF MODERN ART *by Herbert Read*
M8 CREATIVE INTUITION IN ART AND POETRY *by Jacques Maritain*
M9 OUTLINES OF THE HISTORY OF GREEK PHILOSOPHY *by Eduard Zeller*
M10 LANGUAGE AND THOUGHT OF THE CHILD *by Jean Piaget*
M11 SEVEN TYPES OF AMBIGUITY *by William Empson*
M12 ESSAYS ON FREEDOM AND POWER *by Lord Acton*
M13 THE MAN OF LETTERS IN THE MODERN WORLD *by Allen Tate*
M14 THE ORDEAL OF MARK TWAIN *by Van Wyck Brooks*
M15 SEX AND REPRESSION IN SAVAGE SOCIETY *by Branslaw Malinowski*
M16 PRAGMATISM *by William James*
M17 HISTORY AS THE STORY OF LIBERTY *by Benedetto Croce*
M18 NEW DIRECTIONS 15: INTERNATIONAL ISSUE
M19 MATTHEW ARNOLD *by Lionel Trilling*
M20 SHAKESPEAREAN TRAGEDY *by A. C. Bradley*
M21 THE DEVIL'S SHARE *by Denis de Rougemont*
M22 THE HERO WITH A THOUSAND FACES *by Joseph Campbell*
M23 BYZANTINE CIVILIZATION *by Steven Runciman*
M24 ESSAYS AND SKETCHES IN BIOGRAPHY *by John Maynard Keynes*
M25 NIETZSCHE *by Walter Kaufmann*
M26 THE MIND AND HEART OF LOVE *by M. C. D'Arcy*
M27 CONGRESSIONAL GOVERNMENT *by Woodrow Wilson*
M28 TWO ESSAYS ON ANALYTICAL PSYCHOLOGY *by C. G. Jung*
M29 THE WRITINGS OF MARTIN BUBER *edited by Will Herberg*
M30 BERLIOZ AND HIS CENTURY *by Jacques Barzun*
M31 FREEDOM, EDUCATION, AND THE FUND *by Robert M. Hutchins*
M32 A PREFACE TO LOGIC *by Morris R. Cohen*
M33 VISION AND DESIGN *by Roger Fry*
M34 FREUD OR JUNG? *by Edward Glover*
M35 THE MAKING OF EUROPE *by Christopher Dawson*
M36 THE FORMS OF MUSIC *by Donald Francis Tovey*
M37 THE VARIETIES OF HISTORY *edited by Fritz Stern*
M38 THE ESSENCE OF LAUGHTER *by Charles Baudelaire*
M39 EXISTENTIALISM FROM DOSTOEVSKY TO SARTRE *edited by Walter Kaufmann*
M40 ITALIAN PAINTERS OF THE RENAISSANCE *by Bernard Berenson*
M41 SIGHTS AND SPECTACLES *by Mary McCarthy*
M42 MOHAMMED AND CHARLEMAGNE *by Henri Pirenne*

M43 THE WHEEL OF FIRE *by G. Wilson Knight*
M44 GOTHIC ARCHITECTURE AND SCHOLASTICISM *by Erwin Panofsky*
M45 FREUD AND THE 20TH CENTURY *edited by Benjamin Nelson*
M46 POLITICS AND THE NOVEL *by Irving Howe*
M47 A SHORTER HISTORY OF SCIENCE *by William Cecil Dampier*
M48 A GUIDE TO CONTEMPORARY FRENCH LITERATURE *by Wallace Fowlie*
M49 THE RENAISSANCE OF THE 12TH CENTURY *by C. H. Haskins*
M50 NEW POETS OF ENGLAND AND AMERICA *selected by Hall, Pack, and Simpson*
M51 ST. AUGUSTINE: HIS AGE, LIFE, AND THOUGHT
M52 CIVILIZATION ON TRIAL *and* THE WORLD AND THE WEST *by Arnold Toynbee*
M53 RELIGION AND CULTURE *by Christopher Dawson*
M54 PROUST: A BIOGRAPHY *by André Maurois*
M55 ST. THOMAS AQUINAS *by Jacques Maritain*
M56 MEMOIRS OF A REVOLUTIONIST *by Dwight Macdonald*
M57 DEBATES WITH HISTORIANS *by Pieter Geyl*
M58 POLITICS: WHO GETS WHAT, WHEN, HOW *by Harold Lasswell*
M59 GODS AND HEROES OF THE GREEKS *by H. J. Rose*
M60 RELIGION IN AMERICA *edited by John Cogley*
M61 MEN AND IDEAS *by Johan Huizinga*
M62 WITCHCRAFT *by Charles Williams*
M63 SCENES FROM THE DRAMA OF EUROPEAN LITERATURE *by Erich Auerbach*
M64 THE HUMAN MEANING OF THE SOCIAL SCIENCES *edited by Daniel Lerner*
M65 ARISTOTLE *by W. D. Ross*
M66 THE DISINHERITED MIND *by Erich Heller*
M67 THE BOOK OF JAZZ *by Leonard Feather*
M68 THE WORLD OF ODYSSEUS *by M. I. Finley*
M69 THE SCROLLS FROM THE DEAD SEA *by Edmund Wilson*
M70 GREY EMINENCE *by Aldous Huxley*
M71 THE LOGIC OF THE SCIENCES AND THE HUMANITIES *by F. S. C. Northrop*
M72 HISTORY 1
M73 ON MODERN POETS *by Yvor Winters*
M74 THE MAIN STREAM OF MUSIC AND OTHER ESSAYS *by Donald Francis Tovey*
M75 JONATHAN EDWARDS *by Perry Miller*
M76 THE CONFEDERACY *edited by Albert D. Kirwan*
M77 TALENTS AND GENIUSES *by Gilbert Highet*
M78 APES, ANGELS, AND VICTORIANS *by William Irvine*
M79 PAINTING AND REALITY *by Etienne Gilson*
M80 MOZART'S LIBRETTOS *translated by Robert Pack and Marjorie Lelash*
M81 PHILOSOPHY IN THE MIDDLE AGES *by Paul Vignaux*
M82 THE RECOLLECTIONS OF ALEXIS DE TOCQUEVILLE *edited by J. P. Mayer*

M83 HISTORY 2
M84 ON LOVE *by José Ortega y Gasset*
M85 THE ROMANTIC ENLIGHTENMENT *by Geoffrey Clive*
M86 ANSWER TO JOB *by C. G. Jung*
M87 NEWMAN *by Louis Bouyer*
M88 THE NOBLE SAVAGE 1 *edited by Saul Bellow, Keith Botsford, and Jack Ludwig*
M89 AMERICA AND THE IMAGE OF EUROPE *by Daniel J. Boorstin*
M90 PHILOSOPHY OF SCIENCE *edited by Arthur Danto and Sidney Morgenbesser*
M91 AMERICAN FOREIGN POLICY *edited by Robert A. Divine*
M92 DIONYSUS IN PARIS: A GUIDE TO CONTEMPORARY FRENCH THEATER *by Wallace Fowlie*
M93 THE KING AND THE CORPSE *by Heinrich Zimmer*
M94 THE BEDBUG AND SELECTED POETRY *by Vladimir Mayakovsky*
M95 HISTORY 3
M96 GOD AND THE WAYS OF KNOWING *by Jean Daniélou*
M97 AN OUTLINE OF PHILOSOPHY *by Bertrand Russell*
M98 SENATOR JOE MC CARTHY *by Richard H. Rovere*
M99 ON ART AND ARTISTS *by Aldous Huxley*
M100 I REMEMBER *by Boris Pasternak*
M101 A HISTORY OF THE UNITED STATES: FROM THE AGE OF EXPLORATION TO 1865 *edited by Hugh T. Lefler*
M102 THE NOBLE SAVAGE 2 *edited by Saul Bellow, Keith Botsford, and Jack Ludwig*
M103 THE IDEAL READER *by Jacques Rivière*
M104 THE PERSIAN LETTERS *by Montesquieu*
M105 THE AMERICAN PRAGMATISTS *edited by Milton R. Konvitz and Gail Kennedy*
M106 JERUSALEM AND ROME: THE WRITINGS OF JOSEPHUS *edited by Nahum N. Glatzer*
M107 LORD WEARY'S CASTLE *and* THE MILLS OF THE KAVANAUGHS *by Robert Lowell*
M108 THE GRASS ROOTS OF ART *by Herbert Read*
M109 LECTURES ON MODERN HISTORY *by Lord Acton*
M110 THE MEANING AND MATTTER OF HISTORY *by M. C. D'Arcy*
M111 THE AUTOBIOGRAPHY OF EDWARD GIBBON *edited by Dero A. Saunders*
M112 AESTHETICS TODAY *edited by Morris Philipson*
M113 THE NOBLE SAVAGE 3 *edited by Saul Bellow and Keith Botsford*
M114 ENCOUNTERS IN HISTORY *by Pieter Geyl*
M115 A HISTORY OF THE UNITED STATES: FROM 1865 TO THE PRESENT *edited by Frank W. Klingberg*
M116 THE NAZIS: A DOCUMENTARY HISTORY *edited by Walther Hofer*
M117 HISTORY 4
M118 THOMAS MANN: THE IRONIC GERMAN *by Erich Heller*
M119 OUTLINES OF CLASSICAL LITERATURE *by H. J. Rose*

M120 GOD AND THE UNCONSCIOUS *by Victor White*
M121 HELLENISTIC CIVILIZATION *by W. W. Tarn*
M122 A GUIDE TO CONTEMPORARY ITALIAN LITERATURE *by Sergio Pacifici*
M123 THE SUPREME COURT OF THE UNITED STATES *by Paul A. Freund*
M124 THE RENAISSANCE *by Walter Pater*
M125 THE NOBLE SAVAGE 4 *edited by Saul Bellow and Keith Botsford*
M126 THE MERIDIAN COMPACT ATLAS OF THE WORLD
M127 AMERICA IN THE WORLD *edited by Oscar Theodore Barck, Jr.*
M128 THE DECLINE OF THE INTELLECTUAL *by Thomas Molnar*

MG28 THE SOUL AFIRE *edited by H. A. Reinhold*

MG29 AN INTRODUCTION TO THE LITERATURE OF THE OLD TESTAMENT *by S. R. Driver*

MG30 EARLY GREEK PHILOSOPHY *by John Burnet*

MG31 ROMAN SOCIETY IN THE LAST CENTURY OF THE WESTERN EMPIRE *by Samuel Dill*

MG32 THE HISTORY OF ROME *by Theodor Mommsen*

MG33 THE NEW ARCHITECTURE OF EUROPE: AN ILLUSTRATED GUIDEBOOK AND APPRAISAL *by G. E. Kidder Smith*

MG34 A DICTIONARY OF CLASSICAL ANTIQUITIES *by Oscar Seyffert*

MG35 PROLEGOMENA TO THE HISTORY OF ANCIENT ISRAEL *by Julius Wellhausen*

MG36 A HISTORY OF AESTHETIC *by Bernard Bosanquet*

MG37 AN ENCYCLOPEDIA OF RELIGION AND RELIGIONS *by E. Royston Pike*

MG38 CLEAR WRITING *by Leo Kirschbaum*

MG39 THE FEDERALIST *edited by Jacob E. Cooke*

MG40 FRENCH PHILOSOPHERS FROM DESCARTES TO SARTRE *edited by Leonard M. Marsak*

MG41 SCIENCE & TECHNOLOGY STOCKS: A GUIDE FOR INVESTORS *by Grant Jeffery*

MG42 THE PLAYS OF CHRISTOPHER MARLOWE *edited by Leo Kirschbaum*

LA28 RELIGION IN THE MAKING *by Alfred North Whitehead*
LA29 EXISTENCE AND FAITH: SHORTER WRITINGS OF RUDOLF BULTMANN *edited by Schubert M. Ogden*
LA30 REMBRANDT AND THE GOSPEL *by W. A. Visser 't Hooft*
LA31 GOD'S KNOTTY LOG: SELECTED WRITINGS OF JOHN BUNYAN *edited by Henri A. Talon*
LA32 THE PRIVATE DEVOTIONS OF LANCELOT ANDREWES *edited by F. E. Brightman*
LA33 HOW MY MIND HAS CHANGED *edited by Harold E. Fey*
LA34 THE INFIDEL: FREETHOUGHT AND AMERICAN RELIGION *by Martin E. Marty*
LA35 LITURGIES OF THE WESTERN CHURCH *edited by Bard Thompson*

MERIDIAN BOOKS

published by The World Publishing Company
2231 West 110 Street, Cleveland 2, Ohio

JEWISH PUBLICATION SOCIETY SERIES

JP1 FOR THE SAKE OF HEAVEN *by Martin Buber*
JP2 STUDENTS, SCHOLARS AND SAINTS *by Louis Ginzberg*
JP3 A HISTORY OF MEDIAEVAL JEWISH PHILOSOPHY *by Isaac Husik*
JP4 JEWISH LIFE IN THE MIDDLE AGES *by Israel Abrahams*
JP5 STUDIES IN JUDAISM *by Solomon Schechter*
JP6 HISTORY OF THE JEWISH PEOPLE *by Max Margolis and Alexander Marx*
JP7 GOD IN SEARCH OF MAN *by Abraham Joshua Heschel*
JP8 INTRODUCTION TO THE TALMUD AND MIDRASH *by Hermann L. Strack*
JP9 KIDDUSH HA-SHEM *and* SABBATAI ZEVI *by Sholem Asch*
JP10 JUDAISM AND MODERN MAN *by Will Herberg*
JP11 PRINCE OF THE GHETTO *by Maurice Samuel*
JP12 A HISTORY OF THE MARRANOS *by Cecil Roth*
JP13 THREE JEWISH PHILOSOPHERS *edited by Hans Lewy, Alexander Altmann, and Isaak Heinemann*
JP14 THE JEW IN THE MEDIEVAL WORLD *by Jacob R. Marcus*
JP15 THE JEW IN THE LITERATURE OF ENGLAND *by Montagu Frank Modder*
JP16 A HISTORY OF THE CONTEMPORARY JEWS *by Solomon Grayzel*
JP17 THE ZIONIST IDEA *edited by Arthur Hertzberg*
JP18 MODERN NATIONALISM AND RELIGION *by Salo W. Baron*
JP19 GERMANY'S STEPCHILDREN *by Solomon Liptzin*
JP20 NATIONALISM AND HISTORY: ESSAYS ON OLD AND NEW JUDAISM *by Simon Dubnow*
JP21 THE CONFLICT OF THE CHURCH AND THE SYNAGOGUE *by James Parkes*
JP22 THE DEVIL AND THE JEWS *by Joshua Trachtenberg*
JP23 JUDAISM AND CHRISTIANITY *by Leo Baeck*
JP24 AMERICAN JEWRY AND THE CIVIL WAR *by Bertram W. Korn*